"*Compassionate Justice* is an impressive addition to the burgeoning literature on restorative justice. However, it is much more than that. This is a theologically rich account of the foundations and contradictions of substantive justice viewed though the lens of the two most beloved biblical parables: the Good Samaritan and the Prodigal Son. It is imaginative and compelling and powerfully demonstrates the author's deep understanding of justice issues and his commitment to the ethical ideals of mercy and compassion."
—Warren Brookbanks
Professor of Criminal law, University of Auckland, New Zealand

"This is a beautifully written and thoughtful reflection on two familiar parables and the normative implications of the central moment in each: when the protagonist is 'moved by compassion.' An especially important contribution to restorative justice literature."
—Daniel W. Van Ness
Prison Fellowship International

"As with his earlier publications, such as *Beyond Retribution*, Marshall has given us a profound book in highly readable form. His blend of biblical scholarship and contemporary insights from the social sciences and humanities will be of interest not only to Christians but to others concerned about justice in today's world."
—Howard Zehr
Professor of Restorative Justice, Eastern Mennonite University

"Marshall is one of our most creative thinkers in the fields of biblical studies and social justice, and a pioneering advocate of restorative justice. Shedding new light on two of Jesus' best-known parables, this engaging and accessible study challenges us to profoundly rethink our attitudes to justice and compassion, and act accordingly."
—Andrew Bradstock
Howard Paterson Professor of Theology and Public Issues, University of Otago, Dunedin, New Zealand.

"I love the way *Compassionate Justice* combines thick exegesis of Jesus with public ethics, dialoguing incisively with philosophy and public policy on criminal justice . . . showing how Jesus deepens and sharpens the discussion."
—**Glen Stassen**
    Professor of Christian Ethics, Fuller Theological Seminary

"No biblical scholar in the world has searched the Bible more faithfully for its support of the idea of restorative justice than has Christopher Marshall. Nor has any scholar sought more faithfully to promote that justice in the public life of his country. Here, in an intensive study of two of Jesus' parables, he tells me as a fellow Christian that 'justice' in our minds ought to equal 'healing,' not 'punishment.' In the Good Samaritan and the Prodigal Son, it is clear that for Jesus the remedy for human misbehavior is the mercy of healers, not the retribution of punishers."
—**Donald W. Shriver**
    President Emeritus, Union Theological Seminary, New York

COMPASSIONATE JUSTICE

THEOPOLITICAL VISIONS

SERIES EDITORS:

Thomas Heilke
D. Stephen Long
and C. C. Pecknold

Theopolitical Visions seeks to open up new vistas on public life, hosting fresh conversations between theology and political theory. This series assembles writers who wish to revive theopolitical imagination for the sake of our common good.

Theopolitical Visions hopes to re-source modern imaginations with those ancient traditions in which political theorists were often also theologians. Whether it was Jeremiah's prophetic vision of exiles "seeking the peace of the city," Plato's illuminations on piety and the civic virtues in the Republic, St. Paul's call to "a common life worthy of the Gospel," St. Augustine's beatific vision of the City of God, or the gothic heights of medieval political theology, much of Western thought has found it necessary to think theologically about politics, and to think politically about theology. This series is founded in the hope that the renewal of such mutual illumination might make a genuine contribution to the peace of our cities.

FORTHCOMING VOLUMES:

Artur Mrówczynski-Van Allen
Between the Icon and the Idol: Man and State in Russian Thought and Literature: Chaadayev, Soloviev, Grossman

Charles M. Collier
A Nonviolent Augustinianism? Hisotry and Politics and Theologies of St. Augustine and John Howard Yoder

Compassionate JUSTICE

An Interdisciplinary Dialogue with Two Gospel Parables on Law, Crime, and Restorative Justice

CHRISTOPHER D. MARSHALL

 CASCADE *Books* • Eugene, Oregon

COMPASSIONATE JUSTICE
An Interdisciplinary Dialogue with Two Gospel Parables on Law, Crime, and Restorative Justice

Theopolitical Visions 15

Copyright © 2012 Christopher D. Marshall. All rights reserved. Except for brief quotations in critical publications or reviews, no part of this book may be reproduced in any manner without prior written permission from the publisher. Write: Permissions, Wipf and Stock Publishers, 199 W. 8th Ave., Suite 3, Eugene, OR 97401.

Cascade Books
An Imprint of Wipf and Stock Publishers
199 W. 8th Ave., Suite 3
Eugene, OR 97401

www.wipfandstock.com

ISBN 13: 978-1-61097-807-1

Cataloging-in-Publication data:

Marshall, Christopher D.

    Compassionate justice : an interdisciplinary dialogue with two gospel parables on law, crime, and restorative justice / Christopher D. Marshall.

    xii + 372 p. ; 23 cm. —Includes bibliographical references and index(es).

    Theopolitical Visions 15

    ISBN 13: 978-1-61097-807-1

    1. Christianity and justice. 2. Jesus Christ—Parables. 3. Restorative justice—Religious aspects—Christianity. I. Series. II. Title.

HV8688 .M36 2012

Manufactured in the U.S.A.

For Willard M. Swartley
with respect and gratitude

ὁ ἀγαπητὸς ἀδελφὸς καὶ πιστὸς διάκονος ἐν κυρίῳ (Eph 6:21)

Contents

Preface ix
Acknowledgments xi
Introduction 1

PART 1: Restoration and the Victim (Luke 10:25–37)

1. A "Magnificent Little Story" and the Task of Public Ethics 15
2. A Parable of Law, Crime, and Justice 29
3. Loving Life and Doing the Law 55
4. Victimization and the Law of Neglect 82
5. The Samaritan and the Rule of Compassion 111
6. Good Samaritans, Bad Samaritans, and Modern Legal Theory 140

PART 2: Restoration and the Offender (Luke 15:11–32)

7. Offending, Restoration, and the Law-Abiding Community 181
8. Offending as Relational Rupture 195
9. A Better Justice 217

PART 3: Just Compassion

10. Public Compassion 249
11. Compassion and the Criminal Justice System 283

Bibliography 323
Scripture and Ancient Sources Index 343
Author Index 354
Subject Index 360

"Render just judgments, show kindness and mercy to one another."

Zechariah 7:9 (NRSV)

Preface

When it comes to writing books, I believe in evolution rather than creation. Or, to be more precise (and theologically sound), creation by means of evolution. This book evolved from an initial hunch that the parable of the Prodigal Son, which of course I knew in broad outline but had not given much concentrated time to studying, might have something valuable to say to me as a father of two fine young adult sons. As I followed up my intuition and immersed myself in the story, I soon discovered that the parable not only deepened my appreciation of fatherhood, it also triggered a range of recognitions and responses stemming from my long involvement in the work of restorative justice. I came to see that restorative justice theory provided a helpful new lens for understanding this remarkable story, while the story in turn deepened and enriched my conception of restorative justice.

My next hunch was that the same would probably apply to that other most celebrated of Jesus' parables, the parable of the Good Samaritan. Here evolution underwent a surprising mutation, as I was led into the literature of social psychology, jurisprudence, and moral philosophy. Once again, I found this rich vein of scholarship casting new light on a well-worn parable and the parable more than returning the compliment.

Evolution, as all good theists know, is not ultimately a random process. An invisible hand guides it towards some ultimate goal, some final *telos* when the bloody tooth and claw of the evolutionary past, and still of the present, will finally make sense, or at least be swallowed up in perfect peace. Perhaps a teleological hand can also be glimpsed in this present study as well. Who knows? The final outcome might even show faint signs of intelligent design, an inner coherence focused particularly on the need of compassion in the work of corrective justice.

The best-known fact about evolution, of course, is that it takes vast stretches of time to happen. This book has not taken millions of years to emerge, but sometimes has it felt like it. I am very grateful for Tom Noakes-Duncan, who served as my research assistant in 2010 at Victoria

University of Wellington and who conquered the mysteries of End Note on my behalf. In addition to his practical help, Tom's friendship and fellowship were a great blessing during the year. I am also extremely thankful to my son Peter Marshall for his legal advice and editorial expertise made available during a busy time of his life, and to Victor Lipski for his careful and competent proofreading, editorial advice, and preparation of the indexes. I would like to say that any remaining legal blunders and stylistic infelicities are their fault, not mine, but that would be untrue. Thanks also to the staff at Wipf and Stock Publishers for their courteous and thorough work in preparing the manuscript for publication

In his helpful discussion of the priority of love in the panoply of human virtues and its relationship to social justice, Timothy Jackson observes that the biblical conception of justice is so all-encompassing that it invites a story rather than a definition, poetry rather than theory, imitation rather than contemplation, metaphors and parables rather than abstract principles.[1] The following study contains its fair share of definitions and abstract principles since much of the literature it engages with on law, crime, and justice, not to mention biblical studies, is distinctly theoretical in nature. But the book's overriding concern is to return again and again to the stories, metaphors, and parables that Jesus told in Luke 10 and 15 to find guidance on the meaning of justice and the need of compassion. I call this continual looping back to the parables a dialogue, because dialogues are two-way conversations where each conversant is affected by what the other says. In this case, the stories of Jesus are freshly illuminated by commentary from the social sciences and legal philosophy, while modern justice discourse is enriched and critiqued by the parables and metaphors of Jesus.

But the dialogue partners are not of equal volume. The voice of one is more insistent than the other. Nor are the issues at stake ultimately abstract or theoretical in character; they are desperately practical. They are to do with "life" and with "living" (10:28; 15:30), with hurt and with healing, with transgression and redemption, and on such matters Jesus claims to speak with distinctive authority. "Do this," he says, "and you will live" (10:28). In what follows, we will contemplate his two great parables of restorative justice. But contemplation is not finally enough; it must give way to imitation. "Go you and do likewise" (10:37).

1. Jackson, *Priority of Love*, 31, 34, 67.

Acknowledgments

In the course of its development, small sections of this book have been published elsewhere. Mention should be made of: "Offending, Restoration and the Law-Abiding Community: Restorative Justice in the New Testament and in the New Zealand Experience," *Journal of the Society for Christian Ethics* 27/2 (2007) 3–30; "'I Have Sinned Against Heaven and Against You': Sin as Relational Rupture in the Teaching of Jesus," in *A Thinker's Guide to Sin: Talking About Sin Today*, edited by Neil Darragh, 65–73 (Auckland: Accent, 2010); and, "'Go and Do Likewise': The Parable of the Good Samaritan and the Challenge of Public Ethics," in *Ethics and Public Policy: Contemporary Issues*, edited by Jonathan Boston, Andrew Bradstock and David Ong, 49–74 (Wellington: Victoria University Press, 2011).

Introduction

Of all the memorable parables recorded in the Gospels, the two that have become most firmly lodged in popular consciousness and affection are the parable of the Good Samaritan and the parable of the Prodigal Son. Found only in the Gospel of Luke (10:25–37; 15:11–32), these parables give expression to some of Luke's most characteristic thematic and stylistic concerns. Yet their ultimate origin is almost certainly to be found in the teaching of the historical Jesus himself. They offer unrivaled insight into his apprehension of God, religion, community, and morality. There are motifs in both narratives that have precedents and parallels in wider literary and religious tradition. But the Gospel stories remain highly distinctive. They stand in a class of their own for their simplicity, beauty, depth of insight, and sheer unsettling power.

It is not surprising, then, that the impact of these two parables reverberates so strongly through subsequent history. Both stories have been deeply formative of Christian thought and practice. The Good Samaritan has set the benchmark for works of Christian charity and service, and the Prodigal Son has profoundly shaped Christian spirituality and theology. The influence of the two stories has spilled over to wider culture as well. The Prodigal Son has furnished the subject matter for innumerable works of art and literature, while the Good Samaritan has informed research and debate in a number of academic disciplines. Indeed, two more fecund stories in the development of the spiritual, aesthetic, moral, and intellectual traditions of Western civilization are difficult to imagine.

The traffic has been largely one-way, however. While the parables have contributed to developments in the study of psychology, philosophy, art, literature, jurisprudence, and political studies, biblical interpreters have been slow to return to the exegetical table with the fruits of these developments. The Good Samaritan, for example, has helped furnish analytical categories for the study of altruism and other prosocial behaviors, and from this research much has been learned about why people do or do not intervene to help others in situations of need. But Gospel scholars have seldom brought this body of knowledge back to the task of understanding why the characters in the parable are depicted as responding in the way they do. We should not imagine, of course, that either Jesus or Luke was in possession of the technical knowledge that modern psychology has accrued about helping behaviors, or that in telling and retelling the parable they were intending to answer the sorts of questions that interest social scientists today. There are also significant differences between the social world presupposed in the parable and the contemporary world explored by social researchers. But none of this precludes us from using the findings of experimental psychology to try to understand better the personal and relational dynamics depicted in the story. To communicate its message, the parable portrays familiar human responses to stressful situations, and behavioral research can help sharpen our appreciation for why these responses have remained so troublingly familiar to listeners down through the ages.

One of the ancillary aims of the present study, then, is to bring some of the research findings inspired *by* these biblical stories back *to* the reading of the stories themselves. It offers a fresh reading of two well-known parables that draws historical exegesis into conversation with insights from social psychology, moral philosophy, and legal theory. It does so on the assumption that what gives these stories such perennial power is their portrayal of universal human fears, faults, and foibles in the face of circumstances that are morally ambiguous and personally demanding.

But the traffic needs to flow in the opposite direction as well. Just as social research can enrich our appreciation of what is going on in the story-world of the parables, so the parables may have something useful to contribute to academic discourse on topics such as altruism, the proper limits of social responsibility, the relationship between justice and mercy, the connection between law and morality, and the meaning of human love. They may also have something to offer to political debate and policy formation on a wide range of humanitarian and social justice issues. As the influence of the Christian voice in the public arena of Western society continues to wane, the potential for biblical stories such as these to shape and direct popular sentiment and political decision-making is also declining. This calls for new efforts from those of us who believe that the stories of Jesus still have something crucial to say in our context to demonstrate how these parables can speak meaningfully to issues of shared concern today and why secular society should still give ear to their message.

This book represents a modest contribution to this goal with respect to one area in particular, that of criminal justice. I have had a long-standing interest in the intersection of biblical ethics and criminal justice theory and practice. In a previous book, *Beyond Retribution: A New Testament Vision for Justice, Crime and Punishment*, I offered an extended analysis of biblical teaching on crime and punishment from the perspective of restorative justice theory. My goal in that book was partly to allow restorative justice insights to cast new light on early Christian texts concerning justice and punishment, and partly to furnish a biblical and theological basis for Christian involvement in criminal justice reform in a restorative direction (a two-way traffic of ideas, in other words). The extent to which I read restorative justice conceptions into the biblical text from outside, or draw out of the text what is already there but frequently missed by modern interpreters, is hard to say. In biblical studies it is nearly always a mixture of both. But the book demonstrates how bringing a restorative justice lens to the task of New Testament interpretation can be enormously productive. It affords, for example, a fresh way of thinking about the great Pauline doctrine of justification by faith, the logic of which makes far better sense when conceptualized within a restorative rather than a retributive justice frame of reference.

The essential argument of *Beyond Retribution* is that the first Christians experienced in Christ and lived out in their faith communities an understanding of justice as a power that heals, restores, and reconciles rather than hurts, punishes, and kills, and that this understanding ought to drive a Christian contribution to the criminal justice debate today.[1] Human justice-making should be patterned after divine justice-making. And since the justice of God disclosed in the life, death, and resurrection of Christ is a redeeming or *restoring* justice, so the pursuit of justice in general society should also be qualified by a commitment to restorative methods and outcomes. This is not to suggest that the New Testament furnishes us with a ready-made set of policies that can be transposed directly into the criminal justice domain today. That is obviously not the case. What it does offer us, however, is a vision of what human life and

---

1. Marshall, *Beyond Retribution*, 33, 256–59.

human relationships ought to be like—and indeed *can* now be like—in consequence of the revelation of God's restoring intervention in Christ to put the world aright, and it invites us to imagine forms of social policy that bear witness, however imperfectly, to that reality. While the New Testament does not prescribe a package of criminal justice policies and practices, it does point us in a direction, and that direction is decidedly restorative in nature.

In the present study, I narrow the focus considerably. I shift from mapping the overall perspective of the earliest Christian community on issues of crime and punishment to examining how this perspective finds expression in just two brief parables. Both parables, I propose, may be fruitfully read from a restorative justice perspective, and both have something valuable to contribute to contemporary discourse on a number of themes, especially on the role of compassion in social life and legal practice. One parable deals with the restoration of *victims* to wholeness and the response of the legal establishment to their plight; the other deals with the restoration of contrite *offenders* to good standing in society and the hostile reactions that often greet their reintegration on the part of more respectable members of the community. In both cases, the categories and concerns of restorative justice theory afford a new framework for understanding the meaning of the parables, and the parables in turn offer helpful insights into the philosophy and practice of restorative justice.

WHAT IS RESTORATIVE JUSTICE?

The term restorative justice was coined in the 1970s to describe a way of responding to criminal offending that concentrates on relational, emotional, and material repair more than on conviction and punishment. A variety of alternative labels have been proposed for such an approach, such as "transformative justice," "relational justice," "reparative justice," "therapeutic justice," or "collaborative justice," but it is restorative justice that has stuck. The term is now used throughout the world, and in some jurisdictions the language of restorative justice has even been incorporated into statute law. In New Zealand, for example, there is now explicit reference to restorative justice in the Sentencing Act 2002, the Parole Act 2002, the Victims' Rights Act 2002, and the Corrections Act 2004. The terminology has also been used in conventions issued by multinational bodies such as the United Nations, the Council of Europe, and the European Union, calling on member states to introduce or expand restorative options in their domestic justice systems.[2]

Not surprisingly, as use of the terminology has increased and spread, so too has the variety of ways in which it is understood and applied. Restorative justice has been termed one of the current "big ideas" in legal studies, and big ideas, of their very nature, have a tendency to become almost infinitely capacious. The secondary literature on restorative justice is now immense, with discussion ranging well beyond the disciplinary field of legal and criminal studies.[3] The principles of restorative justice have been extended into a variety of other arenas as well, including community policing, education, environmental debates, workplace disputes, family mediation, human-rights advocacy, military disciplinary procedures, and intra-communal peacemaking initiatives. The most recent book to cross my desk is on restorative justice and social work.[4] It is now commonplace to speak of restorative justice, not simply as an idea, but as a broad-based *social movement* for the promotion of restorative living in every sphere of life.[5]

One consequence of this explosive growth is that the precise definition and normative contours of restorative justice have become increasingly contested. Fortunately this debate need not detain us long here. For present purposes, it is sufficient to understand restorative justice as a way of responding to wrongdoing and conflict that seeks, above all else, to repair the harm suffered, and to do so, where possible, by actively involving the affected parties in mutual dialogue and decision-making about their needs and obligations. The distinctiveness of such an approach in the legal domain should not be underestimated. It is not simply a minor variation on the current justice system, a way of oiling its wheels so that it

---

2. See, for example, United Nations Office on Drugs and Crime, *Compendium*, 132–36.

3. To nominate any "best available study" on restorative justice would be invidious, so extensive is the field. But mention may be made of the collections of essays in *Handbook on Restorative Justice*, edited by Van Ness and Johnstone, and *Restorative Justice: Critical Concepts* (4 vols.), edited by Carolyn Hoyle. For a single volume study, see Van Ness and Heetderks Strong, *Restoring Justice*.

4. Beck, Kropf, and Leonard, *Social Work and Restorative Justice*.

5. See, for example, Umbreit and Armour, *Restorative Justice Dialogue*, 1–34; Maxwell and Liu, *Restorative Justice*. On restorative living, see Zehr, "Ten Ways." See also Van Ness, "Restorative Justice: A Modest Proposal."

becomes more efficient or more effective. It is a fresh way of conceptualizing the criminal justice problem, a "third way" between the retributive and rehabilitative models that have long dominated penal philosophy, a different paradigm for thinking about crime and its impact.[6]

For some theorists, the distinctiveness of the restorative paradigm lies in its *processes or practices*. Restorative justice is a particular process in which all those affected by an incident of wrongdoing come together, in a safe and controlled environment, to share their experiences and resolve together how best to deal with its aftermath. For others, the distinctiveness of restorative justice lies in its *values or commitments*. For these thinkers, restorative justice is different because it prioritizes the values of healing and respect, participation and truth telling, mutual care, reconciliation and peacemaking, and social transformation.

There is no need to set these "process" and "values" conceptions against each other. Both must be held together, for it is the values that determine the process and the process that makes visible the values. If restorative justice privileges the values of respect and truth, for example, it is crucially important that the practices followed in a restorative justice encounter exhibit equal respect for all parties and give ample opportunity for everyone present to speak their truth freely. On the other hand, as long as these values are honored, there is room for a diversity of processes and a flexibility of practice.[7] There is also room to broaden the reach of restorative justice to embrace the concept of living restoratively in all dimensions of personal and social existence.

So restorative justice is *both* a distinctive dialogical process *and* a distinctive set of relational and therapeutic values, with each requiring the other in order to be effective.[8] Having said that, what is most crucial as restorative justice continues to grow and diversify, and especially as it becomes more integrated into mainstream justice systems, is that its undergirding values are safeguarded. Advocates of restorative justice often agitate for the provision of restorative avenues within or alongside existing judicial structures, paid for by the state and supported by public agencies like the police, the courts, the prison system, the parole board,

---

6. The seminal work is Zehr, *Changing Lenses*. See also Zehr, *Little Book*.

7. On this, see Boyack et al., "Good Practice," 265–76. See also the superb essay by Pranis, "Restorative Values," 59–74.

8. Strang and Braithwaite state that a combination of values and process conceptions should be seen as a "normative ideal" for restorative justice, *Restorative Justice*, 13.

the probation service, and the legal fraternity. There is much to be said in favor of this as one way of promoting justice and penal reform. But there is always the danger that, in the course of becoming more respectable, restorative justice will be co-opted by the prevailing order and, bit by bit, forced to conform to an alien set of values—such as the need to process cases as quickly and cost-efficiently as possible, to employ only paid professionals to handle them, to measure success in the politically expedient terms of reduced recidivism rather than participant satisfaction, to fixate on the current sacred cow of enhancing public security and minimizing risk, and to bury the creativity and disruptive potential of restorative encounters beneath a mountain of official paperwork and bureaucratic checklists.

But if restorative justice is to make a real difference, its practitioners must be "in the world but not of the world" (John 17:15). They must be trusted participants in the public justice system, yet self-consciously drink from a different stream and cherish a different set of values. Values do not exist in a vacuum, of course; they are held by flesh-and-blood people belonging to particular historical communities. If it is to flourish, then, restorative justice must be anchored in alternative "communities of value," that is, in communities of people who accord the highest importance to the values of mutual care and accountability, honesty and compassion, confession and forgiveness, and peacemaking.

One such community of value ought to be the Christian church. After all, Christians boast a religion that centers on grace, repentance, and reconciliation—convictions that also lie at the heart of restorative justice. One would therefore expect Christians to be vigorous supporters of judicial and penal reform in a restorative direction. Sadly, this has not been the case historically (with some notable exceptions) and is not always the case today (again with notable exceptions). Perhaps part of the mission of the restorative justice movement is to remind the Christian community of what it supposedly believes and ought to practice more consistently, to call the church's attention back to what Jesus himself expounded in his teaching and embodied in his life. Nowhere in Jesus' teaching are the principles and priorities of restorative justice more vividly and memorably represented than in the two magnificent parables we are about to consider.

AN OVERVIEW OF THE BOOK

This book is divided into three sections. Part 1 is devoted to the parable of the Good Samaritan. Chapter 1 begins by noting the use made of this parable by that great social prophet of the twentieth century, Rev. Dr. Martin Luther King Jr., for whom it was obviously a source of personal inspiration and guidance. Dr King's appeal to the parable attests to its enormously persuasive power in the history of Christian thought and practice, and in Western civilization as a whole.

Chapter 2 sets out four reasons why the parable may be helpfully read as a narrative of restorative or therapeutic justice. The most obvious is that the story itself recounts an episode of criminal violence and its consequences. Less immediately obvious, though hugely significant, is that Luke places the parable in a distinctly legal setting and makes extensive use of legal themes and categories. The story is told to a "lawyer" (Luke 10:25) and involves a discussion about "what is written in the law" and how it should be "read" (10:26). These are features that bring the parable within the orbit of legal hermeneutics.

Chapter 3 examines the discussion that transpires between Jesus and the lawyer about the meaning of the love commandments in the Torah and considers the complicated question of the relationship between love and law. Tellingly, Jesus and the Jewish lawyer are portrayed as standing in total agreement on the primacy of love to the law and on the necessity of legal obedience for receiving eternal life. Where they differ is on the meaning of the term "neighbor" in the commandment, "You shall love your neighbor as yourself" (Lev 19:18.) The lawyer sticks to the letter of the law and endorses its straightforward contextual meaning. Jesus rejects any attempt to delimit the concept on purely legal grounds and insists that all human beings, including even one's enemies, count as neighbors to be loved and, whenever they are harmed, restored to wholeness.

Jesus accomplishes this redefinition by positing a hypothetical scenario in which two legal specialists, a priest and a Levite, encounter a "half dead" (Luke 10:30) victim on the road from Jerusalem to Jericho. Chapter 4 first examines the rich insights the story affords into the experience of criminal victimization and traumatology, and then asks the question, Precisely why did the two legal experts not stop to help the victim? What dissuaded them from doing so? Here knowledge gained from research on altruism and the so-called bystander effect assists in clarifying the many variables that could have influenced their decision. Put differently, the parable dramatizes the operation of an avoidance mechanism that is recognizable to us all, and psychological research helps pinpoint the various circumstantial and dispositional factors that can trigger this mechanism.

Chapter 5 is devoted to the remarkable depiction of the Samaritan's response to the needs of the victim, an erstwhile enemy. Here we see the therapeutic side of restorative justice in its purest, most unqualified form. Every detail of the description of the Samaritan's response illuminates what is entailed in restoring victims to health and freedom after the devastation they have suffered. The Samaritan not only serves as an exemplar of individual benevolence; there are also intimations in the story of the need for systemic and structural transformation as a necessary ingredient of a genuinely restorative expression of justice.

Chapter 6 returns to the relation of love and law and to its bearing on the task of legal reasoning. Jesus uses the story of the Good Samaritan to illustrate what it means to satisfy the legal injunction to love one's neighbor as oneself. But what about *bad* Samaritans? What about those who flout their social duty towards neighbors in serious need? Is there a case for using law to punish bad Samaritans and compel good Samaritanism? Or are Anglo-American jurisdictions correct in leaving the decision about whether to assist those in life-threatening situations over to individual conscience?

Part 2 addresses the parable of the Prodigal Son. We begin again, in chapter 7, by reviewing the immense cultural and theological impact of this remarkable parable, the longest and most complex one Jesus ever told. It too may be read as a narrative of restorative justice, with a focus less on the experience of criminal victimization than on the nature and impact of individual offending. Restorative justice has taught us to understand criminal offending primarily as a matter of relational breakdown and disrespect, and this, as we see in chapter 8, applies perfectly to the role of the younger son in the story. His sinfulness resided not so much in his hedonistic excess as in his callous disrespect for his father and his rejection of family responsibilities. Restorative justice has also helped us appreciate that wrongdoing creates a range of obligations on the part of offenders that must be discharged if justice is to be secured. For the younger son, these obligations include contrition, confession, correction of life, and atonement or reconciliation.

Chapter 9 examines the restorative gestures of the father and the resistance to them on the part of the older brother. Just as the Samaritan's actions elucidate what is entailed in restoring victims to wellness, so the father's actions spell out what is required to restore offenders to right relations. Most striking is the public bestowal of honor on the repentant boy. Some theorists have used the concept of "re-integrative shaming" to account for the positive impact that restorative processes can have on offenders. But according to our parable, it is not the reinforcement of shame but the symbolic conferral of honor that carries restorative power.

Central to the literary and poetic structure of both parables is compassion. The turning point is reached when the central character is "moved with compassion" (10:33; 15:20) at the suffering he observes and responds with a clear-sighted determination to restore the sufferer to well-being. Compassion is the key ingredient that inspires and enables justice to be done. In Part 3, therefore, we stand back from the parabolic narratives to analyze the meaning of compassion itself and to probe its connection to justice. Chapter 10 offers a definition of compassion and discusses the strengths and weaknesses of being guided by compassion in the task of moral reasoning. It also explores the need for compassion in public life. It asks how compassion can best be cultivated in individual citizens and in societal institutions, and discusses the role biblical narratives can play in promoting this.

Chapter 11 examines the place of compassion in the justice system. Drawing on the work of feminist legal scholarship on empathy, it argues that compassion has an essential role to play in legal deliberation. Certainly there are dangers in allowing emotions to influence legal process. But there are also dangers in pretending emotion can be wholly excluded from the picture, and notable benefits to be derived from employing a reflective or educated compassion in judicial discovery, analysis, and decision-making. What has been lacking in most of the previous discussions of legal empathy, however, is an appreciation of the importance of empathetic engagement between victims and offenders. This is where restorative justice, with its central procedure of facilitated encounter between victims and victimizers, has a unique contribution to make. It represents a form of justice-making that is energized and enriched by the space it gives to reciprocal compassion.

In the closing pages of the book, I offer a defense of restorative justice against the charge mounted by legal academic Annalise Acorn that it trades in "compulsory compassion" and promotes a "dewy-eyed justice." Acorn's accusation not only misconstrues the character of restorative justice, it is accompanied by a troubling complacency towards the violence and brutality of the current penal system. It also contradicts what I contend in this book is the controlling theme of Jesus' two great parables of restorative justice. Both parables teach that it is only by being "moved with compassion" at the reality of human suffering—whether it be the suffering endured by crime victims or the suffering of remorse and exclusion experienced by perpetrators—that we are adequately equipped to understand and achieve what is needed to bring about true justice, a justice that heals, restores, and reconciles and thereby reflects the prodigality of God's mercy.

PART 1

Restoration and the Victim

(Luke 10:25–37)

THE GOOD SAMARITAN

Just then a lawyer stood up to test Jesus. "Teacher," he said, "what must I do to inherit eternal life?" He said to him, "What is written in the law? What do you read there?" He answered, "You shall love the Lord your God with all your heart, and with all your soul, and with all your strength, and with all your mind; and your neighbor as yourself." And he said to him, "You have given the right answer; do this, and you will live."

But wanting to justify himself, he asked Jesus, "And who is my neighbor?"

Jesus replied, "A man was going down from Jerusalem to Jericho, and fell into the hands of robbers, who stripped him, beat him, and went away, leaving him half dead.

Now by chance a priest was going down that road; and when he saw him, he passed by on the other side. So likewise a Levite, when he came to the place and saw him, passed by on the other side.

But a Samaritan while traveling came near him; and when he saw him, he was moved with compassion. He went to him and bandaged his wounds, having poured oil and wine on them. Then he put him on his own animal, brought him to an inn, and took care of him. The next day he took out two denarii, gave them to the innkeeper, and said, 'Take care of him; and when I come back, I will repay you whatever more you spend.'

Which of these three, do you think, was a neighbor to the man who fell into the hands of the robbers?" He said, "The one who showed him mercy." Jesus said to him, "Go you and do likewise."

1

A "Magnificent Little Story" and the Task of Public Ethics

On April 4, 1967, the great American civil rights leader, Rev. Dr. Martin Luther King Jr., delivered a speech to a gathering of the organization "Clergy and Laity Concerned about Vietnam," at Riverside Church in New York City.[1] Professing his wholehearted support for the aims of this organization, King recounted how, over the preceding two years, he had moved steadily to "break the betrayal of my own silences" on the war. Colleagues had questioned the wisdom of his doing so, fearing it would detract from his focus on civil rights. But coming out against the war, he explained, was not only consistent with his being a recipient of the Nobel Peace Prize, which had been conferred in 1964, it was also consistent with his commitment to the ministry of Jesus Christ. "To me the relationship of this ministry to the making of peace is so obvious that I sometimes marvel at those who ask me why I am speaking against the war."

King proceeded to denounce the dishonorableness of America's intentions in Vietnam, and to detail the enormous suffering that three decades of war had inflicted on the people of that blighted peninsula. He called for an end to aerial bombardment, the declaration of a unilateral cease fire, the opening of negotiations with the Viet Cong, and the setting of a firm date for the withdrawal of foreign troops from the country. He also proposed that all young men in America should register as conscientious objectors, and encouraged ministers of religion to give up their ministerial exemptions from military service and also to enroll as conscientious objectors.

1. King Jr., "Beyond Vietnam."

But King went further. True to his trade as a preacher and social prophet, he asserted that the war in Vietnam was but a symptom of a far deeper malady in the American spirit. "If America's soul becomes totally poisoned," he intoned, "part of the autopsy must read Vietnam." A nation that is prepared to send its poor Negro and white boys to kill and die together in the villages of Southeast Asia, but is unable to seat them together in the same schools or to house them in the same city blocks, is a nation in spiritual decline. A society that chooses to invest its vast economic resources in the demonic destructiveness of militarism, rather than in rehabilitating the poor, is a "society gone mad on war."

What America needed, King declared, was "a radical revolution of values," entailing a shift from being a "thing-oriented" society to becoming a "person-oriented" society, and accompanied by a reordering of priorities so that the pursuit of peace takes precedence over the pursuit of war. Without such a moral and spiritual revolution, America would never be able to conquer "the giant triplets of racism, materialism and militarism." He continued with these memorable words:

> A true revolution of values will soon cause us to question the fairness and justice of many of our past and present policies. On the one hand, we are called to play the Good Samaritan on life's roadside; but that will be only an initial act. One day we must come to see that the whole Jericho road must be transformed so that men and women will not be constantly beaten and robbed as they make their journey on life's highway. True compassion is more than flinging a coin to a beggar; it is not haphazard and superficial. It comes to see that an edifice which produces beggars needs restructuring.
>
> A true revolution of values will soon look uneasily on the glaring contrast of poverty and wealth . . . and say: "This is not just." . . . A true revolution of values will lay hands on the world order and say of war: "This way of settling differences is not just." This business of burning human beings with napalm, of filling our nation's homes with orphans and widows, of injecting poisonous drugs of hate into veins of people normally humane, of sending men home from dark and bloody battlefields physically handicapped and psychologically deranged, cannot be reconciled with wisdom, justice, and love. A nation that continues year after year to spend more money on military defense than on programs of spiritual uplift is approaching spiritual death.

A "Magnificent Little Story" and the Task of Public Ethics

The Vietnam era is now over, and many things have changed in American society since. But Dr. King's searing critique of American militarism, and its inextricable connection with racism and social injustice, remains as pertinent today as it did forty-five years ago (read "Afghanistan" in place of "Vietnam," and the speech could have been delivered last week).

A PROPHETIC METHOD OF SOCIAL ANALYSIS

King's speech is also an instructive example of a particular way of addressing the ethical dimensions of public life. It is the method of the social prophet rather than the now much more familiar method of the trained policy analyst or political strategist or media commentator. King's speech is fundamentally an antiwar homily, not an analysis of domestic social and political policy. But he refuses to compartmentalize the nature of justice, and moves backwards and forwards between the tragedy of Vietnam and the violence and poverty of America's urban ghettoes as two sides of the same coin. One of the things that impelled King to raise his voice against the war, he explained, was the incongruity of commending nonviolent social change to the rejected and angry young men on the streets of America's cities while the American government modeled a way of solving its problems overseas by employing "massive doses of violence." Little has changed in the intervening decades. King's style of social commentary, then, is one that exposes the interconnectedness of all spheres of collective life, and that insists on the need for consistency between what the state expects of its citizens and how the state itself behaves.

A second noteworthy feature of King's approach is that he does not begin with some speculative theory of justice, or a precast list of ethical principles, or a code of universal human rights, which is then applied to social reality in order to determine the appropriate course of action. Instead King begins, on the one hand, with a personal confession of his own complicity in the social problems he is describing, and, on the other, with an account, again grounded in personal experience, of concrete situations of poverty, violence, racism, and injustice, both at home and abroad. What social justice requires, King assumes, cannot be discerned in the abstract from the safe distance of a policy analyst or an academic theorist. It can only be found by looking at the actual, embodied suffering of the victims of oppression and injustice, and questioning the structural arrangements that perpetuate their suffering.

Certainly King repeatedly appeals to the great ethical principles of fairness, wisdom, equality, freedom, truth, humility, justice, and especially love, and he acknowledges the ambiguities that invariably surround the great issues of social life. But the primary challenge is not so much to define what these ethical principles mean in theory or in practice, as it is to listen to the poor, the weak, the victims of inequality and violence, and even to those who count as national enemies. Guidance will come primarily from heeding "the mandates of conscience and the reading of history," and above all from the dictates of compassion, not from detached philosophical or sociopolitical analysis.

A third feature of King's approach is his appeal to religious or spiritual resources to envision social change. This is not surprising, given King's credentials as a Baptist preacher and the religious makeup of his audience. He speaks of his own commitment to Jesus Christ and emphasizes the universal brotherhood of all men under God's Fatherhood. At one point he quotes a Vietnamese Buddhist leader and later appeals to the common "Hindu-Moslem-Christian-Jewish-Buddhist belief" that love is the supreme unifying principle in life and the key that unlocks the door to ultimate reality.[2] Along with quotations from John F. Kennedy, Arnold Toynbee, and several black poets, King quotes two biblical texts verbatim (Isa 40:4/Luke 3:5; 1 John 4:7) and alludes to a third: the parable of the Good Samaritan (Luke 10:25–37).

It is this allusion to the story of the Good Samaritan that is most intriguing, and occasions the detailed exploration of this story I offer in this book. King cites the parable to make the point that while we have a moral obligation to alleviate the suffering of the poor and disadvantaged, by itself that is not enough. Charity must be accompanied by efforts at structural and systemic transformation. "We are called to play the Good Samaritan on life's roadside; but that will be only an initial act. One day we must come to see that the whole Jericho road must be transformed so that men and women will not be constantly beaten and robbed as they make their journey on life's highway." King's appeal to the

---

2. "One of the most fundamental religious intuitions is that love lies at the heart of ultimate reality," Oord, *Defining Love*, 175. For an overview of the role of love in the major relgous traditions, see Martin and Runzo, "Love." On the distinctively trinitarian conception of divine love in Christianity, see Volf, "God Is Love."

Good Samaritan in this speech is only fleeting, but it carries tremendous rhetorical power, for it evokes one of the most seminal narratives in the Western cultural tradition. Indeed, it is hard to think of another story that has been more influential in molding personal and political virtue than the parable of the Good Samaritan. It is a story that may still serve, even in contemporary secular society, as a useful reference point for measuring policy options and guiding ethical decision-making.

This may seem a curious thing to contend for a short, fictional narrative devised two thousand years ago and reflecting vastly different cultural circumstances to our own. But it is worth recalling just how fundamental storytelling is to the construction of social solidarity and identity, and to the development of collective morality. Human beings are, by nature, storytelling creatures, compelled to make sense of our experience by recollection and narration. We use narratives to formulate and convey our understanding of ourselves and the world we inhabit. As communities, we use narratives to express our common origins, history, memories, and ideals, and religious narratives to connect historical experience to matters of ultimate concern. We also use stories to foster moral commitment and to sharpen ethical sensitivities. Stories, it seems, are socially formative and morally effectual in a way that abstract rules and philosophical principles are not.

Stories are not alone in possessing such constitutive power. Shared customs, laws, rituals, ceremonies, and sacred symbols also play an important role, though often these too have a distinctly narrative quality about them. But most of all, it is the stories we tell and accord authority to because of their truthful insight into moral experience that best enable us to identify the virtues and values we consider desirable, to elicit social obligation towards them, and to encourage and sustain shared moral vision. One way to think of public policy, then, is as the attempt to enact procedurally and politically the moral vision and priorities that our foundational moral and religious narratives embody and articulate.

All this may seem blindingly obvious. Yet it is often the most obvious truths we overlook, particularly in the public policy domain, where administrative and fiscal technicalities quickly control and eventually swamp any appeal to larger visionary resources. Moreover, there is a telling critique of modern political liberalism that focuses on its failure to recognize the unitive and generative function of shared narrative traditions. According to the tenets of post-Enlightenment liberalism, the best, perhaps the only, moral and political community we can have today is one based on the guarantee of individual liberty, the freedom of private citizens to do as they please so long as they do not violate the freedom of others. But liberalism mistakenly assumes that such freedom and rationality can flourish independently of any undergirding narrative that is commonly held to be true. We are free insofar as we have no common story that constrains us.

Liberalism celebrates the importance of personal autonomy, pluralism, and tolerance, but liberal society is deficient in the narrative resources needed to cultivate moral character and promote hopeful living, or even, for that matter, to appreciate the deepest meaning of human freedom.[3] To develop communities that embody and elicit virtues such as trust, compassion, patience, hope, gratitude, hospitality, and forgiveness, we need more than a list of political principles or ethical values or codes of human rights. We also need unifying, authoritative, and empowering *stories* that educe and enact moral truth, for moral character and virtue are inherently narrative-dependent phenomena.[4]

Martin Luther King intuitively recognized this in evoking the story of the Good Samaritan. In a few deft words, he triggered recollection of one of the most inspiring and provocative narratives in the Christian tradition. He did so in a way that both affirmed the parable's traditional emphasis on charitable concern for the needy and pushed beyond its conventional interpretation to stress the additional need for structural reform, for a repaving of the Jericho road. Intriguingly, exactly one year later, in the final sermon Dr. King ever preached—the famous "I Have Been to the Mountaintop" speech, delivered to striking sanitation workers in Memphis, Tennessee, on the day before his assassination—he returned to the story of the Good Samaritan, and at much greater length. This time he appealed to the parable to stress the need to over-

---

3. In the philosophical traditions of antiquity, both pagan and Christian, human freedom was understood to mean the fulfillment of one's true essence or nature, one's flourishing as the kind of being one properly is. In post-Enlightenment modernity, however, freedom has become increasingly understood as the individual's emancipation from all constraint and the freedom to choose whatever one desires, whether or not it is consistent with one's created being. For a recent discussion, see Hart, *Atheist Delusions*, esp. 19–26.

4. Among Christian ethicists, Stanley Hauerwas is probably the most influential critic of liberalism in this respect. For a representative sample of his writings, see Berkman and Cartwright, *Hauerwas Reader*.

come fear and never to neglect engaging individually with situations of injustice, rather than simply convening meetings of the "Jericho Road Improvement Association" to investigate the causal roots of the problem.[5] Quite clearly, King's leadership of the civil rights movement, and all that it stunningly achieved for American society, was energized and informed by his frequent meditation on the "magnificent little story" of the Good Samaritan.[6]

THE PARABLE'S POTENT CULTURAL LEGACY

The parable of the Good Samaritan was originally told by Jesus in reply to a question from "a certain lawyer" about the scope of the term "neighbor" in the biblical commandment, "You shall love your neighbor as yourself" (Luke 10:25–29). In response, Jesus offers the lawyer not an analytical definition of jurisprudential terminology, but an imaginary tale that illustrates what it means to be a neighbor in practice.

Of all the stories Jesus told, none has been absorbed more deeply into the moral and legal traditions of Western society than has this extraordinary little story. Its influence far exceeds the boundaries of strictly religious or theological discourse. The parable still frequently figures as a starting point for discussions in moral philosophy and social and experimental psychology about altruism and the nature of social responsibility, while in legal theory it continues to inform debates about the relationship between morality and law and the scope of personal liability. It has also played a huge role in medical ethics, and in shaping the practice codes of other helping professions.[7] The parable is commonly cited to encourage charitable activity at the local level and to inspire philanthropy on the global stage, especially in the form of emergency aid and relief assistance. In the political arena, Good Samaritanism is sometimes used to justify military interventions in failed states for humanitarian reasons

---

5. King Jr., "Mountaintop."

6. King Jr., *Stength to Love*, 30–38. Interestingly, shortly after the historic Selma-to-Montgomery march in 1965, sociologist Joseph Gusfield described it as "one of the greatest outpourings of mass Samaritanism in American history" (Gusfield, "Social Sources," 183).

7. The parable has even inspired the names of some helping professions, such as the well-known telephone counseling service called "Samaritans," begun in England in 1953 and since spread around the world. See Varah, "Why Samaritans."

or to uphold human rights or to come to the aid of oppressed minorities.[8] Most recently, the concept has figured in debates about immigration, extradition, and the treatment of asylum seekers, and the obligations of hospitality towards refugees and displaced populations.[9]

These diverse applications of the parable help explain its powerful and perennial potency. Its intellectual and cultural legacy has been enormous. As a commentator once remarked, the parable of the Good Samaritan has built hospitals all over the world, and if it were truly heeded it would end racism, eliminate national hatreds, and abolish war.[10]

Perhaps the most remarkable legacy of the parable, however, is the continuing currency in secular society of the expression "good Samaritan" as a metaphor for selfless concern for others. At the time of writing this, news reports in New Zealand were dominated by the story of a middle-aged businessman, Austin Hemmings, who was stabbed to death on a busy street in Auckland City at 5:30 p.m. when he went to the assistance of a woman being bothered by a man. Hemmings was regularly described in news bulletins as a "good Samaritan," and when, a few months later, he was named New Zealander of the Year, one newspaper headline read: "Good Samaritan, Best New Zealander."[11]

For Jesus' first audience, by conspicuous contrast, "Samaritan" was a pejorative term indicating someone odious and sinister, and the notion of a "good Samaritan" was an oxymoron. According to John's Gospel, Jesus himself was once slurred with the accusation "You are a Samaritan and have a demon," as though one disparaging identity necessarily implied the other (John 8:48).[12] Today, however, as the newspaper headline shows, the epithet is synonymous with goodness, courage, compassion, and self-sacrifice, a remarkable semantic inversion directly attributable

---

8. The titles of two recent books are revealing, even if the parable itself is not discussed in detail in them: Brysk, *Global Good Samaritans*; Chang, *Bad Samaritans*.

9. See, for example, Schaab, "Neighbor?," 182–202; Carroll R., *Christians at the Border*, 116–26; Soerens and Hwang, *Welcoming*, 91–92. Surprisingly, no mention is made of the parable in Hoffmeier, *Immigration Crisis*.

10. A. T. Robertson is quoted to this effect by Jones, "Love Command," 240.

11. Vass, "Good Samaritan."

12. The slur hurled at Jesus could refer either to the supposed illegitimate origins of the Samaritans (and thus indirectly of Jesus' own illegitimate birth) or, more likely, to the belief that the supposed magical powers of the Samaritans derived from demonic sources. In any event, "the charge of being a Samaritan and the charge of being possessed are two alternate ways of saying the same disparaging thing," Meier, *Marginal Jew*, 3:549.

to Jesus' arresting parable. So effective was Jesus' parabolic rebranding of Samaritans as paragons of virtue rather than embodiments of vice that even in our own biblically untutored times it is still possible, as I saw recently in a suburban newspaper, to advertise for community volunteers under the banner, "Become a Samaritan! Help us to help others."

Few readers today would be able to explain anymore why the term "Samaritan" carries such positive connotations. A recent survey of levels of biblical literacy in Britain found that 60 percent of respondents were entirely unaware of the story of the Good Samaritan, which is even higher than the 57 percent who had never heard of the biblical figure of Joseph or his brothers, despite the hit musical *Joseph and the Amazing Technicolor Dreamcoat*.[13] As popular exposure to the biblical stories, characters, and themes that have traditionally nourished the moral reservoirs of Western society steadily declines, and Christianity recedes in memory to little more than a faded cultural relic, so too does the potential of master narratives such as the Good Samaritan to mold and direct shared morality or public-policy decisions. This is surely regrettable for, as we will see in the journey ahead, this magnificent little story has an almost inexhaustible capacity to shed light on the moral dimensions of a wide range of issues, including issues of criminal justice.

"HEAR THEN THE PARABLE"

The parable of the Good Samaritan has been described as "one of the most brilliant miniature stories ever composed."[14] The story is brief—a little over one hundred words in the Greek text—and uncomplicated in structure and plot line. But the narrative is full of action (with repeated verbs of movement), rich in detail (with mention of nakedness, wounds, oil, wine, bandages, donkeys, inns, and money), and packed with emotional interest (with explicit reference to compassion, mercy, and love). The story exhibits a range of rhetorical devices, including suspense, surprise, coincidence, contrast, reversals, parallelisms, inclusions, and climactic speech. No fewer than six characters or groups of characters make up the *dramatis personae* (not counting the donkeys!): the victim, some robbers, a priest, a Levite, a Samaritan, and an innkeeper. It is this

---

13. The initial findings of the survey are reported in Smith, "Britain 'Knows Little.'"
14. Wright, *Victory*, 306.

wide array of actors that gives the deceptively simple story its subversive effect. Each character occupied a recognizable place in the social hierarchy of the time, and each would have triggered a range of expectations and feelings on the part of the first audience: their initial deference or respect for some characters would soon have given way to disappointment or dislike as the story unfolded, while visceral feelings of contempt for other characters would have been confounded by the unexpected kindness they exhibit.

At one level, the moral of the story is patently obvious: it conveys a straightforward lesson about neighborliness.[15] It teaches that a real neighbor is one who shows mercy to those in need, whatever their personal standing may be. Since love for neighbor is mandated in divine law (Lev 19:18), the flip side of the message is also obvious: "Anyone who knows the right thing to do, and fails to do it, commits sin" (Jas 4:17). Sin is not only the active commission of evil, such as that perpetrated by the marauding bandits; it is also the willful neglect of doing good, such as displayed by the priest and the Levite. Whatever other shades of meaning may be perceived in the parable, this ethical-religious message about the extent of neighborly duty should never be obscured.

But the story is intended to be much more than a sentimental tale about philanthropy. The fact that it is a hated and heterodox outsider who exhibits true conformity to the moral vision of God's law, while two temple officials signally fail to do so, invests the story with wider repercussions. As N. T. Wright observes, "A story like this contains so much of the significance of Jesus' ministry, of the redefinition of the kingdom, of numerous overtones that resonate in various directions, that it is well-nigh impossible to tie it down to any particular theme, or indeed stereotypical literary category."[16] As well as stressing the ethics of care, the story deals with social, racial, and religious prejudice; the contested boundaries of covenantal identity; national enmities, and the individual impact of severe violence; the efficacy of the temple system; the relative importance of ritual and moral performance in the Torah; and, as we will explore in some detail, the response of the law and the legal establishment to the event of criminal victimization.

---

15. Forbes, *God of Old*, 69.
16. Wright, *Victory*, 305.

To acknowledge these multiple resonances is not to open the door to every possible wind of interpretation. Parables may be polyvalent, in the sense that they are capable of diverse and equally legitimate readings, but they are not infinitely pliable. For any particular interpretation of a Gospel parable to be credible, it must be demonstrably faithful to how the story itself is constructed and told, do justice to the historical and cultural points of reference implied in the text, make sense of the narrative and conceptual context in which the parable occurs in the Gospel tradition, and cohere with what we know of the larger message and perspective of its narrator.

Admittedly, such hermeneutical exactitude has not always been evident in the history of parabolic interpretation. The early Church Fathers subjected the parables to a sophisticated allegorical interpretation that aimed to distil a deeper spiritual significance behind the literal or surface meaning of the text. The Fathers did not for a moment deny the literal or historical meaning of the words on the page, but they considered this the least interesting semantic dimension of the text. Much more rewarding was what the parable revealed about soteriology, Christology, ecclesiology, and sacramental theology.

In the case of the Good Samaritan, patristic exegetes were virtually unanimous in viewing it as an allegory of salvation history, with almost every detail of the story being pressed into allegorical service. The victim was taken to represent the human race plunged into sin and ruin, the robbers to symbolize the devil's persecutions, the priest and the Levite to signify the inadequacy of the Old Testament dispensation, and the mysterious helper to denote the saving grace of Christ.[17] Scholars today typically pour scorn on these ancient christological renderings of the parable, with Augustine's classic decoding of its details, which influenced

17. On the allegorical interpretation of this parable in Christian history, see Wailes, *Medieval Allegories*, 209–14; Just Jr., *Luke*, 17–81; Roukema, "Good Samaritan," 278–95; Higton, "Boldness," 447–56. The most sustained modern attempt to read the parable allegorically is that of Gerhardsson. In his analysis, the victim represents Israel, the Samaritan signifies the true shepherd who is the Son of Man, the priest and the Levite represent the false leaders who do not care for the sheep, and the robbers stand for the enemies of the people of God. The original parable was allegedly changed in the early church, prior to its reception by Luke, to become an illustration of the discussion about neighbors. See Gerhardsson, *Good Samaritan*. For a critique, see Snodgrass, *Stories*, 356–57, cf. 698 n. 83, for other modern interpretations that rely on allegory. Interestingly, J. A. Fitzmyer dismisses claims that the parable is anti-Semitic as a subtle kind of modern allegorizing, Fitzmyer, *Luke*, 2:885.

most subsequent interpretation, a particularly common target for derision. Klyne Snodgrass is representative of the current consensus when he rules that "all attempts to find Jesus (or Israel) mirrored in the parable are illegitimate allegorizing."[18]

Now there is no denying that at the heart of patristic and medieval allegorizing lay a fatal flaw, namely, a lack of accountability to the historical matrix in which the parables were first uttered. In the hands of later ecclesiastical interpreters, Jesus' parables lost much of their subversive power and became simply a confirmation of the Church's existing dogma and theological prejudices. For this reason, there can be no going back to the ahistorical allegorizing of the past. But this does not mean that the parables are thereby stripped of all christological significance, as though Christology were merely the bastard child of a mistaken literary methodology. Certainly there is little to suggest that Jesus intended the Good Samaritan to be a thinly veiled self-reference, or a cipher for defending his own religious and moral conduct from criticism. But it is still the case that the Samaritan in the story does what Jesus himself is also portrayed as doing throughout his career, especially in the Gospel of Luke: he brings a divine-like compassion to bear on abject human need, disregarding the conventional boundaries of ritual and religion to do so.

The Samaritan in the parable personifies and performs what Ian McDonald fittingly calls an "alien grace," that same disturbing grace evident in the activity of Jesus in the wider gospel tradition.[19] The Samaritan alien enacts the true meaning of the Torah's love commandments, which, for Luke, are most fully expressed in the historical activity of Jesus. In Luke's Gospel, as John Nolland explains, "Jesus' call for love of God has its best commentary in Jesus' own passion for God, his intimacy with God, and his fidelity to God: just as his call for love of neighbor has its best commentary in the life of this friend of tax collectors and sinners, who saw the service of others as his sacred calling."[20] Fulfilling the law means a passion for God and compassion for others.

---

18. Snodgrass, *Stories*, 356. Gerhardsson observes that twentieth-century exegetes have been as united in their opposition to christological readings of the parable as the Early Fathers were in support of it: Gerhardsson, *Good Samaritan*, 585.

19. McDonald, "Alien Grace," 35–54.

20. Nolland, *Luke*, 585. "Jesus' habitual association with sinners and outcasts is one of the most widely accepted axioms in New Testament scholarship" (Forbes, *God of Old*, 293); cf. Schaab, "Neighbor?," 190–92. Snodgrass objects that even if this is true, it is not Christology in the usual sense (*Stories*, 356). But what is "usual" parabolic Christology?

Significantly, "compassion" in Luke's Gospel is used only of God (1:78, cf. 1:50, 54) and of Jesus (7:13), and of the two most extraordinary parabolic characters of all: the father of the Prodigal Son (15:20) and the Good Samaritan (10:33).[21] Both these parables are used to dramatize a divine reality invading the conventional world of first-century society, a reality activated by and embodied most fully in the larger gospel story by the person of Jesus himself. In this sense, as McDonald observes, "the Fathers were right to look for something beyond the literal or historical dimension in the parable of the Good Samaritan."[22] Certainly it is primarily a didactic tale about moral responsibility towards outsiders. But there is a theological weight or christological texture to the account that should not be missed, even if it is not the governing concern. Birger Gerhardsson's christological allegorizing is unwarranted overkill, but he is surely right to suspect that the departure point for the dominant christological reading of the parable in subsequent centuries is to be found in the parable itself.

This christological dimension is not only evident in the theological writings of the Fathers. It is also evident in many of the artistic representations of the parable, both ancient and modern, which sometimes show greater sensitivity to wider theological resonances of the story than do some professional exegetes. At St. Michael's Anglican Church in Kelburn, near to where I live and work in New Zealand, a splendid stained glass window recounts the parable of the Good Samaritan in a distinctly christological context. The four central panes of the window are devoted to scenes from the parable. But the narrative is framed by two panes on top that quote the Johannine love commandment, "This is my commandment, Love one another as I have loved you," and two panes at the bottom, one depicting Jesus raising Jairus's daughter from her deathbed, together with the words, "He went about doing good," the other of him sharing

---

21. Interestingly, Luke omits all the references to Jesus' "compassion" present in his Markan source (Mark 1:41, cf. Luke 5:13; Mark 6:34; 8:2, cf. Luke 9:13; 10:2; Matt 9:36; 14:14; 15:32; Mark 9:22, cf. Luke 9:38, 41), while retaining or inserting it in a non-Markan source (Luke 7:13, cf. Mark 17:13), though he does retain Mark's reference to Jesus' "mercy" (10:47/Luke 18:38, cf. Luke 17:13). Presumably this is a stylistic rather than a theological adjustment, since the link between Jesus and divine compassion and mercy is well established in the Gospel, and elsewhere in early Christian tradition (Luke 7:13; 17:13; 18:38, cf. Phil 1:8; 2:1; 1 Tim 1:2; 2 Tim 1:2; 2 John 3).

22. McDonald, "Alien Grace," 44–45. Peter Jones allows for "Christological implications," since Jesus and the Samaritan see the world the same way (Jones, "Love Command," 237–38).

a meal with the two travelers on the road to Emmaus, under the rubric, "This cup is the new covenant sealed in my blood." The message conveyed by this framing arrangement is plain: the love shown by the Samaritan in the parable, and the mutual love Jesus enjoins on his disciples, is defined and embodied by Jesus' own deeds of deliverance, table fellowship, and self-sacrifice. Two other sayings of Jesus embedded in between the two halves of the parable reinforce this message: "I am the true vine, you are the branches," and "By their fruits you shall know them."

The parable itself is depicted in four scenes in the middle of the window. The first has the traveler being attacked. The second shows the victim lying twisted and crumpled on the roadside, naked but for a modest loincloth, with two figures in the distance moving away from him, one slightly ahead of the other: the priest and the Levite. Standing beside the victim is a third character looking along the road at the two departing figures, one of whom has his face turned back towards the victim and his companion. The stationary figure beside the victim has his arms extended at his sides, forearms slightly bent at the elbows, with palms open, in a gesture of utter bewilderment at how the travelers ahead of him could have stepped over the body at their feet and continued unaffectedly on their journey. You can almost read his thoughts: "Where on earth are you going! Didn't you see this man? Can't you see he needs help? Why didn't you stop?"

But who is this stationary character on the road? It is not the Samaritan, who first appears in the third windowpane devoted to the story, dressed in different clothes and headgear and with his donkey in train, and there is no third bypasser in the parable itself. Who, then, is this interloper? Presumably the mysterious stranger is intended to represent the conscience or voice of Jesus himself, the one who tells the story, and whose intercession on behalf of the victim is ignored by the religious leaders, who have more important things on their mind, but is heeded by the social outcast who arrives next on the scene. The passing Samaritan enacts the loving and compassionate response that Jesus requires, and that he himself embodies, and in so doing, we will argue, displays the law's true purpose of restoring justice.

2

A Parable of Law, Crime, and Justice

The parable of the Good Samaritan is found only in the Gospel of Luke, where it gives expression to some of Luke's most characteristic thematic and stylistic preferences. These include a particular interest in Samaritans; an emphasis on the plight of the disadvantaged and the need for positive action on their behalf; an attention to the geographical setting of events, with a particular focus on Jerusalem; and a preference for certain words and turns of phrase.[1] A handful of scholars have suggested that the Gospel writer himself composed the parable in Greek.[2] But the vast majority traces the story back to the historical Jesus, even though, as is almost always the case, the dominical tradition has undergone redactional adaptation at the hands of the evangelist and of earlier tradents. We possess now only the Lukan rendition of the parable, yet from the beginning of his work Luke claims to be faithfully transmitting the actual teaching of Jesus, albeit in his own words (1:1–4; cf. Acts 1:1), and there is no good reason to distrust this claim with respect to this parable.

---

1. On Lukan stylistic and thematic concerns in the parable, see Snodgrass, *Stories*, 344, 697 n. 61.

2. For example, Sellin, "Lukas," 166–89; 66, 19–60; Goulder, *Luke*, 487–92. Creed thinks the parable was originally composed in Greek (*Saint Luke*, 150–52). Others find signs of an Aramaic or even Hebrew *Vorlage* (Gerhardsson, *Good Samaritan*, 19, 24). For a critique of Goulder and Sellin, see Nolland, *Luke*, 588–90; Forbes, *God of Old*, 58–59 n. 16; Wilson, *Luke and the Law*, 16–17. Esler is happy to consider the parable a Lukan creation, but thinks that whoever composed it understood the message of Jesus so well it is immaterial whether it is authentic or not (Esler, "Intergroup Conflict," 325, 50–51).

Even if it were possible to reconstruct with confidence the tradition-prehistory of the extant parable—and, frankly, it is not—that would do little to establish the ultimate provenance or authenticity of the story itself.[3] In oral transmission, a story can be told a thousand times, and with a thousand tiny variations, and still be an "authentic" recounting of the same essential, inherited story.[4] Walter Wink's assessment of the origins of the account is probably as far as we can go. "The fact that Jewish hearers are in mind (not Gentiles, or Samaritans, or even Christians), the total simplicity and directness of the parable, unencumbered as it is by later concerns of the church, and the utterly radical notion of love which it presents, suggest to me that either Jesus or someone who had fully internalized his thought composed it."[5] The parable is totally consistent with the most radical of Jesus' teachings, Wink observes, and can legitimately be regarded as representative of his outlook, whether or not he said it in precisely the terms, or in exactly the setting, that Luke recounts it in.

The most contested feature of Luke's editorial work on the parable relates to its literary setting. It is told by Jesus in response to a question from a lawyer about what he must do to inherit eternal life. The parable is folded in between the two halves of the conversation between Jesus and his interlocutor (10:25–29, 36–37). Some scholars maintain that the parable does not answer precisely the question put by the lawyer, and propose that the association of the parable with the dialogue is secondary and unhistorical, even if the parable itself is authentic. These critics suggest that Luke has taken the tradition of Jesus' encounter with the scribe in Jerusalem recounted in Mark 12:28–34 and Matt 22:34–40,[6] attached to it an originally independent parable that deals with a wholly unrelated

---

3. On the limitations of classical redaction criticism, see Marshall, *Faith*, 8–33.

4. For an important discussion of the significance of oral transmission for assessing the shape and fidelity of the Gospel tradition, see Dunn, *Jesus Remembered*. Also relevant is Bauckham, *Eyewitnesses*.

5. Wink, "Compassionate Samaritan," 206–8.

6. Every conceivable option has been suggested for identifying the source of this tradition. Some propose a Q tradition shared by Matthew and Luke; others appeal to a special M or L tradition; some think that Luke and Matthew had access to different recensions of the Markan story; some think Mark and Q overlapped, with the later evangelists conflating them in different ways; many allow for some independent oral or written source that Matthew and Luke have combined with Mark and subjected to redaction. For a brief review of options, see Wink, "Compassionate Samaritan," 206–8; Wilson, *Luke and Law*, 14; Meier, *Marginal Jew* 4:523, 611 n. 158.

issue, and transferred the redactionally forged unit, which John Dominic Crossan describes as "a beautifully constructed double controversy dialogue," to an earlier setting in his narrative.[7] Crossan goes on to argue that the fusion of the parable with the dialogue has had the effect of distorting the true message of the story. The parable originally functioned as a metaphorical allusion to the disturbing irruption of the kingdom of God into human consciousness. But in its Lukan context, it is transmuted into a simple injunction to moral excellence.[8]

This negative judgment about the current setting of the parable is not entirely persuasive, however. Something must have triggered the telling of the story, and it is hard to imagine a more suitable occasion than the one Luke supplies.[9] The parable dovetails perfectly with the two questions raised by the lawyer about the nature of legal performance required to gain future life (*poiein* vv. 25, 28, 37) and about the scope of the biblical idiom "neighbor" (*plēsion*, vv. 27, 29, 36), and there is no need to see this arrangement as wholly editorial.

The main reason for suspecting a secondary conflation is that in both the dialogue with the lawyer in Luke 10 and in the interchange with the scribe in Mark 12/Matthew 22, the conversation deals specifically with the centrality of the twin love commandments in the Torah (Deut 6:4-5; Lev 19:18). But apart from some overlap in content, the accounts have little in common,[10] and it is quite conceivable that they reflect, not just variant accounts of a specific incident in Jesus' career, but two different historical episodes.[11] It seems clear from the wider gospel tradition that

---

7. Crossan, *In Parables*, 61. Others who see the link as secondary include Montefiore, *Rabbinic Literature and Gospel*, 344-49; Creed, *Luke*, 150-52; Gnilka, *Jesus*, 244; Scott, *Hear Then*, 191-92; Witherington III, *Jesus the Sage*, 192.

8. Crossan, *In Parables*, 57-66; idem, "Parable and Example," 285-307.

9. So I. H. Marshall, *Luke*, 445-46; Snodgrass, *Stories*, 348-50; Wright, *Victory*, 305-6; Derrett, *Law*, 222-27; Stein, "Interpretation of the Parable," 287-90; Gerhardsson, *Good Samaritan*, 28 ("Luke 10:25-37 was a unity from the first"); cf. Nolland sees an original minimal connection with a discussion about the idea of "neighbor," which Luke has "displaced with a heavily edited version of the tradition about the greatest commandment in the law," *Luke*, 580. For Bauckham, "the Lukan setting at least dramatizes the kind of context of legal debate to which the parable was originally addressed," "Scrupulous Priest," 476.

10. For a list of the key differences, see Nolland, *Luke*, 583.

11. So Marshall, *Luke*, 441, 445; Fitzmyer, *Luke*, 877; Manson, *Sayings*, 260-62; Cranfield, "Good Samaritan," 368; Banks, *Jesus*, 164; Forbes, *God of Old*, 56-57. This is, however, still a minority view.

Jesus considered love to have hermeneutical precedence in the interpretation of the Torah and to be the lodestar for his own activity,[12] and, as T. W. Manson observes, in the oral culture of the day, "the only way of publishing great thoughts was to go on repeating them in talk and sermons."[13] The importance of the love commandments was therefore probably a recurring topic of conversation between Jesus and his hearers, just as it was in other early Jewish settings. The same applies to the question of how to gain entry to the future world, which also crops up more than once in the Jesus tradition and in rabbinic discourse (cf. Mark 10:17; Matt 19:16; Luke 18:18).[14] Hence it is by no means improbable that two distinct recollections of exchanges between Jesus and other theological teachers of his day on the significance of the twin commandments would survive in the Synoptic tradition. It is also not improbable that Luke would choose

---

12. See Gnilka, *Jesus* 238-47; Manson, *Teaching*, 302-8; Burridge, *Imitating Jesus*, 50-55, cf. 258-60; McKnight, *Jesus Creed*, passim; Snodgrass, *Stories*, 349 ("The two love commands are the heart of Judaism and the foundation of Jesus' ministry, his creed from which all else stems..."). Meier argues that the historical Jesus certainly prioritized love in the Torah (as the Markan tradition indicates) but did not see the love commandments as the hermeneutical principle to the whole Torah (which is a later Matthean development of the tradition; Meier, *Marginal Jew*, 4:478-646). Two points may be noted in response. First, Meier's focus on distilling the words of the historical Jesus from the gospel tradition by means principally of the criteria of discontinuity and multiple attestation involves a significant degree of uncertainty and produces a relatively minimal basis for appreciating Jesus' actual perspective. It is true that in Mark Jesus only affirms the priority of love. But this need not mean that the category of priority exhausts the hermeneutical potential Jesus perceived in the love commands. Certainly one of Jesus' earliest Jewish interpreters, the evangelist Matthew, understood Jesus to accord to love a greater interpretive significance than Meier allows. This leads to the second point. Meier too readily assumes that Matthew's perspective on Jesus and the law, because of its redactional features, is almost wholly unhistorical and unreliable. But redactional reworking need not entail historical fabrication. Nor need Matthew's position be viewed in such sharp contrast to Mark's. After all, if Jesus deemed love of God and neighbor to be the "greatest" commandments in the law, as Mark indicates, this surely implies a range of legal implications, such as Matthew's Gospel articulates. Meier is content to say that, "as opposed to Matthew's reworked version, Jesus simply states that love of God is the first commandment, that love of neighbor is the second, and that no other commandment is greater than these. That is all" (653). But it is inherently implausible that Jesus thought no further about issues of such import. If a first-century Jewish-Christian thinker like Matthew discerned more to it than that, how can a twenty-first-century critical scholar be so confident he was wrong to do so?

13. Manson, *Sayings*, 260.

14. For a survey and discussion of these texts, see Haacker, "'What Must I Do?,'" 140-53.

to omit Mark's story of Jesus' encounter with the scribe in Jerusalem in the corresponding section of his Gospel because he felt the issues had already been thoroughly canvassed in the earlier pericope with the lawyer. This seems inherently more plausible than the alternative explanation that Luke has elected to rewrite Mark's account radically by placing the words of Jesus on the lips of an antagonistic interrogator, combine it with a thematically unrelated parable, and relocate the conflated unit to a different segment of his narrative, the Great Journey narrative of chapters 9–19.

There is even less reason to consider Luke's use of the parable to grant the lawyer moral direction ("Go you and do likewise," v. 37) to be a fundamental misunderstanding of the parable's poetic artistry and existential purpose, as Crossan alleges. The much-discussed difference between metaphorical "parables" and paraenetic "example stories" is one of degree rather than kind.[15] Some parables have a more marked metaphorical or eschatological function of opening people's eyes to the presence of the kingdom of God in the mission of Jesus and its radical implications. Others, like the Good Samaritan, deal more directly with the subject matter at hand, in this case the interpretation of a specific commandment in Scripture. Yet the moral perspective the parable offers on the subject is still eschatologically conditioned. The parable's radical reinterpretation of the love commandments derives, ultimately, from eschatological presuppositions. The Torah is viewed in the parable from the standpoint of its eschatological *telos* now being glimpsed in the career of Jesus, a perspective that entails not a rejection of the Torah but a radicalization of its key ethical demands, together with a sublimation or relativizing of its overall importance in the new age (cf. Luke 16:16).[16] This is not to say that the parable is *about* eschatology *per se*; it is mainly and plainly about ethics. But the ethics in question are *eschatological* ethics—ethics that, while

---

15. See the full-scale treatment by Tucker, *Example Stories*. More briefly, Snodgrass, *Stories*, 13–15, 350–52.

16. There is no more disputed and complex question in Gospel studies than that of Jesus' relationship to the Torah. In broad terms, there is much to be said for Schnelle's suggestion that in Jesus' teaching, protology (an appeal to God's original will in creation) and eschatology (an appeal to the in-breaking of God's new order) combine to decenter the role of the law (". . . for Jesus, it was not the gift of the Torah but the love of God in his kingdom that was the open door through which every person could come to God"), as well as to sharpen its demands in the ethical realm while relaxing its demands at the ritual level. Schnelle, *Theology*, 133–43 (quotation at 143). On the interpretation of the notoriously ambiguous unit Luke 16:16–18, see Wilson, *Luke and the Law*, 43–51.

grounded in existing law, are transfigured in light of the dawning reign of God. For when Samaritans love nameless Jews in such an extravagant manner, and Jews acknowledge the exemplary righteousness of their Samaritan rivals, nothing less than the kingdom of God must be at hand.

This interpenetration of ethics and eschatology helps account for the parable's striking mix of realism and unrealism. From one angle, the story is completely realistic. It describes a common experience in everyday life, an act of predatory violence on a vulnerable stranger. It also portrays familiar human vices and emotions, such as fear, pride, greed, and disgust; it trades on the instinctive human solidarity people feel with innocent victims of violence or injustice; and it summons pursuit of the most noble of human virtues, such as love, justice, and compassion. The reading it advocates of Lev 19:18 is also realistic, in that its commentary on the commandment is theologically defensible and pragmatically achievable. Indeed, the story is so realistic and so unusually precise in its geographical setting[17] that some commentators have suggested it recounts an actual historical event, which Jesus merely appropriated for pedagogical purposes.[18] This seems highly unlikely, although, as we will see shortly, there is a partial precedent in biblical history that Jesus could well have had in mind when constructing his account.

But, from another angle, what transpires in the parable is so shocking, so contrary to normal expectations, so *unrealistic*, that it betokens an entirely different world-order in operation, a world in which enemies act like friends and outcasts perform deeds of covenant faithfulness. It advocates not a straightforward grammatico-historical exegesis of Lev 19:18, but a dramatic extension of its intended meaning in light of new realities. Its radical answer to the question of who is my neighbor, and its characterization of neighbor love as more than simple benevolence, inevitably raises the question, Whence comes such extravagant love for such unlikely neighbors? The parable points beyond what is humanly

---

17. The only other geographically located parable is that of the tax collector and the Pharisee in the temple (Luke 18:9–14).

18. In the judgment of Plummer, "the narrative is not fiction, but history. Jesus would not likely invent such behavior, and attribute it to priest, Levite, and Samaritan, if it had not actually occurred. Nowhere else does he speak against priests or Levites. Moreover the parable would have far more point if taken from real life" (*St. Luke*, 285–86). Cf. also, Jeremias, *Parables*, 203; Geldenhuys, *Luke*, 311; Kistemaker, *Parables*, 167. Lenski is ambivalent: *Luke's Gospel*, 603.

commonplace or naturally attainable and beckons its hearers to open themselves to an eschatological power that transforms existing values and enables a generosity of spirit and of service to the needy that goes far beyond what is merely reasonable or routine. It both enjoins a universal moral obligation ("Go you and do likewise") and underscores the need for divine empowerment to fulfill this obligation to the unlimited and continuous degree that the parable envisages.[19]

A PARABLE OF RESTORATIVE JUSTICE

The parable of the Good Samaritan has been subjected to countless interpretations down through Christian history, and the secondary literature on it is immense. The parable has been applied to virtually every area of ethical reflection, including certain aspects of legal ethics and practice. Its main role in legal philosophy has been to inform discussions about negligence and duties of care in tort law and to launch discussions in criminal law about the legitimacy of so-called bad Samaritan laws that criminalize failure to render assistance to people in life-threatening situations, as well as debates about the appropriateness of laws that indemnify good Samaritans from being sued for causing damage in the act of rescue. We return to these fascinating and important questions in chapter 6. But these matters do not exhaust the potential of the parable for informing a Christian approach to law, crime, and justice. There is still ample room for fresh work in this area, and in particular for exploring the implications of the parable for developing the theory and practice of restorative justice, which is my own primary interest. The parable's particular pertinence to issues of criminal justice in general, and restorative justice in particular, is evident in at least four ways.

---

19. Our human capacity to express love at any level ultimately depends, from a theological perspective, on divine causation (cf. 1 John 4:19). But nowhere is this more evident than in the phenomenon of enemy love. Oord notes that biologists often use ideas such as group-selection and genetic heritage to explain altruism towards members of one's own group, tribe, or community, while social scientists can appeal to various prudential considerations to account for it. However, "No good theory exists to account for the love expressed to strangers and enemies. The love of the good Samaritan remains unexplained." It is best understood, Oord proposes, as an obedient response to a maximally extensive God who inspires creatures to strive for universal brotherhood and sisterhood, consistent with his own love. "Because of God, good Samaritans are possible." Oord, *Defining Love*, esp. 173–212 (quotes at 184 and 199).

A Focus on Victimization

First, inasmuch as the story recounts an innocent man's mistreatment at the hands of violent assailants, it offers a window into the bitter experience of criminal victimization. This is the most obvious connection with the theme of criminal justice, though it is rarely spelled out in any real detail, even in essays specifically on victimology.[20] Admittedly, nothing is said in the account about the man's subjective responses to his assault or its aftermath, and in many respects the crime victim is the least developed of all the characters in the story. He never speaks for himself and, after being bashed unconscious in the opening scene, he never performs any actions for himself. As far as we know, he remains comatose until the very end.

But such impassiveness does not mean that his role in the story is wholly incidental, as some commentators claim. According to Birger Gerhardsson, for example, "It is clear that the parable is not concerned with the injured man; he is only the required object for the action of the narrative and the limelight is upon the three who come across him."[21] But that is completely mistaken. On the contrary, the entire account is told from the victim's point of view. It is *his* plight that holds the story together. What is fundamentally at stake from beginning to end is the value, or lack of value, that attaches to the person of the victim.

As the first character to appear in the story, listeners are immediately drawn to identify with the victim in his everyman role (*anthrōpos tis*) as he undertakes a routine journey on a familiar highway, with all its attendant dangers. He is also present in every scene of the drama.[22] As a storytelling device, this enables hearers to participate fully in the ebb and flow of events by identifying with him. The victim is also the only figure to be encountered directly by every other individual in the story. His predicament constitutes a fixed point at the center of the narrative structure, with two characters moving towards him (the robbers to hurt him,

---

20. For a useful collection of Christian reflections on victimolgy, see Lampman and Shattuck, *God and the Victim*.

21. Gerhardsson, *Good Samaritan*, 10.

22. Snodgrass denies that the victim is present in the final scene of the story (v. 35), *Stories*, 354. But it is natural to assume that when the Samaritan says to the innkeeper, "take care of him," the object of his instruction is physically present, especially given the likely architecture of the inn.

and the Samaritan to heal him), and three moving away from him (the robbers to abandon him, and the priest and the Levite to ignore him).

A lot is said in the account about the physical traumas (*ta traumata* v. 34) the man suffered and of his need for prolonged recuperation (v. 35). The passiveness of the man throughout most of the story is actually an intentional facet of his characterization as a victim. He first appears as an active and independent agent, traveling down the road from Jerusalem to Jericho, and it is only as the direct outcome of his assault that he is reduced to a condition of utter dependency on the ministrations of others. His vulnerability is symptomatic of the enforced disempowerment that constitutes the very essence of criminal victimization and often attends its aftermath.

His disempowered condition is highlighted at both the beginning and the end of the story. Twice he is referred to as "the one who fell into the hands of robbers" (vv. 30, 36). There are even parallels between what he endures on the road down from Jerusalem (*hodeuōn* v. 33) and what Jesus himself passively suffers at the end of his journey up to Jerusalem (*hodos* 9:53, 57; 10:4 cf. 1:76, 79; 3:3–5; 7:27), where he too is stripped (23:34, cf. 11, 53), physically beaten (22:63–65, 23:16), consigned to the company of criminals (22:52; 23:18–25, 32), and left to die (23:46–49). These parallels need not mean that the victim is intended to serve as an image or cipher for the crucified Christ, though some commentators have discerned such an intention.[23] But they certainly indicate that the victim's silence and lack of self-assertion in the story are not signs of his secondary importance but rather are basic to the depiction of his victimized state.

There is good reason, then, to agree with Robert Funk that the parable offers "a view from the ditch."[24] It invites hearers to consider harmful events and legal responses to them from the perspective of the victim.

---

23. Graves takes the victim, not the Samaritan, as a symbol for Christ, and proposes that the parable serves as an invitation to "share in the passion of Christ who set his face toward Jerusalem" ("Moral," 273). Cranfield has a similar intuition: "Not only is Christ the Good Samaritan *par excellence*; he is also to be recognised in the wounded man by the roadside" (Cranfield, "Good Samaritan," 371); cf. Schaab, "Neighbor?," 191.

24. Funk, "Good Samaritan," 74–81. Cf. Also, Bornkamm, *Jesus*, 112–13; Schrage, *Ethics*, 74; Forbes, *God of Old*, 69; McDonald, "View," 28–29, and "Alien Grace," 43; Gagnon, "Second Look," 6; Bauckham, "Scrupulous Priest," 485–86; Roukema observes that, even in later allegorical interpretations, with their strong christological focus, hearers must first identify with the wounded man before they can identify with the one who helps him ("Good Samaritan," 73).

For it is only by identifying with the victim that we can rightly assess the actions of every other character in the story. It is also not coincidental that the one who instinctively acts to alleviate the victim's condition, a Samaritan trader operating in Judean territory, could himself be viewed as a victim of religious and political discrimination, one subject to suspicion, prejudice, and numerous prohibitions. When Jesus concludes the parable by asking the lawyer, "Which of these three do you think was a neighbor to the one who fell among robbers?" (v. 36), he is indicating that the question, "Who is my neighbor?" is really a *victim's* question, which can only be answered from a victim's point of view.

The best way to determine the identity of one's neighbors, the parable suggests, is to project oneself imaginatively into a situation of utter desperation and debilitation and ask, "From whom, in that situation would I accept help?" If, as a victim of severe violence facing a lingering death, the lawyer would accept help from anyone willing to give it, regardless of their status or identity, then he too must be willing to render such help to anyone who needs it, irrespective of their status or identity. Robert Gagnon thus helpfully characterizes the parable as a kind of visualization of the Golden Rule (Luke 6:31): "Do to others as you would have them do to you, *in your hour of greatest need.*"[25] True insight comes from standing in solidarity with victims. The best vantage point for clarifying one's moral responsibility when harm has occurred is in the dirt and blood alongside the wounded party, not at the safe distance of a detached jurist debating the details of the relevant legislation. The lawyer is thus directly challenged to adopt a "victim's perspective" in determining what the law means when it summons him to love his neighbor as himself.

A Duty of Concern for Victims

This leads to a second way in which the parable is relevant to criminal justice concerns: it reflects extensively on the duty of care or solicitude owed to the victims of crime by other members of the community.[26] More

---

25. Gagnon, "Second Look," 7.

26. By "duty of care" here, I am not referring to the technical concept in tort law in which people are legally obligated to adhere to a reasonable standard of care in undertaking acts that may foreseeably harm others. I am using the term in the looser sense of a moral duty people owe to others to be positively concerned for their welfare. The term "duty" itself can be used in a weak sense to designate what people ought to do

words are devoted to describing the actions of the Samaritan than those of the two temple officials combined, with the rule of end-stress dictating that, as the last major character to appear, he is the one who enacts the dominant message of the story. His compassionate deeds are spelled out in extraordinary detail, partly to overcome the prejudicial stereotyping of Samaritans in the minds of Jesus' listeners that might lead them to dismiss or minimize any generic reference to his mercy, but mainly because the individual actions themselves give concrete content to the meaning of neighbor love.

As we will see in a later chapter, in each of the Samaritan's deeds, from his initial first aid to his provision for the long-term convalescence of the victim, there are important clues as to the nature of one's social responsibility towards those who suffer unjustly at the hands of others. Nothing is said about the need to catch and punish the offenders (most muggers never get caught anyway); all emphasis is placed on the need to restore and heal the victim. As Scott recognizes, "The man's restoration is the narrative's goal."[27] Moreover, in his devotion to this task, the Samaritan is not singled out as an exceptionally meritorious individual worthy only of gaping admiration. He is offered as a concrete example to be emulated by hearers (v. 37), as one who demonstrates what it means to perform the law's true meaning (v. 36) and thereby to secure the law's ultimate gift of eternal life (v. 28).

Several scholars have suggested that the parable was inspired by the episode recorded in 2 Chron 28:5–15 in which four Samarian elders respond mercifully to the needs of Judean prisoners of war brought to Samaria as slaves by Pekah, king of Israel, following his defeat of King Ahaz. "Then those who were mentioned by name got up and took the captives, and with the booty they clothed all that were naked among them; they clothed them, gave them sandals, provided them with food and drink, and anointed them; and carrying all the feeble among them on donkeys, they brought them to their kindred at Jericho, the city of palm trees. Then they returned to Samaria" (28:15).

There are striking similarities here with Jesus' parable. In both cases, the victims are naked; in both, they are clothed by people from Samaria, and also anointed; in both, they are transported on donkeys; and in both,

---

as decent human beings, and in a stronger sense to denote what people are obliged to do to in light of other people's rights.

27. Scott, *Hear Then*, 193.

their final destination is Jericho. Conceivably Jesus had this earlier act of kindness by the residents of the northern kingdom in mind when he constructed the parable. Interestingly, Michael Knowles characterizes the historical episode as a form of restorative justice. "Notwithstanding the fact that their own army has caused the victims' suffering, the four Samarians assume responsibility for making amends, demonstrating a kind of restorative justice as an act of faithfulness to God."[28]

This too is what the kind-hearted Samaritan demonstrates in the parable, even though he is not in any way to blame for the victim's plight. In the absence of others to help, including those who caused the harm, he assumes a stance of restorative care towards the victim. His actions reverse, step by step, the damage inflicted by the robbers. They beat him; the Samaritan pours on oil and wine to heal him. They left him half-dead; he conveys him to an inn. They robbed him; he contributes financially to his needs. They showed him no mercy; he treats him with compassion. They negated his value as a human and discarded him as a lifeless object; the Samaritan affirms his dignity and treats him as intrinsically valuable. It is these restorative actions that are held up as paradigmatic for the audience: "Go you and do likewise" (v. 37).

Hence the parable is relevant to the theme of restorative justice because it depicts the traumatic experience of criminal victimization and because it commends a positive ethic of care towards victims of crime. There is also a third way in which the story bears directly on our subject: it affords a highly instructive perspective on the function of law with respect to human distress, as well as a critical look at the proclivity of the legal establishment to exploit the ambiguities of legal justice to evade the higher dictates of love.

A Perspective on Law

For our purposes, it is hugely significant that the parable is told in response to a question from a lawyer about the scope of the law legislating care for one's neighbor (Lev 19:17–18). This is the only parable in the Gospels that is expressly used to explain or defend an item of legal interpretation, something commonplace in rabbinic parables.[29] We know from elsewhere in the Gospel tradition that Jesus engaged in legal debates

---

28. Knowles, "Victim Wearing?," 148.
29. McArthur and Johnston, *They Also Taught*, 169–71.

on many occasions. But this is the only instance where he uses a parable to elaborate and defend his own legal reasoning. Arguably, the pericope follows a midrashic style known as *yelammedenu rabbenu*, "let our master teach us," with the parable serving as a kind of narrative exegesis of the scriptural texts cited by the questioner.[30] The parable is framed by the two halves of the conversation between Jesus and his interlocutor, both of which follow the question-and-answer format commonly used in legal debates at the time.

	1	2
Question (lawyer)	10:25	10:29
Counter-question (Jesus)	10:26	10:30–36
Answer (lawyer)	10:27	10:37a
Answer (Jesus)	10:28	10:37b

What this arrangement means is that the parable comes to us, not as a free-floating humanitarian tale, nor as one component of a larger parabolic collection, but as a commentary on, and support for, a particular item of legal analysis. In the next chapter we will consider more closely what the category of "law" involved at this time. For now it is enough to draw attention to the pronounced legal atmosphere of the account, which is often missed or minimized by modern interpreters but is of considerable importance to understanding the parable's implications. In fact, the pericope is positively saturated with legal terminology, allusions, procedures, and assumptions. These merit laying out in some detail at this point in our investigation since their presence underscores again the potential relevance of the parable to issues of legal theory and restorative justice practice.

To begin with, the man who stands to challenge Jesus is expressly identified as "a certain lawyer" (v. 25), a representative of the legal profession. The term "legal profession" is not inapt here, since the complexity of Jewish law demanded specialist training to understand and apply

---

30. The structure is: a) introductory question on a text of Scripture (vv. 25–27); b) a second Scripture (v. 28); c) exposition (using a parable with catchwords "neighbor" (vv. 27, 29, 36) and "do" (v. 28, 37a, 37b); and d) final remarks alluding to original text or allusions to second text (v. 37), Blomberg, *Interpreting*, 231. Green terms the passage a "narrative exegesis," *Luke*, 425–26.

it correctly, and there existed a recognized cadre of people who provided legal services, much like lawyers or solicitors today.[31] One notable difference was that judicial functions in the early Jewish community went largely unremunerated. "He who takes payment for judging," the Mishnah declares, "his judgments are null; he who takes payment for testifying, his testimony is null."[32]

The word "lawyer" (*nomikos*), like the related term "teacher of the law" (*nomodidaskalos*), is comparatively rare in the New Testament but invariably occurs in contexts that deal with the administration or understanding of the law.[33] In Luke, the term seems to be equivalent in meaning to the more technical term "scribe," which also denotes specialist legal expertise (cf. 5:17 and 5:21). Most commentators assume that the lawyer in Luke 10 is a Pharisee, since lawyers are found elsewhere in Luke's narrative in the company of Pharisees (5:17; 7:30; 11:45; cf. Acts 5:34). This is probably correct, though it is worth noting that the Sadducees, who were mainly priests, also had scribes and lawyers,[34] and at least one Jewish scholar has proposed that the lawyer who interrogated Jesus was a Sadducean priest.[35] When not performing cultic duties (which occupied only five or six weeks a year),[36] well-educated priests

31. Sanders, *Judaism*, 180, cf. 171–73; Schürer, *History* 2:322.

32. *m. Ber.* 4:6; *m. Abot* 4:5, cf. 1:13. Payment was forbidden for both the educational and judicial activities of the sages, though the prohibition may have been adhered to only in the judicial sphere. The Gospels accuse the scribes and Pharisees of greed (Mark 12:40; Matt 23:6; Luke 20:47; 16:14), which, even if a conventional criticism of opponents, requires some basis in fact to be effective.

33. Gutbrod, "νόμος κτλ," 4:1088 (see Luke 5:17; 7:30; 10:25; 11:45; Matt 22:35; Acts 5:34; 1 Tim 1:7; Titus 3:9; the Matthean reading is textually uncertain and may be a secondary assimilation).

34. Cf. Schürer, *History*, 2:329. Schürer notes that the New Testament designation of certain doctors of the law as Pharisees implies that others were Sadducees. Furthermore it is inconceivable that any party that acknowledged the Torah would not have its own professional interpreters. The term "scribe" in Luke is sometimes associated with the Pharisees (5:21, 30; 6:7; 11:53; 15:2; cf. 20:39, 46) and sometimes with the chief priests (9:22; 19:47; 20:1, 19; 22:2, 66; 23:10).

35. So Mann, "Sadducean Priests"; cf. Burge, *Jesus*, 56. Gerhardsson thinks that the inquiry about "eternal life" makes it unlikely the lawyer was a Sadducee, *Good Samaritan*, 11 n. 2.

36. Priests were on duty in the temple only one week in twenty-four, plus the three pilgrimage festivals, totaling five to six weeks a year. Priests and Levites were forbidden to work the land, and so took other employment; at least some would have devoted considerable time to legal exposition and advice.

served as legal arbiters, teachers, and consultants.[37] Ezra was the biblical ideal; he was both a priest and "a scribe skilled in the law of Moses" (Ezra 7:6). Similarly the heroic Maccabean martyr Eleazer is described as "a man of priestly family, learned in the law" (*to genos hiereus tēn epistemēn nomikos,* 4 Macc 5:4), and a "priest worthy of the priesthood" by living "in harmony with the law and philosopher of divine life" (7:6–7). So it is possible that Jesus' legal interlocutor had a much closer association with the temple system than is usually assumed, which may help explain why Jesus cast cultic office-bearers as key players in the parable.

Be that as it may, the term *nomikos* marks him out as a highly educated legal specialist with a professional concern for how the law related to the pragmatics of everyday conduct. He was both a scholar-teacher of the law, with ongoing responsibility for "defining and perfecting the legal principles underlying or deriving from the Torah,"[38] and a judicial practitioner who offered legal services and advice. He taught the law, elaborated the law, and applied the law. Legal experts like him were highly revered in the wider community. In the eyes of the masses, Safrai explains, "there was an aura of sanctity and moral grandeur about them."[39] They exercised a significant role in the political structures of society and served as learned counselors in the courts of justice. Interestingly, the Greek word *nomikos* is sometimes also used in rabbinic writings to make it clear that Jewish teachers of the law were comparable to Roman jurists and teachers of public law in the great Hellenistic cities.[40]

The legal mood of the episode is also evident in the way in which the lawyer addresses Jesus as a "teacher" (*didaskale* v. 25), a term that meant only one thing in the Jewish community of his day: recognized expertise in scriptural exposition. This in itself is interesting, for the Gospel traditions afford us no clue as to where Jesus, a tradesman from Nazareth, acquired such proficiency in the Torah. That he possessed such proficiency is beyond dispute. Not only is he able to range freely across the vast array of commandments in the law to answer questions from inquirers, he also employs identifiable hermeneutical techniques in

---

37. For a detailed analysis of the evidence, see Sanders, *Judaism*, 170–89. Sanders firmly rejects the view of Schürer and Jeremias that legal responsibilities were largely usurped by lay scribes and Pharisees.

38. Schürer, *History*, 2:330.

39. Safrai and Stern, *Jewish People*, 620.

40. So Schottroff, *Parables*, 132, 238 n. 1; Schürer, *History*, 2:324 n. 4.

doing so. Anyone could claim to be a charismatic prophet, John Meier observes, but the kind of halakic expertise Jesus displays required disciplined study, though where he obtained such training may never be known, and the authority he exuded seems anything but derivative.[41]

Luke's picture, then, is of two legal experts engaging in the cut and thrust of legal disputation. Both men ask questions of the other, and both give answers. The lawyer's opening question does not raise any technical issue of textual interpretation; instead, it poses the more fundamental jurisprudential question, "What must I do to inherit eternal life?" (v. 25). This question assumes an axiomatic link between concrete obedience to the law ("What must I *do*?") and access to eternal life. Jesus makes this link totally explicit with his counter-question: "What is written in the law? What do you read there?" This is the first time the word "law" (*nomos*), which in the Greek sentence is placed in the emphatic initial position, appears on the lips of Jesus in Luke's narrative,[42] while the phrase "how do you read" was a standard rabbinic formula for inviting legal exposition (v. 26). Both dialogue partners, in other words, assume that the law is normative; both share the assumption that the ultimate purpose of the law is to ensure life (Lev 18:5), including life in the world to come (cf. Dan 12:2); and both take for granted that dedicated individual performance of the law's injunctions is essential if one is to benefit from the Torah's salvific promise ("What must I *do*?"—"*Do* this and you will live"). The critical issue is not the soteriological function of the law, but how to discern the irreducible essence of legal obligation.

When the lawyer nominates two specific stipulations in the law as the quintessence of its teaching, Jesus declares his reading to be "correct" (*orthōs* v. 28), and affirms that obeying these commands is the prerequisite of securing life, recalling Lev 18:5; 25:18; Deut 5:33; 6:24; 30:6, 15–20. At this point, Duncan Derrett proposes, "Jesus is depicted as a legislator.

---

41. Meier, *Marginal Jew*, 4:572–76, 647–63. Meier suggests that Jesus may well be the first Jew we know of to formulate a legal argument on the basis of the hermeneutical rule of *gezera sawa*, according to which texts using the same words may be interpreted on the same basis. Meier discerns in Jesus' teaching on the law an omnipresent implicit tone of, "it is so because I say it is so." He speculates (655–58) that Jesus may have regarded himself as the Elijah-like prophet of the end time, one of whose tasks was to resolve disputed halakic problems (Mal 4:4–5).

42. This is not the first time in Luke that Jesus addresses legal matters, however; see, e.g., 5:33–38; 6:3, 6.

He plays a role similar to that of Moses."⁴³ But, in typical legal fashion, the lawyer is not content with such a vague level of generality; the term "neighbor" in the second commandment requires technical definition. This is no minor matter of academic exegesis for the lawyer. What is at stake is nothing less than his practice of legal piety. It is in order "to justify himself" (*dikaiōsai heauton*)—that is, to defend his own conception of legal justice (*dikaios*), and hence his own daily lifestyle—that he pushes Jesus for definitional precision.

Presumably the lawyer realizes that his own classification of neighbor as a fellow Israelite devoted to covenantal faithfulness with God is more restrictive than the one Jesus appears to accept. Other teachers of the law had already grumbled about Jesus' liberal intercourse with the lawless, with sinners and tax collectors (7:39, cf. 29–30; 5:17, 21, 30; 6:7, 11). This simmering disquiet is significant, since majority opinion in legal interpretation was considered to be an important indicator of what was true for all Israel.⁴⁴ So the lawyer, taking the approach of an analytical jurist, asks Jesus to rule on those whom he thinks fall within the scope of the term "neighbor." The reason for seeking such a ruling was not so much to clarify whom he was obligated to love (he already knew that), but whom beyond his preferred in-group he was free *not* to love. Behind his perfectly respectable legal inquiry, in other words, lay the deeper concern of ensuring that the law functioned to sustain group boundaries by confirming the absence of positive duties to any beyond the borderlines.

In response, Jesus postulates a hypothetical test case for analysis. Constructing imaginary scenarios was a common method of pursuing halakic discussion. The story is intended, it seems, to draw the lawyer's attention to the hermeneutical priority of mercy in assessing the provisions of the law (cf. Hos 6:6; Mic 6:8). The episode itself is set in an effectively law-free zone, between two urban centers where the coercive power of the ruling establishment is concentrated and in command.⁴⁵ In this liminal, lawless space, a traveler falls victim to violent outlaws and is left for dead. The first two passersby to happen upon the victim are clerics, certified guardians of the law. According to Josephus, priests functioned as the rulers and judges of the nation, with authority to try

---

43. Derrett, *Law*, 222–23.
44. Schürer, *History*, 2:332.
45. Cf. Lindberg, *Political Teachings*, 186–87.

cases and punish malefactors.[46] Priestly responsibilities included legal instruction (the temple was a major center of Torah training),[47] and forming the temple police force was among the duties that fell to Levites (cf. Luke 22:47).[48] They also had some responsibility for Torah instruction, and served as judges in Judean towns and villages.[49]

Both characters, therefore, had more than a passing acquaintance with the law and so ought to have known in principle what the law required of them. But they falter in their duty towards their neighbor, not because they deliberately flout the law, but because they fail to prioritize restorative mercy in their application of the law's manifold stipulations. As we will see later, they act in a legally defensible manner in avoiding contact with the victim—like the lawyer, they would be perfectly able to "justify themselves" in their decision—but they nonetheless undermine the deepest values of the law in the process.

What fundamentally upholds the law's authority, the parable implies, is not a strict definition of neighbor, but a generous definition of love. For love, of its very nature, does not begin by deciding in advance on its appropriate object of concern: it discovers its object in the actuality of person-to-person relationships. Love requires actual relations with others. One cannot love in the abstract but only in the act of personal encounter. True love of neighbor, moreover, demands more than a negative respect for the neighbor's right not to be harmed, which is the primary intention of Lev 19:18. It also requires a positive dedication to restoring

---

46. For references and analysis, see Sanders, *Judaism*, 171–72.

47. "Temple and Torah formed an unbreakable whole: the Torah sanctioned and regulated what happened in the Temple, the Temple was (in much of this period) the practical focal point for the observance of Torah, both in the sense that much Torah-observance actually consisted of Temple-ritual, and in the sense that the Temple was the major place for the study and teaching of Torah" (Wright, *People*, 227–28).

48. Jeremias considers there is little doubt that the guards sent to arrest Jesus included Levitical police (Mark 14:43; Matt 26:47; Luke 22:47; John 18:3, 12). Among other things, the police would have protected the temple from Samaritans (Jeremias, *Jerusalem*, 209–11). Other Levitical duties included janitorial upkeep of the temple, preparation of the cereal offerings, and charge of the temple treasury.

49. So Wink, "Compassionate Samaritan," 209–10. Sanders notes that, at least in late biblical times, "Priests and Levites were often scribes, a title that covers a range of activities: copying texts, drawing up legal documents, and serving as experts on the law." This situation became even more pronounced in the first century (Sanders, *Judaism*, 170–71).

the well-being of those who have been injured by the deeds of others, regardless of their social identity or status.

Whereas those in the professional legal system fail to fulfill the law in this way in the name of honoring certain of its stipulations, the Samaritan, whom the lawyer would have judged to be habitually in contempt of the law, achieves what the law truly requires, in both letter and in spirit, by giving primacy to love and mercy over all other technical considerations. The lawyer is forced by the events of the story to take the side of the one whom he would have normally judged to be a flouter of the law against those whom he had hitherto considered to be its most faithful interpreters. In so doing, the one who tried to justify himself through his professional command of the law is summoned to confront the lack of justice in the assumptions he makes about the law's jurisdiction and implications.

Clearly, then, the parable has much to say about law, legal interpretation, and the hazards of professional dereliction of duty by those who are well versed in the law's decrees. The parable commends a style of legal reasoning that may differ significantly from that followed by other legal practitioners of the time, but it is still a species of legal reflection and thus may have something to contribute to thinking about legal theory and practice today.[50]

In view of this, it is curious that several Gospel scholars deny that the parable of the Good Samaritan has anything to do with Jesus' stance on the law, a subject that Luke allegedly had little interest in, unlike Matthew or Mark. Philip Esler, for example, states, "I do not consider that the parable as a whole concerns how the law should be interpreted or that it presents Jesus as caught up in the process of legal interpretation."[51] S. G. Wilson likewise insists that neither here nor elsewhere in his Gospel is Luke concerned with discussing or defining the law's true meaning; he is only concerned with *doing* the law. For this evangelist, theoretical debates about the relative merits of the commandments are "a false trail" that should be avoided in favor of pragmatic obedience to what the law says.[52] Pheme Perkins concurs that Luke is "not at all interested in the question of the law and even changes the [scribe's] question so that

---

50. See Saiman, "Legal Theory," 97–130.
51. Esler, "Intergroup Conflict," 335 n. 16.
52. Wilson, *Luke and Law*, 15, cf. 24.

it focuses on salvation in general."[53] Richard Burridge, too, emphasizes that Luke's focus is on eternal life and salvation, "rather than focusing on Jesus' interpretation of the law and its many commandments in the manner of a rabbinic anecdote."[54]

Now, the larger question of how Luke conceives and presents Jesus' attitude towards the law remains a matter of considerable scholarly debate.[55] The reason for this debate is that Luke sends mixed signals on the issue. On the one hand, Luke's Jesus explicitly and repeatedly affirms the law as a trustworthy expression of God's will and as an adequate guide for those who wish to enter the kingdom of God (e.g., 10:25–26; 11:42; 16:29; 18:18). In no sense does he set out to contradict or abrogate the Torah; rather, he faithfully upholds it. On the other hand, there are points at which Jesus' teaching or conduct appears to undermine the status of the law and some of its specific commands, whether by ignoring it (6:1–5), supplementing it (18:18–19 cf. 16:16), or calling it into question (6:1–11; 9:60; 11:41; 13:10–17; 14:1–6; 16:18 cf. 5:12–13, 33–34). In his benchmark study *Luke and the Law*, Wilson concludes that it is virtually impossible to discern a consistent pattern from Luke's evidence. "He presents Jesus as sometimes opposed to and sometimes in league with the law."[56]

It is not clear how this ambiguity is best explained.[57] But, in general terms, Luke seems less concerned with the details or relative merits of the law's constituent provisions than with the broad function of the law as a testimony to, and reinforcement for, the disclosure of God's eschatological will in the person and teaching of Jesus. It is not the meaning of the law *per se* that interests Luke so much as the meaning of Christian discipleship. The demands of discipleship stand in direct continuity with the law's central requirements and are consistent with them, yet they are not contained or exhausted by the law. The rich young ruler is beckoned by Jesus both to obey the commandments in order to attain eternal life, and also to do the "one thing still lacking: sell all that you own and distribute the money to the poor . . . then come, follow me" (18:18–23). The lawyer to whom the parable of the Good Samaritan is told is encouraged to obey

---

53. Perkins, *Love Commands*, 22–23; also Banks, *Jesus*, 170, cf. 246–48; Meier, *Marginal Jew*, 4:526.

54. Burridge, *Imitating Jesus*, 258.

55. For a survey of recent scholarship, see Loader, *Jesus' Attiutude*, esp. 273–300.

56. Wilson, *Luke and the Law*, 57.

57. For a brief survey, see Burridge, *Imitating Jesus*, 250–60.

the law's injunctions to love God and his neighbor as himself, but he is also implicitly summoned to love even his enemies as if they were his neighbors (10:25–37), which is more than the law ever envisages.

So Luke's depiction of Jesus' attitude to the law has its own characteristic features.[58] But Luke is still interested in *law*, and the law still occupies an important place in his narrative.[59] Moreover, his approach to the law still constitutes an *interpretation* of the law's meaning and function, even if it does not take the form of extended analysis of the law's prescriptions and jurisdiction. Wilson's suggestion that Luke is interested in practical obedience to the law *rather* than theoretical reflection on its meaning creates a false alternative. Theory and practice are not mutually exclusive; indeed, they are mutually indispensable, for how can one obey the law without considering its meaning? Esler's assertion that the Good Samaritan episode does not depict Jesus as "caught up in the process of legal interpretation" is equally dubious. Even if we take Luke's account of the interchange with the lawyer as a redactional modification of the Markan-Matthean episode with the Jerusalem scribe, and see the addition of the parable as secondary and artificial, neither of which is certain, it is inherently unlikely that, having juxtaposed the two units, Luke would see little connection between Jesus' discussion with a lawyer about the law and the events depicted in the parable. On the contrary, we have seen that the pericope as a whole has a pronounced legal mood throughout and entails issues of legal interpretation, even if its message is that the law *by itself* is not enough to generate the radical love God requires, since it is the legal specialists who fail in their moral duty, while the marginalized outsider succeeds.

---

58. For an exhaustive comparison of the Gospel writers, see Loader, *Jesus' Attitude*.

59. Luke uses *nomos* nine times in the Gospel and fifteen or sixteen (cf. 24:6 v.l.) times in Acts. The majority of these references refer to prescriptions in the Mosaic Torah; the remainder speak of the predictive aspect of the law. This reflects normal Jewish and Christian usage of the term. In addition, Luke speaks of "Moses," "custom" (*ethos*), and "commandment" as ways of referring to the law. Loader writes: "Luke has much in common with Matthew in affirming the place of the law . . . *for both the issue is a live one*. Yet they appear to operate in very different settings. Matthew is in a Jewish setting, Luke in a primarily Gentile setting" (Loader, *Jesus' Attitude*, 389 [my emphasis]).

A Declassification of the Adversary

This brings us to the fourth way in which the parable of the Good Samaritan bears on the concerns of criminal justice and legal practice. It directly challenges our propensity to dehumanize others by categorizing people dualistically as friend or foe, good or bad, guilty or innocent, even as victim or offender. What transpires in the story reverses conventional expectations about how people ought to behave, and thus challenges social constructions of good and evil. As John Donahue observes, "it subverts our tendency to divide the world into insiders and outsiders. It makes us realize that goodness may be found precisely in those we most often call evil or enemy."[60]

Jesus uses the parable to expound the meaning of the commandment "You shall love your neighbor as yourself" (Lev 19:18), and it continues to be used in both philosophical and legal ethics for unpacking the meaning of neighbor love. But had Jesus simply wanted to emphasize the need to show charity towards those in distress, any three individuals would have sufficed as actors in the drama, as long as the third one did the right thing. Had he only wanted to take a potshot at priestly myopia or legal pettifogging, the third person down the road could simply have been an Israelite layperson. Had he intended simply to reiterate the common mytheme, found in several popular tales, that there is virtue in rendering assistance even to those undeserving of aid, he would have cast the Samaritan as the victim and the rescuer as a Jew.[61]

But Jesus deliberately casts a hated national enemy as the one who upholds covenant commitments and fulfills the love commandments. In doing so, he effectively achieves two things: he expands the meaning of neighbor love to include enemy love, and he nullifies the identification of religious opponents with the enemies of God.[62] Both moves were

---

60. Donahue, *Gospel in Parable*, 134, and "Who Is My Enemy?," 142–43.

61. So Scott, *Hear Then*, 200–202.

62. Contra Montefiore, *Rabbinic Literature*, 344–49; and Schottroff, *Parables*, 135, who deny an emphasis on enemy love. Snodgrass rightly observes, "With its underlying theme of racial hostility the parable is very close to Jesus' emphasis on loving one's enemies" (*Stories*, 358). But this may be too reticent. Gnilka is closer to the mark when he insists that "the story *needs* to be read as an example narrative and depicts love of one's enemy," *Jesus*, 245 (my emphasis). So too McDonald, "Alien Grace," 46; Reiser, "Love of Enemies," 425; Perkins, *Love Commands*, 59–65; Burridge, *Imitating Jesus*, 259–60; Matera, *Ethics*, 88. Schrage rightly notes that enemy love rather than neighbor

phenomenally daring. With few exceptions, it was taken for granted in antiquity that one should love one's friends and harm one's enemies (cf. Matt 5:43). Jesus, by startling contrast, deemed love of friends to be ethically unremarkable (Luke 6:32–34; Matt 5:46–47), while valorizing love for one's enemies as a sign of true fidelity to the character of God, "for he is kind to the ungrateful and the wicked" (Luke 6:27–31, 35–36; Matt 5:44–45).[63]

This is shocking enough. But what is doubly shocking in the parable is that the one who displays such God-honoring enemy love was himself deemed by Jesus' hearers to be an enemy of God, a "foreigner" (Luke 17:18), who knew not the God of Israel he falsely claimed to worship (cf. John 4:22) and upon whom divine judgment could legitimately be called down (Luke 9:51–55). Jesus could have enrolled a Samaritan as the crime victim and had a noble Jewish benefactor stop to render him assistance. That would have exemplified love for enemy well enough. But it would not have deconstructed the destructive stereotyping of Samaritans as evil adversaries, and could even have reinforced his audience's sense of moral superiority towards them.

To reverse the roles of hero and villain in this way was an incredibly audacious thing to do. Kenneth Bailey explains how, even after living in the Middle East for over twenty years, he never had the courage to tell Palestinians a story about a noble Israeli, or Armenians a tale about a noble Turk. "Only one who has lived as a part of a community with a bitterly hated traditional enemy can understand fully the courage of Jesus in making the despised Samaritan appear as morally superior to

---

love is at the heart of Jesus' ethics (*Ethics*, 77–79). On love of enemy in Jesus' teaching, see esp. Meier, *Marginal Jew*, 4:528–76.

63. Montefiore has argued that Jesus' distinctive broadening of neighbor love to embrace all people is progressively narrowed again in the rest of the New Testament to become the same in-group reality as it was in Jewish tradition. "Thus what was distinctive about Jesus' teaching about neighborly love came to be altered until it was similar to the best Jewish teaching on love, except the mutual love was demanded within a religious rather than a national group, and became grounded on different theological doctrines" (Montefiore, "Thou Shalt Love," 169, 157–70). This judgment, however, rests on the assumption that a predominant focus on intra-communal love in the pastoral literature of the early church somehow excludes a parallel commitment to extra-communal or enemy love. But this is an argument from silence, and not necessarily reflective of the reality (cf. Gal 6:10).

the religious leadership of his audience. Thus Jesus speaks to one of the audience's deepest hatreds and painfully exposes it."[64]

The story of the Good Samaritan shows how the boundaries that divide people into mutually hostile groups are destabilized by two primal experiences: by the experience of profound need, and by the experience of profound love. Under normal circumstances, the traveler on the road to Jericho would have been regarded by the priest and Levite as a neighbor, and thus owed the obligation of neighbor love. But once he is beaten, stripped of all visible signs of identity, and left half dead, he becomes, as we will argue later, a threat to their cultic purity and is treated by them as a pariah, even as a would-be adversary. Though innocent of any wrongdoing, he is perceived as a threatening source of contamination, and in that sense a potential cause of offense, and is shunned accordingly. The Samaritan, by contrast, is so moved with compassion at the plight of the victim that an erstwhile Judean enemy is transformed into a neighbor and treated as such. Impelled by compassion, the Samaritan extends to an anonymous stranger the intimacy of care befitting a close friend or a brother, without giving a moment's thought to his ethnic origins or religious loyalties. As Pheme Perkins observes, the Samaritan behaves toward the Jewish victim as though the whole sorry history of hatred between the two groups had never existed.[65]

Such a self-sacrificing act of friendship towards enemies is a profoundly disconcerting thing for the human psyche to envisage, for it undermines stereotyped definitions of "us" and "them." It disrupts assumptions about how the real world operates and requires us to contemplate hitherto unimaginable possibilities. This is why the deliberate fostering of interpersonal relationships across opposing group lines is such a powerful, though underappreciated, tool for conflict transformation. Arguably the best (and perhaps the only) way to initiate change in the consciousness of mutually hostile groups towards peaceful coexistence is by the building of one-to-one friendships among some individuals from both sides. Such relationships, by their very existence, complexify reality and disallow the wholesale demonizing of the other group. Just as the impact of collective violence is ultimately experienced by individual actors and disseminated through networks of personal relationships, so the

---

64. Bailey, *Poet and Peasant*, 48.
65. Perkins, *Love Commands*, 63.

impact of individual acts of peacemaking can accumulate over time and spread through the relational networks that tie communities together, until a tipping point is reached and society-wide shifts in consciousness occur.[66] As stories spread of opponents acting out of character, they erode the foundations of prejudice and stereotyping upon which centuries-long structures of animosity often rest.

The parable teaches, then, that the familiar and comforting correlation between friend and foe with good and evil, is deceiving and dangerously unreliable. The innocent can be treated as though they were guilty, while those who are judged guilty of evil may prove capable of greater good than those who condemn them. Nowhere is this lesson more relevant than in the sphere of criminal justice, where the repeated labeling of serious offenders as irredeemably evil or inhuman (and of their victims as contrastingly noble or virtuous) has a particularly pernicious impact on the mood of society and the direction of public policy. The parable also teaches that such destructive dualisms are in no way more powerfully deconstructed than by simple acts of goodness on the part of individuals who reach across the divisions of fear and loathing to treat the "other" as brother, the foe as friend, and the foreigner as neighbor.

Perhaps this is harder to do for those who, like the two clerics in the parable, belong to tightly defined groups, take their cues entirely from like-minded members of their own exclusive circles, and perceive threats to themselves on all sides. It is a little easier, perhaps, for those who, like the Samaritan, are themselves marginal figures and are less constrained by existing social classifications, though the personal costliness of transcending social and ideological boundaries remains considerable for them as well. At the end of the day, however, the parable suggests that it is not one's social location that finally dictates one's response to strangers in need or unknown victims of crime. Rather, it is one's capacity for compassion, and one's determination to let compassion overrule all the situational and institutional forces that push in the opposite direction. It is the actor who prioritized mercy that the lawyer is beckoned to emulate: "Go *you* [*su*] and do likewise."

---

66. See an extended discussion of what he calls "citizen diplomacy" in Gopin, *To Make the Earth Whole*.

SUMMARY

For these four reasons the parable of the Good Samaritan may usefully be read as a parable about law, crime, and restorative justice. It vividly depicts the impact of criminal offending on victims and the complex of individual and personal needs that radiate out from that experience. It reflects on the obligation of care that is owed to the victims of crime, a duty incumbent on their neighbors to address their personal needs, even over the long haul, and to restore them to community. This duty exists whether or not it is possible to hold the offenders directly accountable for the harm they have perpetrated. It explores, in particular, the responsibility of the legal fraternity towards victims and insists that the demands of justice, to which the law bears witness, cannot be ascertained apart from a commitment to radical love that trumps self-serving uses of the law to preserve the status quo.

Finally, it suggests that when love is present, the reassuring and ordering dualisms that divide people into good and evil, friend and foe, offender and victim, are relativized, if not nullified entirely. For no one is ever beyond the reach of mercy, and none is ever exempt from the obligation to show compassion for those who suffer tragic events. With this in mind, we turn now to examine how these themes are developed in Luke 10, beginning with consideration of the episode that elicited the telling of the parable.

3

Loving Life and Doing the Law

The parable of the Good Samaritan is told by Jesus in response to a question from a lawyer about what he must do to "inherit eternal life" (v. 25)—that is, what is needed in order for him to attain with the faithful to life in the age to come, when Israel's destiny will reach fulfillment and the present world will be restored to wholeness under God's effective rule.[1] I have argued that the connection between the parable and the lawyer's question is likely to be original. But even if it is editorial, Luke plainly intends us to see a close connection between the theme of the parable and the legal issues raised in the conversation between Jesus and the lawyer. Before turning to the parable itself, we need to consider the issues of life, love, and law that arise in the lawyer's cross-examination of Jesus.

> Just then a lawyer stood up to test Jesus. "Teacher," he said, "what must I do to inherit eternal life?" He said to him, "What is written in the law? What do you read there?" He answered, "You shall love the Lord your God with all your heart, and with all your soul, and with all your strength, and with all your mind; and your neighbor as yourself." And he said to him, "You have given the right answer; do this, and you will live." But wanting to justify himself, he asked Jesus, "And who is my neighbor?" (vv. 25–29)

---

1. The combination of "inherit" and "eternal life" does not occur in the Old Testament but is found elsewhere in Jewish literature (*Pss. Sol.* 14:10; *1 En.* 40:9; *T. Job* 18). The inheritance promised to the people of Israel in Scripture is the land or the kingdom of the Messiah (e.g., Gen 28:4; Deut 1:8; 2:12; 4:1, 22, 26; Ps 37:9, 11, 22, 29, 34; Isa 60:21, cf. Acts 7:5), both derived from the promise to Abraham. "Eternal life" is the condition that the faithful dead are raised to enjoy in the restored land (cf. Dan 12:2, LXX).

The fact that the lawyer "stood up" to ask his question and salutes Jesus courteously as "teacher" suggests that he has been seated among those whom Jesus has been instructing. His inquiry is prompted by what he has previously seen and heard of Jesus' activity. The question he poses—"What must I do to inherit eternal life?"—is legitimate enough. It is the same question put to Jesus on another occasion by the rich young ruler,[2] and it was probably a commonplace in religious discussions of the time. It is said of Rabbi Eliezer (ca. 90 CE) that his pupils would ask him: "Our master, teach us the ways of life, so that through them we may merit the world to come."[3]

But this lawyer's question is not a neutral request for theological information or spiritual guidance. It was framed, Luke says, in order to "test" or tempt Jesus (*ekpeirazōn auton*). Not all commentators regard this test as hostile or mischievous in intent. Some think the lawyer simply wants to clarify Jesus' qualifications as a layman to pronounce on legal issues, or to probe the extent of his scriptural knowledge. His goal is not to trap Jesus but to give him an opportunity to display his credentials.[4] But this seems incongruous. The verb *ekpeirazein* carries negative connotations elsewhere in the New Testament (cf. Luke 4:2),[5] and the fact that the lawyer's follow-up question is prompted by a concern to "justify himself" indicates that he feels threatened by Jesus' stance on legal issues. Elsewhere in Luke's account, the legal authorities are habitually hostile to Jesus' message and praxis. They are frequently criticized by Jesus for their arrogance and self-promotion (16:15; 18:10–12; 20:20, cf. 5:32) and for

2. Luke 18:18; Mark 10:17; Matt 19:16; cf. Acts 13:46, 48.

3. The Talmud text reads: "When R. Eliezer fell ill, his disciples came in to pay a call on him. They said to him, 'Our master, teach us the ways of life, so that through them we may merit the world to come.' He said to them, 'Be attentive to the honor owing to your fellows, keep your children from excessive reflection and set them among the knees of disciples of sages, and when you pray, know before whom you stand, and on that account you will merit the life of the world to come'" (*b. Ber.* 28b).

4. So Manson, *Sayings*, 260; Plummer, *St. Luke*, 284; Marshall, *Luke*, 442; Nolland, *Luke*, 582–83, 585. Snodgrass is ambivalent (*Stories*, 353).

5. The compound verb *ekpeirazein* is infrequent in biblical Greek (Deut 6:16; 8:2, 16; Ps 78:18 [LXX 77:18]; Matt 4:7; Luke 4:12; 10:25; 1 Cor 10:9) and refers to testing in a negative sense, except in Deut 8:2, 16. But *ekpeirazein* appears to be synonymous with *peirazein*, which is sometimes used positively (John 6:6; 2 Cor 13:5; Rev 2:2). Those who construe its use in Luke 10 as hostile include Forbes, *God of Old*, 59; Green, *Luke*, 425, 428; Fitzmyer, *Luke*, 880; and Loader, *Jesus' Attitude*, 329 (who speaks of the lawyer's "aggression").

their "neglect of justice and the love of God" (11:42; 16:13–14; 20:47).[6] The same situation probably pertains here. This lawyer too is perturbed by what he has witnessed of Jesus' teaching and conduct, especially his easygoing association with marginal people and his lack of attention to certain purity strictures,[7] and maybe even his toleration of Samaritans (cf. 9:52–56), and so he rises to challenge Jesus publicly on the extent to which his daily practice coheres with the plain teaching of Jewish law.[8]

The first-person phrasing of the query—"What must I do?"—is formulaic and probably disingenuous. In the only previous mention of lawyers in the Gospel, we are told that whereas tax collectors and the crowds "acknowledged the justice of God" (*edikaiōsan ton theon*) by being baptized by John as an act of repentance, "the Pharisees and the lawyers rejected God's purpose for themselves by refusing to be baptized by him" (7:29–30). The same presumably applies to this lawyer. He also refuses to embrace the inclusive justice of God enacted by Jesus, and seeks instead to defend his *own* justice (*dikaiōsai heauton*) by means of a public debate that will openly display the extent to which it is he, the legal rigorist, and not Jesus, the social liberal, who stands in agreement with Scripture.[9]

To initiate the dispute, he asks Jesus what he must do to inherit eternal life. Likely Jesus had acquired a reputation for discoursing on this particular topic (cf. Luke 18:30; Mark 10:30; Matt 19:29; 25:46); in any event he was bound to have a personal opinion on a matter of such topical concern. Some commentators think the question is incoherent since "doing" and "inheriting" are incompatible notions: an inheritance comes of right; it is not achieved by performance.[10] They therefore indict the lawyer for self-righteously seeking to earn his own salvation through some

---

6. See Powell, "Religious Leaders," 93–110.

7. Cf. Luke 4:24–30, 40–41; 5:12–15, 27–28, 29–32, 33; 6:6–11, 19; 7:11–17, 25, 33–34, 35–50; 8:26–39, 40–56; 9:52–56.

8. The parable is, at least in part, a defense of Jesus' approach to issues of cleanness and uncleanness, since two ritually pure and two impure characters appear in it. So Witherington, *Sage*, 196; Snodgrass, *Stories*, 72, 358; cf. Malina and Rohrbaugh, *Social-Science*, 318–20.

9. Malina and Neyrey read the episode as a "challenge-riposte" (a public competition for honor) between Jesus and the lawyer. Malina and Neyrey, "Honor," 50–51; Malina and Rohrbaugh, *Social-Science*, 306–7; Esler, "Intergroup Conflict," 335–36.

10. Cf. Graves, "Moral," 272.

decisive or meritorious feat of legal obedience. One commentator even proposes that the lawyer's head was filled with nothing but Pelagianism![11]

But this appraisal is not only anachronistic, it entirely misconstrues the Jewish setting of the discussion. In Jewish thought, it was communal possession of the Mosaic Torah, not individual accomplishment, that was the basis of future confidence, so that in a real sense eternal life was inherited through membership of the law-blessed community. At the same time, having a legal corpus as the ground of present identity and future security necessarily involves a dimension of individual human achievement, for a law that does not oblige concrete compliance from its constituency is not truly a law at all. Even if it were widely presumed that "all Israelites have a share in the world to come," as the Mishnah states, it is only because they submit obediently to the law's demand for righteousness (the Mishnah continues, "As it is written, 'your people shall all be righteous, they shall inherit the land forever'"), and anyone who stubbornly resists doing so will face final exclusion.[12] Hence *doing* the

---

11. Lenski, *Luke's Gospel*, 596, cf. 602. Others who discern some kind of meritorious works-righteousness include Plummer, *Luke*, 289; Bailey, *Poet and Peasant*, 35–37; Morris, *St. Luke*, 187–88; Caird, *Saint Luke*, 147; Ellis, *Luke*, 160.

12. The Mishnah reads: "All Israelites have a share in the world to come, as it is said, 'Your people also shall all be righteous, they shall inherit the land forever; the branch of my planting, the work of my hands that I may be glorified (Isa 60:21)'. And these are the ones who have no portion in the world to come: he who says, resurrection of the dead is a teaching that does not derive from the Torah law, and the Torah does not come from Heaven, and an Epicurean" (*m. Sanh.* 10:1). In the Mishnaic tractate *Pirke Abot*, which links ethical instruction through a chain of tradition to the Torah, there is a saying that affirms that the "disciples of Abraham our father" will, by cultivating the virtues of goodness and humility, "inherit the Garden of Eden and inherit the world to come, as it is said 'That I may cause them that love me to inherit substance, and that I may till their treasuries." The "disciples of Balaam the wicked," by contrast, will "inherit Gehenna" (5:22). Often in Second Temple Jewish literature (as indeed in the New Testament), there is a tension between the affirmation that God wills and expects perfect obedience to his law, and the recognition that it is still possible to be righteous, and thus gain entrance to the coming world, without perfection, since God is merciful and forgiving and provides for effective atonement in the sacrificial system. The *Book of Jubilees*, for instance, assumes that the majority of Israel who seek to remain within the covenant belong to the elect of Israel, notwithstanding their need for mercy and forgiveness. At the same time, there is a warning that those who "commit sin or transgress the ordinances or break the covenant will be recorded in the heavenly tablets as adversaries, and they will be destroyed out of the book of life, and they will be recorded in the book of those who will be destroyed and with those who will be rooted out of the earth" (30:21–22).

law and *inheriting* eternal life are by no means incommensurate notions; they are two sides of the same coin.

THE LAW OF LIFE

The "law" at stake in all this, of course, was the biblical Torah and its associated hermeneutical traditions. The Hebrew word *torah* (like its Greek equivalent *nomos*) has a broad semantic range, including "instruction," "teaching," "directives," "commandment," and, when applied to the teaching given by God to Moses on Mount Sinai, "divine revelation." The various legal rulings that make up the Mosaic Torah were initially passed down in oral form by community leaders, such as parents, elders, priests, and judges, and gradually they coalesced into discrete collections or codes. In time these codes were brought together and committed to writing, and were embedded in the larger story of Israel's origins and historical vocation that spans the five books of the Pentateuch. The whole product was naturally referred to as the "Law of Yahweh" or the "Law of Moses," since it comprised God's revealed will for his people delivered through the agency of Moses and embodied in the historical experience of the Israelite people.

It is crucial to appreciate the irreducible complexity that surrounds the category of "law" in the Bible and in early Judaism, especially when seeking to draw links or analogies with the modern phenomenon and practice of law. We have already noted one aspect of this complexity: biblical law includes both *legislation*, in the sense of specific directives relating to moral, cultic, domestic, and civil concerns, and a range of foundational *narratives* from which moral and religious guidance may be drawn. Generally in the New Testament, and consistently in the Synoptic Gospels, "the law" (*ho nomos*) refers to the Mosaic Pentateuch in both its legislative and narrative dimensions, which, together with the Prophets, constituted the canon of Jewish Scripture at that time ("the law and the Prophets"). Sometimes in the New Testament the term is applied to specific prescriptions within the Pentateuch, sometimes to associated narratives, sometimes to its prophetic anticipations of the future.

In later rabbinic usage, the term Torah has an even wider array of applications, ranging from individual commandments, to the Decalogue as the heart of the legal corpus, to the Pentateuch as the heart of the Scriptures, to the Israelite Scriptures or "Tanakh" in their entirety, to the contents of particular biblical scrolls. Following the compilation of the Mishnah (ca. 200 CE), the term was expanded to embrace, not only the written word of Scripture but also the teachings and writings of the rabbis of the first six centuries of the Common Era, eventually collected in the Talmud. According to the Talmudic doctrine of the Dual Torah, God's revelation at Sinai was imparted in two media: the Written Torah and the Oral Torah. The latter was comprised of explanations and amplifications, and was faithfully handed down from generation to generation until it was reduced to writing in the Mishnah. From thence, the term Torah became virtually synonymous with the religion or worldview of Judaism as a whole.[13]

The formal doctrine of Oral Torah was not current at the time of Jesus or the Gospel writers. But it was still the case in the first century that alongside the Written Torah there existed extensive traditions of oral analysis and interpretation that carried binding authority for those who accepted them, what in Mark's Gospel is called "the tradition of the elders" (Mark 7:3). The emergence of such hermeneutical traditions was to be expected. After all, if the Torah's words express the eternal mind of God, it was only logical to assume that they possessed an inexhaustible reservoir of meaning.[14] Furthermore, no legislative code can cover every conceivable contingency in life, and if the Torah was to regulate the conduct of all Jews at all times and in all places, as was intended, it needed constant interpretation and adaptation. The tendency to expand and update the Torah is detectable within the prehistory of constituent law codes themselves, and the process of amplification and adaptation continued into the Second Temple period in a variety of ways.

Competing interpretations of the Torah were thus the hallmark of the various religious movements that comprised the first-century Jewish community, such as the Pharisees, the Sadducees, the Essenes, and the Samaritans, as well as of subgroups within these movements, and there were probably local and regional variations as well. Prominent religious teachers within these various streams regularly issued legal rulings or opinions on contested matters of practice, which, for their constituencies, had prescriptive authority (cf. Mark 7:1–7; Matt 23:1–36). By the

---

13. See Neusner and Green, *Dictionary*, 637–43.

14. For a lyrical account of this perspective on the Torah from a modern Jewish scholar, see Soloveichik, "Torah and Incarnation," 44–48.

time of the Mishnah, such rulings were referred to as "halakah" (literally "walking," "conduct," "behavior"). This term was not current in the first century, though the practice it denotes certainly was, so that it is quite appropriate to speak of Jesus or other teachers of his day issuing halakah.[15]

The interrelationship between these halakic traditions and the written or biblical law itself is by no means easy or straightforward to determine. On the one hand, there was still a degree of fluidity in the written text of the Torah itself, with the various textual traditions circulating in Palestine containing variant readings at many points. Moreover, veneration for the Written Torah did not prevent some groups from rewriting its stories and laws to reinforce their own group's beliefs and practices (as, for example, in the *Book of Jubilees* ca. 161–152 BCE). On the other hand, the boundary between the written law and its oral reception was not always clear-cut. Not only were there rival interpretations of the commandments current in the halakah, but the legacy of long-standing oral commentary on the law was such that it sometimes led to peculiar assumptions about the actual content of the written Torah. John Meier gives examples of competent early Jewish teachers asserting that the Written Torah contained Sabbath commandments that, from a historical-critical perspective, simply do not exist, although they were assumed to exist in some sense.[16]

All this makes it extremely difficult to assess the attitude of Jesus to the Mosaic law. This is an issue that has been vigorously debated in New Testament scholarship for a very long time. John Meier begins his painstaking analysis of this question by dismissing all available treatments of the topic as substantially mistaken. Not only do most of them fail to wrestle adequately with the enormous complexities surrounding the content, shape, meaning, and diverse interpretations of first-century Jewish law, but, more fatally, they fail to differentiate carefully enough between the historical Jesus' approach to the law and that of the later Gospel writers. The besetting sin of much previous scholarship, Meier argues, has been to read Jesus through the lens of Matt 5:17–48, with its list of so-called antitheses. But the structure, wording, and theological perspective of this convoluted text, Meier insists, reflects Matthew's distinctively Jewish–Christian catechism on Jesus and the law and cannot

15. So Meier, *Marginal Jew*, 4:8, 30–37.
16. Ibid., 32–38.

be taken as a reliable gauge for how the historical Jesus himself engaged with the Torah. This can only be discovered by "using the scientific tools of modern historical research as applied to ancient sources,"[17] which Meier proceeds to do in the ensuing seven hundred pages of his book.

Whatever one thinks of the thick wedge Meier drives between the historical Jesus and the perspective of Matthew,[18] the Gospels leave us in no doubt that Jesus frequently engaged in public debate and discussion on the meaning and implications of the Torah, both in whole and in part. That is hardly surprising. As Meier points out, anyone ascending the public stage in first-century Palestine and presenting himself as a religious teacher or "rabbi" would, of necessity, have to expound the Torah, especially someone claiming for himself a unique eschatological significance, as Jesus unquestionably did.

THE LAW'S CHIEF DEMANDS

Yet the Torah that Jesus referenced, and which every Jew revered, was a complex tapestry of hundreds of moral, civil, and ritual stipulations, whose exact application to the exigencies of daily life must necessarily be a matter of continual discernment. How, then, can anyone be certain that he or she has accomplished precisely what the law expects? What must one actually *do* in order to satisfy the law's true intent, and thus secure its eternal benefits? This is the question the lawyer puts to Jesus, though he articulates it in terms of the law's ultimate promise of life rather than in terms of its interior meaning (Lev 18:5; 25:18; Deut 5:33; 6:24; 30:6, 15–20). Even so, his question was presumably intended to elicit from Jesus a summary of the law's most fundamental or ineluctable requirements, perhaps captured in a single paradigmatic commandment, the fulfillment of which would comprehend all other precepts in the law and guarantee participation in the age to come.

An interest in identifying the law's most foundational convictions —such as purity of heart, justice, mercy, peace, honest dealings, faithfulness—is apparent in the Old Testament itself,[19] as well as in postbiblical

---

17. Ibid., 6.

18. See above 32 n. 12.

19. See, for example, Mic 6:8; Hos 2:19–20; Pss 15:2–5; 24:3–6; Isa 66:2; Jer 22:3–4; Zech 7:9–10; 8:16–17.

Jewish literature[20] and at several points in the Gospel tradition.[21] The aim, of course, was never to filter out those *mitzvot* that were considered to be unimportant or superfluous or inconsequential—an unimaginable possibility for a body of law that had been divinely given! The aim rather was to capture, in a precise normative statement, the law's undergirding values or controlling convictions that must be lived out in daily practice, and prioritized in the application of the law's manifold provisions, so that the law's gift of life may be appropriated with confidence.

Jesus responds to the lawyer's request with a counter-question that invites him to nail his own colors to the mast: "What is written in the law? What do you read there?" (v. 26) This was a standard rabbinic formula for eliciting the recitation or exposition of Scripture.[22] What is most striking at this point of the interchange is the extent of the common ground between Jesus and his questioner. There is agreement between them that access to the future world is a valid concern and should not be taken for granted, that the requirements of entry are disclosed in the Torah, and that performance of the law is not only desirable and feasible but also absolutely essential. There is no trace of anxiety on either side about the dangers of legalism or self-righteousness, much less of Pelagianism. The key issue is not *whether* law-keeping is necessary for salvation but *how* the law is to be construed.

In answer to Jesus' question, the lawyer brings together two widely separated commandments in the Torah: the *Shema* from Deut 6:4-5, which pious Israelites were expected to recite twice a day and which was

---

20. Philo and Josephus are representative of Jewish intellectuals who appropriated the Hellenistic practice of summing up human obligations towards the divine as *eusebeia* ("reverence," along with, in Philo's case, *hositēs*, "holiness") and towards one's fellows as *dikaiosunē* ("justice," "righteousness") or *philanthrōpia* ("love of humans"). Rabbinic literature reflects a tendency, attested in both Diaspora and Palestinian Judaism in the pre-70 period, to summarize the commandments under some general principle or rubric or norm (in rabbinic writings referred to as "a *kelal*," a rule or principle, or a "great *kelal*," e.g., *m.Sabb* 7.1). See further Meier, *Marginal Jew*, 4:499-528.

21. Luke 11:42/Matt 23:23; Luke 18:18-23/Matt 19:16-22/Mark 10:17-22; Mark 12:28-34/Matt 22:34-40.

22. Some scholars think the phrase here has the force of, "How do you recite?" Jeremias, *Theology* 1:187; Marshall, *Luke*, 443. Others think it means, "How do you expound?" since the lawyer goes beyond simple citation of the *Shema*; Derrett, *Law*, 223-24. Bailey thinks both nuances are present, *Poet and Peasant*, 37; cf. Daube, *Rabbinic Judaism*, 432-33.

foundational to Jewish piety in the home, synagogue, and temple,[23] and the formulation of the Golden Rule in Lev 19:18, located in the midst of the Holiness Code (Lev 17–26). "He answered, 'You shall love the Lord your God with all your heart, and with all your soul, and with all your strength, and with all your mind [cf. Deut 6:5]; and your neighbor as yourself [cf. Lev 19:18].'"

Three things are noteworthy here: it is the *lawyer*, not Jesus, who nominates the twin love commandments as the law's center of gravity; in doing so, he conflates two distinct commandments into a *single* obligation, governed by a single verb; and he construes the obligation of love to be principally a matter of formal *obedience* rather than emotional experience. Each of these points warrants further reflection.

The Question of Originality

The first thing to note is that it is the lawyer, not Jesus, who offers the love commandments as a summation of the law's teaching and as a condition for eternal life. This is not depicted as a hermeneutical innovation on the part of Jesus, though Christian readers often regard it as such. It comes rather from the expert Jewish lawyer. It is possible of course that he is only echoing what he had first learned from Jesus' teaching.[24] But there is absolutely no hint of this in the text. On the contrary, Jesus expressly asks the lawyer to draw on his own legal knowledge and insight ("What do *you* read there?") to answer his question. The foundational importance of the love commands, in other words, appears to be another area of commonality between Jesus and the Torah scholar.

This is hardly surprising. Love of neighbor was already central to Jewish ethics at the time,[25] while love for God, even in Deuteronomy,

---

23. In the rabbinic era, the *Shema* consisted of Deut 6:6-9 + 11:13-21 + Num 15:37-41. At the time of Jesus, however, the texts used for recitation varied in length and content. There is substantial evidence for the importance of this prayer to Jewish people in Jesus' day (Deut 6:7, cf. *m. Ber.* 1:1-4; *m. Tamid* 5:1; *b. Ber.* 21b, 47b; Josephus, *Ant.* 4.8.13 §212-13; Philo, *Spec. Laws* 4:141; cf. Str-Bill 4:189-207).

24. Manson, *Sayings*, 260.

25. See, for example, Sir 7:21, cf. vv. 30-36; *Jub.* 7:20; 36:78. Interestingly, in later rabbinic discussion the love of neighbor commandment was often understood to require humane forms of capital punishment (*b. Pesah.* 74a; *b. Ketub.* 36b; *b. Sotah* 43a; *b. B. Qam.* 47b; *b. Sanh.* 10a; 42a; 52b; 84b), though it is sometimes cited in connection with other, more private matters (*b. Nid.* 16b; *b. Qidd.* 41a).

is seen as comprehending and explaining all the other commandments (Deut 11:1, 13–21; 19:9; 30:16, cf. Josh 22:5; 23:11). Also, the fact that the identical form of the verb for "love" is used in Torah texts demanding love of God (Deut 6:5; 11:1) and love of neighbor (Lev 19:18, 34) would have helped draw these passages together in the minds of many Jewish interpreters.[26] There are several early Jewish sources where the *topos* of love for God and love of neighbor are closely juxtaposed, and although the pre-Christian provenance of some of these references is uncertain, and none of them is strictly identical to what we find in the Gospels, there is nothing improbable in Luke's portrait of Jesus and the lawyer concurring in an ongoing Jewish culture of discussion about the function of the love commandments in epitomizing the meaning of the law.[27] The available evidence suggests that Jesus adopted a particularly lucid and compelling position on the absolute priority of love and the inseparability of both commands, a position that has had an enduring impact on subsequent Christian tradition.[28] But he did not initiate the discussion itself, nor did he articulate a highly idiosyncratic or intrinsically controversial view on the matter.

This, in any event, is how *Luke* portrays the historical situation. Luke plainly has nothing invested in implying that Jesus' perspective on the centrality of love was in any way novel. Yet not all scholars consider Luke to be historically reliable at this juncture. Enormous scholarly effort has been expended trying to ascertain the extent to which Jesus' teaching on the double love commandments was innovative or unique. One strand of opinion appeals to the numerous anticipations, parallels, intimations, and echoes of the two love commandments in Jewish literature at the time, and argues that Jesus was representative of a broader tendency among legal interpreters to nominate love of God and love for neighbor as the perfect summation of God's will. The Decalogue, for example, was commonly understood to consist of two sections—responsibilities towards

---

26. So Gerhardsson, *Good Samaritan*, 6; Snodgrass, *Stories*, 349; Nolland, *Luke*, 581–82.

27. *Jub.* 36:4–8; 1QS 1.1–3, 9–10; *T. Iss.* 5:2; 7:6; *T. Dan.* 5:3; Philo, *Spec. Laws* 1:299–300; 2:63. For other references, see Snodgrass, *Stories*, 700 n. 97; Nolland, *Luke*, 580–82. A useful summary is found in Allison, *Resurrecting Jesus*, 153–60.

28. Elsewhere in the New Testament, love of neighbor alone is used to summarize the law (Gal 5:14; Rom 13:9; Jas 2:8). Reference to both commands occurs in other early Christian literature (*Did.* 1:2; *Barn.* 19:2, 5; Justin, *Dial.* 93:2–3; *Mart. Pol.* 3:3).

God and responsibilities towards neighbors—each of which could be summarized in terms of the duties of love.[29]

Another strand of scholarship draws attention to the distinctive features of Jesus' appropriation of the love texts that sets it apart from all other instances.[30] In the latest volume of his magisterial study *A Marginal Jew*, John Meier identifies four aspects of Jesus' teaching on the double love commandment in Mark 12:28-34 that are historically unique: (i) he quotes both Deut 6:4-5 and Lev 19:18b word for word, rather than paraphrasing or alluding to these texts, something that happens nowhere else in available sources; (ii) he cites both biblical texts back to back, employing the hermeneutical device of *gezera sawa* in which disparate texts are brought together on the basis of the recurrence of similar or identical words in each; (iii) he orders the commands numerically, insisting that Deuteronomy 6 is the "first" commandment and Leviticus 19 the "second"; and (iv) he affirms the superiority of these two commandments over all other stipulations in the Torah.[31] The combination of these four features is found nowhere else in Jewish or (interestingly) in

---

29. Cf. Sanders, *Judaism*, 230-35.

30. Scholars who stress the distinctiveness of Jesus' appeal to the love commandments usually point out that it is only in the Gospels that we find the explicit quotation of the two written commandments side by side, not a paraphrase of them or a reference to the ideals they embody; cf. Schrage, *Ethics*, 70-71; Gnilka, *Jesus*, 238-47. The juxtaposing of the two commandments in this way serves to generate new meanings, with love for God and love of neighbor becoming mutually interpretive; cf. Patrick, "Understanding," 101-29. Most distinctive is the absolute priority that is given to the love commandments over all other commandments in the law, so that other commands are subordinated to them or may even be disregarded in the name of obeying the love commandment (Mark 3:1-6; 7:1-23; 12: 33; Luke 14:1-6; John 5:2-18). The acuity of Jewish ethics lies in its multiplication of detailed ethical commands rather than in the attempt to reduce the law to master themes. Jesus, however, assigns absolute, not just relative, importance to the twin love commandments. They stand in a class of their own and take absolute precedence, as a canon within a canon. Accordingly, "there is no real parallel to the elevation of love to pre-eminence by Jesus" (Davies and Allison Jr., *Matthew*, 169). Manson notes that while there were discussions in rabbinical circles about the greatest commandment, these debates related to haggadah (material for edification) and were not intended to be binding legal discussions. Sometimes rabbis were simply nominating their favorite commandment; at other times they were identifying which command had logical priority as the source of other commands. There was never any suggestion that the chosen command was intended to abate the importance of, or the obligation to obey, all the other commands (Manson, *Teaching*, 302-8).

31. Meier, *Marginal Jew*, 4:499-528, 572, 647-63.

later Christian literature, so on the criterion of dissimilarity Meier judges Jesus' teaching on the topic to be historically reliable.

At one level this isolation of a distinctive twist to Jesus' teaching may be an important contribution to the so-called quest for the historical Jesus. But the comparative originality of Jesus' perspective on the matter was, it appears, neither as evident nor as important to the Evangelists as it is to some modern critical historians. If Jesus was the very first Jewish preacher to combine and quote the twin love commandments in this way, obviously Luke did not consider this feat to be so revolutionary or hermeneutically perceptive that he was unwilling to transfer the formula to the lips of an antagonistic opponent and have Jesus merely concur with his interrogator. He is more than happy to portray Jesus as endorsing an already established hermeneutical axiom in Jewish teaching. Even in the corresponding Markan account, which, unlike the Lukan version, Meier favors as historically dependable, there is evidence of a shared viewpoint between Jesus and his scribal interlocutor. In that episode, it is Jesus who nominates the two commandments to characterize the law. But no sooner has he done so than the scribe instantly agrees with him, reciting the commandments a second time and saying he has spoken "truly" (12:32), a response that indicates that the scribe already knew the answer he was looking for when he constructed the question.

We are left then with a puzzling state of affairs. Only in the Synoptic tradition do we find the verbatim citation of Deut 6:4–5 and Lev 19:18 in direct sequence and their explicit elevation to absolute preeminence in the law, and in all likelihood this was a recurrent theme in the teaching of Jesus. On the other hand, the Gospel writers avoid suggesting that Jesus was alone in possessing this insight, ascribing it even to a hostile opponent who was out to "test" Jesus (Luke 10:25), as well as to a supportive scribe who, though "not far from the kingdom of God" (Mark 12:34), was still not an overt supporter of Jesus. It is conceivable that both questioners came to juxtapose the two Torah verses in their minds as a direct result of having heard Jesus do so previously; it was his teaching that helped them crystallize their own position. But there is no intimation in either story that this was the case, and certainly Luke thought there was nothing exceptional about grounding the law's complex superstructure on the foundational injunctions to love God wholeheartedly and to love one's neighbor as oneself.

The Conflation of the Twin Commands

This leads to the second notable feature of the lawyer's response: he conflates the two commandments into a single unit without differentiation, governed by a single imperative. By contrast, in the parallel story of Jesus' encounter with the Jerusalem scribe in Mark 12/Matthew 22, a clear distinction is maintained between the two injunctions. In Mark's version, Jesus identifies love for God as the "first" commandment (12:28-29), and love of neighbor as "the second" (12:31), and stipulates that "no other commandment is greater than *these*" (12:31). The scribe concurs, reiterating the wording of each commandment separately and adding the comment that observance of them "is much more important than all whole burnt offerings and sacrifices" (12:33). The scribe is not suggesting that the cultic commandments are unimportant or unnecessary, only that the love commandments are much more important and that none of the law's requirements must ever be observed at their expense.

In Matthew's rendition, love for God is also marked out as the "greatest and first commandment" (Matt 22:38), and love of neighbor as "a second," even though it is "like" the first in character (Matt 22:39). This hierarchical enumeration of "first" and "second" keeps the two commandments quite distinct. At the same time, the two are conceived as indivisible, for it is only as a unified pair that they answer the question about "the greatest commandment" and furnish the hook on which "hang [*krematai*] all the law and the prophets" (22:40, cf. 7:12).[32] Exactly what this latter phrase means is uncertain.[33] But whether it indicates that love is the supreme principle from which all other commandments may

---

32. Meier considers it intrinsically improbable that Jesus would use the originally pagan precept of the Golden Rule, which has no theistic content, to capture the teaching of the Law and the Prophets, as Matt 7:12 indicates. He thinks there is no firm evidence that Jesus himself ever cited the Golden Rule at all, especially since it contradicts his withering attack on the ethic of reciprocity in Luke 6:27-36, cf. *Marginal Jew*, 4:551-57, 653-54. But Meier's skepticism is unwarranted. If the Jewish-Christian Matthew, who saw Jesus' teaching and career as the fulfillment of the law, could employ the Golden Rule in this way, it is hard to know why Jesus would have shrunk from doing so, especially when the proverb was already well established in Judaism. The contrast Meier draws between the Golden Rule and Jesus' critique of reciprocity is vastly overstated and somewhat simplistic. It is also worth observing that the force of Matt 7:12 may simply be that the Golden Rule is consistent with the Law and the Prophets, not the summation of it.

33. See Davies and Allison, *Matthew*, 254-56.

be deduced, or that love summarizes all the imperatives of the law, or that love is the ultimate purpose of the law, the implication is the same: the provisions of the law cannot be properly understood or applied without conscious reference to love. Obedience to the law must be motivated by a preeminent devotion to God and by a corresponding determination to treat one's neighbors as of equal value as oneself (cf. Matt 7:12).[34]

In the Markan-Matthean tradition, then, the two commandments are distinguished yet held in dialectical tension. Neither commandment is collapsed into the other, and neither is viewed in isolation from the other. The two injunctions are separate, yet inseparable, and only together do they comprise the master key to the law's interpretation and application.

In Luke's account, however, the lawyer blends the two commandments into a single obligation controlled by a single verb: "You shall love the Lord your God with all your heart . . . and your neighbor as yourself." His merging of the commandments is echoed and endorsed in Jesus' reply: "You have given the right answer; do *this*"—not *these*—"and you will live." The twin commands are not simply juxtaposed; they are effectively combined. The inference seems to be that love for God includes and enables love of neighbor, while love of neighbor expresses and requires love for God.

This does not mean the two objects of love are considered identical or interchangeable, with love for God and love for neighbor being two ways of saying the same thing. It means, rather, that there can be no love for God without love for neighbor, and no love for neighbor that does not involve pleasing or obeying God. To love God wholeheartedly—that is, to love him with the totality of one's physical, moral, intellectual, and emotional capacities, as the *Shema* decrees—requires loving one's neighbor as well, and loving one's neighbor is an integral part of one's total response to God and depends, ultimately, on reflecting God's love for them. Luke's account underscores even more emphatically than

---

34. Meier ascribes this statement to Matthew rather than Jesus, and insists there is no evidence of Jesus seeing love, or anything else, as a central organizing principle in the law. It is impossible to identify any logical link between Jesus' individual legal pronouncements and the theme of love, so that his legal teaching remains largely *ad hoc* and unexplained (*Marginal Jew*, 4:653–55). Again it is notable that Meier denies, on methodological grounds, what Matthew considers historically self-evident, which raises the question of who was closest, temporally and culturally, to the subject matter to make the call.

Mark's or Matthew's that God cannot be loved in isolation but only in and through loving other people.

Another variation in Luke's account is that the unified love commandment is not explicitly characterized by the lawyer or by Jesus as the "first" or "greatest" decree in the law. The significance in this difference should not be overstated, however. Some scholars take it as an indication that Luke was positively opposed to any attempt to draw theoretical distinctions among the Torah's various commandments, preferring instead to emphasize the pragmatic need to obey the law rather than to analyze it.[35] But this reads too much into the discrepancy. While the language of priority is not found in Luke's account, the implication of selecting specific provisions in the law to epitomize its message has much the same effect. For if the ultimate purpose of the law is to confer life, as Jesus and the lawyer agree, and if what enables the law to deliver its promise of life is love for God and neighbor, then by implication love must be the law's primary demand and its greatest theme. That is why Jesus deems the lawyer's choice of the double commandment to be the "right" (*orthōs*) way of "reading" (*anaginōskeis*) what "is written in the law" (*en tō nomō gegraptai*). The lawyer has correctly identified the law's cardinal commandments.

The difference, then, between Luke's story of the encounter with the lawyer and the episode with the scribe in Jerusalem recorded in Mark and Matthew is more one of style than substance. All three accounts agree that love of God and love of neighbor are of supreme importance among the law's manifold demands and that all the law's remaining commandments must be enacted in the service of love. Love summarizes the law's diverse requirements, it satisfies the law's true intention, and it delivers the law's greatest blessing. Without love, it is impossible to fulfill the law. The accounts also agree that love for God and love of neighbor are inseparable obligations. One cannot be achieved without the other. This is most strongly emphasized in Luke's story where the lawyer effectively amalgamates two existing directives into a new commandment, a single double-pronged obligation governed by the same verb. This reformulation underscores that love for God includes and enables love of neighbor, while love of neighbor expresses and requires love for God. To love God wholeheartedly requires loving one's neighbor as well, and loving one's neighbor is an essential part of one's obedience to God. God cannot be

---

35. So, for example, Wilson, *Luke and the Law*, 15; Banks, *Jesus*, 170; Meier, *Marginal Jew*, 4:526.

loved in isolation but only in and through concrete relationships with one's neighbors (cf. 1 John 4:20).

The lawyer obviously understands this point well, and Jesus deems his apprehension of the law to be totally "correct." Now he must put into practice what he perceives to be true in principle, and in so doing he will secure eternal life for himself: "Do this and you will live" (v. 28).

Love as Legal Obligation

This brings us to the third observation about the lawyer's answer. It is an observation that may help explain the paradoxical tension we find in the Gospel tradition (and elsewhere in the New Testament, especially in Paul) between a profound respect for, and endorsement of, the law on the one hand, and a transcending or relativizing of the law on the other. Commentators have frequently noted this tension, and although there are differences of opinion over where the balance lies between the poles, there is a general agreement that the main reason for the tension is eschatological. That is to say, it stems from the fact that Jesus and his followers thought that a new age was pressing in on them urgently. A new reality was dawning that required a re-visioning, in some sense, of the law's role and meaning, an affirming of its essential message and authority yet a transcending of its function.

Now, eschatology is undoubtedly the key factor in accounting for the tension. But the tension is already implicit, I suggest, in the simple act of giving absolute priority to specific commandments within the law, a trend that was already underway in Jewish jurisprudence at the time and furthered by Jesus. The tension became much more pronounced in the Jesus movement because of the eschatological transformations that attended Jesus' life, death, and resurrection. But the lawyer's choice of the double love command as a sort of canon within a canon already invites the kind of intra-canonical critique that permits the relativizing of certain of the Torah's demands in service of deeper truths.

This tendency is also encouraged by the decision to prioritize *love* among the law's many commandments. It is important to note that when Jesus endorses the lawyer's identification of the supremacy of love, he is not referring to some abstract philosophical principle or moral virtue or emotional experience exterior to the law itself; he is referring to positive stipulations within the Torah's own legislative architecture. Love of God and love of neighbor are legal imperatives ("you shall love") that must be obeyed ("do this and you will live"). They are *commandments*. At the very least, this suggests that the love in question does not come easily or naturally. Love is a difficult undertaking that involves conscious effort, continual practice, and considerable self-discipline. It is not merely an emotion, for emotional feelings cannot be elicited by bald command but are contingent upon circumstance and temperament.

Some moral philosophers have argued that it is a mistake to make the principle "love your neighbor as yourself" the central pillar of universal morality because it is impossible to have an affectionate attachment to all people equally. Nor can persons have the same feelings for others that they have for themselves: there is a qualitative difference between self-attachment and attachment to others.[36] In reply to this objection, it is usually pointed out that in Jewish and Christian tradition, as well as in secular rationalism, neighbor-love is understood in terms of benevolent *action*, not affective feelings.[37] "In Jewish Scripture and tradition," E. P. Sanders explains, "the commandment to love is inseparable from the commandment to act. Love may include feeling, but in law it involves concrete and specific actions."[38] John Meier makes the same point. He comments that first-century Jews would have had no problem with the idea of love being commanded, for they understood love as "first of all a matter of willing and doing good, not feeling good."[39] It is only because Jesus understood love in such activist terms that he could speak of loving one's enemies. He was not telling his disciples to have warm emotional feelings for their enemies, in which case they would cease to be enemies, but rather was calling on them to *do* good to their opponents, however they felt about them.[40] C. H. Dodd's classic definition of Christian agape as "energetic and beneficent good will which stops at nothing to secure the good of the beloved object" captures well the action-emphasis of neighbor-love in biblical perspective.[41]

---

36. Hanfling, "Loving My Neighbor," 145–57.
37. Radcliffe, "Neighbour Love," 497–502.
38. Sanders, *Judaism*, 232.
39. Meier, *Marginal Jew*, 4:527, cf. 490, 530.
40. Ibid., 530.
41. Dodd, *Gospel and Law*, 42.

All this is true insofar as it goes. Biblical love is undoubtedly an action more than a sentiment. But, as we will see, the parable of the Good Samaritan suggests that Jesus believed there is more to love than benevolent activism. The Samaritan's merciful actions in the parable are the direct result of his being "moved with compassion" at what he saw (*esplangchnisthē*, v. 33). The verb describes a gut-wrenching surge of emotion that overwhelmed him, and it is this emotional reaction that marks the critical turning point in the story.[42] The neighbor-love displayed by the Samaritan, in other words, is not a clinical, cold-hearted attention to the victim's essential welfare needs but a sympathetic sharing in his personal suffering and isolation. Just as love for God cannot be reduced to exterior actions alone but engages the whole heart, mind, strength, and soul,[43] so love for neighbor cannot be limited to benevolent deeds alone but involves empathetic feelings, thoughts, and motivations as well.

This is an important consequence of the amalgamation of the dual love commandments into a single imperative that interpreters (and perhaps even Luke's lawyer) often miss. It is not uncommon in theistic traditions to see a deep affinity between one's love of God and the emotional

---

42. Menken, "Position," 107–14. See further below, chapter 5, 121ff.

43. There is a bewildering range of variations in the list of human faculties mentioned in the *Shema*, as well as the prepositions used with them, in the MT, the LXX, and the Synoptic Gospels, and in the various textual traditions of each (see Meier, *Marginal Jew*, 4:587–88 n. 31). Little can be deduced about literary relationships between the Synoptics on the basis of these variations, since the oral and textual traditions were still in a state of flux and liturgical modifications would have been commonplace. Marshall notes that Luke's version of the great command reflects LXX of Deut 6:5, though with a different preposition (*ek* rather than *en*), the use of "strength" rather than "power," and with a fourth item, "all your mind," added (Mark also has four, but in a different order, while Mathew only has three, like the Hebrew text). "The prepositional phrases together indicate the totality of mind and will that must be brought to the worship of God. No clear distinctions can be made between the different aspects of human personality here listed. They were, however, differentiated in rabbinic theology" (*Luke*, 443–44). It is possible to ascribe distinct, though overlapping, meanings to the individual items in light of wider Old Testament usage (such as "heart" designating spiritual consciousness and moral understanding, as well as emotional responsiveness; "soul" denoting physical vitality; "might" referring to physical energy and action, and which later commentators took to include personal resources or property; and "mind" to refer to intelligence, thoughts, and volitions). But what is significant is the force of the piling up of the faculties as a group to "sum up the totality of personal life" (Fitzmyer, *Luke*, 880).

intensity of human love, especially romantic love;[44] it is less common to reverse the relation and understand love for one's fellow human beings as demanding the same intensity and passion that one has for God. But this is precisely what the parable implies. It teaches that the wholeheartedness of the covenant love enjoined in the Torah for God must also be extended to one's neighbors as well. Both parties are to be loved with the whole of one's heart, soul, mind, and strength ("whole" is reiterated four times in v. 27). In both cases, the love entailed is volitional, rational, practical, *and* emotional in character.

The law *commands* such all-embracing love not because it equates love with external acts alone, or because love can be induced on demand, but because it considers love to be an intentional commitment *before* it is either an emotion or an action, yet a commitment that necessarily issues in both affective and active outcomes. Unlike modern Western law, biblical law is not content to restrict itself to outer conduct alone, but seeks to inculcate a whole orientation to life that involves the entire person. It presupposes an integrated anthropology in which words, deeds, feelings, and thoughts influence each other reciprocally and that together give expression to the fundamental religious orientation of the heart, which is the control center of the human person. In demanding such wholehearted love from its subjects, biblical law addresses itself to the very seat of the personality. It beckons the human heart to orient itself cognitively, volitionally, emotionally, and continuously to the fullness of relationship with God and richness of relationship with others for which it has been created.

So love belongs, both rhetorically and substantively, to the law itself. Love is intrinsic to the law's structure. But in a profound sense, love also transcends the sphere of law entirely. What love requires cannot be defined adequately in legal terms, and it cannot be enforced by threatened sanctions. "A man can be compelled to abstain from work on the Sabbath," T. W. Manson observes, "but he cannot be compelled to love God with all his heart."[45] Love is, in essence, a free and voluntary response that cannot be legislated for in any detailed way. Significantly, neither of the

---

44. Common to both religious love and romantic love is the emphasis on personal transformation and interpersonal union, and such experiences cannot be attained by willpower alone but require emotional engagement. See the useful discussion by Martin and Runzo, "Love," in *Oxford Handbook*, 311–32.

45. Manson, *Teaching*, 305.

love commandments in the Torah specifies what "love" involves. As laws, they are as minimally legal as possible. No specific actions are prescribed as the outworking of love for neighbor, and those that are forbidden in the immediate context (such as taking vengeance or bearing a grudge or nursing hatred) describe the negative preconditions of love rather than its positive enactment. Similarly, love for God is not tied to a particular set of actions but is described as a comprehensive devotion to God and to God's will that infuses every aspect of existence. The open-endedness of both commands stems from the inherent nature of love. There is a kind of spontaneity and recklessness to love that defies legal description and resists institutional control. In summoning wholehearted love for God and neighbor, therefore, the law necessarily points beyond itself.

This is why in wider New Testament teaching the deepest meaning of love is disclosed, not by the law, but by the flesh-and-blood example of Jesus Christ. "We know love by this," John writes, "that he laid down his life for us, and we ought to lay down our lives for one another" (1 John 3:16). For the first Christians, Jesus perfectly embodied what love involves within the constraints of normal human existence, and those who "abide in him" are empowered to love as he loved. "Whoever says, 'I abide in him,' ought to walk just as he walked" (1 John 2:6). The Apostle Paul, in particular, looks outside the law for the wherewithal to satisfy the law's requirements (cf. Rom 8:1-4). The entire law can be summarized, Paul says, by the love commandment. "Owe no one anything, except to love one another; for the one who loves another has fulfilled the law. The commandments, 'You shall not commit adultery; You shall not murder; You shall not steal; You shall not covet,' and any other commandment, are summed up in this word, 'Love your neighbor as yourself.' Love does no wrong to a neighbor; therefore, love is the fulfilling of the law" (Rom 13:8-10; Gal 5:14). But the means by which one fulfils this law is by "putting on the Lord Jesus Christ" (Rom 13:14), crucifying the flesh and its passions, and living by the Spirit, whose fruit is the way of love (Gal 5:24-26, cf. Rom 5:5; 15:30).

Love, then, is simultaneously a law within the Law but also more than a law. It satisfies the law yet transcends law at the same time. The obligation to love may be formulated rhetorically as a legal imperative, for it requires a free, volitional commitment in order for it to happen. Yet the personal experience and practical outworking of this love carries us beyond the sphere of law entirely. When the commandments speak of love, they envisage a response of the whole personality—heart, mind, soul, and body—that the law can invite but not generate, specify but never fully comprehend. Supremely, for the first Christians, the meaning of this love was disclosed in the example of Jesus, and the capacity to emulate his love was thought to be imparted, not by submission to the Torah, but by participation in the life, death, and resurrection of Christ and by the gift of his Spirit. These realities, of course, are not explicit in Jesus' exchange with the lawyer. But the parable Jesus will soon tell him certainly indicates that something more is needed than autonomous benevolent action truly to accomplish the loving intent of the law.

BUT WHO IS MY NEIGHBOR?

So far, we have seen that it is the lawyer, not Jesus, who isolates the two love commandments as the means to attain the law's promise of eternal life, and that he understands love for God and love for neighbor to be mutually indispensable and mutually interpretive mandates. But this carries a significant implication. If love for the covenant God is indivisible from, and manifested in, love for one's neighbor, and if the neighbor is to be loved "as oneself"—that is, as someone of equal standing as oneself before Israel's God—then it follows logically that the neighbor in question must be a fellow member of the covenant community of Israel. This is precisely the meaning of "neighbor" in Lev 19:18. It stands in parallel with "your kinsman," "your brother," and "your people" in vv. 16–19, and designates, in Fichtner's words, "fellow-members of the . . . community who share in the election and the covenant and the implied duties and rights."[46] Neighbor is, in other words, a legally defined category. It designates not just those who live in physical proximity, but also those who share lawfully in full covenantal status with all the attendant rights and obligations. To love one's neighbors, then, does not mean to act benevolently towards one's fellow human beings in general but rather to uphold, protect, and, if need be, restore the rights, dignity, and status of those within the social and cultic community of Israel. It is to accord them all the entitlements, privileges, and material support that belong as of right only to other citizens of the covenant.

---

46. Fichtner, *"plēsion,"* 4:314–15.

This begs the question of what constitutes citizenship. The category of covenant membership was capable of expansion to include resident aliens and proselytes who embraced the Jewish faith, whom the law says are also to be loved (Lev 19:34; Deut 10:19), or of contraction to exclude, along with Gentiles and Samaritans, fellow Jews who, though of Israelite stock, were deemed to be derelict in their observation of the essential disciplines of their ancestral way of life and so forfeited their covenant standing. The precise scope of neighbor was therefore a matter open to legal debate, and such a debate appears to have been current at the time of Jesus.[47]

The lawyer alludes to this debate by asking Jesus, "Who then is my neighbor?" (v. 29). McFarland considers the question to be a perfectly reasonable one. Given that nothing less than eternal life was at stake, the question is a sign of "no greater presumption or recalcitrance than the ethically serious efforts of participants in contemporary debates over abortion and euthanasia to find a coherent definition of the person."[48] Yet in Luke's view, there was more on the lawyer's mind than ethical seriousness. He was anxious to "justify himself." This statement has been interpreted in a variety of ways, ranging from an embarrassed effort to justify his initial simplistic question, to a prideful attempt to prove that he merited salvation.[49] The best way to understand it, I suggest, is as a reference to his desire to justify or vindicate his own understanding and practice of the law—his own legal "rightness" or justice (*dikaios*)—focused in

---

47. The more restrictive interpretation was evident in certain sects and groupings at the time (cf. Str-B 1:353–57; *TDNT* 4:316). The Qumran community excluded outsiders (1QS 1:9–10; 2:24; 5:25; 1QM 1:1, cf. Josephus, *War*, 2:139), and some Pharisees were inclined to exclude the '*am ha'eretz* (cf. Str-B 2:514–17). The rabbis discussed extensively the limits of interaction with non-Jews (*m. Abod. Zar.* 1:1; 2:1–2; 4:9–10). One text includes one rabbinical saying to the effect that traitors and enemies should be pushed into the ditch and not helped out (*b. Abod. Zar.* 26a-b, cf. Jeremias, *Parables*, 202–3).

48. McFarland, "Who Is My Neighbor?," 59.

49. Available explanations include: 1) a desire to justify his original question (Plummer, *Luke*, 285; Creed, *Saint Luke*, 152; Jeremias, *Parables*, 202; Marshall, *Luke*, 447; Fitzmyer, *Luke*, 886; Wilson, *Luke and the Law*, 15); 2) a desire to regain his dented honor (Malina and Neyrey, "Honor," 50–51; Green, *Luke*, 429); 3) a desire to commend himself as fully righteous and thus merit praise from Jesus (Bailey, *Poet and Peasant*, 39; Lenski, *Luke*, 602; Ringe, *Luke*, 157); 4) a semi-Pelagian wish to merit final salvation (Cranfield, "Good Samaritan," 370; Morris, *Luke*, 188; Ellis, *Luke*, 160); 5) a desire to vindicate his status as a covenant Jew who will be vindicated when God acts in history (Wright, *Victory*, 307).

particular on his maintenance of purity in all his dealings with others. He subscribes to a stricter definition of neighbor than Jesus appears to adopt. But such strictness, he believes, is justified as a necessary outworking of his undivided devotion to God and to God's law.

But his quest to pin down the precise limits of neighbor has a negative corollary. It presupposes that there are certain people who can be justly regarded as non-neighbors, as persons to whom no duty of love is owed and whom in some cases one might even be justified in hating (cf. Luke 4:29; 6:22, 27; Matt 5:43). For the meticulous lawyer, neighbor is a term that limits one's liability. He assumes his obligations to other people derive wholly from their legal standing in the community, and their legal standing is a matter of empirical judgment. His relational obligations to others can be categorized and ticked off with the same precision and objectivity with which he can specify and accomplish his ritual obligations.

It is at this point that Jesus, for the first time in the story, parts company with the lawyer. The parable he composes shifts attention from "neighbor" as a static identity conferred on others by the law to "neighboring" as an open-ended task that one must perform in all one's interpersonal relationships. For Jesus, the key issue in the interpretation of Lev 19:18 is not the definition of "neighbor," as the lawyer assumes, but the meaning of "love." For neighbors are not simply created by legal fiat; they are discovered through love, and love is a quality of human relationships before it is a category of law. When love and compassion are present, the parable teaches, the identification of neighbors takes care of itself, for one's capacity to feel compassion for another human being is already a sign that one stands in a neighborly relationship to that person, with all its consequent obligations, independently of any status the law might or might not confer on them. Compassion is the emotional signal that we all participate in a common stream of broken humanity, and it is this shared humanity, not the jurisdiction of law, that evokes the obligation to love others as creatures of equal worth and rights as oneself.

The parable serves, then, to expand the existing understandings of neighbor to embrace anyone in need and everyone in relationship. The social and political implications of this interpretive shift have been enormous. Meier prefers to credit Luke rather than Jesus for this ingenious broadening of the term neighbor, since there is no hint in the Markan tradition that Jesus understood "neighbor" any differently than does Lev

19:18b. By modern liberal standards, and even compared to Luke and Matthew, the historical Jesus' construal of the Levitical commandment remained "distressingly provincial," says Meier.[50] But this is a debatable conclusion to reach. Just because Mark's Jesus does not thematize the subject in the same manner that occurs in Luke does not mean that he subscribed to a more conventional definition of neighbor. If the scope of the term was a matter of spirited debate during Jesus' time, as seems to be the case, and if there was something about the inclusive praxis of Jesus that led Luke to discern in his parable of the Good Samaritan a dramatic expansion of "neighbor" in Lev 19:18, why could not Jesus himself also have done so? The difficulty with positing a provincial Jesus whose views are subsequently radicalized by the third Evangelist's appending of the parable of the Good Samaritan to a redacted version of the Markan tradition lies in explaining why such radicalization occurred in the first place, unless there was something in the tradition to encourage it. Even if Luke were the first person to use the parable as a commentary on Lev 19:18, the fact that he did so would indicate that there was a momentum in this direction already at work in his sources. This impetus must have come from somewhere or someone. Luke claims it came from Jesus, and there is no need to doubt him.

SUMMARY

Luke's account of the conversation between Jesus and the lawyer over the correct way of reading the law is as important for what it denies as for what it affirms. It denies that Jesus was the first Jewish teacher to emphasize the foundational significance of the two love commandments in the Torah, or that he was the first to bring them together into a mutually dependent, mutually interpretive relationship. Some of his erstwhile critics and opponents shared this perspective, even if Jesus emphasized it with unmistakable clarity. The story also denies that Jesus questioned the salvific function of the Torah or minimized the necessity of legal obedience. "Do this and you will live" could scarcely be more unambiguous! Finally, the story denies that Jesus championed love instead of law, or that he considered love and law to be mutually exclusive regimes. Love belongs to the law, it takes the form of a legal requirement, and it satisfies

---

50. Meier, *Marginal Jew*, 4:651, cf. 492–93.

the deepest intent of the law. At the same time love, being what love is, necessarily transcends the law. It transcends it both in the sense that the law cannot exhaustively describe or prescribe what love requires and it cannot empower or energize the love it enjoins. Love is a demand, but it is also a gift; it is a legal obligation, but also an act of self-determination and freedom; it is a volitional commitment, but also an affective and sympathetic involvement; an external action, but also an interior motivation.[51]

It is here that Jesus differs from the lawyer. Both accept that love of God and love of neighbor are essential for eternal life. But whereas the lawyer thinks that the critical issue is the scope of the term "neighbor," Jesus considers the key question to be the scope of "love." The lawyer reduces love to its legal minimum by restricting the category of neighbor to fellow members of the covenant community, which, in his favor, corresponds to the plain meaning of Lev 19:18. Jesus, however, maximizes the category of neighbor because he refuses to reduce love to its legal dimensions. Neighbors are not chosen or created by law; they are found and cultivated through human encounter.[52] Because love of neighbor is inseparable from love of God, and because love of God is comprehensive in character, engaging the entire personality in undivided commitment, there can be no limits to what love requires and no exceptions to its attentiveness. All human beings count as neighbors to be loved, even those who on other scores might count as enemies. Indeed, love for enemy is the supreme testimony to the freedom and grace that is love, for it is a love that loves without expecting reciprocity.

For Jesus, love of neighbor is indiscriminate and unconditional in character precisely because it is love, the same limitless love that God exhibits towards his creatures (Matt 5:45–48; Luke 6:35–36) and personally embodies (cf. 1 John 4:7–12). So radical is Jesus' concept of love, and so unrestricted its application, it raises the question of where such love comes from and how it can be appropriated. Love, of its very character, I have suggested, necessarily transcends the realm of law. Yet when love

---

51. For a similarly rounded account of love, see Oord, *Defining Love*, esp. 11–30, where he defines love as follows: "To love is to act intentionally, in sympathetic response to others (including God), to promote overall well-being."

52. "For Jesus, my neighbor is anyone to whom I draw near. And I ought to draw near to all women and men, particularly my enemies (Matt 5:44) and the poor and plundered whom I meet along the pathway of my journey on Earth" (Boff, *When Theology Listens*, 33–34).

is conceived as profoundly as Jesus conceives it, it transcends the law to nothing less than eschatological proportions.

In responding to the lawyer's question about the limits of neighbor love, Jesus does not engage in abstract philosophical reflection or exegetical-linguistic debate on the details of the Written Torah. Instead he tells a story. It is a story that operates at multiple levels and that requires the lawyer to approve of the extralegal activity of a non-neighbor in preference to the law-informed behavior of two cultic experts from his own community. In this way Jesus confronts the one who would "justify himself" with the true meaning of justice and the true meaning of love. It is time now to enter the story world of Jesus' great parable of neighbor-love and restorative justice to discover what each means in practice.

4

Victimization and the Law of Neglect

The parable opens with "a certain man" (*anthrōpos tis*) journeying down from Jerusalem to Jericho. Importantly, no indication is given of the man's ethnic or religious or social identity, only his basic humanity, though Jesus' Jewish audience would have naturally assumed him to be a Jew in the absence of indications to the contrary. He is pictured "going down" to Jericho because Jerusalem was located some eight hundred meters above sea level, whereas his city of destination lay at or below sea level, entailing a descent of some thirty meters for every kilometer traveled.[1] The road was steep in places and also treacherous, twisting through barren terrain honeycombed with caves and gullies that provided ample hiding places for the many robbers who infested the area. It was extremely dangerous territory to pass through, and remained so for most of subsequent history. St. Jerome (ca. 342–420 CE) ascribed its Arabic name, "The Ascent of Blood" (*Tala'at ed Damm*), to "the blood that is often shed there by robbers." He thought it was a fitting name, for "the Lord also reminds us of this bloody, bloodthirsty place in the parable of the man who went down from Jerusalem to Jericho."[2]

The twenty-five kilometer journey would normally have taken at least six hours to complete on foot. But on this occasion the man's progress is cut short by a violent attack. His assailants are described as *lēstais* ("robbers"), a term that indicates that they were not opportunist thieves

---

1. Wilkinson, "Way," 10–24.

2. Quoted in ibid., 18–19; Creed, *Saint Luke*, 152. The biblical Hebrew name *Ma'ale Adummim* (Josh 15:7; 18:17) probably meant "The Ascent of the Red Places," since there are several outcrops of red sandstone in this area.

(*kleptais* cf. Luke 12:33, 39; John 12:6) but well-armed brigands or outlaws who preyed on vulnerable travelers in the countryside. Conceivably they were social bandits, poor people driven to crime by severe economic circumstances. Social banditry is a common phenomenon in agrarian societies during periods of social, political, and economic upheaval. Unemployed workers or peasants driven off their land through debt, famine, or excessive taxation resort to brigandage in order to survive, and their primary victims are typically the ruling elites whom they hold responsible for their plight. According to Josephus, brigandage was a widespread problem in first-century Judea, and even the Romans struggled to control it. He tells of one episode during the reign of Herod the Great in which the ancient equivalent of special forces were lowered down the cliff faces in baskets to storm the caves where the bandits were holed up.[3]

Given the sociopolitical context of social banditry, some commentators suggest that Jesus' first hearers would have felt immediate sympathy for the robbers mentioned in the parable, viewing them as Robin Hood–type figures who struggled valiantly on behalf of the little people against social and economic oppression.[4] But this seems implausible. The social origins of criminal behavior rarely generate genuine sympathy for its perpetrators amongst those who have not themselves turned to violent crime and who ever remain its potential targets, whether directly or indirectly as a result of official reprisals. The penalty for brigandage at this time was death, and fear of being attacked by bandits was widespread in the populace. According to Josephus, the only thing the Essenes, whom he describes as "despisers of riches," carried with them on their travels were weapons for protection against brigands.[5]

In any event, the parable scarcely portrays the robbers in a positive light. They are responsible for extreme violence against a nameless victim whose simple humanity is highlighted while his social status is left deliberately ambiguous. It is ambiguous because the only thing seized from him by his attackers is his clothing: "in addition to beating him they stripped him" (*hoi kai ekdusantes auton kai plēgas epithente*). Throughout Luke's two volumes, clothing is a consistent indicator of wealth and status,[6] so it

---

3. Josephus, *War* 1:311.
4. Malina and Rohrbaugh, *Social-Science*, 404, cf. 347; cf. Ringe, *Luke*, 158; Oakman, "Peasant?" 121.
5. Josephus, *War* 2.124, cf. 2.228.
6. See Luke 7:25; 15:22; 16:19; 20:46; Acts 12:21; 16:14.

is possible that the stripping of the victim implies he was a wealthy man whose expensive clothing was worth stealing. On the other hand, it could indicate that he was so dirt poor that he possessed only the rags on his back, which the bandits took in spiteful frustration.

Whatever his social rank, the man is treated cruelly by his assailants and left for dead. The dramatic description of his attack captures no fewer than five common aspects of the experience of criminal victimization. These need to be spelled out carefully at the beginning of the story, for if the man is ever to be restored to well-being, each dimension will need to be addressed. These five features also correspond to a remarkable degree with the findings of modern research into the experience of criminal victimization.

THE IMPACT OF VICTIMIZATION

First, and most basically, the man's victimization was an occasion of *profound disempowerment*: "he fell into the hands of robbers" (*lēstais periepesen*). Without warning, total strangers invade his life, disrupt his normal routine, seize control of his person, and reduce him to abject impotence. He is subject to actions over which he has absolutely no control. As we noted previously, from this point on in the narrative the man is portrayed as completely passive, utterly dependent on the goodwill of others for his very survival. His assailants have reduced him to a state of radical helplessness. This, at its most elemental level, is what victimization is: an uninvited and debilitating powerlessness.

The man's victimization was also an experience of *physical violation*: "they beat him," literally to within an inch of his life, leaving him "half dead." The phrase used for his beating (*plēgas epithentes*, "laying on blows") is the same expression used for the ferocious flogging dished out to Paul and Silas in the Philippian jail (Acts 16:23, cf. 2 Cor 6:5; 11:23). The word translated "half dead" (*hēmithanē*) is exceedingly rare in biblical Greek, although Moulton and Milligan point to a striking parallel in a later papyrus document where a woman lays a complaint about an episode of domestic violence in which her brother and sister-in-law "nearly killed me by numbers of blows and left me half dead."[7] Clearly, then, the man was subjected to severe violence. Later, his rescuer must

---

7. Moulton and Milligan, *Vocabulary*, 280 (citing P.Ahm II.141:13). The only occurrences of *hēmithanē* in biblical Greek are 4 Macc 4:11 and here in Luke 10:30.

dress and bandage his oozing wounds before attempting to move him to safety. Some commentators conjecture that such a severe beating implies that the man resisted his attackers and tried to defend himself.[8] But it could equally be an act of wanton violence against someone unfortunate enough to have only his clothes to surrender as loot. Either way, his attackers violate his bodily integrity, and he is discarded like a worthless piece of garbage.

Third, his victimization was an experience of *psychological humiliation:* "they stripped him" (*ekdusantes auton*). Clothing in the ancient world was an essential means of signaling one's wealth, class, or religious function, and the ability to recognize one's social peers by their appearance was enormously important. This is particularly clear in Luke's writings, where wearing ornate clothing is a sign of personal dignity, honor, and worth (7:25; 15:22; 16:19; 20:46; Acts 12:21; 16:14), and being divested of apparel is a sign of shame and degradation, whether chosen willingly as an expression of faith and service (3:11; 9:3; 12:22-23, 27), or suffered involuntarily through judicial punishment or criminal wrongdoing (6:29; 22:63; Acts 16:22-23, 27). The victim's stripping in the parable, therefore, implies his humiliation as much as material deprivation.

Moreover, he is not only robbed of personal dignity, he is also stripped of his social location, for with his stolen clothing went all available markers of his ethnic identity and social belonging. Naked and unconscious, and thus unable to speak, all external clues as to his individual, cultural, or religious identity are taken away. In effect, he is dehumanized, for the wearing of clothes is a distinctively human cultural practice that exhibits the wearer's essential humanity. (Thus stripping detainees naked is a recognized technique interrogators and torturers use to dehumanize them and to overcome the prevailing moral and cultural norms that discourage the abusive treatment of fellow human beings.)[9] Stripped of all human dignity, the victim is reduced to an absolute minimum: an exposed, anonymous, insensible creature whose only claim on anyone else's attention is his acute need.[10]

8. So Jeremias, *Parables,* 203; Bailey, *Poet and Peasant,* 42.

9. On the link between dehumanization and abuse, see Zimbardo, *Lucifer Effect,* 307-13, 396, 402.

10. It is unlikely that his clothing itself would have been an indication of his ethnicity, since there is little evidence that Jews wore clothes that distinguished them from Gentiles, although long robes, prayer tassels, and phylacteries were used by some as symbols of religious commitment (Matt 23:5; Mark 6:56, cf. Luke 15:22).

Fourth, the victim's experience was one of *social isolation:* "they went away, leaving him" (*apēlthon aphente*). He is left alone in a lonely place to die a lonely, lingering death. So isolated is he that it is only "by chance" (v. 31) that his battered and bruised body is seen by anyone at all. Even then the first people who come across him elect to leave him in his abandoned state. He is twice forsaken: first by his attackers, then by his potential rescuers, whose indifference to his plight is a cruelty of equal magnitude. Victims of severe violence often speak of the disconnection they feel from those around them, even from close friends and family members, who are unable or unwilling to fathom their pain or bridge the gap to their desolate condition. The aloneness they experienced in being singled out for an attack by their assailant is compounded by the profound sense of loneliness they know in struggling with its aftermath. They feel enclosed in a shell of isolation.

Finally, the victim's experience was one of *enduring vulnerability:* "they left him half dead." His suffering commenced at the time of the assault, but his anguish is not yet over. For the remainder of the story, the victim hovers between life and death. Those who stumble upon him on the road have a choice: They can either, like the priest and the Levite, regard him as good as dead already, beyond any worthwhile effort to restore, or, like the merciful Samaritan, they can defy the logic of death and seek to fan the flicker of life back into flame. There is no middle way. Those who encounter victims can either surrender to the logic of destruction unleashed by the crime and reckon their powerless, violated, humiliated, and abandoned state to be hopeless, or they can strive to bring hope and healing and restoration to the victim, however remote that may seem at the time. The first option is starkly illustrated in what happens next in the story, as two passing clerics elect to pass by on the other side.

In these four or five key phrases, then, the parable affords a piercing insight into what it means experientially to become the victim of violent crime. It is only in the last few decades that social scientists and psychotherapists have sought to gain a better understanding of the distinctive traumas experienced by crime victims and to map the constellation of personal and communal needs that flow from the criminal event. Each person's experience is different, of course, but certain common themes recur in the way crime victims describe their struggles to come to terms with what has happened. These themes are strikingly similar to the themes highlighted in Jesus' parable where, in a few carefully chosen words, he characterizes the universal experience of those who fall foul of the malevolence of others.

Howard Zehr, frequently called "the grandfather of restorative justice," has made a special effort in his career to listen to the voices of crime victims and their advocates.[11] The victim community is sometimes suspicious of restorative justice as being an offender-centered intervention, though in reality it strives to be victim-focused in its procedures and principles. In a sensitive essay, Zehr sets out how restorative justice is uniquely placed to meet some of the deepest needs victims have in the wake of the crime, such as the need for answers to their questions, the need for vindication or validation of their suffering, and the need to feel safe again in an unsafe world.[12]

Zehr also explains why it is that victimization often has such a devastating impact on people. To become the victim of a significant crime undermines the four central pillars on which people base their sense of security and belonging in the world. We all need a sense of *autonomy*, a feeling we have some degree of control over our own lives; a sense of *order*, a belief that the world is a structured or predictable place where events can be understood and explained; a sense of *relatedness*, of having positive relationships with other people, knowing who can be trusted and where we fit in to the networks of reciprocity that unite us; and a sense of *meaning*, an ability to make sense of what is going on around us and how it squares with our sense of personal identity and purpose. The trauma of victimization strikes at all four levels. It is an all-encompassing crisis that upsets the normal physical, emotional, mental, social, and spiritual equilibrium by which people live their lives, and it can cause acute problems in each of these areas. The victim's sense of autonomy is overwhelmed by a crippling sense of powerlessness; a sense of order gives way to disorder; feelings of relatedness are displaced by feelings of aloneness and alienation; and meaningfulness dissolves into bewilderment, confusion, and sometimes despair. Two words that perhaps best capture this crushing ordeal of victimization are *disempowerment* and

---

11. See Mika et al., *Listening Project*.

12. Zehr, "Restoring Justice," 131–59. More generally on the victim movement, see Strang, "Victim Movement," 69–82, and the useful essays in part 10 of Hoyle, *Restorative Justice*, 3:1–134

disconnection, and no two terms better summarize the portrayal of the hapless victim on the road from Jerusalem to Jericho.

It is the disconnection that victims experience that helps explain why it is that other people often find it so difficult to attend to their needs. Victims have a way of making others feel anxious and unsure as well. Everyone needs to feel that the world is a safe and predictable place, that we have some measure of control over our lives. But the randomness of crime challenges that perception. Victims remind us of our vulnerability and insecurity. In witnessing their suffering, doubts arise about our own safety. Victims frighten us. This accounts for the widespread tendency to blame victims, especially rape victims, for their predicament. If we can explain their adversity in terms of their own foolishness, we reassure ourselves that it might never happen to us, so long as we avoid *their* mistakes.

It is because victims evoke such anxieties in others that we try to keep them at a safe distance, which exacerbates their feelings of isolation. One might expect things to be different for victims who belong to faith communities, such as churches and synagogues, since such communities usually strive be places of hospitality and support. But this is not always the case. In fact, in some ways victims constitute an even more threatening presence in the religious community than they do in the wider community. The stark reality of their victimization raises profoundly unsettling questions about faith—questions about the origins of evil and God's presumed control of the world, about the arbitrariness of suffering and the effectiveness of prayer, about the value of spiritual commitment when God seems to fail those who trust in him. The inadequacy of stock answers to such questions is threateningly exposed by the hard facts of the victim's experience, and fellow believers either fall into an awkward silence or resort to trite and formulaic answers. I once spoke to a man whose daughter had been killed by a drunk driver. One of the hardest things for him in the aftermath of the tragedy was going back to church. "People were so busy defending God," he said, "they weren't able to sense what we were going through." Could this be a clue to the mindset of the two religious professionals who appear next in the parable? Were they also too busy defending God or the things of God to attend to the needs of the victim?

THE JUSTIFICATION OF PROFESSIONAL NEGLECT

By good fortune, the victim was not the only traveler on the Jericho road that day. A priest and, later, a Levite were also heading down the highway. They were probably returning home after completing their eight days of rostered service in the Jerusalem temple (cf. Luke 1:8). Jericho was a popular residence for temple functionaries, with perhaps up to half of the twenty-four courses of priests (1 Chron 24:1-19) and Levites (1 Chron 15:4-12) who served the temple residing there. The priests maintained the regular schedule of sacrifices and offerings in the sanctuary, while the Levites supplied a range of support services, including provision of the instrumental and choral music that accompanied morning and evening worship.[13]

As holders of sacerdotal office in a strongly hierocratic society—that is, one stratified according to religious function and authority—both the priest and the Levite would have enjoyed great social prestige. They would have been widely revered for the purity of their bloodline and their commitment to ritual holiness. Very likely they wore long white linen garments to signify their exceptional sanctity.[14]

As we noted earlier, along with their other tasks, priests and Levites exercised an important judicial function. They were specialists in the interpretation and application of the law, and in particular of the Holiness Code, which tightly regulated their professional and private conduct. Originally, priests exercised sole prerogative in the interpretation of the law in Israel, and, as Safrai notes, were "regarded as the natural and self-evident authorities in interpreting Scripture."[15] Over time, a lay order of Torah scholars emerged alongside them, who also commanded great public respect for their expertise. Yet, contrary to what is sometimes thought, priests never relinquished their role in legal instruction and administration. E. P. Sanders sets out the evidence for their continuing legal responsibility and concludes: "Priests and Levites were the employees of the

---

13. The term "Levite" originally designated descendents of the tribe of Levi (Gen 29:34), but in the Bible the term is used for those who, though not descendents of Aaron, were entrusted with minor service relating to the temple. Their status varied in the course of biblical times, but they soon acquired a status entitling them to receive tithes for priestly service (Neh 10:37-38). See further Schürer, *History* 1:227-313; Jeremias, *Jerusalem*, 207-21; Safrai and Stern, *Jewish People*, 580-612; Sanders, *Judaism*, 77-102.

14. For evidence, see Knowles, "Victim Wearing?," 162-64.

15. Safrai and Stern, *Jewish People*, 580.

nation for the purposes of maintaining the worship of God in the Temple, and teaching and judging the people . . . . [T]he nation's official teachers and magistrates were the priests, and . . . a good number of them spent their time on these tasks when they were not on duty at the Temple."[16]

This means that the priest and the Levite who appear on the road would have known all too well that the law enjoins Israelites to render aid to their neighbors in need.[17] They would have also been familiar with the biblical injunction, "When you see the naked, cover them, and do not hide yourself from your own kin" (Isa 58:7). Jews were generally renowned for showing kindness to their fellow countrymen, impelled in part by the plain demands of Scripture.[18] Yet, in sharp variance to biblical injunction, the priest and the Levite turn aside from the sufferer on the roadside and leave him untouched to die alone. Why do they do so? Why do they display such appalling indifference to him? Why does the parable cast the priest and the Levite in such a negative light?

Several answers have been given to this question. Some interpreters attribute the failure of the two clerics to little more than a personal weakness or simple apathy. They were busy men and couldn't be bothered with the inconvenience of stopping to assist someone in need, and since they were alone on the road, they could hasten on without anyone else noticing their selfishness.[19] Others think they were fearful that the robbers who attacked the man might still be lurking in the area and could ambush them as well.[20] Maybe they thought the whole situation was a setup: the man on the ground could be feigning victimization in order to lure passersby into a trap. Perhaps they went into a state of nervous shock and simply kept moving as a way of dealing with the anxiety they felt. Or maybe they felt physically revolted at the disgusting condition of the body. It has been found that people are substantially less inclined to render assistance to persons in need when it involves them coming into

16. Sanders, *Judaism*, 182.

17. E.g., Exod 22:21–27; 23:6–12; Lev 19:9–18, 33–34; 23:22; Deut 15:7; 22:4; 24:11–21; 29:9–15.

18. Of the Jews, Tacitus writes, ". . . among themselves they are inflexibly honest and ever ready to show compassion, though they regard the rest of mankind with all the hatred of enemies" (*Histories* 5:5, cf. Juvenal, *Satires* 14:103–4).

19. Cf. Farrer, *St. Luke*, 205; Johnson, *Luke*, 3:175.

20. Cf. Snodgrass, *Stories*, 355–56; Ringe, *Luke*, 159; Lenski, *Luke's Gospel*, 604–5; King Jr., "Mountaintop."

contact with their blood or bodily fluids.[21] It is also the case that people who say cleanliness is an important personal value are generally less helpful than those who consider it to be of lesser importance.[22] This natural aversion to blood and high valuation of cleanliness would have been particularly pronounced in first-century Jewish priests, for whom blood and bodily fluids were also potential vehicles of ritual contamination.

Or perhaps the clerics simply considered it beneath their dignity to help someone of lower status.[23] The victim's ethnic pedigree and moral reputation were equivocal at best, and perhaps, like ben Sirach, they believed themselves to be under a positive obligation to withhold assistance from the ungodly.[24]

> If you do good, know to whom you do it,
> and you will be thanked for your good deeds.
> Do good to the devout, and you will be repaid—
> if not by them, certainly by the Most High.
> No good comes to one who persists in evil
> or to one who does not give alms.
>
> Give to the devout, but do not help the sinner.
> Do good to the humble, but do not give to the ungodly;
> hold back their bread, and do not give it to them,
> for by means of it they might subdue you;
> then you will receive twice as much evil
> for all the good you have done to them.
>
> For the Most High also hates sinners
> and will inflict punishment on the ungodly.
> Give to the one who is good,
> but do not help the sinner. (Sir 12:1–7; cf. 25:21)

---

21. Schroeder et al., *Psychology of Helping*, 46.

22. Staub, "Distressed Person," 329. This is probably because people who value cleanliness highly are often more conventional in their values, and there is a tension between convention and creative concern for others.

23. Green, *Luke*, 430–31. According to *b. B. Mes.* 32 a–b, 33a, 30a, distinguished persons were relieved of the duty to aid others in need if it was beneath their dignity to do so.

24. Cf. Bailey, *Poet and Peasant*, 43–44; Meier, *Marginal Jew*, 4:534. The parallel with Jewish laws relating to lost property is instructive. There is a clear duty to return property to its true owner (Exod 23:4; *b. B. Mes.* 32a), but, as Besser and Kaplan explain, there is no obligation to restore lost property to a Gentile or a heretic, lest one ends up supporting the ways of the wicked in the world. Besser and Kaplan, "Good Samaritan," 198.

The clerics knew that they were enjoined in Scripture to love all who loved the God of Israel (cf. Lev 19:17; Prov 8:17). But this naked, unidentified stranger could well be a flagrant sinner who hated God, and who should therefore be hated in return by the righteous (Ps 139:21–22).[25] Presuming him to be a sinner would also help explain his suffering: something bad had happened to him because he deserved it. After all, if sinners and criminals are ritually unclean, as Levitical law indicates, it is not too difficult to reverse the equation and assume that the manifestly unclean and contaminated are probably also sinners and criminals. In short, according to this view, the priest and Levite would have been willing to help the right person, at the right time, in the right circumstances. But this was the wrong person, at the wrong time, in the wrong circumstances, and it was certainly no time to hesitate. Better be safe than sorry.

Now none of these personality or dispositional considerations can be ruled out in the explanation. Fear, pride, and selfishness are universal human failings, and apathy can numb moral sensitivity (though contrary to what we might expect, apathy is the least common reason for people failing to assist others in extreme need).[26] But there must have been more to the clerics' decision than personal haughtiness, apathy, cowardice, or laziness, even if these traits were also present in some measure. It can hardly be accidental that both characters have a professional association with the Jerusalem temple. Presumably there was something about their cultic connections or vocational priorities that conspired with their normal human self-centeredness to overrule their *prima facie* legal and moral duty to rescue a neighbor in need.

In this connection, several commentators emphasize systemic rather than personal forces at work in their decisions. They propose that the clerics failed in their duty of rescue because they were cogs in a corrupt and debilitating sacred caste system. Many detect in the parable a polemic against the efficacy of sacrifice and temple performance in general,[27] while others imagine a more targeted assault upon the priestly aristocracy, who were complicit in the social and economic exploitation of the common people, not least through their control of the sacrificial system.[28]

25. Cf. Pss 5:5; 26:5; 68:1; 81:15; 89:23; 2 Chron 19:2; 1QS 1:3–4, 9–10.

26. Freedman, "No Responses," 175; Schroeder, *Psychology of Helping*, 25–58.

27. Wright sees part of the message of the parable as involving "the firm relativisation of cult and sacrifice," *Victory*, 305. Also, Jones, "Love Command," 237.

28. So McDonald, "Alien Grace," 49; Stassen and Gushee, *Kingdom Ethics*, 338–39.

The former is doubtful, however, since the overall attitude towards the temple and the priesthood in the Gospels, and especially in Luke's writings, is positive. Luke's narrative opens and closes in the temple (1:5–25; 24:53), and the temple is also a place of prayer for the early Christians (Acts 2:46; 3:1; 5:12, 25). Twice Jesus sends healed people to the priests for confirmation of their recovery (5:14; 17:14), and in Acts 6:7, a large number of priests become Christian believers. Certainly there is a relativization of the temple in Jesus' ministry and an expectation of its imminent destruction (21:5–6, cf. Mark 13:1; Matt 24:1–2). But there is no sustained attack upon priestly religion as such, and there is no reason to assume that the priest and the Levite in the parable abandoned the man in the ditch purely because they were wicked priests.

The latter explanation is also doubtful. It rests on the assumption that priests were typically wealthy and powerful individuals who comprised the upper stratum of Jewish society.[29] But most priests and Levites were probably poor,[30] especially those residing outside of Jerusalem, even if, as sacred figures, they were still revered as persons of noble heritage and function.[31] Traces of anticlericalism in Jewish sources are largely confined to criticism of the resident hierarchs who ran the temple and who were widely regarded as corrupt. But there is nothing to suggest that the priest and the Levite in the parable were members of the small patrician elite who controlled the religious and political establishment in Jerusalem and milked the system for personal gain.

If the failure of the priest and the Levite, then, was not due solely to personal cowardice or pride, or to their aristocratic lineage and institutional corruption, what other explanation could there be? Some commentators refuse to speculate on this, claiming their motivation is unknowable and irrelevant to the story.[32] Yet this is far from the case. Certainly the parable lacks the interior monologues we find in some

---

29. Scott, *Hear Then*, 197. Bailey assumes the priest was aristocratic and surmises that he would have been riding down the road, whereas the Levite would have been on foot (Bailey, *Poet and Peasant*, 43–44). But this outruns any evidence.

30. Bauckham, "Scrupulous Priest," 479 n. 11, citing Josephus *Ant.* 20:181, 20:207; Snodgrass, *Stories*, 354–55.

31. Stern, *Jewish People*, 580. Josephus writes, "The family from which I am derived is not an ignoble one, but has descended all along from the priests; and as nobility among several people is of a different origin, so with us to be of the sacerdotal dignity, is an indication of the splendor of a family" (*Life* 1:1).

32. Schottroff, *Parables*, 135–36; Gnilka, *Jesus*, 245; Schrage, *Ethics*, 74–76.

other parables (such as the parable of the Prodigal Son), which provide a window into the characters' inner thought world.[33] But there are still several important clues in the narrative as to why the priest and the Levite responded the way they did.[34] Careful consideration of each of these narrative clues, together with insights drawn from the wealth of recent social-science research into the psychology of altruism and bystander intervention, allows us to construct a credible explanation that integrates psychological, socioreligious, systemic, and, in particular, legal considerations.

EXPLANATORY NARRATIVE CLUES

The first clue is the description of the victim as "stripped" and "half dead." Death was a major source of ritual impurity in Jewish society. According to the Torah, contact with a corpse, and with anything a corpse had touched, brought impurity for seven days, which required a set of purification measures, at some financial cost to the beneficiary, to eradicate (Num 19:11–16, cf. 5:2). Such defilement was, of course, unavoidable in social life. In every community, people die regularly and their bodies need to be disposed of, and there was a clear duty on members of the Jewish community to attend to the needs of the dying and the deceased, as long as the resulting impurity was dealt with appropriately. Priests, however, were under a unique obligation to avoid all contact with corpses, except in the case of immediate family members (Lev 21:1–4; 22:4–7; Ezek 44:25–27), though even this exception was not permitted for the high priest (Lev 21:11) or a Nazirite (Num 6:6–12). There was, in other words, a clear *legal* duty on the priest, and probably also on the Levite, to avoid corpse-pollution.[35] Since the body on the Jericho road appeared to be lifeless, it posed a serious threat of ritual defilement for them.

---

33. On this narrative device in Luke's parables, see Sellew, "Monologue," 239–53.

34. Contra Scott, *Hear Then*, 197 ("In the end there is no final resolution for the priest and Levite's motivation, because the parable offers no clues.")

35. Strictly speaking, the prohibition in Lev 21:1–4 applies only to corpses of fellow Israelites, though the principle was probably extended to Gentile corpses as well (cf. Num 19:11–16, the "dead body of any human being"). The prohibition also applies directly to priests, and we cannot be sure it would have been extended to Levites as well. But it is not improbable it would, given their close links with temple worship.

This explains the second clue in the account: the priest and the Levite, having "seen" the man's derelict condition, did not merely fail to stop; they deliberately "passed by on the other side" (*antiparēlthen*). This is the only occurrence of this compound verb in the New Testament, and it presumably indicates that they crossed to the opposite side of the road in order to continue on their journey. They distanced themselves as far as practicable from the body, since impurity could be contracted, not only by touch, but by coming too close to a corpse, and specifically from standing over it, as corpse impurity was believed to travel vertically through the air.[36] Even if they thought the man was still alive, there was always the possibility that he might die as they drew close enough to check his pulse, in which case they would be defiled.

The third clue in the story is the contrast afforded by the Samaritan, whose actions are described in exact parallel to those of the priest and the Levite, except in one crucial respect.

the priest . . .	saw him (*kai idōn*) . . .	and passed by on the other side (*antiparēlthen*)
the Levite . . .	saw him (*kai idōn*) . . .	and passed by on the other side (*antiparēlthen*)
the Samaritan . . .	saw him (*kai idōn*) . . .	and had compassion (*esplangchnisthē*)

The Jewish clerics "see" the victim's state and "pass by on the other side" out of concern to preserve their ritual purity. The Samaritan, who from a priestly perspective was the very epitome of uncleanness, not least because he refused to acknowledge the legitimacy of the Jerusalem temple and its purification regimes, "sees" the victim and responds with "compassion." Disregarding all other scruples, the unclean Samaritan does what the priest and the Levite failed to do: he heeds the evidence of his eyes and the superior dictates of compassion.

The best explanation, then, of why the two temple figures refuse to help the victim is that they were concerned, above all else, to avoid corpse contamination. Some scholars reject this explanation on the grounds that the men had completed their cultic duties in Jerusalem and were

---

36. Bauckham, "Scrupulous Priest," 477–78; Bailey, *Poet and Peasant*, 44–45; Derrett, *Law*, 213, notes that rabbinic texts instruct people to remain at least two meters (four cubits) from a corpse.

now heading home, so that sustaining ritual cleanliness was no longer so important for them, especially not for the Levite. They also note that the victim wasn't actually dead anyway, so technically not a source of defilement.[37] But this objection underestimates the extent to which the custodians of Israel's law internalized purity concerns and let them permeate every fiber of their existence.[38] The Torah provided them with a comprehensive "purity map" that categorized times, places, persons, things, foods, conditions, and bodily states according to degrees of purity or pollution.[39] The Pharisees, as is well known, were marked by a concern to extend the rigorous standards of cultic purity into everyday life, and Luke records them as being in constant controversy with Jesus over purity norms relating to times (6:1–11), places (19:45–46), dietary practices (11:37–38) and, most of all, people. Jesus touched lepers (5:13), menstruating women (8:43–48), and corpses (8:54), and he had meals with impure people (5:29–30; 10:7–8). To the Pharisees, he appeared to treat purity regulations with benign neglect, if not downright contempt. It was this factor, as I proposed earlier, that probably provoked the lawyer to "test" Jesus with his question about eternal life (v. 25).

But at the very head of the purity stakes were not the Pharisees but priests and Levites, and their concern to exhibit and preserve ritual distinction would have run very deep indeed. For them to contract avoidable defilement in any circumstances would have been a disruptive, expensive, and shameful experience. Most of all, however, it would have involved them in a clear violation of the law. They stood under a legal requirement not to defile themselves through contact with a corpse. They would have therefore instinctively recoiled from drawing too close to the

37. So Jeremias, *Parables*, 203–4; Gourgues, "Priest," 79–80; Green, *Luke*, 430; Schottroff, *Parables*, 135; Ringe, *Luke*, 159; Gnilka, *Jesus*, 245 n. 98; Liefeld, "Luke," 943; Snodgrass, *Stories*, 355–56.

38. "Commentators who refuse to acknowledge that a purity issue is at stake because purity is not specifically mentioned in the parable have failed to enter imaginatively the first-century Jewish world, in which confronting a priest with a dying man on a deserted road could scarcely fail to raise the issue of corpse-defilement for any informed hearer, (Bauckham, "Scrupulous Priest," 477).

39. For a brief overview, see Malina and Rohrbaugh, *Social-Science*, 318–20. The use of rabbinic sources for determining legal perspectives in the Second Temple period is, of course, disputable. But there is enough evidence from Qumran and elsewhere to show that there was continuity from the Hasmonean period through to the early rabbinic period in the type of halakic discussions that took place, not least over purity matters.

bloodied, unconscious figure on the side of the road, fearing him to be recently deceased or in the last stages of expiring.

But—and this is a crucial point—their legal duty was not as unambiguous as they imagined. The law also imposed a strong obligation to come to the aid of their neighbors in time of need, even, in some cases, where that neighbor was a personal foe (cf. Lev 19:17; Prov 25:21–22, cf. 24:17–18). The commandment about loading and unloading a distressed donkey was taken as paradigmatic of this duty (Exod 23:4–5; Deut 22:2; cf. 2 Macc 2:14).[40] The obligation was not absolute. Exceptions applied, and the rescuer was not obligated to help if it entailed suffering substantial personal loss in the process.[41] But the duty to rescue was more untrammeled when human life was at stake. A later Talmudic ruling captures the underlying rationale clearly. "How do we know that, if one sees his fellow drowning in a river, or being dragged off by a wild beast, or mugged, he is liable to save him? Scripture says, 'You shall not stand by the blood of your neighbor' (Lev 19:16)."[42] In such circumstances, nothing, including purity considerations, must stand in the way of intervention.[43] If his intention were to save the victim's life, even a priest could justifiably incur ritual defilement. Preservation of human life—or at least the lives of fellow Jews, for in Jewish law philanthropic duties were limited to fellow Israelites, and certainly never extended to Gentiles—was the supreme responsibility the law enjoined.[44] As Besser and Kaplan explain in their comparative study

40. Cf. *m. B. Mes.* 2:10; *b. B. Mes.* 32a–33a.

41. Passersby are exempted from the duty to rescue if they are too old or weak to help, or too far away. Moreover, the duty to aid "exists only as long as the rescue activities cause no loss to the rescuing party. If he is to suffer a loss he will not be obligated to act gratuitously" (Besser and Kaplan, "Good Samaritan," 207–8).

42. *b. Sanh.* 73a. The biblical allusion here is to Lev 19:16 ("you shall not profit by the blood of your neighbor," NRSV), interpreted as, "you shall not stand idly by the blood of your neighbor." Further on in the same Talmudic discussion, the question is posed: "How do I know that one must save his neighbor from the loss of himself?" The answer given is by a citation of Deut 22:2, "Then you shall restore him to him." The passage refers to restoring a neighbor's lost property, but the Talmudic interpretation extends it to his own person, viz., if he has lost himself, he must be helped to find his way again, which includes rescuing him from danger.

43. "Laws were suspended when life was endangered" (Snodgrass, *Stories*, 355, 703 n. 131).

44. Neusner and Avery-Peck observe that "altruism within Judaism is embodied in stories that presuppose the Israelite identification of actors and beneficiaries" (43). There is no generalized affirmation in classical Judaism of altruistic conduct towards

of Jewish and American law, "In Jewish law, saving a human life is a positive religious commandment set forth by God in the Torah. It is forbidden to stand idly by when one's neighbor is attacked. Violating a negative commandment such as this, although it is not punishable because the breach involves no action, is nevertheless a grave sin."[45]

There was also a very strong legal requirement for Jews to bury the dead, even ahead of meeting other religious obligations. According to the Mishnah, "One whose dead is lying before him [awaiting burial] is exempt from the recitation of the *Shema* and from [wearing] phylacteries . . . (and) from [reciting] the prayer."[46] This obligation extended to burying neglected corpses one might stumble across unexpectedly (cf. Tob 1:17–19), a duty that fell to the first person on the scene. If that person happened to be a high priest or a Nazirite, there was a difference of legal opinion as to whether either or both should be prepared to contract corpse contamination in order to deal with the situation.[47] But there appears to have been a common rabbinic halakah at the time of Jesus that gave precedence to the obligation to bury an abandoned corpse over the laws forbidding the contracting of corpse-impurity by priests.[48]

Interestingly, some modern European legal codes, including those of Denmark, Italy, Iceland, and Turkey, have imposed a similar duty

---

other human beings at large. On the contrary, humanity is sharply divided into those who know and love God (fellow Israelites) and those who serve idols and hate God (Gentiles, who are regarded as "an undifferentiated phalanx of enemies of God"). With respect to the latter, "even ordinary transactions that express simple compassion are subjected to doubt (*m. Abod. Zar* 2:1)" ("Altruism," 41–42). Neusner and Avery-Peck argue at length that "there is no doctrine of altruism in classical Judaism" (51), inasmuch as the modern conception of altruism rests on assumptions about human nature, society, and motivation that are foreign to biblical and rabbinic tradition. In Jewish understanding, it is simply not possible to perform actions that go beyond what the Law requires or that bring no reward to the doer, for God has told people in the Law how to behave and promises to reward every good deed and to punish every evil one, whether in this life or the next. See further Neusner and Avery-Peck, "Altruism," 31–52.

45. Besser and Kaplan, "Good Samaritan," 218, cf. 193–219. The authors note that Samaritans were excluded from this obligation, since they were schismatics and unwelcoming of Jews (218 n. 130).

46. *m. Ber.* 3:1

47. *m. Naz.* 7:1; *b. Naz.* 47b–49a, *b. Meg.* 3b, *b. Zebah.* 100a.

48. For a discussion on this, see Bauckham, "Scrupulous Priest," 481–84; Scott, *Hear Then*, 195–97.

to attend to bodies chanced upon that appear lifeless. This duty is not merely an expression of human decency, nor a regard for public hygiene. It is a logical extension of the concern to preserve human life. Where a person has only recently died, it may be hard for a casual observer to determine whether death has in fact set in, and so to prevent mistakes, legislation requires that the body must not simply be disregarded.[49]

What all this means, then, is that when the priest and the Levite came across an apparently lifeless body on the side of the road, they were confronted with a legal conundrum. Was the man dead or alive? Should they observe the Torah on avoiding corpse-contamination, which was a higher duty on them than on ordinary Israelites? Or should they observe the Torah on love of neighbor, preservation of life, and respect for the bodies of the deceased?[50] There was an apparent clash of commandments, so that from a strictly legal point of view they could justify either course of action. How then were they to resolve this dilemma?

LEGAL REASONING IN AMBIGUOUS SITUATIONS

In such situations, one rule of thumb might be to follow the commandment that one was sure could be fulfilled. In this case, there was no certainty that the clerics could save the victim's life (Lev 19:16), but they could certainly avoid ceremonial defilement (Lev 21:1–3).[51] Furthermore, they could reason that whereas the duty to avoid contact with a corpse is expressly stipulated in the written text of Scripture, the duty to bury neglected corpses or to preserve human life is more a matter of secondary deduction, and therefore of lesser bearing. Moreover, these stipulations pertain specifically to fellow Israelites, and since there was no way of being sure that the naked, motionless stranger was not a foreigner, they might not even be pertinent.[52]

There was also no way of knowing just how endangered the man's life was without seriously risking a legal breach. The priests might have told themselves that, in such circumstances, they had no lawful duty to

---

49. Feldbrugge, "Good and Bad Samaritans," 647.

50. So Donahue, *Gospel in Parable*, 131; Bailey, *Poet and Peasant*, 43–47; and esp. Bauckham, "Scrupulous Priest," 476–85.

51. Wink, "Compassionate Samaritan," 209.

52. Cf. Besser and Kaplan, "Good Samaritan," 204 n. 49. Even confirmation of his circumcision would not guarantee his Jewishness, for he could be a Samaritan.

resolve the man's ambiguous condition, given the potential risks of doing so, before deciding on their responsibilities with respect to him. In any event, there was always the possibility he was not in any immediate danger of dying, and could survive long enough for someone else to reach him in time.[53] Human life, in other words, may *not* be at stake at all, and leaving him as they found him was not causing him any additional harm.

Of course, the quandary they faced was not simply an issue of academic jurisprudence. One of the ways of resolving the problem would be much more costly for them individually than the other, and it is commonly known that levels of helpfulness decrease as the associated costs involved increase.[54] Stopping to assist the man would be personally inconvenient, physically demanding, and financially draining. As well as having to assume responsibility for procuring the victim's burial if he were found to be deceased, the priest would have to rend his expensive garment and undergo a period of compulsory impurity, during which time neither he nor his family could eat of the tithes, which constituted their primary means of material support.[55] He would then have had to return to Jerusalem for ceremonial cleansing. Helping the victim, in other words, would mean a loss of time, a loss of energy, and a loss of income.

But even more pressing were the nonmaterial costs involved. The priest and the Levite had to be prepared to violate their deepest held values relating to ritual cleanliness and their own professional honor. They were fresh from a week of temple duties, where their ritual distinction had been of paramount importance. Now they are confronted with the possibility of compromising their sanctity through contact with

---

53. Underestimating the seriousness of a victim's plight is a common psychological mechanism people use for exonerating themselves of responsibility to act on their behalf; cf. Lichtenberg, "Absence," 84.

54. Cf. Staub, "Distressed Person," 399; Schroeder, *Psychology of Helping*, 38–58.

55. Bailey explains that for a priest to contract corpse defilement would mean that he could not officiate at any service or wear his phylacteries until he had undergone purification at the eastern gate of the temple, which would have been expensive (it required the purchase and burning of a red heifer), time consuming (it involved a return trip to Jerusalem and took about a week to complete), and deeply humiliating (it was shameful for a priest to contract impurity)(Bailey, *Poet and Peasant*, 45). Derrett adds the observation that the priest and his household could not eat of the tithe while the priest was defiled, and priests depended on tithes (Derrett, *Law*, 214–16). Wink points also to a Talmudic ruling that defiled priests should be subject to a disciplinary flogging (*b. Sotah* 43b–44a)(Wink, "Compassionate Samaritan," 209–10).

the bloodied corpse of a total stranger. Doubtless they would have been swept with feelings of revulsion at the thought of doing so, and, we know, feelings of disgust are a major impediment to compassion.[56] The incentive to leave it to the next person down the road would have been almost overwhelming. It must have been so. Why else would they cross the road and continue on their journey?

INSIGHTS FROM THE "BYSTANDER EFFECT"

In recent decades, there has been considerable research on what factors encourage or inhibit people from intervening to help others in distress. The initial impetus for this research came from the brutal murder of Kitty Genovese by a serial rapist and murderer in Kew Gardens, a quiet, middle-class neighborhood in the New York borough of Queens, at 3:00 a.m. on March 13, 1964. According to the conventional account (aspects of which have recently been contested),[57] no fewer than thirty-eight neighbors heard the attack in progress, just outside their apartment building, but not one of them came to Kitty's aid, nor even so much as called the police. This incident spawned a flurry of studies by social scientists on bystander apathy and prosocial behaviors,[58] together with renewed debate about whether laws should be passed making it a criminal offense to withhold lifesaving assistance.[59]

In a later chapter, I will consider some of the legal issues that have arisen out of this "duty-to-rescue" debate. Here I want to review what recent research has taught us about the psychology of altruism and bystander inaction, since it could offer fresh insight into the dynamics portrayed in the parable. Caution is required, of course. Most of the experimental

---

56. The role of disgust, together with its close cousins of shame and envy, in impeding compassion is well argued by Nussbaum, *Upheavals*, esp. 342–53, 423–25.

57. The story of Kitty Genovese's murder is cited in virtually all introductory textbooks in psychology. On the symbolic role and historical reliability of this story, see Manning, "Kitty Genovese," 555–62.

58. Several thousand studies have been conducted on bystander behavior. For a comprehensive survey, see Schroeder, *Psychology of Helping*. On the dozens of factors that may inhibit bystander intervention to deal with harmful behaviors in the workplace, see Rowe et al., "'Unacceptable' Behavior," 52–64.

59. Soon after the murder, a conference was convened at the University of Chicago Law School in 1965, the proceedings of which are found in Ratcliffe, ed., *Good Samaritan and the Law*.

work has been carried out on modern Western subjects, and there are likely to be significant variations in how bystanders in different cultural contexts "instinctively" respond. Even so, the thousands of studies carried out on prosocial behavior suggest that there are common human reactions to stressful situations that plausibly are echoed in the parable.

Researchers have found that people's willingness to get personally involved in aiding strangers may be impaired by several factors. One obvious disincentive is concern for personal safety (fear of retaliation was a common defense offered by Kitty's neighbors). Another is the existence of ambiguity about whether the victim really needs or deserves help. A further inhibiting factor is where the victim is clearly dissimilar to the bystander in terms of race, class, rank, religion, or ethnicity, or is physically unattractive. On this point, research findings are clear and consistent: *people are more likely to help those who appear similar to themselves than those who are dissimilar.*[60] This propensity is even more pronounced in collectivist cultures and in tightly knit social groupings where group boundaries are firmly enforced.

Another constraining factor, somewhat surprisingly, is the presence of other people in the vicinity. Their presence leads to what social psychologists call a "diffusion of responsibility" taking place. This occurs where bystanders offload any personal sense of responsibility to intervene by diffusing or distributing that obligation among other potential rescuers.[61] Research findings on this point are also consistent and unequivocal: *the larger the number of bystanders present, the less likely any one of them is to intervene.* There are several possible explanations for this puzzling state of affairs. One is that we tend to assume that other people are better equipped than we are to supply what is required. Another is that people instinctively conform themselves to group expectations. Especially in ambiguous situations, we monitor the reactions of others to determine the proper response for ourselves. If others are inactive or unsure of what to do, we replicate their diffidence. It is as though everyone is waiting for someone else to lead the way, fearing social disapproval for acting peremptorily or inappropriately.

60. Schroeder, *Psychology of Helping*, 48, cf. 225, 262. This response is partly because bystanders perceive similar people to be less threatening, and partly because they can more easily identify with the experience of such persons.

61. Darley and Latané, "Bystander Intervention," 377–83; Schroeder, *Psychology of Helping*, 25–58.

Now the priest and the Levite in the parable were totally alone when they came across the victim. Theoretically this should have intensified their sense of individual responsibility, though we also know that anonymity is a major contributor to antisocial behavior.[62] But the succession of travelers on the Jericho road indicates that it was frequently enough traveled for them to assume that, in due course, others would be available to help. They may have eased the sense of inner conflict they felt at not stopping to aid the victim by comforting themselves with the knowledge that people would soon arrive on the scene who would be better equipped to effect the rescue since they would not be constrained by clerical restrictions.

Another factor influencing bystander behavior is whether the potential helpers are in a hurry to reach their destination. In one well-known experiment, it was found that the subjects' sense of hurry was a more reliable predictor of a helping response than were their personal beliefs.[63] People running late for an appointment who are confronted with a situation of need experience an acute sense of conflict between the immediate demands of the victim and the expectations of those relying on their arrival.[64]

Admittedly, hurry is a culturally specific category. Modern Westerners are much more susceptible to feelings of time pressure than are people in other cultures, and in smaller, village-based societies, the demands of the present often take priority over those of the future. But underlying the phenomenon of hurry is the more universal problem of dealing with competing demands on one's attention and resources. Faced with the discomfort of resolving this dilemma, a common strategy people use is cognitive reinterpretation. This is where the apparently pressing problem of the moment is reinterpreted as being not as serious or urgent

---

62. On the role of anonymity in facilitating antisocial behavior, see Zimbardo, *Lucifer Effect*, 25, 298–307.

63. Darley and Batson, "Jerusalem to Jericho," 100–108. This study found that those recently reminded of their moral and religious duty to help were almost twice as likely to assist a person in need than those who had not (53 percent versus 29 percent), but their actions correlated much more strongly with whether they were in a hurry. Only 10 percent of subjects who were running late were prepared to help compared to 63 percent of those with time available.

64. See the study by Batson et al., "Failure to Help," 97–101. Cf. Darley and Batson, "Jerusalem to Jericho," 100–108.

as it initially seemed to be. This can occur very quickly and without any conscious awareness of it having happened.[65]

That the priest and the Levite were in a hurry is not expressly said in the parable, but is probably implied by the explicit mention of their destination and by their act of "passing by on the other side" to continue their progress. Moreover it can be assumed from the dangerous terrain they were traveling through. That they cognitively reinterpreted the plight of the victim as not requiring any urgent remedy is also implied by their response.

There has also been extensive research on the extent to which holding religious beliefs may affect an individual's willingness to act altruistically. This is a difficult area to measure accurately and there are several variables involved. But some findings suggest that while religious belief—or, at least, the right kind of religious belief—may assist in clarifying the *theoretical* duty believers stand under to care for the needy, it does not necessarily promote increased levels of altruistic *activity*. Believers may possess a keener sense of their moral obligation than nonbelievers, but they are no more successful in discharging this obligation in practice. The ethical and religious norms they hold to, in other words, are only one of the potential determinants of their behavior, and are not necessarily the most decisive. Personality traits and situational factors, including hurry, are just as relevant, if not more so.[66]

Two other points from this research are pertinent to our parable. One is that highly devout individuals—those whose religious identity is a matter of deep personal commitment and is integrated into their total way of living and being—seem to be less inclined than nonreligious actors to render aid to individuals who belong to groups that contravene their own religious group's social norms. Assistance is less readily forthcoming where the potential recipient is perceived to represent a threat to the believer's own core moral and religious values.[67] This is clearly the

---

65. Schroeder, *Psychology of Helping*, 32–36, 220–29.

66. Batson points to the "disappointingly weak empirical relation between principled morality and pro-social action. . . . It is at least possible that moral principles are used more to censure and extol others' action than to motivate our own" (Batson, "Prosocial Motivation," 333–81).

67. "Despite the call to universal compassion, we found no evidence that intrinsic religion led to a universalizing expansion of in-group boundaries to include all human beings on equal terms . . . . Devout, intrinsic religion may well be a source of

situation in the parable, where the victim, as a source of ritual pollution, represented a tangible threat to the clergymen's most treasured values. Their religious convictions served to reinforce and give transcendent validity to feelings of exclusivity and detachment from outsiders, and such religiously intensified detachment is a known impediment to altruism.

The famous study by Samuel and Pearl Oliner of people who rescued Jews from the Nazis in Europe during World War II found that non-rescuers tended to have very exclusive or constricted sets of relationships. While religious belief itself was not a strong indicator of whether a person became a rescuer, those who understood their religion to mandate inclusiveness and attachment towards all other human beings were notably more inclined to rescue than those whose interpretation of religion supported their social prejudice.[68]

The other point is that deeply religious people are often inclined to view behaviors that jeopardize their religious norms and beliefs to be every bit as threatening to their sense of personal integrity and well-being as actions that put them in physical peril. It is commonly accepted that no one is under any moral or legal duty to put one's own physical security at risk to save another person. But what about other kinds of risk, such as risk to one's moral values or religious commitments? Highly devout people may actually be more ready to risk their physical well-being than to compromise their principles. Parents who believe in faith healing, for example, have been known to allow their sick children to die rather than jeopardize their religious beliefs by seeking medical help. For deeply pious believers, even martyrdom is preferable to religious malfeasance.

This again is pertinent to the parable. If the priest and the Levite had stopped to tend to the man in the ditch, they would have certainly increased their exposure to physical attack, since his assailants could still be lurking in the rocks. But the greater peril for them was what contact with a corpse meant for their sense of religious identity and public vocation. Was it worth the cost? Could not the next person down the road

---

other personal and social benefits, but our results suggest that it is not a source of the universal compassion that is often considered a defining feature of world religions" (Batson et al., "'Who Is My Neighbor?'" 456–57); cf. also Batson, "Good Samaritans?" 758–68; Rigby and O'Grady, "Agape and Altruism," 719–73.

68. Oliner and Oliner, *Altruistic Personality*, esp. 154–57. Also Oord, *Defining Love*, 85–90.

take responsibility for dealing with the problem? Surely, in the larger scheme of things, more good would come from them remaining dedicated to their core religious tasks in the community than from soiling their hands with the commonplace job of disposing of a neglected body?

The issue for the clerics, then, was not so much what the law told them to do, but what it told them *not* to do. It told them to love their neighbor, preserve human life, and afford the dead a dignified burial. But it also told them not to touch corpses or compromise their ritual sanctity. These formal vocational prohibitions became so deeply internalized in their psyches that they displaced the law's injunctions to neighbor love and victim care, and led them to perpetrate a kind of legitimized professional neglect. The law's negative proscriptions trumped its positive prescriptions, and the victim was left alone to die a solitary death.

SUMMARY

On encountering the battered body of the victim on the edge of the road, the priest and the Levite had to decide on the spot how they should balance differing obligations in the law. The decision had to be made quickly, and there were situational and systemic, not just dispositional, forces at work. Neither character need have been exceptionally cruel or wicked, and it was certainly not the case that they simply failed to notice the victim's predicament (which sometimes happens when people are in a hurry). Instead, they faced a situation of conflicting duties. According to Derrett, "the ethics of the time gave no decisive guidance."[69] The right response was, at the very least, halakically debatable.[70]

But while both options could claim support from an academic point of view, one was much more costly for the temple officials than the other. One simply entailed crossing to the other side of the street and leaving the dirty business to the next guy on the scene. The other option would involve an interruption to their schedule, heightened risk of physical attack, considerable financial expense, temporary disqualification from professional duties, and a willingness to tolerate instinctive feelings of revulsion and contamination, all on the off chance that the victim might still be alive and could be restored to health. These were no trifling considerations,

---

69. Derrett, *Law*, 216; cf. Wells, "Jericho Affair," 17.
70. Bauckham, "Scrupulous Priest," 484.

especially for those whose very existence focused on rigid adherence to conventional religious values. The priest "saw" the victim from some distance away, and chose the easier path of avoidance. Likewise the Levite, who perhaps out of curiosity came a little closer to the victim ("he came to the place," v. 32),[71] on witnessing his condition, crossed the street and continued briskly on his way. That they both "saw" the victim underscores their accountability to act; that they crossed to the other side communicates their decision not to look any further at what they had seen, to put it out of their minds and carry on with business as usual.

Psychology experiments have shown that people are significantly more inclined to help when a victim is directly in their path and there is no easy way of escape. Where the victim can be avoided by circling around or crossing to the other side, the likelihood of help decreases. Tellingly, where the escape option is chosen, people usually try to avoid looking directly at the victim. Recounting one experiment, Ervin Staub explains:

> Films made during the experiment showed that a number of subjects in the *easy escape* group looked at the confederate and immediately turned their head, never looking back again. Whether they avoided further exposure to the distressed person in order to minimize their psychological involvement and any possibility of internal conflict, or were trying to maintain the appearance of not having noticed the event so they could thereby minimize the possibility of blame, is, of course, unknown.[72]

The priest and the Levite certainly noticed the event. But by crossing the road they disengaged their eyes, and therefore their hearts, from the reality they had encountered. They saw only a bleeding body or a contaminating corpse to be dealt with, not a human being like themselves, one in desperate need of rescue. The victim's abandonment was intensified by the callousness of professional neglect—and it was a technically lawful

---

71. The insertion of *genomenos* before *kata ton topon* makes *elthōn* belong to *hidōn*, "came and saw." According to Alfred Plummer, this implies the Levite first inspected the victim closely before passing by (*St. Luke*, 287). But it is uncertain that both *genomenos* and *elthōn* are original. One or other term is omitted in several manuscripts. I. H. Marshall favors the longer text with the redundancy, however, and notes that it gives the sense of the Levite reaching the spot, actually going up close to the man, but not stopping to help (*Luke*, 448–49). Creed contrasts the "dainty neglect of the priest" with the "cold curiosity" of the Levite (*Luke*, 205; cf. Bailey, *Poet and Peasant*, 47).

72. Staub, "Distressed Person," 307.

neglect at that. Instead of asking what needed to be done to rescue the man from death or dishonor, they hurriedly determined what needed to be done to safeguard their own sanctity and professional welfare, and proceeded accordingly. Their legal role provided them with a convenient means of avoiding the full reality of the human pain they encountered and accepting personal responsibility for it. To this day, the "judicial can't"—the attitude that says, "Sorry, my hands are tied; I don't make the rules, I simply apply them"—remains a bolt-hole for legal professionals unwilling to confront the human suffering and moral evil the law can sometimes permit. As one legal scholar explains: "The judicial conscience is an artful dodger and rightfully so. Before it will concede that a case is one that presents a moral dilemma, it will hide in the nooks and crannies of professional ethics, run to the cave of role limits, seek the shelter of separation of powers."[73]

In opting for the least costly, and professionally least disruptive, course of action, the priest and the Levite took shelter in a narrow kind of role morality, and it is conceivable that other legal authorities of the time may have thought they did the right thing in prioritizing their priestly vocation. But the logic of Jesus' story is that they did the *wrong* thing. They subverted the law's deepest principles by exploiting its technical complexities and ambivalences for their own advantage. What ultimately permitted such casuistic evasion of the law's overriding concern for human welfare and mutual responsibility was a want of compassion, and in two respects. They failed personally to exhibit compassion for the derelict man on the roadside, and they failed hermeneutically to recognize the priority of compassion over cultic restrictions on their conduct in the Torah. They failed to slow down on their journey long enough to absorb the anguish of the victim and to be emotionally affected by it, and they failed to acknowledge what the prophets repeatedly emphasize: that God desires mercy more than sacrifice, lovingkindness more than temple performance, redeeming justice more than judicial meticulousness.

For such a failure, these two paragons of Israel's law stand condemned by their own actions, and they are shamed by what happens next in the story. The fact that even the self-justifying lawyer to whom the parable is addressed implicitly acknowledges their failure to dis-

---

73. Cover, quoted in Henderson, "Legality and Empathy," 1590.

charge the law's central injunction to neighbor love for want of mercy (vv. 36–37) indicates that any appeal the clerics might make to cultic or legal technicalities to justify their actions would simply betray the degree of hermeneutical selfishness at work. Recoiling from the costliness of mercy, they opt for a reading of the law's priorities that most suited their own interests. It was no defense to claim that they were simply obeying the letter of the law. For the Torah itself warns that the hard of heart are ill-equipped to discern the true measure of God's law (Deut 4:29; 8:2; 10:16; 11:18; 30:6; cf. Isa 29:13; Jer 31:33; 32:40), and are liable to co-opt the law for self-serving ends.

Marc Gopin is a Jewish specialist in conflict studies who has engaged in dialogue with religious leaders and diverse faith communities throughout the Middle East for more than twenty-five years. Gopin has observed that even deeply conservative religious people can display an astonishing degree of independent judgment in arriving at their moral and religious convictions. "They are continually making their own judgments and interpretations of right and wrong. They never quote me obscure religious law about exclusive or racist positions. They always cite their own interpretations and impressions of what is right, drawing on a variety of influences, from their own news analysis to their memories of favorite religious stories or verses."[74] Gopin takes heart from this fact, seeing it as a sign that there is more freedom of religious conscience in the world today than we usually think, even in highly traditional societies. But the flip side is also true. Religious conservatives who insist on the harsh enforcement of religious strictures at the expense of human mercy often do so because they derive some personal benefit from their rigidity, if only at a psychic level.

The priest and the Levite probably fall into this category. Systemic, dispositional, normative, and environmental factors all contributed to the decision they made to ignore the victim. We gather this both from the details in the story that reflect the social world of first-century Judaism and from the thousands of modern studies that have been conducted into the psychology of altruism and bystander activity. But the parable suggests that the astonishing independence of hermeneutical judgment that Gopin acclaims, and that the clerics fail to exhibit, depends, ultimately, on the existence or strength of one key ingredient—compassion.

74. Gopin, *Make the Earth Whole*, 19–20.

It is compassion, or, to use the more sterile term preferred by psychologists, "empathetic concern," that makes all the difference.

The next man on the scene, the merciful and resourceful Samaritan, amply demonstrates this truth. It is because he feels compassion, and practices mercy, that he is possessed of the necessary hermeneutical insight to know what the law truly demands and what is actually required in order to inherit eternal life.

5

The Samaritan and the Rule of Compassion

We have seen how recent social-science research has established that there is a multiplicity of factors that promote or inhibit people from rendering aid to other persons in need. Personality and situational variables interact in complex ways, and a range of personal, social, and institutional norms governing how people ought to behave in given circumstances condition both sets of variables. Simple apathy is rarely a significant factor in accounting for bystander inaction. It is not that people fail to care. More often it is that they fail to know how to express their care, or whether their feelings of care constitute a firm moral obligation to help in this particular instance, or whether there are other things they should care about more at this time. A capacity for empathetic arousal at the distress of others is a universal human trait. It emerges in infants across all societies within a day or two of birth, and in all known cultures there is a high valuation placed on interpersonal helpfulness. But this general predisposition to altruistic engagement is refracted through a prism of cognitive, affective, normative, and circumstantial considerations to produce a series of uncertain outcomes. As Ervin Staub puts it, "behavior that manifests concern about others' welfare is fragile, and easily yields to counterinfluences."[1]

The truth of this statement can be seen in the reactions of the priest and the Levite in the parable. They saw the condition of the bruised and battered victim on the side of the road and were disturbed enough at what they had witnessed to cross to the other side of the street to avoid further exposure. They registered the victim's distress and reacted to it,

1. Staub, "Distressed Person," 315.

and in that sense they cared. But they chose not to come to his assistance because they cared *more* about other important matters in their lives at the time, particularly in their professional lives.

The next traveler down the road was "a certain Samaritan" (v. 33). Jesus' first audience would have been taken aback at the appearance of a Samaritan in the story. They would have naturally expected the third character to be an Israelite layman, since the threefold division "priests, Levites, and all the children of Israel" was a standard way of summarizing the religious diversity of the nation and the hierarchy of value within it.[2] Yet not only does Jesus use a Samaritan in place of an Israelite, he portrays him as responding in a way that puts the Jewish characters to shame. His hearers would have probably anticipated some additional act of villainy towards the victim from the cold-blooded Samaritan; instead, he enacts the very demands of the law that the Jewish clerics honor in the breach.

The jarring nature of this reversal of roles cannot be emphasized too strongly. All the evidence we have suggests that relations between Jews and Samaritans in the first century were implacably hostile. Each group viewed the other in the darkest of terms, and tensions between the two communities were widespread and deep-seated.[3] It is only by appreciating the full extent of this culture of mutual loathing that we can begin to comprehend the far-reaching ramifications of Jesus' casting of a Samaritan as the hero of the story.

GROUNDS FOR SUSPICION

Jesus' Jewish audience would have responded to the arrival of a Samaritan on the scene with extreme suspicion and distaste. They would have assumed the worst about him on a number of grounds. To begin with, they would have viewed him as a religious pariah. As is often the case in

---

2. So Gourgues, "Priest," 710–12; Crossan, "Parable," 63–64; Gnanavaram, "'Dalit Theology,'" 73; Jeremias, *Parables*, 204; Snodgrass, *Stories*, 355; Scott, *Hear Then*, 198–202. Interestingly, Scott suggests that the absence of an Israelite layman in the narrative forces the audience to identify with the Jewish victim.

3. "Each of these sources—Josephus, the New Testament Gospels, and the rabbinic literature—agrees that in the first century C.E. tensions were rife between the Jews and the Samaritan sect. The key dispute over the proper place of worship no doubt spilled over into civil, community, and economic matters" (Anderson and Giles, *Keepers*, 48). So too, Jeremias, *Jerusalem*, 352–58; Ferguson, *Backgrounds*, 534–36; Esler, "Intergroup Conflict," 329–32; Meier, *Marginal Jew*, 3:532–49, 594 n. 128.

religious disputes, much of the antipathy between Jews and Samaritans stemmed from the fact that they shared a great deal in common. Both worshipped the same God, Yahweh; both honored the Mosaic Torah as authoritative and, consequently, practiced circumcision and observed biblical purity laws; both considered themselves to be the authentic bearers and guarantors of the Israelite heritage; and both disdained the other as covenantal impostors.

The historical origins of the Samaritan community are difficult to ascertain. This is partly because the label "Samaritan" can be understood in a variety of ways depending on whether it is construed as a geographical, ethnic, or religious designation (or a combination of all three),[4] and partly because the extant historical sources on Samaritan origins are a mixture of myth, legend, and propaganda.[5] The term "Samaritan" or "Samarian" in the Old Testament refers to the inhabitants of Samaria, which was the capital of the northern kingdom of Israel. It does not designate the distinctive religious sect of the later Second Temple period. Exactly when this distinct religious community first emerged is unknown. Many scholars imagine a decisive schism or cleavage occurring between Jews and Samaritans at some point in the early Hellenistic period, perhaps occasioned by intense disagreement over the centrality and significance of Jerusalem and its sanctuary. Other scholars postulate a gradual drifting apart of the two communities, or a series of ruptures interwoven with periods of unity. Still others question whether it is meaningful to speak of the two communities dividing off from each other at all, as though they had once been part of the same entity. John Meier, for example, thinks it best to conceive of Samaritanism and Judaism as two parallel expressions of the ancient religion of Israel, which centered on the worship of Yahweh and the way of life spelled out in the five books of

---

4. The term "Samaritan" is sometimes used in a *geographical* sense to denote the inhabitants of the region called Samaria, on the western side of the Jordan River, south of Galilee and north of first-century Judea; sometimes in an *ethnic* sense, to designate the presumed descendants of the Israelite tribes of Ephraim and Manasseh (the main components of the northern kingdom of Israel); and sometimes in a *religious* sense to describe a group of Semites who worshipped the God of Israel in a manner that was distinct from how the Jews worshipped. For this tripartite classification, see Meier, *Marginal Jew*, 3:533–35.

5. See Hjelm, "Samaritans and Jews," 9–59. Hjelm notes that despite a huge amount of research, "very little is, in fact, known of either the origin or the development of the Samaritan people," 29.

Moses. This core religion, which was shaped and reshaped by the impact of Assyrian, Babylonian, Persian, and Hellenistic empires, crystallized into these two distinct forms in the final centuries before the turn of the Common Era. "Neither religion was immediately derived from the other and neither broke away from the other."[6]

Whatever their original connection, by the Roman period each community defined itself over against the other, as well as in opposition to the wider pagan world. The Samaritans honored their own version of the Pentateuch and gave allegiance to their own sanctuary on Mount Gerazim (cf. Deut 11:29; 27:12), near the city of Shechem, with their own line of Levitical priests (cf. John 4:20). Relations between the two groups no doubt fluctuated from relative cordiality during times of peace to fiery animosity during periods of stress. At the time of Jesus and the early Christian movement, lines of antagonism were very clearly drawn, though commerce and contact between the communities still occurred, ideally subject to certain restrictions.[7] Jewish authorities, for example, did not regard Samaritans as reliable witnesses to agreements, and it was forbidden to accept certain offerings from them or to eat Passover with them.[8]

From a Jewish point of view, Samaritans occupied a liminal position between Israelites and Gentiles (a perspective evident in the New Testament as well).[9] They shared many common beliefs and practices with Jews, and some later rabbinic authorities counted them as still under the umbrella of Israel.[10] But it appears the majority of early Jewish teach-

---

6. Meier, *Marginal Jew*, 3:541.

7. Snodgrass explains that "Samaritan women could serve as midwives and wet nurses. Rabbinic regulations permit buying bread and wine from Samaritans and other business arrangements, allow a Samaritan to be included in the number who needed to say a common table grace, to say a benediction, and to pay tithes, and a Samaritan to be a *haber* (an associate).... [T]he sources indicate commerce and contact between Jews and Samaritans were a normal part of life" (Snodgrass, *Stories*, 347).

8. *b. Git.* 10a, 10b.

9. A text from the "Seven Jerusalem Booklets" at end of the fourth Seder of the Babylonian Talmud declares: "The usages of the Samaritans are in part like those of the Gentiles, in part like those of Israel, but mostly like Israel," cited by Anderson and Giles, *Keepers*, 47–48. In *b. Abod. Zar.* 15a, Samaritans are not suspected of bestiality and incest in the same way that Gentiles are.

10. Common beliefs included strict monotheism; the importance of Moses and the authority of the Pentateuch; a range of ritual practices, such as circumcision, Sabbath observance, ablutions, and prayers; belief in final judgment; and messianic expectation. On Samaritan religion, see Anderson and Giles, *Keepers*, 117–33.

ers considered them to be apostates—less repugnant than pagans, to be sure, but still "foreigners" or aliens to the commonwealth of Israel (Luke 17:18, cf. Matt. 10:5–6) and without a share in the world to come.[11] Even if they acknowledged a similar Torah, they certainly did not interpret it correctly, however strictly they enforced its constituent commandments, and their refusal to accept the legitimacy of the Jerusalem temple meant they disobeyed a great deal of it in practice. Jesus' words to the woman at the well in Samaria in John 4 encapsulate crisply their perceived heterodoxy: "You worship what you do not know; we worship what we know, for salvation is from the Jews" (John 4:22).

The Samaritan in the parable would have been despised, secondly, for his corrupt bloodline and unclean condition. Whereas the Jewish priest and Levite epitomized genealogical purity *par excellence*, belonging to classes that practiced strict endogamy, the Samaritan occupied the opposite end of the spectrum. The Samaritans regarded themselves as true Israelites who stood in unbroken descent from the patriarchs. But this was refuted by most Jews who viewed them as half-castes rather than blood relations, the alleged offspring of intermarriage between Israelites and pagans. They often called them "Cutheans" or "Cuthites" (viz., people from the pagan region of Kuthah) to distinguish them from fellow Israelites. According to the polemical text of Sirach 50:25–26, Cutheans are "not even a nation at all" and are despised by God.[12]

The basis for this indictment came from 2 Kings 17:24–41, a passage that tells of how the Assyrians in the eighth century BCE settled foreign deportees from Babylon and surrounding districts in Samaria to replace Israelites who had been deported. These new settlers, the biblical narrator says, merely incorporated the veneration of Yahweh into the continuing worship of their own gods and its associated customs, including child sacrifice. Josephus and later rabbinic interpreters used this story polemically to explain the historical origins of their Samaritan

---

11. According to the Mishnah, those that have no share in the world to come include "he that says there is no resurrection of the dead prescribed in the law." It appears that early Samaritan belief resembled that of the Sadducees in repudiating resurrection, though this changed later (ibid., 125, cf. 47).

12. On the complex philological features of the Sirach text, see Meier, *Marginal Jew*, 3:539–40.

rivals and thus to belittle them as the product of religious syncretism and racial admixing.[13]

Another common Jewish misgiving about Samaritans was the manner in which they observed ritual law. In the eyes of many Jews, Samaritans were perpetually unclean, not least because they did not accept the prescribed mechanisms administered by the Jerusalem temple for cleansing away impurity. They considered themselves to be the "Keepers" of Torah (*samerim* in distinction from *someronim*, "inhabitants of Samaria"), and they observed its festivals and decrees quite strictly in their own way. But the recommended default setting for Jews when it came to Samaritan purity norms was skepticism and distrust.[14] Marriage with Samaritans was forbidden because Samaritans were considered too lax in their observance of the laws of levirate marriage[15] and because Samaritan women were viewed as perpetual menstruants from the cradle to the grave, conveying uncleanness to everything they touched or overshadowed.[16]

Food was also an issue. Rabbi Eliezer used to say, "One who eats bread [baked] by Samaritans is like one who eats pork."[17] Jews serious about maintaining ritual distinction would likely have shrunk from all physical contact with Samaritans, and on journeys from Galilee to Judea, highly observant Jews would cross and recross the Jordan to avoid going through Samaritan territory (cf. Matt 10:5), though others would opt for the more direct route. In John 4, Jesus passes through Samaria on a journey from Galilee to Jerusalem and pauses for a rest at a well in the Samaritan city of Sychar. When he asks a woman for a drink, she expresses astonishment at his request. "How is it that you, a Jew, ask a drink of me, a woman of Samaria? Jews do not share things in common with Samaritans" (John 4:8–9).

A third ground for hostility to the Samaritan in the parable would have been his perceived association with inter-communal violence. Jewish hearers would have instinctively viewed him as—to use modern military

---

13. Modern DNA testing suggests there may be some basis to such a reading of the story (Shen et al., "Reconstruction," 248–60).

14. Cf. *m. Nid.* 7:4–5.

15. So Cowley, "Samaritans."

16. *m. Nid.* 4:1, cf. 7:1; *b. Nid.* 31b, 56b. Even if this extreme ruling was not current at the time of Jesus, the underlying attitudes that gave rise to it probably were (cf. Wink, "Compassionate Samaritan," 210).

17. *m. Seb.* 8:10.

parlance—"a hostile," a member of a dissident group that had been actively involved in perpetrating violence against the Jewish community and so deserving retaliatory violence in return. Josephus refers to several episodes of violence between the two groups that must have left a legacy of bitterness and hatred. He recounts how the Maccabean prince John Hyrcanus (134–104 BCE) was "greatly displeased with the Samaritans for the injuries they had done to the people of Marissa, a colony of the Jews." As part of his campaign against Antiochus IV, John destroyed the sanctuary on Mount Gerazim and sacked the city of Shechem. John's sons completed the destruction of other Samaritan cities.[18] Josephus also tells of an incident during the procuratorship of Coponius (ca. 9 CE) when some Samaritan commandos defiled the Jerusalem temple on the eve of Passover by spreading human bones around the entrance.[19] Philip Esler terms this an act of "pure mischief making," typical of groups locked into extreme antipathy towards one another.[20]

Another story that underscores the propensity of both communities to mutual violence occurred shortly after the time of Jesus, during the tenure of Cumanus as governor of Judea (52–59 CE). Some Samaritan villagers ambushed a group of Jewish pilgrims passing through Samaria on their way to Jerusalem and killed one of their number. The Roman procurator accepted a bribe not to punish the crime, so a group of Jewish vigilantes attacked and burned a Samaritan village in revenge. Those involved in the episode were subsequently rounded up and crucified, but a complaint was taken all the way to Emperor Claudius, who decided in favor of the Jews and had the leaders of the Samaritan delegation executed.[71]

Similar levels of hostility are reflected in rabbinic literature and in the Gospel narratives as well.[22] In Matthew 10, Jesus instructs the dis-

---

18. Josephus *Ant.* 13:275–81. Historians disagree on whether the temple and city were sacked at the same time or on separate occasions. Some date the destruction of the temple in 128 BCE and the city in 107 BCE, but others combine the events.

19. Josephus *Ant.* 18:29–30.

20. Esler, "Intergroup Conflict," 331.

21. Josephus *Ant.* 20:118–26; *War* 2.232–46.

22. According to the Mishnah, Jews had to change their custom of using signal fires to signal the New Year because Samaritans lit fires to confuse them (*m. Ros Has.* 2:2). According to the Talmud, Jews are not liable to the death penalty for killing a Samaritan and may withhold wages from a Samaritan (*b. Sanh.* 57a). *Y. Abod. Zar.* 5:4 allows Jews to charge interest to Samaritans. The Baraitha (an extra-Mishnaic Tannaitic teaching) on Exod 21:35 ("and if one man's ox hurt his neighbor's") states explicitly: "If the ox of

ciples to avoid Samaritan towns since their mission is only to "the lost sheep of the house of Israel" (vv. 5–6). In Luke 9, Jesus' party is shunned by a Samaritan village because "his face was set towards Jerusalem," provoking the disciples to want to burn the village in retaliation (vv. 52–53). In John 8, Jesus' Jewish opponents taunt him with the question, "'Are we not right in saying that you are a Samaritan and have a demon?' Jesus answered, 'I do not have a demon!'" (vv. 48–49).

A fourth ground for repugnance towards the Samaritan in the parable was his occupational status. Though not stated explicitly, there are several indications that he was a merchant or trader plying his regular business route from Jerusalem to Jericho. He is depicted as "journeying" (v. 33) and speaks of his plan to make a return trip in the future (v. 35). He knows of an inn in the region (almost certainly in the vicinity of Jericho since there is no evidence of inns in the wilderness),[23] and seems to have had some acquaintance with the innkeeper.[24] It was traders and other transients with no familial claims on anyone else's hospitality that mainly frequented inns. The reference to "his own animal" (*to idion ktēnos*) is also telling. It suggests that he had more than one animal with him. The others presumably were beasts of burden carrying a cargo of oil and wine (cf. v. 34).[25] Archaeological research confirms that Samaria was a center for commercial oil and wine production, and there was a market for such goods in both Jerusalem and Jericho.[26]

One further clue to his occupation is the amount of money the Samaritan carries. He has sufficient funds to cover his personal needs as well as the expenses incurred by the victim. Jesus' hearers would have likely attributed his prosperity to extortionate business practice, since

---

an Israelite has gored the ox belonging to a Samaritan, there is no liability." Here the Samaritan is expressly excluded from inclusion in the category of "neighbor." These witnesses are later than the first century, but probably reflect long-established attitudes and perspectives.

23. Bailey, *Poet and Peasant*, 52.

24. Jeremias, *Parables*, 204.

25. Although *ktēnos* may designate a mount for riding (Acts 23:24), it can also designate a pack animal, such as an ass or donkey. Here it could imply that the Samaritan is accompanied by beasts of burden carrying commercial goods; so Knowles, "Victim Wearing?," 151; Derrett, *Law*, 209; Bailey, *Poet and Peasant*, 50–51; Jeremias, *Parables*, 204.

26. See Knowles, "Victim Wearing?," 152–55.

traders were notoriously dishonest.[27] They were despised equally by the common people, who saw them as exacerbating the economic problems that afflicted them, and by the elites who saw their "new wealth" as a threat to their own honor and status.[28] The Samaritan's willingness to trust an innkeeper may also have been seen as a reflection of his own dubious character. Innkeepers were an even more disdained group than traders, and decent people avoided their establishments. "A man who trusted an innkeeper," Derrett observes, "knew what he was about."[29] His itinerant lifestyle and constant interaction with all sorts of unsavory individuals would have also made it impossible for him to observe even the most basic biblical laws concerning food preparation and ritual purity, albeit according to Samaritan customs.

Taken together, these four considerations made a Samaritan the most improbable hero imaginable for Jesus to conjure up. He was representative of a despised and apostate minority, someone who would have been thought to share in the collective responsibility of his people for violent antagonism towards the Jewish community, a man of impure stock and unclean practice, and the member of a disliked and distrusted occupational group.

Yet this unlikely character becomes the savior of the stranger on the roadside. John Nolland complains that commentators are prone to exaggerate the trouble the Samaritan goes to on behalf of the victim and to inflate the relationship that emerged between them. "The Samaritan took responsibility for the needs of the situation," Nolland writes, "but he went about his business the next day, leaving the continued care of the injured man in the hands of the innkeeper. We know nothing of a personal relationship."[30] But such a matter-of-fact summary of the Samaritan's response scarcely does justice to the literary elegance and emotional power of Luke's description. The Samaritan's actions are recounted in exquisite detail because they serve to exemplify what is entailed in accepting someone in need as a neighbor towards whom love is enjoined, a love moreover that is patterned after love for God. Just as love for God is to be all-encompassing, involving the whole of one's heart, soul, mind,

---

27. Malina and Rohrbaugh, *Social-Science*, 347; Ringe, *Luke*, 158.
28. Oakman, "Peasant?," 121–22.
29. Derrett, *Law*, 210. Cf. Oakman, "Peasant?," 122–23.
30. Nolland, *Luke*, 596.

and strength, so the Samaritan's love for the Jewish victim is depicted as engaging all the powers of his personality: his sight, his heart, his hands, his strength, his time, his possessions, and his intelligence.

AN ALL-ENCOMPASSING ENGAGEMENT

First to be engaged were the Samaritan's *eyes*: like the priest and the Levite, "he saw" (*kai idōn*) the victim. But, unlike them, he saw him up close. He drew near to his actual person. Whereas the priest came down "that road" (*en tē hodō ekeinē*), and the Levite came to "the place" (*kata ton topon*), the Samaritan drew "near to *him*" (*kat' auton*). Whereas the other travelers looked at the victim as involuntary spectators, the Samaritan entered volitionally into his personal space and got personally involved. The three travelers all had the same physical evidence to go by. For all three, the naked, motionless body was without visible signs of ethnicity or social status and for all intents and purposes appeared to be dead. But for the Samaritan alone, the ineradicable humanity of the victim overruled all other concerns about his ethnicity or social status or ritual pollution and compelled participation in his rescue.[31] His "seeing," therefore, was more than mere physical perception. It was a positive ethical achievement, for what he saw was not a mere object of curiosity or contempt but a vulnerable fellow human being.

It is for that reason that the next thing to be engaged was his *heart* or *his feelings*: "he was moved with compassion." The reference to compassion comes exactly halfway through the narrative and shatters the parallelism between the three bypassers. All three "see" the victim, but whereas the first two respond with self-protective caution, the third is overcome with compassion (*esplangchnisthē*). This passive deponent verb occurs in the New Testament only in the Synoptic Gospels. It features in just three of Jesus' parables, and on each occasion signals an important shift in the drama.[32] The term denotes a gut-wrenching surge of emotion, a

---

31. For a moving reflection on the difference between responding to an act of evil as a spectator and as a participant, see Brown, "Holocaust," 223–39.

32. Luke 10:33; 15:20; Matt 18:27. The metaphorical meaning of *splangchnizomai* as having compassion or showing mercy occurs only in the writings of Judaism and Christianity (the verb is found only once in secular Greek, with the meaning of reading or prophesying from the entrails of a sacrificial animal). The verb is sometimes used in Jewish literature to depict God's eschatological mercy (e.g., *T. Zeb.* 8:1–2; *T. Ab.* [B] 12).

deep physical stirring in the innards, since the intestines (*to splangchna*) were thought to be the seat of the natural passions (hence God's compassionate heart is described in Luke 1:78 as *splangchna eleous,* "bowels of mercy"). In Luke's Gospel, compassion is supremely a divine attribute. It is, says John Donahue, "that divine quality which, when present in human beings, enables them to share deeply in the sufferings and needs of others and enables them to move from one world to the other: from the world of the helper to the one needing help; from the world of the innocent to that of the sinner."[33]

Just as God has compassion on expectant Israel and comes to her rescue in Luke's infancy narrative (1:78, cf. v.50), just as Jesus has compassion when he sees the desolate widow in the village of Nain burying her dead son and restores him to life (7:13), and just as the father of the prodigal son (himself an image for God) is filled with compassion when he sees his starving boy stumbling up the road and rushes to embrace him (15:20), so the Samaritan is consumed with compassion when he sees the condition of the battered victim. In this respect, he imitates the character of God, for in Jewish tradition, "to walk after the Lord your God" (e.g., Deut 10:12; 13:5; 28:9) was understood to involve emulating God's compassionate example of feeding the hungry, clothing the naked, visiting the sick, comforting the sorrowful, and burying the dead.[34] Jesus casts a Samaritan as the human embodiment of divine benevolence.

Its application to Jesus (e.g., Luke 7:13; Mark 6:34; 8:2; Matt 9:36; 14:14; 15:32; 20:34) is part of the "messianic" characterization of him as the one who embodies God's role as eschatological savior.

33. Donahue, *Gospel in Parable*, 132. Cf. Elliott, "Temple," 228–39.

34. Schottroff, *Parables*, 137, points to a Talmudic text that is worth quoting in full: "What is the meaning of the following verse of Scripture: 'You shall walk after the Lord your God' (Deut. 13:5). Now is it possible for a person to walk after the Presence of God? And has it not been said, 'For the Lord your God is a consuming fire' (Deut. 4:24)? But the meaning is that one must walk after the traits of the Holy One, blessed be he. Just as he clothes the naked, as it is written, 'And the Lord God made for Adam and for his wife coats of skin and clothed them' (Gen. 3:21), so should you clothe the naked. [Just as] the Holy One, blessed be he, visited the sick, as it is written, 'And the Lord appeared to him by the oaks of Mamre' (Gen. 18:1), so should you visit the sick. [Just as] the Holy One, blessed be he, comforted the mourners, as it is written, 'And it came to pass after the death of Abraham that God blessed Isaac his son' (Gen. 25:11), so should you comfort the mourners. [Just as] the Holy One, blessed be he, buried the dead, as it is written, 'And he buried him in the valley' (Deut. 34:6), so should you bury the dead" (*b Sotah* 14a).

Modern research has confirmed the importance of emotional or affective engagement in motivating people to give aid to the needy. It has also shown that it is easier to arouse emotional engagement in potential donors by exposing them to the needs of a single identifiable sufferer than by recounting the distress of abstract masses. As philosopher Peter Singer explains, the "identifiable victim effect" leads to "the rule of rescue": *we will expend more effort and resources to rescue a recognizable victim than to save a "statistical life."*[35] Witnessing the suffering of an individuated victim tugs at the heartstrings and inspires greater sacrifice than we are prepared to make for the undifferentiated collective. Mother Theresa is reputed to have said, "If I look at the mass I will never act. If I look at the one, I will."[36]

There is an important sense in which the Samaritan's heart overruled his head. As someone who was also subject to the law of Moses, the Samaritan could well have proceeded by way of legal calculation, first determining whether the victim was a fellow Israelite (that is, a fellow Samaritan), then choosing to show love for him as a neighbor. Social psychologists have found that empathetic concern is more likely to arise when the potential helper recognizes a special bond with the person in need. People are much more inclined to help members of their own tribe or group than they are to help strangers.[37] But the Samaritan is completely indifferent to the man's social or ethnic identity. His automatic response is one of compassion, not calculation. The casuistic strategy adopted by the priest and the Levite is simply not part of the Samaritan's moral universe. Instead, he follows the rule of compassion.

Of course, having one's heart in the right place is rarely enough in order genuinely to help someone in need. Compassion may inspire the decision to help, but some level of cognitive reasoning is also required in order to ensure that any help offered will actually prove beneficial. Deciding *how* to help, in other words, is just as critical as deciding *whether* to help. In fact, even the decision whether to help is not the automatic product of compassionate feelings. An overpowering surge of emotion may prove paralyzing in an observer and fail to generate any concrete actions at all. Or, more familiarly, those who feel compassion

---

35. Singer, *Life*, 46–50.
36. Quoted in ibid., 49.
37. Schroeder et al., *Psychology of Helping*, 263.

may be tempted to consider the emotional sensation itself a sufficient response to satisfy their consciences; nothing further is required, it is enough to *feel* sorry for the sufferer to prove one's moral virtue. A welling up of sympathetic feelings only results in positive ethical engagement when it is channeled through, or interpreted by, a set of personal or social norms that mandate decisive action in such circumstances and that dictate the form such action should take.

This is true of the Samaritan, for the next thing to be activated were his *hands and feet:* "he went and bandaged his wounds." His interior experience of compassion was translated into exterior deeds of deliverance,[38] and it was his act of "*doing* mercy" (*ho poiēsas to eleos*), not his emotional arousal, that fulfilled the Torah (v. 37). His movement towards the victim counteracted the man's isolation and rejection. His bandaging of his wounds addressed his most urgent physical needs and set him on the road to ultimate recovery (cf. Jer 30:17). In dressing his wounds, the Samaritan used his own possessions. The dressings would have been torn from his clothing or headgear (he is unlikely to have carried ready-made bandages in his load), and the oil and wine would have come from his commercial cargo. Oil was a household remedy for pain relief and wine was commonly used as disinfectant (Isa 1:6; Mark 6:13; Jas 5:14). Under normal circumstances, a Jewish recipient would have recoiled from such intimate contact with the unclean property of an unclean foreigner, especially a recipient who had only recently been a visitor to or resident in the Holy City.[39] But here the Samaritan's impure property serves paradoxically to mediate divine-like compassion to the forsaken casualty, and thereby becomes the means of satisfying the requirements of God's law.

Oil and wine were not only used as medicinal remedies; they also played an important role in temple worship as sacrificial libations (Lev 23:13, cf. Rev 6:6). One need not posit elaborate allegorical associations to recognize an additional layer of symbolic significance in the Samaritan's use of oil and wine to minister to the victim. In showing practical concern for the welfare of the victim, irrespective of purity considerations, the Samaritan offers true worship to God. By loving his neighbor in this uninhibited way, he expresses his wholehearted love for God and fulfils what God's law mandates. Micah declared that what God requires—more

38. Cf. Stassen and Gushee, *Kingdom Ethics*, 336–37.
39. Derrett, *Law*, 220–21; Funk, "Good Samaritan," 79; Marshall, *Luke*, 450.

than ten thousand rivers of oil poured out in temple worship—is justice, mercy, and humility.[40] Cultic sacrifice remains obligatory and important, but in the absence of an inward purity of heart and an outward commitment to justice and mercy, it fails to please God.[41]

The Samaritan enacts the truth of this message, in contrast to the priest and Levite. They would have just recently poured oil and wine on the temple altar in Jerusalem in profound devotion to God, but they failed to manifest their worship in merciful justice toward the crime victim. It is the hated Samaritan who offers the worship of justice and mercy in pouring oil and wine on the victim's wounds. In so doing he manifests the deepest intentions of the law, something the lawyer himself readily acknowledges when he nominates the "one who performed mercy" as the person who most acted like a neighbor (v. 37).

Next the Samaritan enlists his *power to change the victim's circumstances*: "he put him on his own animal and brought him to an inn." He picked the defenseless man up in his arms, heaved him on to his mount, and removed him to a place of greater security. The implication of putting the victim on "his own animal" is that the Samaritan dismounted and went ahead on foot leading the animal by a tether.[42] This would not only slow his progress through unfriendly territory but also, more significantly, involve him in assuming the position of a servant leading an animal ridden by a social superior.[43] In seeking to transform the victim's circumstances, therefore, the Samaritan expresses both personal humility and profound respect for the victim. He also displays great courage. Kenneth Bailey makes the observation that in deciding to take the wounded man into town and be identified with him, the Samaritan ran the risk of being perceived as the culprit responsible for his injuries, which could trigger personal retaliation from the man's kinfolk. Commonly in Middle Eastern communities, "the stranger who involves

---

40. Mic 6:7–8; cf. Hos 6:6; Isa 58:5–9; Matt 23:23.

41. Meier warns against being led astray by what specialists in Semitic languages call "dialectical negation." Since Hebrew lacks comparative adverbs and adjectives, comparisons must be expressed in other ways. To say, "I desire mercy not sacrifice" means, "I desire mercy *more than* (not, instead of) sacrifice" (Meier, *Marginal Jew*, 4:44).

42. The phrase *ēgagen auton* in v. 34 could mean "led it (the animal)," rather than "brought him (the man)," to the inn.

43. Bailey notes that the "social distinctions between riders and leaders of riding animals is crucial in Middle eastern society" (*Poet and Peasant*, 51).

himself in an accident is often considered partially, if not totally, responsible for the accident. After all, why did he stop? Irrational minds seeking a focus for their retaliation do not make rational judgments, especially when the person involved is from a hated minority community."[44] That the Samaritan accepts such heightened risk attests to the genuineness of his love, for sincere love (unlike mere charity) invariably involves risk.

Once at the inn, the Samaritan devotes *time and attention* to the victim's recovery: "and he took care of him." The inn would have had little in common with the purpose-built guesthouses of later times. Inns or khans in the first century were basically stopping places for travelers who had no local ties of hospitality to draw on.[45] They were places where wayfarers could rest and water their animals and enjoy some level of safety from wild beasts and marauding bands of robbers in the countryside. Typically, they were walled enclosures, open to the skies, with animal stalls along the sides and a well in the central courtyard, and possibly a tower at the entrance to watch for bandits. Lodgers provided their own food and slept alongside their animals on straw or pallets. Inns were uncomfortable and unwholesome places. Jewish moralists, in particular, considered them to be dens of iniquity and sexual perversion.[46] They were also dangerous places. One first-century Roman writer, Columella, warned his readers of the "depredations of passing travelers" on the highways, while a contemporary in Palestine recommended that before spending a night at a wayside inn, the wayfarer should first make a will![47] For all this, lodging at an inn was still preferable to being alone and exposed on the open road in pitch darkness, and in this instance it was the victim's only chance of survival.

Remaining with his charge overnight, the Samaritan does not sleep but continues to work at reversing the damage inflicted by the robbers. They had assaulted him, humiliated him, and left him to die in isolation. The Samaritan, by contrast, has washed the man's wounds, afforded him the dignity of riding on the donkey while he walked on foot, and now, at the inn, he offers protection and companionship throughout the night. The victim is not abandoned for a second time, but is sustained in

---

44. Ibid., 52; also, Wells, "Jericho Affair," 17.
45. Jones, "Love Command," 233; Elwell and Comfort, *Dictionay*, 635.
46. *m. Abod. Zar* 2:1 alleges that bestiality, fornication, and murder occurred in Gentile inns.
47. MacMullen, *Roman Social Relations*, 4.

a relationship of sheltering care. At daybreak, the Samaritan must depart on his regular business, though the patient is still not fit to travel. So the Samaritan "took out two denarii, gave them to the innkeeper, and said, 'Take care of him; and when I come back, I will repay you whatever more you spend'" (v. 35).

There are several remarkable details in this final scene of the story. One is the amount of money involved. It is estimated that two denarii would have covered room and board for several weeks.[48] The Samaritan makes provision, in other words, for the long-term recuperation of the victim. He himself cannot be there to nurse him, so he deputizes the innkeeper to serve as his agent, instructing him to continue rendering the same "care" (*epimelētheti* v. 35) that he himself has offered the victim overnight (*epemelēthe* v. 34). By accepting payment in advance, the innkeeper bound himself to carry out this commission. This is the most extraordinary detail of all. The Samaritan enters into an open-ended financial arrangement with the innkeeper, promising to cover any further expenses he might incur in tending the patient. His solemn promise, "I will repay you" (*apodōsō soi*), is a formula for taking over someone else's debt.[49] Such an undertaking was clearly intended to afford the victim protection from being imprisoned or enslaved for unpaid dues after his recovery (cf. Matt 18:23–25). The Samaritan's chances of being defrauded were considerable; innkeepers were far from trustworthy characters.[50] But the Samaritan makes himself vulnerable to extortion in order to spare the victim the possibility of subsequent victimization.

That the Samaritan exhibits such solicitude for the future experience of the victim, and remains personally implicated in his recovery even though he is physically absent, attests to an important, though uncomfortable, moral truth: *once aid is given, it initiates a chain of events in which the benefactor remains morally implicated.* It is well known, especially in humanitarian work, that every intervention has unintended

---

48. Estimates range from two weeks (Snodgrass, *Stories*, 347; Nolland, *Luke*, 596; Hultgren, *Parables*, 99) to three weeks (Stassen and Gushee, *Kingdom Ethics*, 337; Malina and Rohrbaugh, *Synoptic Gospels*, 347–48) to up to two months (Morris, *St. Luke*, 190; Lenski, *Luke's Gospel*, 607).

49. See Derrett, *Law*, 217–18 n. 4.

50. Oakman thinks Jesus' hearers would have considered the actions of the Samaritan in general to be foolish. Yet it is hard to see evidence for Oakman's claim that "for a peasant audience, the Samaritan's 'aid' has left the man in a worse condition than at first" ("Peasant?," 122).

consequences. Even benevolently intended interventions may sometimes have a damaging impact upon the recipient.[51] Those who instigate an intervention, therefore, are obliged to anticipate, as best they can, the likely consequences of their action and to address any unforeseen negative effects that may arise. They are not morally responsible for these negative outcomes themselves, in the sense of being blamable for them, unless they are the product of gross negligence. But they are morally obliged to be concerned about potentially harmful repercussions of their actions, and, where appropriate, to strive to ameliorate them. Good intentions are not enough. Moral forethought and ongoing monitoring are also required, for well-meaning gestures can easily go awry.[52] The Samaritan in the parable anticipates the possibility that the victim may end up indebted to the innkeeper and thus remain unrestored to wholeness. He therefore assumes personal responsibility to mitigate this potentially destructive outcome.

The Samaritan, then, not only draws the victim into a community of restorative care, he ensures this community will continue on into the future as long as the victim has need of it. He also makes sure that the victim will emerge from his time of weakness and convalescence into a position of independence and freedom. Whether the Samaritan planned to seek reimbursement from the patient when he was well again is not said. He had legal right to seek such a settlement,[53] though he would hardly have expected Jewish courts to enforce any such claim against a Jew on the part of a Samaritan.[54] Yet there is no hint whatsoever in the story that the Samaritan's actions were conditional upon expectation of future recompense. On the contrary, the Samaritan indicates that the purpose of his return visit to the inn is to settle up accounts with the innkeeper, not to recover costs from the patient.

All in all, the Samaritan performs some nine different actions. Such an extraordinary detailing of his endeavors is not accidental. The Samaritan's deeds enact, in concrete terms, what the law means by love of neighbor. I have suggested that his actions are intended to confirm the lawyer's insight that love for neighbor cannot be separated from

---

51. See Angier, "Pathological Altruist."

52. See Driver, "Ethics."

53. On Jewish law on this matter, see Besser and Kaplan, "Good Samaritan," 204, 211–12.

54. See Derrett, *Law*, 218–19.

love for God. They constitute a single reality. Just as love for God must embrace all the dimensions of one's personality—heart, soul, mind, and strength—so too must one's love for others.

The Samaritan exemplifies this duty. He is engaged emotionally, physically, materially, socially, financially, and morally in reaching out to the dying man on the roadside. He goes far beyond what was minimally required to save his life; he shows supererogatory dedication to his full restoration.[55] He offers immediate emergency aid to be sure, but he also acts to transform the victim's environmental circumstances by transporting him to an inn. He replaces his humiliation with the dignity of being served and brings an end to his isolation by enveloping him in a fellowship of care that goes the distance. He nurses him back from the brink of death by tending and soothing his wounds, and, by paying for his upkeep well into the future, he guarantees the victim is not exposed again to the dangers of the road before he is fully recovered. He also ensures he will not be discharged from his sickbed into a prison cell for unpaid dues. The victim's restoration to community, therefore, is a reempowerment and liberation as well as a healing, and for this reason the Samaritan's response qualifies as an exemplary demonstration of restorative or transformative justice in its fullness.

The Samaritan had nothing to gain personally (but had a great deal to lose) from helping the victim in this unrestricted way. But in electing to do so, he, an unclean foreigner, acted more like a neighbor to the man in the ditch than did the man's natural neighbors. Under the guise of upholding the law and preserving their professional honor, the priest and the Levite had discounted the demands of love and misconstrued the law's primary values. Their failure of compassion towards the victim was both a failure of character and a failure of hermeneutical insight, as Jesus makes very plain in his closing interchange with the lawyer.

THE JUDGMENT OF MERCY

The lawyer who rose to question Jesus was concerned to "test" his fidelity to the law by asking him to pronounce on the necessary conditions for

---

55. *Prosdapanēsēs* in v. 35 ("spend further") is translated in the Vulgate as *superogaveris*, whence comes the technical expression in Roman Catholic theology *opera supererogantionis*, "works of supererogation," good works that exceed the basic commands of God and thus earn merit.

gaining entry to the future age (vv. 25–26). The lawyer recognized that his own practice of legal righteousness was much stricter than that of Jesus, and he is anxious to "justify himself" (v. 29) in the face of Jesus' more liberal standpoint. When Jesus replies by asking him to specify what he thinks constitutes the legal basis for eternal life, the lawyer nominates wholehearted love for God and love of neighbor. He does so in a way, moreover, that rightly presumes the inseparability of these twin injunctions. Love for God *requires* love of neighbor, and love of neighbor *expresses* love for God. It expresses love for God because God commands love of neighbor, and one cannot love God without obeying God's commandments. Conversely, if love of neighbor is integral to loving God, it could be reasoned that to qualify as a neighbor, one must also love God and obey God's laws. It is here that the lawyer judges Jesus to be much too easygoing. He therefore seeks to pin Jesus down to a definitive ruling on the question, "Who is my neighbor?" (v. 29). Clearly, if "doing" the law of love is *the* necessary requirement for entry to the new age, an unambiguous definition of the object of such love seems critically important.

Jesus responds to this question with the parable of the Good Samaritan (vv. 30–35). He then invites the lawyer to make his own interpretive judgment on the matter of neighborliness: "How does it seem *to you [dokei soi]*?" he asks. "Which of these three was a neighbor to the man who fell into the hands of robbers?" This question returns to the lawyer's original inquiry, but in a significantly modified form. It no longer focuses on the identity of the *other* as neighbor, but on the questioner's *own* identity as a neighbor.[56] It is not, "*Who is my neighbor?*" but "To whom am *I* a neighbor?" There is a shift from object to subject, from recipient of compassion to agent of compassion, and with it a decisive shift from the realm of legal abstraction to the world of relational engagement, from the priority of carefully delineating the legal rights others possess to concentrating on one's own moral obligations to treat them as persons of equal worth. For no one can simply *have* a neighbor without first *being* a neighbor. Neighbors cannot be defined in the abstract; they can only be discovered in the context of human relatedness.

---

56. Most commentators see this shift from object to subject as highly significant, though some, like Jeremias, see it merely as formal inconsistency with no deeper significance (*Parables*, 205). Wink rightly sees it as the whole point of the story ("Compassionate Samaritan," 211–12).

The issue in the parable, then, is not whether the nameless, naked, half-dead crime victim qualified *in law* as a neighbor, but whether any of the three characters who encountered him honored their relational responsibility towards him as a fellow human being *in fact*. The matter of principle, it should be noted again, is framed entirely from the perspective of the crime victim, whose status as a neighbor is simply taken for granted. For to ask, "Which of these three was a neighbor to the man who fell into the hands of robbers?" already presupposes that the victim is automatically a neighbor, regardless of any secondary qualifications, with inalienable claims upon others. He is a neighbor simply because he is another human being in need. But while everyone *is* a neighbor to their fellows, not everyone *acts* like a neighbor towards others. Neighbor is as neighbor does. So which of the three men, the lawyer is asked, proved in practice to be a neighbor to the man in the ditch?

Posed this way, only one answer is possible, for only one of the three characters did anything at all to benefit the victim. "The one who showed him mercy," the lawyer replies. Perhaps he could not bring himself to utter the loathsome word "Samaritan," as commentators often surmise.[57] But what the lawyer says of the benefactor's actions shows that he recognized in the Samaritan's response three exemplary facets.

First, he acknowledges that the Samaritan exhibited *mercy* (*eleos*) to the victim. Mercy is a quality supremely associated in the biblical tradition with God. It is an expression of God's covenantal faithfulness towards Israel irrespective of her merits. According to the Old Testament prophets, God expects his people to replicate such divine mercy in their transactions with one another, with mercy taking priority over all the sacrificial offerings that the law prescribes for dealing with sin and impurity (Mic 6:7–8; Hos 6:6; Isa 58:5–9). The Samaritan, though outside the Jewish covenant community and lacking the same recognition for the prophets that the priest and the Levite had, in practice upholds the supreme intent of covenant law (cf. Luke 11:42). He understands that "loving neighbor" (*agapēseis ton plēsion*, Lev 19:18) means "loving mercy" (*agapan eleon*, Mic 6:8).

---

57. This is commonly suggested by exegetes, including Creed, *Saint Luke*, 154; Plummer, *St. Luke*, 289; Farrer, *St. Luke*, 206 (who quotes Luther: "He will not name the Samaritan by name, the haughty hypocrite"); Jeremias, *Parables*, 205; Marshall, *Luke*, 450; Jones, *Criminals*, 170.

Second, the lawyer recognizes that the Samaritan performed mercy *as an action*, he did not simply feel it as an emotion (*ho poiēsas to eleos*). The gut-churning "compassion" he felt when he saw the victim (v. 33) translated itself into concrete deeds of deliverance, and it is these *deeds* that constitute "mercy."[58] It is by means of his merciful actions that he proved himself (*gegonenai*) to be a neighbor.[59] As Wolfgang Schrage observes, "His actions make it unmistakably clear that love cannot be identified with feelings and emotions. Love means active and concrete involvement on behalf of those who suffer."[60] Just as love for God in the Old Testament is fundamentally a willing and a doing of God's will, not just an affectionate feeling for God, so love for neighbor is first of all a willing and a doing of good to others, not simply feelings of warmth towards them.[61]

But, as we discussed earlier, the emotional dimension is by no means excluded. The Samaritan loved his neighbor so effectively because he *both* felt compassion *and* acted mercifully. One without the other falls short of genuine love. Compassion without merciful deeds does nothing to help the needy party. Merciful action without compassion does nothing to transform the helper. It also diminishes the victim's sense of being an inherently loveable human being, for to be the occasion of someone else's compassion is to be esteemed as someone worthy of love and respect. As Martin Luther King observes, "The Samaritan used his hands to bind up the wounds of the robbed man's body and he also released an overflowing love to bind up the wounded man's spirit."[62]

In performing deeds of mercy, the Samaritan fulfils the law and meets the crucial condition for gaining eternal life. The lawyer had initially asked Jesus what he must "do" to win eternal life (v. 25), and Jesus had responded he must "do" the law (v. 28). By indicating that the Samaritan "does" mercy (v. 37), the lawyer concedes that the Samaritan meets the requirement of "doing" the law, which opens the door to eternal life for him. Jesus confirms this by issuing his second imperative to the lawyer: "Go you [*su*] and do [*poiei*] likewise [*homoiōs*]" (v. 37, cf. v. 28).

58. On the distinction between mercy and compassion in the philosophical tradition, see Nussbaum, *Upheavals*, 396–99. We return to this theme in chapter 10 below.

59. Nolland thinks it is probably justified to press the perfect tense of *genonenai* "to have become," Nolland, *Luke*, 596.

60. Schrage, *Ethics*, 78.

61. Meier, *Marginal Jew*, 4:490, 491, 527.

62. King Jr., *Stength to Love*, 36.

Every word of this injunction is important. The present tense of the verb *poiei* ("do continually, do repeatedly, do constantly") underscores the perpetual or habitual nature of the specified action. Mercy is not a singular episode in one's dealings with others; it is a comprehensive way of life. The personal singular pronoun "you" (*su*) drives home the individual purchase of this obligation. It operates not simply at a communal or institutional or political level but applies to each and every moral agent within the community as well. The comparative adverb "likewise" (*homoiōs*) guards against subjectivist or idiosyncratic definitions of mercy. Like all the important virtues, mercy is best learned from observing merciful people in action and especially from the experience of having received mercy from others, initially and most influentially from one's parents. The adverb also disallows any kind of moral exceptionalism that permits an evasion of personal responsibility by vicarious reliance on the goodness of heroic proxies. The lawyer is not told to admire the Samaritan as a uniquely virtuous individual; he is told to copy him as a feasible role model. What the Samaritan did as one individual in one specific circumstance to transcend religious enmity and legally protected privilege, the lawyer is summonsed to replicate in all other situations where the same destructive dynamics are at work.[63]

Finally, the lawyer recognizes that the Samaritan's merciful attention was focused on the personhood of the victim: he "showed mercy *to him*" (*met 'autou*).[64] His actions were not the outcome of a careful weighing up of competing legal stipulations to ensure minimal conformity to legal requirements. They were the expression of a reckless compassion for the pressing needs of an actual human being "who fell into the hands of robbers." The Samaritan satisfied the deepest meaning of the law by keeping the humanity and individuality of his victim in full view, which, in this case, entailed disregarding the law's provisions for maintaining strict boundaries around covenantal identity and ritual purity.

The message of the parable, then, is inescapable: *the continual and habitual practice of restorative mercy is an essential individual requirement for entry to the age of salvation.* The Samaritan qualifies to enter; the priest

---

63. So Esler, "Intergroup Conflict," 345–52.

64. Wink translates the prepositional phrase *met'autou* as "with him," and thinks it implies that the Samaritan got down in the ditch with the victim and got blood and filth on his own clothing in order to render aid ("Compassionate Samaritan," 211). But this overpresses the syntax.

and the Levite do not. In this way, as Jones memorably puts it, the parable "exposes any religion with a mania for creeds and an anemia for deeds, an uptightness about orthodoxy not matched by a parallel concern for orthopraxy (cf. I John 3:23)."[65] It also exposes any approach to criminal justice that places a concern for legal technicalities and professional decorum ahead of the needs of actual victims and that diverts the wider social community from its overriding responsibility to work towards the restoration of victims to a place of health, strength, freedom, and autonomy.

Nothing is said in the parable about the need to catch and punish the robbers or to hold them directly accountable to the victim, though the justice of doing so might be assumed. Nothing is said about what the kindhearted Samaritan would have done had he arrived on the scene in the middle of the attack, though he might well have intervened in some (hopefully nonviolent!) way. Nothing is said, of course, about the need to make the highways safer for travelers, nor about the value of drafting more police into the region to deter similar attacks in the future, though deterrence has its place and security is a valid concern. The parable does not address these larger systemic issues, not because they are unimportant to consider in any comprehensive approach to crime, law, and justice, but because the governing concern of this story is the duty of restoration towards the victim, and the priority of this in the interpretation and administration of the law.

This is not to say that systemic concerns are entirely absent from the parable. There are, I suggest, several ways in which the story hints at wider structural considerations that should not be overlooked in ethical appropriations of the parable, especially when it is used as a paradigm of restorative justice.

SYSTEMS, SITUATIONS, AND PERSONALITIES

At the beginning of this study, I quoted Martin Luther King's stirring words, "We are called to play the Good Samaritan on life's roadside . . . but one day we must come to see that the whole Jericho road must be transformed so that men and women will not be constantly beaten and robbed. True compassion is more than flinging a coin to a beggar; it is not haphazard and superficial. It comes to see that an edifice which produces

65. Jones, "Love Command," 241.

beggars needs restructuring." This is undoubtedly correct. Genuine compassion for the poor requires more than charitable relief for their immediate needs; it also requires a commitment to work for social and political change. But it would be a mistake—albeit a very common mistake—to identify the Samaritan's response in the parable as mere charitable giving alone. The Samaritan does much more than fling a spare coin or two in the direction of the victim. He doesn't merely bandage his wounds and leave him on the road to be violated again. Instead, he effects a change in the victim's external circumstances. I have suggested that his action of relocating the victim to the inn and enlisting the innkeeper in his future rehabilitation involved a transformation of his environmental conditions, and in that sense intimates the need for structural change in the quest for restoring justice.

The same could be said about the way the Samaritan forged a personal relationship across the lines of national animosity that divided the two religious communities. To transcend or ignore entrenched hatreds and dehumanizing stereotypes in order to bring healing to traumatized victims on the opposing side is in itself a powerful way of delegitimating prevailing structures of violence and exclusion. The transformative reverberations of such actions are already apparent in the Lukan context itself. For when the Jewish lawyer acknowledges that it was the Samaritan who acted as a neighbor to the victim from Jerusalem, he is already beginning to reconfigure his worldview to accommodate the enemy as a neighbor. He is forced by what he has heard to remove the "cataracts of provincialism"[66] from his eyes and view the "other" as brother and equal, insinuating a massive shift in existing understandings and structural arrangements.

In this connection, it is also possible to detect systemic implications in what the Samaritan does *not* do in the story, in the way the plot of the parable is *not* elaborated, though caution is obviously needed since arguments from silence are notoriously indecisive. It has often been observed that because the Samaritan arrives on the scene after the act of unjust aggression has occurred, the story offers no guidance on the validity of using violence in defense of the innocent or in pursuit of a just cause. The Good Samaritan may serve as a powerful paradigm for therapeutic jurisprudence, but, it is frequently said, the parable has little relevance to questions of corrective or punitive or military justice.

66. I borrow this phrase from King Jr., *Stength to Love*, 33.

At one level, this is true enough. It would be foolish to expect a single brief parable to address all our questions to do with the administration and enforcement of justice in a complex society. But the absence of any hint of counter-violence in the account is still worth remarking on, especially in view of how the story could easily have been told. Richard Hays, a prominent New Testament ethicist, sees significance in the fact that Jesus never told stories in which the good guys kill the bad guys and the New Testament never narrates any act of sword-wielding heroism by Christian believers. In this respect, the New Testament texts are truly unusual in the world's literature. Imagine, Hays asks, if the parable of the Good Samaritan had been constructed along the following lines:

> A man was going down from Jerusalem to Jericho, and fell into the hands of robbers, who started to beat and rob him. A passing priest and Levite, being pacifists, saw the mugging taking place but did nothing. But then, at the last moment, a Samaritan sheriff swooped down from the hills with a (duly deputized) posse. They fell upon the robbers with their swords and killed them, rescuing their victim and making the Jericho road safe for other travelers. Which of these three, do you think, was a neighbor to the man who fell into the hands of the robbers?[67]

Had the parable been told along these lines, Hays observes, some basis might exist for attempts to ground just war thinking in New Testament teaching. But no such basis exists. Quite the contrary, by construing neighbor love as something that compels costly compassion towards an enemy victim of random violence, Jesus' parable surely excludes the legitimacy of using violence in the name of love to render other people as victims, even if they are perceived to be guilty of violent wrongdoing themselves.

So the parable is not entirely innocent of systemic and political implications, and it certainly portrays love of neighbor as more demanding and comprehensive than merely making charitable contributions to the poor. Even so, the parable is not focused primarily on the need for structural transformation in society but rather on the nature of individual responsibility towards the victims of human cruelty. This is not a weakness in the story. Arguably it is its most penetrating and disconcerting dimension. For the parable recognizes that there is something far more difficult

---

67. Hays, "Thorny Task," 83–84.

to achieve than securing social or cultural change. That is to become a truly loving person who engages all the powers of one's personality to bring wholeness and freedom to others. To attain to that kind of love, something more is needed than political reform.

Psychologists have long debated the relative influence of situational and dispositional factors in explaining prosocial and antisocial behavior. The majority view has been that situation is a much more significant determinant of human behavior than personality difference. Countless experiments have shown that if a change is made in the situation a person is in, that person's behavior will also change. Under the influence of environmental forces, people can undergo significant transformations of temperament and behave in ways that would otherwise be considered out of character. This is a critically important insight that precludes the simplistic division of human beings into two groups: those who are naturally good and those who are intrinsically evil. Nowhere is this tendency more marked than with respect to crime, with offenders often being typecast as inherently wicked. But the reality is much more complex than this. The dividing line between good and evil is more permeable than most of us like to believe. As Philip Zimbardo, the architect of the famous Stanford Prison Experiment, argues at length in his illuminating book *The Lucifer Effect*, "Any deed that any human being has ever committed, however horrible, is possible for any of us—under the right or wrong situational circumstances."[68]

Yet, without denying the immense power of situations and systems to influence behavior, psychologists are coming to believe that personality traits continue to have an important role in accounting for prosocial behavior.[69] Some personality types, it seems, are more inclined to altruism than others. Four character traits, in particular, have been identified as important in facilitating altruistic engagement, especially in ambiguous situations: *empathy*, a consistent tendency to respond emotionally to other people's experience and a willingness to see things from the perspective of others; *responsibility*, a sense of accountability for the welfare of others; *efficacy*, a confidence in one's own ability to effect real change; and *extensivity*, an ability to connect with, and feel responsible for, people beyond one's own immediate in-group.

68. Zimbardo, *Lucifer Effect*, 211.

69. Schroeder, *Psychology of Helping*, 171–72. For a full-scale analysis, see Oliner and Oliner, *Altruistic Personality*.

These are precisely the attributes exhibited by the devoted Samaritan and sadly lacking in the priest and the Levite. All three characters were confronted with the same external situation. But only the Samaritan responded with compassion; only he assumed responsibility for the injured party; only he acted with confidence and competence to transform the victim's circumstances; and only he responded to the victim's essential humanity rather than his in-group or out-group identity. None of this could happen *ex nihilo*. The Samaritan's behavior can best be explained as the situational manifestation of established character traits and well-practiced virtues, especially the virtue of mercy, carefully honed over time through the ups and downs of everyday life.

SUMMARY

Once again we have observed in the example of the Samaritan, as in the case of the priest and the Levite, a remarkable resonance between the dynamics portrayed in the parable and the findings of modern social-science research into altruism and prosocial behavior. All three characters were subject to a range of personal, situational, and systemic forces that made concrete intervention on behalf of the wounded man on the side of the road a risky and costly undertaking. Only the Samaritan was able to rise above these pressures and devote himself unreservedly to the rescue and restoration of the victim to a state of wholeness, freedom, and independence. The Samaritan could only do so, presumably, because he possessed a moral character that had been habitually conformed throughout his life to the dictates of compassion.

Jesus offers this compassionate outsider as the definitive role model for the Jewish lawyer to emulate: "Go you and do likewise." The importance of positive role models or mentors in increasing levels of altruism and benevolent behavior in the community is well known to social researchers. Equally well known is the importance of positive social labeling. People tend to live up to, or down to, the identity labels conferred on them by others. Call people generous, and they are more likely to become generous. Call them selfish or criminal or unclean, and they are more liable to behave in corresponding ways. As well as offering the Samaritan as a role model for the lawyer, Jesus elicits a relabeling of him as the "one who was a neighbor" (v. 36) and "one who does mercy" (v. 37). Given the hatred that existed between Jews and Samaritans, such a relabeling of the old enemy as neighbor and friend constituted a radical subversion of prevailing social and political values. This is one of the ways that the parable, even while accenting individual responsibility for the disadvantaged and the need for an inner transformation of character in order to love more wholeheartedly, points at the same time towards the need for structural and systemic change, as the social outworking of love.

For the Jewish lawyer to contemplate such sweeping social change required him to rethink the meaning and purpose of the law. For what transpires in the story elicits a relabeling of the Samaritan not only as "neighbor" and "mercy doer" but also as the "one who does the law" and "inherits life," and who thereby, in effect, embodies God's covenantal justice. The lawyer felt able to "justify himself" (v. 29) when challenged by the gracious inclusiveness of Jesus' lifestyle, believing that his own wholehearted love for God required him to restrict his circle of neighbors to those who loved God in the same way as he did, that is, those who observed God's law with the same exactitude as he did. The priest and the Levite could similarly justify their separation from the unclean victim because the law required of them a different set of responsibilities than it did of other people. Somebody else could attend to the victim while they attended to their own professional duties—duties that, they probably told themselves, fulfilled a higher purpose than dirtying their hands with individual victims. No doubt the Samaritan merchant could have justified a similar course of action as well. After all, he was a foreigner traveling in Judea, and the man beaten to a pulp on the roadside was most likely a Jew, not a fellow Samaritan, and hence not really a neighbor of his in law.

But, overwhelmed with compassion for the crushed humanity of the victim, he sets about to rescue and restore him, step by costly step redressing the damage done to him. He does not first pause to ascertain his neighbor-status in law; instead, he focuses upon his own neighbor-status in fact towards persons in need, and "showed him mercy" (v. 37). His restorative mercy towards the injured man fulfilled both the letter and the spirit of the law. At the same time, it radicalized the reach of the commandment to include within the scope of neighbor even those who are otherwise deemed as enemies and lawbreakers.

In this way the parable teaches that there is more to achieving true justice than enforcing technical conformity to the law. A distinctive feature of biblical law, as we will see in the next chapter, is its combination of enforceable and unenforceable obligations. The Torah includes both concrete prohibitions that invite censure and punishment for their contravening (as does modern Western law) and positive moral exhortations that lie beyond the reach of any coercive sanction (the realm of modern ethics rather than law). Both kinds of obligation are integral to the biblical conception of law, as well as to the biblical conception of justice or righteousness. True justice—that condition of individual and communal "rightness" in its most comprehensive sense—cannot be achieved solely by enforcing negative prohibitions that regulate external behavior. It also requires the cultivation of positive virtues, the sustaining of healthy relationships, and the manifestation of overflowing compassion for those who suffer and those who fail.

Martin Luther King used to say that the ultimate solution to racism lay not in the legal enforcement of civil rights but in the willingness of people to obey the unenforceable obligations of morality. Legal change was still important. But all the law can do is to restrain the heartless; it cannot change the human heart.[70] For that change to happen something more powerful than law is required. It requires the power of love. Without a commitment to love, the fullness of justice cannot be achieved.

This is something biblical law recognizes. By placing the demand for wholehearted love at the very center of its demands, it points beyond itself to a fullness of response that legislation can never hope to comprehend. The Samaritan satisfied the justice that the law commends because he loved the wounded man with all his heart and soul, in a way that transcended any minimally enforceable legal obligation and that prioritized his restoration to wholeness above all other concerns. What might such a commitment to restorative love mean for the practice and development of criminal law today? Is it possible to make any meaningful connections between the realm of biblical law and Jesus' remarkable commentary on it, and the very different reality of modern Western law? How should contemporary law support or encourage good Samaritanism, and should it punish bad Samaritans? These are some of the questions to be addressed in next chapter.

---

70. King Jr., *Stength to Love*, 37–38.

6

Good Samaritans, Bad Samaritans, and Modern Legal Theory

The parable of the Good Samaritan is conventionally understood as a dramatic enunciation of the ethics of charitable care for those in severe need. This is entirely appropriate, especially when the systemic and structural implications we have identified in the story are included in the reckoning. But I have proposed that the parable should also be read as a parable of law, crime, and justice. It offers a penetrating commentary on the bitter experience of criminal victimization, on the duty of restorative care owed to victims of crime by others in the community, and, most tellingly of all, on the proclivity of the law and the professional legal establishment to justify the neglect of victims in the name of serving the higher good of the law itself.

The parable is told to a lawyer who, we have seen, rightly understands that the fundamental concern of the law is to promote wholehearted love for God and neighbor, but mistakenly assumes that the term "neighbor" is a term of limited reference. To explode this restriction, Jesus offers a parabolic commentary on the commandment that portrays a legally suspect Samaritan fulfilling the real intent of the law by showing mercy to a naked and unconscious—and therefore ethnically and religiously "unmarked"—victim, while the two Jewish cultic professionals prioritize provisions in the law that, they thought, permitted them to look the other way.

The parable affirms that the overriding purpose of the law is to serve and protect human welfare so that people afford the same standards of care toward all others that they expect for themselves and that are commensurate with undivided devotion to God. Yet the law can only achieve this objective when it is interpreted and administered through the lens of compassion and mercy. Compassion is a manifestation of the relationality that binds people together in community and that constitutes the very essence of their humanity. Mercy is the concrete embodiment of compassion in deeds of deliverance and restoration. Without compassion and mercy, the parable teaches, it is possible to justify conduct as law-keeping and law-honoring that, in reality, thwarts the deepest objectives of the law.

In light of this message, it is appropriate to complete our analysis of the parable by returning to the issue raised at the outset: the potential of the biblical story for informing discussions of public policy today. It would be unwise, of course, to try to spin an entire theory of law or justice or political order from a single short parable. Parables are not suited to that purpose. They lack the measure, balance, and intricacy required in theoretical or philosophical deliberation. They offer instead a distinctively eschatological, and often shockingly subversive, perspective on the taken-for-granted assumptions and truisms that govern everyday reality. Moving from the counterintuitive world of parabolic communication to the highly rational and technical world of juridical and political deliberation is by no means easy. There are also substantial differences between engaging with the law of God disclosed in Scripture, as the parable does, and exploring the role and character of temporal human law in a secular society. Divine law and human law differ markedly in terms of their perceived origins and formation, their intended jurisdiction, their modes of address, and their underlying anthropological assumptions.

Yet there are two good reasons for seeking to probe the relevance of the parable to social and political deliberation today. One is the extent to which in this parable, and elsewhere in his teaching, Jesus exhibits an approach to legal analysis, or a type of legal theory, that still has application today. By "legal theory" I mean a particular way of thinking about the function, interpretation, and limitations of law in wider human experience. The other reason is to do with the impact the parable of the Good Samaritan has already had on the development of Western law, both civil and criminal. After a brief discussion of these two matters, I will focus attention on just one example of how the parable may inform and enlighten an issue of current public and philosophical debate. That debate concerns the question of whether criminal law should be used to compel people to come to the aid of strangers in life-threatening situations and punish those who don't, or whether such altruistic interventions should be left over to personal choice.

JESUS' METHOD OF LEGAL REASONING

According to Duncan M. Derrett, one of the lessons of our parable is that methods of legal reasoning that balance different stipulations in the law as though they were weights on a scale can, because of our natural tendency to self-deception, permit the very breaches of the law that the method is intended to prevent.[1] The strategy of playing off different commandments against each other to produce a preferred outcome may end up distorting the true objective of the law as a whole. The parable suggests that a different mode of legal reasoning is required, one in which love or compassion for victims serves as the benchmark for determining the application and relative importance of the law's constituent rules and regulations. Instead of sticking to the letter of the law or striving to hold its various prescriptions in some kind of abstract equilibrium, the law must be enacted in such a way that its deepest values and priorities are satisfied.

This appraisal of the hazards of legal reasoning still has pertinence today. Yet the relevance of Jesus' teaching to modern legal theory has attracted very little scholarly attention. According to Jewish scholar Chaim Saiman, this is largely because the delegalization of the Christian religious tradition has been so successful that most contemporary readers of the Gospels fail to recognize that the daily issues Jesus wrestled with in his life and teaching implicate the central questions of legal theory and interpretation.[2] Even in the vast recent literature on "Christianity and the law," virtually no consideration is given to the jurisprudence of Jesus, to what Jesus himself thought about law, lawyers, legal rules, and the legal order. The term "law" in this literature serves instead as a generic label for social and political policy. But if we take law to mean a particular type of reasoning process—a conversation whereby professional jurists analyze legal texts, precedents, and rules to reconcile competing social ideals and values—it soon becomes apparent that Jesus and his followers subscribed to a set of ideas about the law and the place of the law in human affairs that may fairly be regarded as a type of legal theory. It is a theory not in the formal or scientific sense but in the sense that it comprises a collection of interpretive proclivities and jurisprudential assumptions regarding the nature of legal rules and texts and the advisability of refracting difficult social questions through a legislative lens.

---

1. Derrett, *Law*, 222.
2. Saiman, "Legal Theory."

In an astute and even-handed discussion, Saiman suggests that the best way to delineate Jesus' approach to legal reasoning is to compare it with the method employed in the rabbinic tradition. It is well known that in the early centuries of the Common Era, Christianity and Judaism parted company significantly over the role and domain of the law in religious and civil affairs. Whereas the Christian movement sought to reduce the overall density of the Torah's legal regime and relativize its importance, the rabbis moved in exactly the opposite direction. They conceptualized the entire biblical-textual tradition as inherently and irreducibly legal, and considered that studying the law—wading waist-deep into the particularity and peculiarity of its details—to be the highest form of divine service and the most direct path to God.[3] The signs of this divergence are already evident in the Gospels. Jesus adopts a position on the law that is substantially different from that of the Talmudic fathers. Saiman does not attempt to subject the Gospel traditions or the rabbinic sources to historical-critical analysis, and conceivably there was a much smaller contrast between the legal reasoning exhibited by Jesus and that of other first-century rabbis than appears from comparing the Gospels to the much later Talmudic corpus. Nonetheless, Saiman's comparison of the two streams of tradition does serve usefully to crystallize two different approaches to legal analysis.

For the later rabbis, because the biblical commandments embody God's revealed will, it was crucially important, and practically achievable, to know exactly what God commands and exactly when one's duty of obedience had been fulfilled. Since the Torah addresses the whole of life, it follows that each and every contentious issue in social, religious, or economic affairs is, in principle, justiciable and resolvable in terms of a halakic-legal framework. The Torah was understood to exhibit a dense and intricate legal structure whereby each constituent body of laws generates a unique set of rules and regulations that can be used to solve any moral or pastoral problem the community faces. Rulings on narrow points of law in turn generate further levels of meaning that can be extracted by an analytical process of legal deduction. The most legitimate form of interpretation, the rabbis assumed, is one that approaches specific questions of concern in terms of the objective rules and precedents that apply. They were deeply skeptical of any method that bypasses the concrete details of

---

3. On this, see Soloveichik, "Torah and Incarnation."

the commandments in order to discern what some directive or institution, such as the Sabbath, is "really" about.

Jesus occupies a very different discursive space. This is clearly shown, Saiman says, by his debates with the Pharisees over Sabbath observance (Mark 2:23–28; Matt 12:1–8; Luke 6:1–6). It is also shown, we may add, by his interchange with the lawyer over love of neighbor. Evidently for Jesus, the best way to examine important religious and social issues is not to refract them through the prism of the Torah in a positivistic manner, but to examine the deeper principles and ideals at stake, as well as to take into consideration the moral and spiritual motivations of the agents involved. It is not that Jesus rejects positive law as such. But he employs a legal methodology that favors standards over rules, policy over doctrine, context over text, meaning over detail, elementary principles over particular directives. In defending his Sabbath conduct, for instance, Jesus draws attention to the fundamental purpose of the institution rather than the details of Torah legislation: "The Sabbath was made for humankind, not humankind for the Sabbath" (Mark 2:27). Similarly, in ascertaining the scope of the commandment to love one's neighbor as oneself, Jesus focuses on the logic of love rather than the semantics of "neighbor." The lawyer's approach of rulifying, reifying, and legalizing the command misses the point, Jesus implies, for it leads the lawyer to concentrate on the limits of his legal duties rather than the unlimited scope of his relational responsibilities; it encourages him to focus on what the law specifies rather than what love requires.

Saiman notes that the great strength of the rabbinic-Talmudic mode of legal reasoning, which involves the application of rules and precedents to facts and constructs abstract rulings from particular cases, is its predictability, objectivity, and authority. The method guards against the kind of arbitrary subjectivism that gives too much discretion to individual decision-makers and can produce haphazard, self-interested, or even corrupt applications of the law. The weakness of the method is that it can easily become preoccupied with the arcane details of legal minutiae and with the cut and thrust of legal argumentation, and lose sight of the underlying intention of individual laws and of the humane function of the law as a whole. Justice can get lost in the legal shuffle. Because rules, by definition, can never be all-inclusive, strict fidelity to statute law can end up distorting the original intent of the biblical mandates.

This, it seems, is what Jesus was most concerned about among his scribal contemporaries. He feared that the process of interpretation favored by them could have a dehumanizing effect on the law, a loss of emphasis on the actual human consequences of decision-making. For Jesus, one cannot fulfill the Sabbath command without remembering that the Sabbath was made for the benefit of human beings, not vice versa, and that God desires mercy more than sacrifice (Mark 2:27; Matt 12:7). One cannot fulfill the love commandment without appreciating that love transcends all secondary distinctions between people, so that neighbor love is at stake wherever human beings are found. The lawyer sought to ground his own practice of legal justice in definitional exactitude. But such an approach offers no adequate safeguard against the kind of legalized callousness the priest and the Levite exhibited on the Jericho road, which even the lawyer himself recoils from (v. 37). Only an approach to the law that prioritizes compassion and restorative mercy above all else can secure the holistic justice the law intends. A reasoning process controlled solely by positive law, Jesus urges, must give way to a reasoning process informed by love.

To acknowledge the primacy of love within and beyond the law does not mean that every ethical decision is unique, or that the right course of action can be determined on circumstantial grounds alone, or that case law can be dispensed in favor of vague general principles. Jesus does not advocate an unprincipled situationalism. Statute law and legal precedent are still indispensable and in no sense does Jesus abrogate commandments willy-nilly or abolish the regime of law entirely. But within the plethora of injunctions and regulations that make up the law, the obligation to love has supreme importance, and the operationalizing of all other legal norms must constantly be tested against the criterion of love.

Perhaps the chief lesson to be drawn from this discussion for the task of legal reasoning in general is recognition of the need for positive law constantly to be measured against some transcendent, extralegal norm in order to prevent it from becoming oppressive or self-serving. The law is not an end in itself but a means to achieving an end greater than itself. In standard political theory, the transcendent principle to which law is accountable is the norm of justice. That is quite appropriate, and is true of the biblical tradition as well.[4] Only thus is it possible to

---

4. For a simple introduction to law and justice in the Bible, see Marshall, *Little Book*.

speak of unjust laws or lawful injustice. But the contemporary virtue of political or legal justice is a good deal more attenuated than is the biblical conception of justice,[5] and if we conceive of justice in too narrow or too procedural a sense, and isolate it too sharply from the relational qualities of love, it too can become a mask for oppression and neglect.

Modern law, unlike biblical law, never uses the language of love in its provisions. This is because love is presumed to belong properly to the private sphere of interpersonal relationships, not the public sphere of institutional and contractual relationships, which is governed by justice. Such a distinction is alien to the Bible, however, as well as being false to everyday experience, as we will see in Part 3. It is also foreign to Jesus' style of legal reasoning. Jesus' approach beckons us always to assess the content and application of law in terms of its contribution to promoting human flourishing in its most rounded sense, and human beings cannot flourish without love. Concrete applications of the law must be compatible with the dictates of love, even though, as we saw previously, love by its very nature always exceeds legal definition.

Jesus' perspective also invites us to be ever conscious of the innate limitations of law for generating moral and relational fullness of life. The law can summon love of neighbor, but it cannot manufacture the kind of self-sacrificing love shown by the Samaritan. The law can regulate ritual purity, as it did for the priest and the Levite, but it cannot transform the human heart or create virtuous character (cf. Mark 7:1–14; Matt 15:1–20). The Apostle Paul places great emphasis upon this limitation. He argues that while the law is effective in showing up sinful behavior as truly sinful, and in making us aware of our moral culpability for doing wrong, it cannot defeat the power of sin itself. The law is simply not strong enough to do that. In fact, in his most daring discussion of the law, in Romans 7, Paul speaks of how even God's law has been outmaneuvered by sin, like a skillful military tactician, so that what God intended for good (the law) has actually become an instrument for embedding sin ever more deeply in human experience. Something more powerful than a law code is needed to defeat evil and bring true freedom. That something is the redeeming grace of Christ, which happens, significantly, "apart from law," though the law bears witness to it (Rom 3:21, 31, cf. 8:1–4).

---

5. On the meaning of justice in the biblical tradition, see Marshall, *Beyond Retribution*, esp. 35–95.

What does all this mean for assessing the function of law in general today? It means that while the rule of law may be affirmed as of fundamental importance to a healthy political community, as a bastion against tyranny and a tool for securing justice, the law is also an imperfect and limited instrument. It is not a self-validating reality but rather stands accountable to a truth beyond itself. Nor can law reach to the heart of human experience or secure the transformation of moral character that human beings most crave and society most needs. The law is important in regulating external behavior so that we not injure each other too grievously in our social and commercial relationships. But that, pretty much, is where its power ends. The law cannot comprehend the full extent of our moral and spiritual responsibilities to one another, and the moment we think it does, we are in trouble. This, we have seen, is one of the lessons of the parable of the Good Samaritan.

MORALITY, RELIGION, AND LAW

At the beginning of this study, I commented on the far-reaching impact the parable of the Good Samaritan has had on the intellectual and cultural life of Western civilization. It has played a notable role in the development of moral philosophy, social psychology, medical ethics, and a wide range of philanthropic endeavors. It has also played an intriguing role in the evolution of Western law. In a celebrated passage in *Donoghue v Stevenson*, the 1932 case that created the modern tort of negligence, Lord Atkin appealed directly to the lawyer's question in Luke 10:29, "Who is my neighbor?" to assert the existence of a general duty of care, quite apart from the existence of any contractual or other special relationship between the parties. The matter at issue was whether the manufacturer of a bottle of ginger beer was liable for the nervous shock and gastroenteritis suffered by a customer when she discovered she had consumed the remains of a dead snail in her soft drink. Since no formal relationship existed between the complainant and the manufacturer, her claim for damages was initially dismissed. But the House of Lords allowed it on appeal by a 3–2 majority. The leading judgment by Lord Atkin asserted that even where an established duty of care does not exist in common law, there is still a general duty of care flowing from the neighbor principle.

> The rule that you are to *love* your neighbor becomes in law, you must not injure your neighbor; and the lawyer's question, "Who is my neighbor?" receives a restricted reply . . . Who, then, in law is my neighbor? The answer seems to be—persons who are so closely and directly affected by my act that I ought reasonably to have them in contemplation as being so affected when I am directing my mind to the acts or omissions which are called in question.[6]

The result of this determination on subsequent jurisprudence has been far-reaching.[7] Yet while inferring a general duty of care in law from the biblical neighbor principle is fitting, such an inference in no way comprehends the ethical radicalism advocated in the parable of the Good Samaritan (which Lord Atkin does not explicitly mention in his judgment). The message of Jesus' parable is that love for one's neighbor demands much more than a respect for his or her negative right not to be harmed, which is the primary intention of the injunction in Lev 19:18, as the lawyer knew full well. It also requires a positive dedication to restoring the well-being of those who have been harmed by the deeds of others, regardless of their personal status or social contribution. Moreover, those who qualify as neighbors-to-be-loved in this wholehearted way are not only persons who may be directly affected by my actions or omissions. The category includes everyone to whom I stand in relation as a fellow human being, and especially those who are in severe need and within immediate reach of my help.

In short, the parable propounds an unlimited duty of compassionate benevolence to all people in need, including total strangers and even our collective enemies, and offers this as the true intent of the biblical commandment. Quite how such a comprehensive moral duty, even if we accept its normative authority (which not everyone will), can or should be translated into statutory law or public policy in a secular society, is by no means obvious. The relationship between law and morality, and the

---

6. UKHL, *Donoghue v Stevenson* [1932] AC 562, p. 580.

7. The outcome of this case was to furnish grounds for complainants to seek a remedy for damages caused by individuals or companies with whom they had no contractual or other special relationship, provided certain conditions are met. In a 1990 case, *Caparo Industries Plc v Dickman* [1990] 2 AC 605, which revised the neighbor principle to encompass public-policy concerns, a three-stage test for establishing a duty of care was laid down: foreseeability of damage; a relationship of proximity or neighborhood; and considerations of fairness, justness, and reasonableness in law.

relation of each to religion, has been a matter of constant befuddlement in post-Enlightenment legal and political thought. Law and morality are obviously closely connected, since both are concerned to define acceptable standards of conduct and it is impossible to explain the obligatory nature of law without presupposing a shared moral sensibility amongst its constituency. But the two spheres are not identical. Morality and law overlap but they do not completely coincide. Not all morally bad behavior is legally proscribed or punished, and not all morally good behavior is legally defined or protected.

Legal codes are also much more formal than moral codes. They are less sensitive to individual circumstances and more easily controlled or manipulated by those in positions of political authority. Moreover, in the liberal political enterprise there has been a principled aversion to using the law as a means of enforcing morality. This is because laws necessarily involve a restriction on personal freedom, and maximizing individual liberty is considered the most effective way to prevent political tyranny. Such freedom is conceived in essentially negative rather than positive terms—freedom *from* external compulsion or constraint, not freedom *for* particular ends. Criminal law in particular is viewed solely as an instrument for preventing harm, not as an engine for promoting good or for facilitating human transformation.

In biblical thought, the situation is significantly different. Morality and law are much more closely aligned in the Bible and share a common origin in the revealed will of God. The relationship between law and freedom is also conceived differently. Law is not thought to be antithetical to freedom but is considered the necessary foundation for any meaningful experience of freedom. Unwavering submission to God's law brings, not constriction and constraint, but liberty, life, and blessing (Deut 30:15–20). Freedom is understood differently as well.[8] Freedom is not simply freedom of choice or freedom from unwanted intrusions, but freedom to flourish as a created being, a flourishing that comes from enjoying relational integrity with God and with others, not from maximizing individual autonomy.

Accordingly, biblical legislation addresses almost every dimension of human life, both public and private. It is not content to address outer conduct alone, but seeks to inculcate a whole orientation to life that

---

8. Cf. Marshall, *Crowned*, 95–106; Hart, *Atheist Delusions*, esp. 19–26.

involves the entire person. It presupposes an integrated anthropology in which words, deeds, feelings, and thoughts influence each other reciprocally and together give expression to the fundamental religious orientation of the human heart, which is the control center of the human person. Its constituent laws encompass positive aspirations as well as negative prohibitions. Some 40 percent of the commandments in the Torah are moral or spiritual exhortations that carry no penal implications. Of the 60 percent that do forbid specific wrongdoing, punitive sanctions are not always attached. In some cases, enforcement is left over to God or to the law of cause and effect. Of course, obedience to the entire corpus of commandments was considered mandatory, something that spawned intense casuistic deliberation in subsequent Jewish jurisprudence. But clearly not all of the law's prescriptions or ideals could be supervised or enforced by the courts. Some depended on appraisal and enforcement by a higher, divine authority and required the voluntary cultivation of personal wisdom, insight, and virtue rather than enforced compliance.

All these features make biblical law and modern democratic law markedly different phenomena. They diverge in terms of their perceived origins and formation, their intended jurisdiction, their modes of address, and their underlying anthropology. Yet there are also important similarities between the two enterprises. Both deal with meaning and truth; both work with authoritative written texts; both are immensely sophisticated realities with multiple interlocking parts; both require constant interpretation and adaptation to changing cultural and legal circumstances; and both give expression to a set of transcendent moral and spiritual convictions held to be self-validating. There is also an overlap in subject matter between the two endeavors. This is partly because of the influence of biblical values on the development of Western law, and partly because all legal codes, whatever their assumed origins, must address the perennial problems of human existence and social coexistence.

Taken together, these considerations make the task of assessing what pertinence biblical law and teaching may have to the operation of legal and social policy today extremely difficult. One option would be to dismiss the biblical tradition as antiquarian, parochial, and inconsequential for contemporary concerns, as secular policymakers are increasingly wont to do. But that would be to disregard one of the chief wellsprings of Western culture and to deprive us of the insight and wisdom its legal and narrative traditions still have to offer. A better solution is to envisage a dialectical relationship between biblical perspectives and current practice, a dialogue in which current political and policy options are weighed against the values and priorities evident in relevant biblical analogies, with the aim of sharpening moral judgment today and clarifying the ethical commitments on which all sound public policy finally must rest.

To illustrate how such a dialogue may be useful, let us turn to consider the question of whether a duty to rescue should be embedded in statute law today and subject to criminal enforcement or whether it should be left to individual conscience. In view of all that we have discovered about the message of Jesus' parable, about his style of legal reasoning, and about the similarities and differences between biblical law and modern law, should we support the passing of laws that require people to act as good Samaritans and that punish them for being bad Samaritans?

A PLACE FOR "SAMARITAN LAWS"?

We have seen that a crucial issue in the interpretation of the parable of the Good Samaritan is understanding why the priest and the Levite chose to ignore the man in the ditch rather than rescue him and on what basis their decision may be considered blameworthy. The key to answering this question, I have argued, lies in the victim's apparently lifeless condition and the legal ambiguities this created for other characters in the story. When the two clerics stumbled upon the "half-dead" victim, they were confronted with a clash of legal requirements. On the one hand, they stood under a general obligation to come to the rescue of neighbors in need, especially when human life was at stake. On the other hand, they were subject to a peculiar requirement as priests not to defile themselves through avoidable contact with corpses. The unconscious man on the ground could well be dead. Rather than risk the chance of ritual contamination by checking his pulse, they chose to preserve their vocational distinction and leave the messy business of burying a neglected corpse, also a strong legal obligation on Israelites, to the next person down the road.

The temple officials could have defended their decision on strictly legal grounds. There were provisions in the law that they could cite in support of their choice not to get personally involved with this kind of victim in this kind of circumstance. Had the priest and the Levite been subject to Anglo-American law, however, their legal duty would have been much less ambiguous. There is no common law duty on persons to intervene to save someone else in peril, except where such a duty is established by statute or contract, or where it derives from the character of certain fiduciary or professional or personal relationships between the parties, such as parent and child, husband and wife, employer and employee, or where it arises from the formal assumption of care for others. Apart from these exceptions, in both tort law and criminal law, the courts have consistently held that there is no general duty to rescue. There is no legal obligation to save a drowning child or to warn others of dangerous currents in the river. One may lawfully stand by and watch someone bleed to death at an accident scene, as long as one has not personally caused the injury. The decision to rescue is left entirely to individual conscience. No legal liability attaches to failure to intervene.

Ironically, it is only when the bystander *does* choose to intervene that civil liability may arise. The rescuer is required to exercise reasonable care, and may even be liable to compensate for any damage to property or person caused by his or her negligence. If a would-be rescuer drags an injured person from a car following an automobile accident in the belief that the car is about to explode, and causes the victim further injury in the process, the Good Samaritan can be sued for failing to exercise sufficient care, as happened in California in 2008.[9] Thus, from a strictly legal point of view, the wisest thing a bystander can do is precisely nothing.[10] One legal scholar sums up the message of Anglo-American law as follows: "Stay where you are, you're sitting pretty." If intervention is voluntary, yet laden with legal risk when embarked upon, nonintervention is the safest option. "If you are not under a duty to 'fease,' then nonfeasance can never be held actionable. But if you do engage in feasance toward anybody, then under most circumstances you must 'fease' carefully. Moral: Don't ever 'fease' unless you have to!"[11]

---

9. Williams, "Good Samaritans." The Supreme Court of California held, by a 4–3 majority, that Lisa Torti was liable for damages for contributing to the injuries of a coworker whom she dragged out of a car wreck and was rendered a paraplegic as a result. The court ruled that the care she rendered was not medical in nature, and therefore the immunity granted by 1980 Health and Safety Code to medical workers who unintentionally cause damage while rendering emergency aid did not apply to her. In New Zealand, the accident compensation legislation prevents proceedings of this type: section 317 of the Injury Prevention, Rehabilitation and Compensation Act 2001.

10. Besser and Kaplan, "Good Samaritan," 213.

11. Gregory, "Good Samaritan," 23, 28.

That citizens should be legally exempt from liability for failing to perform their moral duty to save human life, while incurring the risk of liability for attempting to discharge that duty, seems peculiar, to say the least. It is equally peculiar that conduct which, in the context of a contractual or professional or intimate relationship would count as criminally negligent nonfeasance and invite severe punishment, in another context attracts no criminal liability whatsoever. A person who intentionally fails to rescue someone with whom he or she is in a legally recognized relationship may be convicted of homicide or manslaughter. But if that person is a mere acquaintance or a total stranger, the non-rescuer is exempt from any such charges.[12]

There are other oddities as well. In a 2009 decision, the House of Lords ruled that the Glasgow City Council was not liable to damages for having failed to alert Council tenants of a known violent resident on their estate who went on to beat his next-door neighbor to death with an iron bar. The court accepted that the harm was foreseeable but upheld the absence in common law of any positive duty to protect or assist others. Such a duty may arise in certain other relationships, but it is not incumbent on a landlord to warn tenants of potential harm from the criminal acts of a third party.[13] Presumably the Council was under an obligation to fix faulty handrails and attend to suspected gas leaks, but it had no responsibility to warn of potential violence from one of its tenants.

These anomalies are grist to the mill for legal scholars and moral philosophers. They sometimes crop up in popular and political discourse as well following particularly galling examples of bystander impassivity. We have already cited the 1964 example of Kitty Genovese in New York City, a woman whose cries for help over a thirty-minute period were ignored by dozens of her neighbors. This incident spawned a deluge of studies on bystander inaction and sparked public clamor about the need for legislative change. A similar outcry accompanied allegations in 1997 that members of the paparazzi had elected not to call emergency services as the Princess of Wales lay dying in front of them and they jostled for the commercially priceless photographs of the accident scene.

---

12. On this anomaly in the Anglo-American system, see McIntyre, "Guilty Bystanders?," 161, 187–91.

13. UKHL, "Mitchell v. Glasgow City Council," 11.

Countless other cases could be mentioned. A recent example in New Zealand concerned a three-year-old child, Nia Glassie, who was subjected to sustained abuse and unfathomable cruelty by no fewer than six adults in her wider family circle, until her little body could take it no more and she died. There was public incredulity at the pitilessness of the atrocity, though child protection experts said it was typical rather than exceptional, and newspaper writers called for extremely harsh punishment of the perpetrators, who included the child's mother and grandfather. But one columnist turned her eloquent rage on the family's neighbors, who knew what was happening but did nothing to stop it.

> They heard the child's cries over the fence; they even witnessed some of the cruelty; but they did nothing, they said, because there were other adults present, and it was therefore not up to them to act. It was the same story at Nia's previous address, where the misery seems to have begun in earnest. There were observers enough who didn't help her there, and I don't let them off the hook, either. They all helped her to die by their inaction, as did her absent father, whose abdication of responsibility, and rejection, seems to have set the tragedy in motion . . . It takes guts to stand up to bullies, especially if they're living next door. People fear retaliation, and don't believe they'll be supported if they speak up. For reporting to be effective, there has to be the right response from the police and welfare, and support. That doesn't always happen.[14]

The refusal of the neighbors to intercede on behalf of a tormented child was, most people would agree, morally monstrous. But should it also have been illegal? Should people who witness child abuse and turn the other way be criminalized, as another commentator argues in connection with the same episode?[15] Is there a case, in other words, for *compelling* people by law to be good Samaritans and penalizing them for being bad Samaritans? Does Jesus' parable highlight the need for further development of the criminal law in this direction?

Interestingly, in most civil law jurisdictions in Europe and in Latin America (and in Quebec in Canada), "bad Samaritan laws" have been on the books for a long time. Bad Samaritan laws are those that make it a

---

14. McLeod, "Hear No Evil."
15. Laws, "Children Who Survive."

criminal offense to withhold aid to persons in serious peril, while good Samaritan laws are those that restrict the civil liability of persons who unintentionally cause harm in the process of providing aid or that compensate the rescuer for losses suffered in the operation.[16] The first country to adopt a bad Samaritan statute was Russia, in 1845, and over the following century or so, most Continental countries followed suit, including Spain, Italy, Germany, France, the Netherlands, and most of Scandinavia.[17]

There are variations in this legislation but a common pattern exists.[18] The duty to rescue generally applies only in circumstances where victims are in mortal danger and unable to save themselves. The duty falls only on those who are consciously aware of the victim's predicament, who are close enough to intervene, and who have the effective means of intervention available to them. It does not apply where rescue is physically impossible or where attempting it would expose the rescuer or anyone else in the vicinity to serious danger. Some statutes impose criminal liability only where the victim has died or been seriously injured as a direct result of the bystander's refusal to act, and usually it is only those who remain totally inactive in face of the emergency that face prosecution. In other words, the offense can only be committed intentionally. It entails a conscious decision to refrain from extending even minimal aid to the victim or seeking to procure the help of others when doing so would create no specific danger to the bystander nor breach any substantial duty owed to other parties. In simple terms, the law forbids the deliberate eschewal of easy rescue of those facing life-threatening danger.

The most glaring exception to this pattern occurs in Anglo-American legal systems. In English-speaking jurisdictions, there has been longstanding resistance to enacting bad Samaritan laws and a general hesitancy towards good Samaritan provisions.[19] As Lord Devlin explained in

16. McIntyre, "Guilty Bystanders?," 158; Malm, "Bad Samaritan Laws," 710.

17. On the way legal and moral thinkers dealt with the issue prior to the Russian initiative, see Kleinig, "Good Samaritanism," 387–91. A draft of the 1833 penal code of Louisiana included such a duty, reflecting the utilitarian views of Jeremy Bentham, so Murphy, "Beneficence," 605.

18. For useful older surveys of European legislation, see Feldbrugge, "Good and Bad Samaritans"; Rudzunski, "Duty to Rescue." On French law, Tunc, "Volunteer." For a more recent comparative survey, see Pardun, "Good Samaritan."

19. On the issue of restitution, see Dagan, "In Defense." In New Zealand, the state assumes responsibility for meeting most of the medical costs incurred by the rescuer by including them under the rubric of an accident.

a lecture to the Medical Society in London in 1960, "The good Samaritan is a character un-esteemed by the English law." English law does not consider that an act done for another person's benefit but without his or her consent to be deserving of reward or of immunity from prosecution if the beneficiary subsequently objects. Devlin attributed this feature of English law to "the great attachment we have to the liberty of the individual" and to a fear that allowing the plea of doing good to others as a basis for overriding the absence of consent will be the thin end of the wedge.[20]

In 1967, the American state of Vermont became the first common law jurisdiction to criminalize bad Samaritans (with a fine not exceeding one hundred dollars) and to protect good Samaritans from civil suits for damages, and a handful of other American states have made failure to notify certain crimes a criminal offense (with relatively modest penalties).[21] In Australia's Northern Territory, the criminal code provides for up to seven years' imprisonment for "callous" failure to rescue, perhaps reflecting the special needs for interdependence in this harsh and sparsely populated environment.[22] But attempts to expand such provisions usually encounter strong opposition. According to one critic of the Anglo-American convention, "there is no doubt that our legal system is

---

20. Devlin, *Samples*, 90.

21. The Vermont statute provides that "(a) A person who knows that another is exposed to grave physical harm shall, to the extent that the same can be rendered without danger or peril to himself or without interference with important duties owed to others, give reasonable assistance to the exposed person unless that assistance or care is being provided by others. (b) A person who provides reasonable assistance in compliance with subsection (a) of this section shall not be liable in civil damages unless his acts constitute gross negligence or unless he will receive or expects to receive remuneration. Nothing contained in this subsection shall alter existing law with respect to tort liability of a practitioner of the healing arts for acts committed in the ordinary course of his practice. (c) A person who willfully violates subsection (a) of this section shall be fined not more than $100.00" (Vt. Stat. Ann. tit. 12, §.519 [1973]). Duty-to-aid provisions are also now in force in some other states, including Minnesota and Rhode Island, while duty-to-report requirements are found in several states, including Massachusetts, Washington, Hawaii, Wisconsin, Florida, New York, and Nevada. The Rhode Island statute reads: "Any person at the scene of an emergency who knows that another person is exposed to, or has suffered, grave physical harm shall, to the extent that he or she can do so without danger or peril to himself or herself or to others, give reasonable assistance to the exposed person. Any person violating the provisions of this section shall be guilty of a petty misdemeanor and shall be subject to imprisonment for a term not exceeding six (6) months or by a fine of not more than five hundred dollars ($500), or both" (R.I. GEm. LAWS § 11-56-1 [1994]).

22. Criminal Code Act s.155.

strongly against the view that I am my brother's keeper, or that I should be punished for not helping him, especially when any risk of danger to myself is involved."[23] Why is this?

RESISTANCE TO SAMARITAN LAWS

Opposition to Samaritan laws stems from a variety of procedural, moral, philosophical, and prudential objections to the principle of using penal law as an instrument for enforcing love of neighbor. But how persuasive are these objections, and how should they be evaluated in view of the message of Jesus' parable?

Practical Objections

It is often urged that bad Samaritan laws, even if desirable, would be unworkable in practice. A range of complicated definitional, procedural, and equity problems would bedevil any attempt to transpose a vague duty to rescue into precise and enforceable legal rules. These include the difficulty of determining when the duty comes into existence, for how long it persists, and on whom it devolves where multiple bystanders are present. Then there are the exorbitant costs of enforcing Samaritan laws and the problem of selective prosecution of offenders. There is also the potential for such laws to be abused. Villains, for example, knowing that the law requires bystanders to intervene, may feign injuries in order to lure would-be rescuers into a trap.

There is also the dilemma of how any risk associated with a potential rescue is to be assessed. What magnitude of risk is needed to absolve bystanders of the obligation to intervene? Would the remote possibility of contracting AIDS from the victim's wounds, for example, be acceptable justification for not intervening? What about fear of possible reprisal from the victimizer? There is also the question of what types of risk are considered relevant. Is it only risk to life and limb? Or do emotional, psychological, spiritual, and vocational risks also count (as they did, we proposed, for the priest and the Levite)? And how are degrees of risk to be measured, and by whom? Is it enough to rely on the subjective perceptions of the participants or are objective criteria needed? Given that the decision about whether or not to intervene typically has to be made

---

23. Woozley, "Duty," 1278.

very quickly, subjective considerations will always be entailed. But how can parties who were not present at the time, such as the police or the courts, assess the reasonableness or accuracy of these perceptions, without opening the door to prejudicial judgments based on the bystander's race, class, gender, education, or appearance?

There is also the difficulty of deciding on what severity of punishment is appropriate for violation of the duty to rescue.[24] Should the penalty be commensurate with the level of harm that subsequently befalls the victim? If the victim dies, for instance, should the bad Samaritan be punished for intentional homicide? Or should the sanctions be relatively modest? Should they serve mainly to draw attention to the existence of societal expectations about the issue and to underscore the moral deficits in the offender? Yet, if the crime attracts little more than a slap on the wrist, does this not send a signal that the breach of social responsibility is comparatively minor? If, on the other hand, the punishment is intended as a deterrent, is there a risk that people might be encouraged to attempt risky rescues well beyond their capabilities for fear of possible prosecution?

Now these are all legitimate concerns, and they present a sizable challenge to the drafters of any such legislation. But complexities such as these are not unique to Samaritan laws. In existing tort law, where there is an accepted duty to act stemming from particular professional, vocational, or personal relationships, similar complications arise but are not insurmountable. The lines of responsibility may be difficult to draw at times, but, as Antony Honoré shrewdly observes, "lawyers are professional line-drawers."[25] Also, the fact that a great many European countries have failure-to-rescue provisions on their books suggests that such laws are not intrinsically unworkable. Critics who allege the impracticality of Samaritan laws often ignore the long history of such provisions working tolerably well in Continental jurisdictions.[26]

---

24. See Davis, "How Much?" The penalties prescribed in existing bad Samaritan legislation, both in common-law and civil-law spheres, tend to be modest. For a theoretical defense of minimal sanctions, see Murphy, "Beneficence," 625–26.

25. Honoré, "Law, Morals," 234.

26. "The short and simple answer to the it-won't-work objection is to point out where and for how long it has been working" (Woozley, "Duty," 1290); so too Murphy, "Beneficence," 621.

Moral Objections

In addition to pragmatic concerns, various theoretical objections have been raised to the idea of criminalizing bad Samaritanism. One such objection centers on the damage allegedly done to the moral integrity of altruism by rendering it a legal requirement. To understand the basis of this objection, we need to consider the nature of altruism and examine its connection to the moral duty of rescue.

Few people would deny there is a clear moral duty to come to the aid of someone in serious peril when that person can be aided without risking grave damage to the rescuer or entailing significant wrongdoing. The rationale for this "duty of immediate rescue" resides fundamentally in the equal value of every human life and the equal respect that each deserves. It also resides in the common commitment implied in the social contract for citizens to be attentive to the conditions of human vulnerability that all share in. The duty is not without its conundrums, of course. One matter that has received considerable attention in recent discussion is the *moral significance of distance* in the duty to rescue.[27] If there is an inescapable obligation to rescue the nearby stranger in life-threatening distress, is there not a similar duty to rescue the distant stranger? If I am morally bound to save a child I find drowning in a local swimming pool, am I not also obligated to expend comparable energy to save a child starving to death in a foreign country? If not, why not?

In a seminal essay published in 1972, "Famine, Affluence and Morality," philosopher Peter Singer argued that we have the same duties of rescue towards the distant needy as we have towards the nearby needy, even if such impartiality runs counter to common human instincts. Singer has not resiled from this position since, though he concedes that the political implications of such a conclusion are too radical to be acceptable to the electorate.[28] Other philosophers have sought to differentiate the duty of immediate rescue from the more general obligations of benevolence owed to the disadvantaged everywhere. They have defended the legitimacy of giving preference to the needs of those who are physically or emotionally closest to us, without lessening the claims that remote strangers also make

---

27. For a discussion of the moral significance of proximity and distance in assessing obligations to the needy, see the various essays in Chatterjee, ed., *Ethics of Assistance*.

28. See Singer, "Outsiders." See also Singer, *Life*.

on our attention.[29] Richard Miller, for instance, argues that appreciating the equal worth of all people does not imply an equal level of concern for all. There may be legitimate reasons for prioritizing the needs of those who stand in a special relationship to us over those who do not.[30]

Arguably the category of special relationships includes those in desperate need whom we personally encounter in the course of our life, or whose sufferings we personally witness. It is this element of personal involvement that is partly why we intuitively feel that nearby rescue is morally more urgent than distant rescue. However fleeting it may be, personal encounter creates a particular relationship between the parties, a relationship that brings with it a responsibility to attend to any sudden peril that may arise. It is remarkable, in fact, how quickly the lives of total strangers become emotionally intertwined following personal contact, and it is by means of this intertwining that the abstract duty of rescue becomes activated or focused on this particular person and this particular event.

Having said that, it remains extremely difficult at the level of moral logic to qualify the duty of rescue on the grounds of arbitrary and accidental considerations of distance. At a physical and psychological level, however, such qualification seems to be essential. It is simply not possible for any individual to sustain an equal level of concern for every needy person on the planet. The human mind is not equipped for this. Indeed, any concerted effort to display a totally undiscriminating and self-subordinating love for everyone equally in the world would soon destroy us as independent moral agents and thus preclude love entirely.[31] There is also an intelligible basis for why it is we feel a stronger sense of obligation towards the needs of those closest to us over those more distant. After all, our very capacity for empathetic concern for others, which steers us towards genuinely moral commitments, arises out of our childhood experiences of intense attachment to parents and relatives. We learn other-regard from the focused attention we receive from our most intimate and

29. See Mantouvalou, "N v UK," 822–25.

30. Miller, "Moral Closeness," 101–22.

31. This is one reason why it would be a mistake to define love as, or to equate it with, self-sacrifice or selfless altruism. These may be a manifestation of love, but love sometimes requires us to eschew self-sacrifice to secure a larger good. Truly loving relationships also require something more than unilateral altruism; they require reciprocal give and take between the partners. Cf. Oord, *Defining Love*, 40–44, 52–60; Jackson, *Priority of Love*, 24–26, 54–56.

closed circle of contacts, and it is to them we first reciprocate such regard. The danger is that we allow our "natural" orientation towards our nearest and dearest to do the whole job of ethics. This would result in an unacceptable partiality. Instead, as Martha Nussbaum argues so eloquently, we must combine our inherent capacity for compassionate concern for those nearby with an ethical theory that pushes us constantly and consciously to expand the boundaries of concern beyond our own in-group to embrace those who are different to us and distant from us.[32] This includes people in desperate need in far-flung places whom we have not personally encountered and whose sufferings we will never directly witness.

So moral philosophers debate the ethical value of distance in the duty to rescue. But whether nearby rescue is considered to be morally more compelling than duties of goodwill to strangers in distant locations, or whether there is no substantive difference between the two circumstances, it is universally agreed that there is a moral requirement on us all to offer achievable and non-life-threatening assistance to those in severe danger whom we personally come across.

It is sometimes urged, however, that the attempt to use the coercive power of the law to encourage or enforce such acts of goodwill is detrimental to morality itself. Endeavoring to legislate for morality not only illegitimately aggrandizes the law by having it displace other forms of social control, it also erodes the very essence of morality itself, which is the free and willing compliance with what is good and true, not an enforced obedience to external rules. The virtue of altruism, in particular, is said to be destroyed if it is governed by the threat of punishment or the promise of reward. In the past, this argument has been used to oppose the awarding of restitution or compensation to good Samaritans who incur personal loss in the process of rescue on the grounds that a debt of gratitude, not material compensation, is the true reward for deeds of benevolence. At the same time, indemnifying good Samaritans against the possibility of being sued for negligence in carrying out their rescue would impugn their moral responsibility to be accountable for the consequences of their actions.[33]

---

32. Nussbaum, *Upheavals*, 386–92.

33. For a discussion of the oddity that we sometimes hold people responsible for the bad consequences of benevolently intended actions, see Driver, "Ethics."

This moral objection to Samaritan legislation is by no means persuasive however. Law and morality are not mutually exclusive domains, nor do they necessarily threaten each other. The law is deeply embedded in society's beliefs and values, and gives expression to a set of agreed moral convictions. Social opinion may change over time about which moral expectations should be inscribed in positive law, but there is nothing intrinsically objectionable to legislating morality. Criminal sanctions serve, among other things, to dramatize and reinforce the system of moral values that already prevail in a given society by naming and punishing behaviors considered especially outrageous. Moreover, transmuting certain moral precepts into legal prescriptions does not thereby diminish their power as moral truth. Nor does it deprive citizens of the opportunity to make free moral judgments about their actions. The moral vileness of murder, for example, is not lessened by the fact that it is illegal, and most people still refrain from killing because of its intrinsic wrongness rather than because of its unlawfulness. In most respects, the criminal law is not needed for citizens who are morally diligent but for those who are morally slack and require the threat of impaired self-interest to discourage them from doing wrong. As John Kleinig observes, criminal law is "not a substitute for morality, but a safeguard when the bonds of social morality threaten to break."[34]

The claim that indemnifying or compensating good Samaritans for their losses undermines the virtue of altruism is also uncertain. Auguste Comte coined the word "altruism" (from the Latin *alter*, "other") in the 1830s as a general term to designate solicitude for others. The concept has since been refined and appropriated by scholars in such diverse fields as psychology, sociology, economics, philosophy, religion, and evolutionary biology. Altruism is now defined in a variety of ways, but at a minimum it designates acts carried out with the primary intention of conferring benefit on others rather than securing obvious or tangible rewards for oneself.[35] Some theorists think altruism requires the complete absence

---

34. Kleinig, "Good Samaritanism," 406. On a related note, Woozley observes: "It is better that people refrain from harming each other, without having laws to make them refrain; but it is better to have laws to make them refrain than they do not refrain. It is better that people prevent harm to each other, without having laws to make them prevent it; it is also better to have laws to make them prevent it than they do not prevent it" ("Duty," 1300).

35. On the definition and psychology of altruism, see Schroeder et al., *Psychology*

of all external obligations. This means that any attempt to make rescue legally obligatory or to offer material reward for carrying it out necessarily erodes the altruistic quality of the act. Yet it is not true that altruism only arises in the absence of formal duty. A firefighter is only doing his job when he risks his life to rescue someone from a burning building. But the degree of courage and self-sacrifice involved are still considered by most people to be a praiseworthy expression of altruism.[36]

Pure altruism, in the sense of a total lack of self-interest, is extremely rare, perhaps nonexistent. Even in the most heroic acts, some degree of self-concern can be detected, even if it is only the wish to act or become or appear to be a courageous person. Virtue may be its own reward, but it is still the virtuous who receive the reward! But altruism is no less authentic for not being totally untrammeled. There is still a genuine selflessness involved in any decision to place the needs of others ahead of one's own immediate interests, and at substantial cost to oneself, even if one derives some emotional, psychic, or moral satisfaction from doing so.[37]

Some theorists argue that genuine altruism is impossible because human beings are innately egoistical. All human behavior, they claim, is fundamentally conditioned by the drive either to promote positive feelings or reduce negative ones. An act may seem selfless on the outside, but deep down it is motivated by the benefactor's need to alleviate the emotional discomfort he or she experiences in witnessing the recipient's distress. Because such "selfish" motivations are unavoidable, true altruism cannot, by definition, exist. Yet there are two reasons to challenge such skepticism. First, it is debatable whether human beings are, in fact, constitutionally and irreducibly egoistic. A case can be made for understanding human personhood ultimately as gift, as the outcome of the altruistic concern of others. Our very existence and development as autonomous persons, capable of moral actions that are sometimes selfish and sometimes generous, actually depends upon the selfless care we receive as newborn infants and children. The human brain, neuroscientists

---

of Helping, 18–20, 63–84. For a review of the philosophical discussion on altruism, see Dagan, "Good Samaritan," 1167–68, 1171–72.

36. On different kinds of duty to rescue, see Honoré, "Law, Morals," 225–42.

37. Recent research has clearly established that doing good deeds heightens a person's sense of well-being, even if those deeds are not in themselves pleasant or immediately rewarding. See the excellent review by Steger, Kashdan, and Shigehiro, "Being Good." See also the extensive discussion in Barasch, *Compassionate Life*, esp. 149–77.

are discovering, is hardwired for empathy, and it is our primal experience of being the objects of unmerited care by others that lights up the circuits. As Timothy Jackson explains, "We all depend on the kindness of strangers—initially our parents and/or their surrogates—to be fed, materially and spiritually. If we do not receive unconditional and unearned care early on, we never grow into responsible agents."[38]

This is one of the reasons why Jackson insists that, among the human virtues, love takes precedence over justice: we become persons capable of acting justly or unjustly only as a result of first being the recipients of love, a love that exceeds what justice requires.[39] Our very being, then, is the product of altruism, and a capacity for altruism is intrinsic to our human identity, albeit subject to constraining factors, including sin. "People get to be people and continue to act like people only when they are extended care *by* others and are schooled in how to extend it *to* others."[40]

Second, it is pointless to construe altruism in a way that is rendered meaningless by the nature of personal agency and reality of human interconnectedness. Human identity is intrinsically social or relational in character, so it is simply not possible to disengage a concern for the welfare of others from all traces of self-interest or self-involvement. Human persons are not isolated atoms. Our sense of selfhood and of possessing independent agency is organically constituted by our interactions with others. This means that, in general terms, we necessarily benefit ourselves when we act for the good of others (cf. Luke 6:38), even if we do not consciously seek such benefit or experience it in some tangible or temporal manner. As Jesus continually stresses in his teaching, self-realization comes through self-transcendence: we find ourselves by losing ourselves in love for others (cf. Mark 8:34–38; John 12:25). Altruism occurs when someone conscientiously acts for the benefit of another, knowing that the immediate costs of doing so significantly outweigh any direct sense of personal profit from the action, and without seeking anything in return.

Of course, there are varying degrees of altruistic motivation. In the case of emergency rescue, if the benefactor knows in advance that any material losses he or she might incur will be remedied by subsequent restitution, the extent of altruism involved may be diminished somewhat.

---

38. Jackson, *Priority of Love*, 57.
39. Ibid., 7, 29, 69.
40. Ibid., 63.

But it is not entirely destroyed. The helper still absorbs some losses that can never be restored, such as the loss of time or energy or mental focus, and elects to become vulnerable to unknowable psychological or physical consequences that may prove beyond repair. Pecuniary restitution is often the easiest reparation to offer. But it serves as little more than a symbolic acknowledgement that those who have suffered detriment as a result of their altruistic actions deserve restorative care every bit as much as those who have suffered it as a result of criminal selfishness.[41]

Certainly it would be unjustly harsh to make the rescued party liable for the payment of such restitution or compensation to the rescuer, especially when their predicament occurred through no fault of their own. The responsibility should be borne by the community as a whole and supplied from public funds. A commitment by society at large to make good, insofar as possible, the losses that good Samaritans experience could fairly be seen as a social investment in boosting levels of mutual care in the wider community. If people can be confident that their material expenses will be reimbursed, they may be more ready to accept the other irrecoverable losses and inconveniences entailed in lending assistance to others. Even a limited or calculated altruism is better than no altruism at all. A truly good Samaritan, like the character in the parable, will give no thought in advance to repayment. But a moderately decent Samaritan is still preferable to a thoroughly bad Samaritan!

Philosophical Objections

Behind the practical and moral objections raised to Samaritan laws often lurks a deeper philosophical objection. It is an objection that centers on the appropriate limits of criminal law in a liberal society on the one hand, and on the need to protect personal liberty from all unwarranted intrusions on the other. The argument has long held sway in the Anglo-American legal tradition that the proper function of penal law is to prevent people from actively doing harm, while it is the job of moral and religious education to encourage people actively to do what is good. This view was classically stated in 1879 by Thomas Babington Macaulay when he wrote, "the penal law must content itself with keeping men from doing positive harm, and must leave to public opinion, and to the teachers of

---

41. On the role of restitution, see Dagan, "Good Samaritan."

morality and religion, the office of furnishing men with motives for doing positive good."[42] To stand by and *allow* harm to befall another person may be morally reprehensible, but it is not the same as directly *causing* such harm. It is therefore not within the proper purview of criminal law to penalize it; were it to do so, it would unjustifiably infringe personal liberty.

In the Western liberal tradition, personal liberty is the supreme value.[43] Each person deserves to be completely sovereign over their own sphere of existence, free of forcible interference from others. The law has the essentially negative task of protecting individual sovereignty by deterring others from trespassing on personal space. Law *per se* is essentially detrimental to human freedom because it restricts personal choice. But this detriment is offset where it achieves a greater good. The only good that justifies the law interfering with individual autonomy is to prevent the commission of harm to others. Individuals may freely consent, in the form of an agreed contract, to have their liberty restricted by external controls. But the only ground on which coercion may be legitimately imposed against someone's free will is to forestall the doing of injury to others. Apart from that, the state should stay out of people's lives. It should remain neutral with respect to matters of value and leave people alone to pursue their own conceptions of the good life as they see fit. The law should not be *moralistic*, in the sense of enforcing morality for its own sake. Nor should it be *paternalistic*, in the sense of imposing constraints for the recipient's own good. It should not intervene to protect agents from the consequences of their own negative actions, nor should it compel them to do positive good. Citizens have a legal duty not to make things worse for one another, but they do not have a positive legal duty to make things better.

Against such a backdrop, Samaritan laws are opposed because they undermine liberal theory at several levels. To begin with, they seek to enforce positive rather than merely negative obligations, and thus expose agents to potentially unlimited, and excessively costly, duties of beneficence to others. If citizens may be obligated to confer the benefit of rescue

---

42. Macaulay, "Indian Penal Code," 314–15.

43. Murphy differentiates between the "Millian" or utilitarian strand and the "Lockean" or libertarian side of the liberal tradition. The former believes the only legitimate reason for restricting individual liberty is if it serves the greater good of others. The latter sees liberty as a natural right that should only be limited for the sake of greater liberty, "Beneficence," 625–43.

on strangers, why should they not also be obligated to devote their personal resources to feeding the hungry or educating the poor? In addition, Samaritan laws treat the omission of an act on the same basis as the commission of an act. This opens the door to all kinds of encroachments on citizens' private affairs. Most importantly, by seeking to coerce a person to make a critical life decision with respect to another, when that person has done nothing to interfere with the other's liberty rights, such laws are a violation of the most fundamental autonomy right individuals possess, namely, the freedom to direct their own lives independently of others. If courts are given the power to punish people for refusing to subordinate their own judgments and wishes to the needs of strangers, the state is no longer being neutral with respect to matters of value and is requiring individuals to conform to the values of the majority. "This subtle coercion towards homogeneous values," H. M. Malm suggests, "is something that a liberal should find distasteful."[44] The basic objection, then, is that Samaritan laws substantially corrode personal freedom. As John Kleinig observes, "In a culture steeped in individualism, nothing produces more hysteria than measures which encroach on individual liberty."[45]

One response to such libertarian cavils is simply to dismiss them as exaggerated and without empirical foundation. "If Good Samaritan law cannot be introduced without undermining the foundations of individual liberty," A. D. Woozley asked several decades ago, "how is it that it is alive and well in Denmark, France, Germany, Holland, and Norway?"[46] There has been no creeping erosion of individual liberty in these countries. Nor has there been any greater frequency of citizens snooping on each other's private affairs, since the laws are sufficiently precise to obviate this outcome. Samaritan laws may technically constitute an infringement of personal liberty. But not all infringements are of equal consequence, nor seriously jeopardize the principle of liberty itself. The restriction of the duty to rescue to relatively easy rescues means that any interference with personal liberty is minimal, especially given what is at stake for the victim.

It is also a strange kind of political morality that finds it acceptable that people should be legally allowed to die for want of help from unwilling bystanders just so those bystanders can retain their freedom to

44. Malm, "Liberalism," 21.
45. Kleinig, "Good Samaritanism," 403.
46. Woozley, "Duty," 1299; so too Feldbrugge, "Good and Bad Samaritans," 654.

exercise the moral virtue of choice. Nor are Samaritan laws the only example of penal law being used to impose positive obligations on people. There are situations of much lesser moral weight where this already happens, such as requiring citizens to serve on juries, or to testify in court when subpoenaed, or to file annual tax returns, or to supply their names and addresses when involved in traffic accidents, or, as in Australia, to vote in state and federal elections.

It is also possible to mount a normative defense of Samaritan laws within the terms of political liberalism itself. One common way of doing this is to challenge the assumption that failing in a positive duty is merely a case of *permitting* harm rather than *causing* harm. There is, to be sure, an important normative distinction between actively harming someone and allowing harm to occur, just as there is a difference between letting a person die (which is to permit an existing process to run its course) and deliberately killing someone (which is to initiate a new process). Negative agency is not the same as positive agency.[47] But the distinction is not watertight, and it could be argued that allowing a harm to continue, when it is within one's power to halt it, is itself a new cause of the harm getting worse. The passive agent cannot be held responsible for the original harm that has befallen the victim. But the agent is responsible for the harm being exacerbated or intensified by the decision to remain uninvolved. On this understanding, Samaritan laws are not a matter of legislating for benevolence, but of legislating against violations of a negative duty not to act to someone else's detriment.

This proposal is not without its problems. There are significant philosophical difficulties in defining causation and in determining the extent to which a failure to act contributes causatively to the harm suffered.[48] Furthermore, not all forms of criminal responsibility depend on causing positive harm to another party. Some acts are criminalized because of their *potential* to precipitate harm (e.g., driving under the influence, or conspiracy to commit a crime, or attempted murder) or because they breach a statutory obligation (e.g., tax evasion). The perpetrating or preventing of actual harm is not the only recognized warrant for imposing criminal liability, so there is no absolute doctrinal requirement to tie required rescue to the positive harm principle.

---

47. Cf. Kleinig, "Good Samaritanism," 403–4.
48. See the discussion in Murphy, "Beneficence," 617–18.

Another strategy for defending Samaritan laws on liberal assumptions is to argue that failure to rescue constitutes a violation of the victim's human rights and therefore should be subject to criminal proscription. The right to rescue is but an extension of the right to life, which is grounded in the intrinsic dignity of every human person. Enactment of the legal duty merely gives formal expression to this preexisting human right. On this understanding, negative freedom (freedom from external constraint) is not the most fundamental expression of freedom but is rather a means to a higher end. The ultimate expression of freedom is self-determination, the ability to act on one's own goals and aspirations. A life-threatening situation places the ability of the victim to achieve such positive freedom in extreme jeopardy, and the negative freedom of the benefactor must give way to this more essential dimension of freedom.

Again, this proposal encounters difficulties. Even if the right to rescue were accepted as an expression of the right to life (which is open to debate), there is still the difficulty of how one moves from the existence of a general right to the imposition of a specific duty of intervention on disinclined bystanders, especially one that requires rescuers to expend their own resources to discharge it. Normally in liberal theory, the corresponding duty called forth by specific rights is the duty not to interfere with the exercise of the other's right; it is not a duty to expend oneself in the interests of the other. A further criticism of rights-based arguments is that they may give rise to the "freerider problem." People may be encouraged selfishly to put themselves in danger in a way that obliges others to render aid, thus taking advantage of their neighbor's goodwill.[49]

Recent litigation attempts to ground required rescue in human rights provisions have not proved highly successful. In the case mentioned earlier where a claim was brought against the Glasgow City Council for failing to warn its tenants of the risks posed by another violent tenant, who went on to murder his next-door neighbor, the court struck down a claim made under Article 2 (the right to life) of the European Convention on Human Rights (ECHR) and s. 6(1) of the Human Rights Act 1998. It did so partly on the grounds that there was no certainty of a real or immediate threat to life and partly because the Council qua landlord was not the body on whom the corresponding duty devolved.[50]

49. Malm, "Bad Samaritan Laws," 713–18.
50. UKHL, "Mitchell vs. Glasgow City Council."

In another case, the European Court of Human Rights held, by a split decision, in May 2008, that the British Government did not breach Article 3 of the ECHR forbidding inhuman and degrading treatment by deporting a seriously ill woman to her country of origin, Uganda, despite the fact that doing so placed her at a high risk of severe suffering and early death. The court ruled that the woman's potential medical complications did not reach the minimum threshold of severity to qualify as severe ill-treatment under Article 3, and that the UK government was not liable to prevent suffering experienced extraterritorially. Critics of the ruling have argued that the decision to deport the woman violated the moral duty to rescue the nearby needy and has "set a precedent that undermines the belief that human rights law has a role to play for those most in need of it." According to Virginia Mantouvalou, the judgment "constitutes a statement that the dignity of the poor and needy foreigner amongst us does not carry equal worth to ours, who are privileged enough to live in affluent communities and who are not prepared to make an effort to rescue them, even at relatively low cost."[51]

Yet another way of defending Samaritan laws on liberal premises is to ground them in the protective functions of the state or in the social contract between individuals that gives rise to human government and generates a regime of agreed entitlements and responsibilities. The state has a duty to protect the general welfare of its people, and one way of doing this is to deputize all citizens to act as monitors of situations of peril. Citizens are placed under a duty to report emergencies or to render easy assistance as a service to the common good. This is not an undue interference with their liberties because it entails only a small amount of effort or minor inconvenience yet reaps considerable collective benefits.

One virtue of this approach is that the duty to rescue is conceived as a matter of public interest, not just as a private transaction between the Samaritan and the person in danger. One difficulty lies in the fictive concept of deputation. It cannot simply be inferred that because the government has a function, it is the responsibility of every citizen to assist in discharging that function. The state has a duty to provide education, for example, but citizens are not automatically required to activate that function if they happen to find themselves in a situation where education is needed. It may be valid to require citizens to be supportive of the

---

51. Mantouvalou, "Duty," 843.

protective tasks of the state (e.g., by notifying the authorities of emergencies); it is more difficult to justify requiring them to intervene personally in situations where protection is needed.[52]

Still another approach is to concede that required rescue is, indeed, a positive legal duty of beneficence but to offer normative grounds for restricting this duty to emergency situations alone, so that it does not threaten the principle of individual liberty nor entail legal moralism. Liam Murphy argues, for example, that the general duty of beneficence devolves principally on the state. Individuals are morally obliged to bear their fair share of the collective burden, but not to assume it all. The state discharges its duty primarily through social policy and through the provision of well-organized and well-trained professional services. The only situation where the involvement of ordinary citizens is indispensable is an emergency situation that requires immediate action by whoever happens to be available. In such cases, the use of a criminal sanction is appropriate to underscore the moral obligations people have to others in such circumstances. In every other situation, alternative remedies are available, and in principle the state should not use criminal law to achieve what is better achieved by nonpunitive means. There are, therefore, both normative and utilitarian grounds for restricting the criminal duty of beneficence to definable emergency situations that entail minimal risk of harm for the rescuer, and that include compensation for any nonphysical losses incurred.

Clearly, then, Samaritan laws constitute something of a challenge to the traditional principles of political liberalism, with its commitment to individual autonomy and minimal coercion. To the extent that the legitimacy of penal law is conceived solely in terms of its function in preventing the causing of positive harm, criminalizing the impassivity of bad Samaritans is difficult to justify philosophically. Some liberal theorists have found various ways to circumvent the dilemma, but none has proved universally persuasive. Samaritan legislation will always be difficult to square with liberal theory and anthropology.

Prudential Objections

In addition to the pragmatic, moral, and philosophical objections discussed so far, there are also prudential objections to passing Samaritan

---

52. So Malm, "Bad Samaritan Laws," 712–13.

laws. That is to say, even if such legislation were morally justified; even if the pragmatic problems could be overcome by skillful legal drafting; and even if these laws could be accommodated within liberal theory, they are still unlikely to achieve much good, and their benefits would not outweigh the problems and the costs involved. The goal of promoting mutual aid in society would therefore be better served by noncoercive means rather than by dint of penal law.

For H. M. Malm, it is the unlikelihood of bad Samaritan laws achieving any positive benefits that militates against having them. None of the advantages sought by such laws would eventuate in practice. If the intention were to save more lives at minimal risk to others, greater good would come from changing laws relating to organ donation from an opt-in to an opt-out arrangement than from criminalizing bad Samaritans. If the goal is to punish people who show outrageous disregard for the welfare of others, the reality is that even in those jurisdictions that have them, such laws are rarely invoked. Even when they are, convictions are infrequent since too many extenuating circumstances usually exist. If the goal is deterrence, it is improbable that the tiny minority of people who are unwilling to stir themselves to assist people in extreme need would be deterred by criminal penalties, and typically modest penalties at that. If the goal is to make a symbolic statement about the kind of values society wants its citizens to internalize, there is the risk that such laws will have the opposite effect. Laws that are perceived as merely symbolic diminish respect for the rule of law and may send the message that the associated values are not greatly prized at all since they are not thought worth enforcing. Malm concludes that rather than punishing bad Samaritans, it would be better to reward good Samaritans for their actions (not necessarily in monetary ways) and to educate people to notify the authorities of harmful circumstances.[53]

John Pardun similarly accepts that while Samaritan laws can be justified within the terms of a liberal polity, the testimony of experience in common law jurisdictions is they have little value. Their putative function of providing a moral compass for social responsibility is undermined by the unwillingness of the courts to enforce them (existing laws in US states have been rarely enforced, and in some cases never). In practice, the laws punish nothing and therefore furnish an ineffective symbolism.

---

53. Ibid., esp. 742–50.

Samaritan legislation is an exercise in futility that is "no more effective than the Good Samaritan parable in the Bible itself. We do not need that lesson recapitulated to know right from wrong."[54]

More could be said about the contested merits of good and bad Samaritan legislation. The arguments are complex and involved. The purpose of rehearsing them here is not so much to arrive at a definitive position. It is rather to illustrate how bringing contemporary legal debates into dialogue with relevant biblical teaching can help clarify the values-commitments and ideological presuppositions underpinning present social and political policy, in particular the supreme value modern society places on individual autonomy. It can also offer a fresh perspective on current debates by viewing the issues at stake from a distinctive viewpoint, one in which law, morality, religion, and personhood intersect with one another in different and deeper ways than is envisaged in the modern liberal order.

SUMMARY

In biblical and Jewish law, intervening to rescue a neighbor from mortal danger or from overwhelming distress was a clear legal obligation. The priest and the Levite in the parable faltered in their legal as well as in their moral duty, a point often lost in contemporary expositions of the story. Admittedly, the biblical commandments they contravened carried no prescribed sanctions, and they could have argued, on technical grounds, for a different set of legal priorities. But as far as the parable is concerned, in electing to place their own professional honor above the needs of the dying stranger, they stood in breach of the most fundamental principles of divine law.

By contrast, the fundamental principle in the current Western legal system is personal liberty, and it is out of reified deference to such liberty that the attempt to require people by law to act magnanimously is considered unacceptable. It is deemed tantamount to legislating for morality, which not only undermines the essence of morality as voluntary compliance with the good but also illegitimately aggrandizes the law by having it displace noncoercive forms of social control, such as education and religion. Yet, as the biblical writers understood well, it is simply

---

54. Pardun, "Good Samaritan," 609.

not possible to treat law and morality as neatly divisible spheres. There is nothing intrinsically wrong with legislating morality. Law inevitably entails the transcription of moral precepts into legal rules, and those precepts lose nothing of their moral persuasiveness for being inscribed in legislation. The law reflects and reinforces, rather than replaces or reduces, the dictates of morality.

It is also hard to understand why a duty to rescue should be considered essential in the context of certain legally defined relationships between the parties but not with respect to mere acquaintances or strangers. The existence of voluntary consent may be inferred in the former case, but in practice such consent is more notional than real. When human life or bodily integrity is at stake, and when the possibility of easy rescue exists, it seems bizarre that the moral duty to assist should be underwritten by the law only when the individuals involved are linked in some lawfully recognized manner that, allegedly, preserves their autonomy. Current law, in essence, reflects the viewpoint of the priest and the Levite more than it does the perspective of Jesus or the merciful Samaritan.

There is a case to be made, then, for a change to current law, so that criminal law better reflects moral truth at this point. Samaritan laws—both those that penalize bad Samaritans for outrageous indifference to the welfare of their fellows and those that protect or recompense good Samaritans for their losses—are best justified in terms of their symbolic import. Such provisions give formal expression to the supreme value of human life, to the bonds of solidarity and empathy that comprise human identity and that bind people together in social community, and to the ongoing need human beings have to be committed to one another's rescue and restoration when severe harm befalls them, whether that harm stems from the experience of criminal victimization or from another cruel twist of fate. There are some things we can never do for ourselves as isolated individuals, and restoration to wholeness in the wake of disempowering or life-threatening circumstances is one of them.

Samaritan provisions also remind us that our obligations to restorative care extend beyond the normal bonds of human affection and relationship to apply to complete strangers in our midst. The absence of a duty to rescue in current criminal law implies that those who are strangers to us have no compelling claim on our attention, which was what the priest and the Levite apparently thought.

In practice, bad Samaritan laws would probably only be invoked in circumstances where there has been blatant contempt for the plight of another. There is good reason to limit the legal duty of rescue to emergency situations alone where rescue can be accomplished at minimal risk to the rescuer, and for employing only moderate sanctions for violation.[55] Such a restricted scope does not impugn the value of the legislation, for its function is more to remind us of our shared moral commitments than it is to regulate precisely our interactions with one another. It is the natural inclination of most people to come to the aid of those in serious distress, so the job of bad Samaritan laws is less to compel compliance to an onerous responsibility from a reluctant constituency than to serve as a symbolic expression of the bonds of mutual concern and solidarity that unite us with one another, as well as to provide the means of exposing and denouncing particularly hideous examples of nonchalance in face of remediable evil, such as abandoning children to abuse.[56]

To say such laws are primarily symbolic is not to say they are *merely* symbolic, in the sense of being unenforced or unenforceable.[57] Rather, it is to say that they serve principally as markers of the borderlines of moral obligation more than as procedural mechanisms for resolving conflict or preventing harm. In the language of Jesus' parable, they symbolize what

---

55. See Murphy, "Beneficence," 644–65.

56. Malm cites the example of David Cash, "a friend of Jeremy Strohmeyer who watched Strohmeyer lure a seven-year-old girl into the restroom of a Nevada casino and begin to molest her. Cash didn't stay to watch the sexual assault and ultimate murder, but neither did he try to help the girl or notify authorities . . . In response to this case, over 20,000 people signed a petition seeking to have Cash punished for his omission. But in the absence of a bad Samaritan law, nothing could be done" ("Bad Samaritan Laws," 742). At the time of writing, legislation is before the New Zealand Parliament that would make failure to protect children, the elderly, and the disabled from abuse a criminal offense, with a maxium penalty of ten years in prison. The duty will fall on all adults living in the household or the relevant institution, and, according to the Minister of Justice, could well extend to neighbors and others in "very close proximity" to the household.

57. Malm opposes merely symbolic (that is, unenforced) laws, since they undermine respect for the rule of law and fail to motivate obedience ("Bad Samaritan Laws," 748). But penal laws are all symbolic to some degree, see Marshall, *Beyond Retribution*, 131–43. Moreover, symbolic does not necessarily mean unenforced. The symbolic power of the law is not wholly dependent on the frequency or intensity of its enforcement. The law serves as only one of an integrated array of norm-enforcing signals society sends about appropriate or inappropriate behavior, as a way of preventing or controlling disorder (cf. Keizer, "Disorder").

it means to be a neighbor to those who fall into desperate straits. Even if they are rarely used in practice, Samaritan laws attest to the fact, sometimes forgotten in liberal society, that it is impossible to be truly free on our own, for we cannot escape from being our brother or sister's keeper.

In the last sermon he preached, Martin Luther King summoned his hearers to cultivate the attribute of "dangerous unselfishness" displayed by the Samaritan in Jesus' parable. King imagined that when the priest and the Levite came across the man in the ditch, they asked themselves, "If I stop to help this man, what will happen to me?" and out of fear for their individual safety they opted not to get involved. The Samaritan reversed the question: "If I do *not* stop and help this man, what will happen *to him*?" That is what makes the Good Samaritan the ideal paradigm for citizens and policymakers ever after.

It is, of course, beyond the reach of criminal legislation or social policy to manufacture such selflessness in the human heart; Jesus' brief parable is infinitely more powerful in that respect. But what the law can do, and arguably should do, is reflect and reinforce the shared moral sentiment of society that there are some circumstances where anything other than a self-subordinating action to rescue a victim would constitute so serious a betrayal of the meaning of our humanity, with all its shared vulnerabilities, that it warrants the strongest condemnation available to us: the censure of penal sanction.

PART 2

Restoration and the Offender

(Luke 15:11–32)

THE PRODIGAL SON

Then Jesus said, "There was a man who had two sons. The younger of them said to his father, 'Father, give me the share of the property that will belong to me.' So he divided his property between them. A few days later the younger son gathered all he had and traveled to a distant country, and there he squandered his property in dissolute living.

When he had spent everything, a severe famine took place throughout that country, and he began to be in need. So he went and hired himself out to one of the citizens of that country, who sent him to his fields to feed the pigs. He would gladly have filled himself with the pods that the pigs were eating; and no one gave him anything. But when he came to himself he said, 'How many of my father's hired hands have bread enough and to spare, but here I am dying of hunger! I will get up and go to my father, and I will say to him, "Father, I have sinned against heaven and before you; I am no longer worthy to be called your son; treat me like one of your hired hands."' So he set off and went to his father.

But while he was still far off, his father saw him and was filled with compassion; he ran and put his arms around him and kissed him. Then the son said to him, 'Father, I have sinned against heaven and before you; I am no longer worthy to be called your son.' But the father said to his slaves, 'Quickly, bring out a robe—the best one—and put it on him; put a ring on his finger and sandals on his feet. And get the fatted calf and kill it, and let us eat and celebrate; for this son of mine was dead and is alive again; he was lost and is found!' And they began to celebrate.

Now his elder son was in the field; and when he came and approached the house, he heard music and dancing. He called one of the slaves and asked what was going on. He replied, 'Your brother has come, and your father has killed the fatted calf, because he has got him back safe and sound.' Then he became angry and refused to go in. His father came out and began to plead with him. But he answered his father, 'Listen! For all these years I have been working like a slave for you, and I have never disobeyed your command; yet you have never given me even a young goat so that I might celebrate with my friends. But when this son of yours came back, who has devoured your property with prostitutes, you killed the fatted calf for him!'

Then the father said to him, 'Son, you are always with me, and all that is mine is yours. But we had to celebrate and rejoice, because this brother of yours was dead and has come to life; he was lost and has been found.'"

7

Offending, Restoration, and the Law-Abiding Community

If the parable of the Good Samaritan is the most widely known of Jesus' parables, and the one that has had the greatest impact at the sociopolitical and institutional level of society, the parable of the Prodigal Son is the most loved of Jesus' parables, and the one that has made the greatest impression at a personal, aesthetic, and spiritual level. It is the moving story of a young man who demands his share of the family inheritance in advance of his father's death, squanders it in wild living in a distant land, and then comes to his senses and returns home deeply chastened, where he is joyfully reconciled with his father and profoundly resented by his older brother. The influence of this parable on Christian thought and practice, and on Western cultural formation in general, has been incalculable. It is the parable most frequently represented in European art and has furnished the subject matter for numerous works of music, choreography, drama, film, literature, philosophy, and spirituality.[1]

At over 390 words in the Greek text, it is also the longest and the most elaborate of Jesus' parables, with a substantial cast of actors and uncommonly well-drawn characterization.[2] The narrative is full of descriptive

---

1. See, for example, Siebald and Ryken, "Prodigal, (who note that it is the parable most frequently alluded to by Shakespeare). More briefly, see Donahue, *Gospel in Parable*, 152; Fitzmyer, *Luke*, 1083.

2. The characters are not as fully developed, of course, as one would find in full-scale dramas or novels or even narrative poetry or epic ballads. But within the limits of the parabolic genre, each character has a marked degree of individuality. Francois Bovon suggests that each character is characterized by a verb chosen with care: the son "came to himself" (v. 17), the father "had compassion" (v. 20), the elder brother

detail and resonant with allusions to, or echoes of, a wide range of biblical stories, characters, and events, as well as wider mythemes and cultural archetypes.[3] It is these features that have attracted extensive allegorizing of the parable at the hands of Christian interpreters down through the centuries.[4] Classical allegorization is now generally repudiated as an appropriate hermeneutical technique for expounding Jesus' parables. Yet the texture of this parable is so richly layered and evocative that it invites interpretation at multiple levels and from a diversity of perspectives. As Kenneth Bailey, a scholar who has spent the best part of his long academic career pondering this one parable, observes: "Nearly everyone who wrestles seriously with this pericope ends up with a sense of awe at its inexhaustible content."[5]

THE MOST BEAUTIFUL STORY EVER TOLD

Reasons why this exquisite parable has exercised such a powerful grip on the Christian imagination are not hard to find. In purely literary

---

"was angry" (v. 28), with the three parts of the story expanding on these three verbs ("First Reading," 60).

3. Parallels of the story have been uncovered in Babylonian and Canaanite literature, in the Lotus Sutra, and in Greek papyri. "Yet none of the parallels or the retellings can measure up to or compare with the moving force of this story put on the lips of Jesus in this Gospel" (Fitzmyer, *Luke*, 1084). Roger Aus highlights parallels with the rabbinic narrative of R. Eliezer ben Hyrcanus, and argues that both stories draw on popular oral motifs of the day ("Luke 15:11–32," 443–69). The story is replete with intertextual echoes from the Old Testament (Aus identifies fourteen Jewish motifs), with the cycle of the Joseph stories in Gen 37–50 affording several reminiscences. The parable also evokes the host of biblical stories involving older and younger brothers, such as Cain and Abel, Ishmael and Isaac, Aaron and Moses, Esau and Jacob, Joseph and Benjamin, in which the younger ones are often rebels and the older ones niggardly and rigid, see Derrett, *Law*, 116–21. Or where favoritism is shown by father to the younger son at the expense of the older, see Scott, *Hear Then*, 112–14. Bailey highlights the parallels with the Genesis story of Jacob and Esau, although his proposal that Jesus consciously reformulated this story in this parable seems forced and implausible (*Jacob*, cf. Moxnes, "Review," 354–56). For a comprehensive discussion of Greco-Roman parallels, analogies, and thematic comparisons, see Holgate, *Prodigality*. Holgate argues that instead of searching for the closest parallel, it is better to ask what accounts for the relationship that exists between the parable and all other uses of common motifs and language.

4. See Tissot, "Patristic Allegories"; Just Jr., *Luke*, 246–53. More briefly, Snodgrass, *Stories*, 126–27. More generally on allegory, see Snodgrass, "Allegorizing," "Modern Approaches," and *Stories*, 1–35.

5. Bailey, *Poet and Peasant*, 158.

terms, it is a masterpiece of storytelling. Sometimes described as the most beautiful story ever told, it is lauded by one literary critic as "an absolutely flawless piece of work."⁶ It employs a wide range of narrative devices and rhetorical techniques, including verbal repetition, structural and thematic parallelisms, the use of interior monologue to disclose the characters' inner thoughts and motivations, a strong emphasis on direct speech as a means of highlighting important issues, and a deliberate withholding of key information on events and persons to create gaps and teasing ambiguities.⁷ The characters are all true-to-life, utterly believable at one level, yet startlingly unconventional at another. The plot is realistic and straightforward, moving in a simple linear sequence through a succession of brief scenes, yet involving ironical reversals and concluding on a strikingly open-ended note. Parables, in general, function as "hermeneutically unfinished stories,"⁸ and nowhere is this more obvious than in the parable of the Prodigal Son. Listeners are left dangling in suspense, not knowing whether the angry elder son relented of his indignation and joined the family festivities or whether he stood his ground on a self-evident matter of principle. As Bernard Scott puts it, "The parable's ending leaves the hearer without an ending."⁹ The resolution of the affair is purposefully unstated, requiring listeners to finish the story themselves and in so doing to ponder deeply where their own sympathies lie in the whole affair.

Equally unresolved in the parable is which of the three main characters is intended to be the major focus of attention. The parable's traditional title suggests that the story is principally about the *younger son*, and there are still scholars who defend this view.¹⁰ Dan Via, for example, observes that it is the youngest son's actions that drive the entire plot and that "the main interest of the story as a whole is seen to be the redemp-

---

6. Robert M. Bridges, quoted in Hunter, *Parables*, 61. Cf. Snodgrass, *Stories*, 117.

7. Cf. Holgate, *Prodigality* 56–65; Ramsey, "Plots, Gaps"; Sellew, "Monologue," esp. 245–47.

8. Kelber, *Oral*, 62. In a helpful analysis, Susan Wittig explains how parables are semantically constructed so as to create a multiplicity of meanings and a variety of significations, "Theory"; cf. Crossan, "Metamodel."

9. Scott, *Hear Then*, 122.

10. The title "Prodigal Son" is found as a marginal note in sixteenth-century English Bibles, and is derived from the Vulgate's *De filio prodigo*. The traditional German title for the parable is *Der verlorene Sohn*.

tion of the prodigal."[11] More commonly today, however, it is the *father* who is viewed as the main actor, since he is mentioned in most scenes of the story (the word *patēr* occurs almost a dozen times in the text), and both halves of the account conclude with his words of celebration. The father's character is the most morally developed of the three main players, with the prodigal son arguably being the least developed.[12] Both structurally and didactically, it is the father's actions and values that are critical to the meaning of the story.[13] Jeremias and Fitzmyer therefore think the account would be better titled, "the parable of the Forgiving Father" or "the parable of the Father's Love,"[14] while Donahue coins the tag, "the parable of the Prodigal Father."[15] Yet a case can also be made for seeing the *elder son* as the focal point of the narrative, especially since it is his sullen response to his father's forgiveness of his brother that gives the parable its sharply polemical edge.[16] The story's end-stress is achieved in the only two-way conversation in the parable, in which the father replies to the stinging criticisms of his firstborn son, who evidently serves as a cipher for the scribes and Pharisees (cf. 15:1–3).

Some suggest that both sons have equal attention. T. W. Manson calls it "the parable of the Two Sons,"[17] Ernst Fuchs, "the parable of the Prodigal Sons,"[18] and Timothy Keller, "the parable of the Two Lost Sons."[19] Several scholars have defended the authenticity and literary integrity of the extant account, which few scholars now seriously question, on the ground that its dyadic structure coheres with other dominical parables

---

11. Via, *Parables*, 164, 167. Also Green, *Luke*, 578 ("... as important as the father is to this parable, centre stage belongs to the younger son").

12. So Ramsey, "Plots, Gaps," 37. The father is consistently patient and gracious, whereas the prodigal's motivations are more ambiguous and the elder son does one thing and thinks another.

13. Holgate, *Prodigality*, 53–54, 67.

14. Jeremias, *Parables*, 128; Fitzmyer, *Luke*, 1084.

15. Donahue, *Gospel in Parable*, 160 (although Donahue rightly notes that it is really a parable about relationships, 152–53). This title is also used by Caputo, *Weakness*, 215.

16. Cf. Bovon (citing D. Buzy), "First Reading," 49. Cf. Hunter, *Parables*, 61.

17. Manson, *Sayings*, 284; Beasley-Murray, *Jesus*, 113; Bailey, *Jacob*, 95.

18. Fuchs, *Studies*, 160–62.

19. Keller, *Prodigal God*, xiv, cf. 17 (Keller's exegesis focuses almost entirely on the elder son).

that involve two contrasting types (e.g., Luke 7:41–42; 18:9–14; Matt 21:28–31; Matt 25:1–13).[20]

But to insist on a dominant protagonist in the drama is to miss the important narrative clue given at the very outset of the story. The parable's pointed introduction—"A certain man had two sons" (v. 11)—functions to direct our attention away from any one individual performer and on to the relational bonds between them. Relational pronouns are repeatedly used when identifying the main characters in the episode: *my* father, *his* son, *your* brother, *my* son, *your* son. The parable evidently is all about interpersonal relationships. Even in the description of the prodigal's degraded lifestyle in vv. 13b–19, fully half the text is occupied by a soliloquy in which the prodigal reflects on his relationship with "my father" (vv. 17–19). It is what Joachim Gnilka calls the "triangular relationship" between the family members that is the main subject of interest.[21] Each son relates differently to his father, though the father's relationship with both boys is notably consistent and equitable.[22] The relationship between the siblings is obviously strained, which perhaps contributed to the prodigal's offending in the first place,[23] with the older son judging himself to be radically

---

20. Bultmann, *Synoptic Tradition*, 196. Another argument in favor of the original integrity of the parable is the presence of pre-Lukan stylistic features in both halves of the story, Fitzmyer, *Luke*, 1085; Marshall, *Luke*, 605–6. For a neat listing of all other relevant considerations, see Forbes, "Repentance and Conflict," 212–13; Manson, *Sayings*, 285–86; Tolbert, "Prodigal Son," 11; Carlston, "Reminiscence." The vast majority of critics consider the parable to be dominical (even the Jesus Seminar renders the whole story in pink), despite the fact that it shows signs of Luke's redactional pen and it coheres with major Lukan themes. Luke Timothy Johnson helpfully observes that the parable combines "the distinctive note of originality we associate with Jesus, and the distinctive literary sensibility of Luke. It is however impossible entirely to disentangle tradition from redaction, precisely because Luke covers the traces of his sources so thoroughly" (*Luke*, 3:239). Luise Schotroff once ascribed the parable to Lukan redaction but then changed her mind. She now ascribes it to "a vital orality" in which there is no one author (*Parables*, 243 n. 20). For an important reassessment of the notion of "anonymous orality," however, see Bauckham, *Eyewitnesses*.

21. Gnilka, *Jesus*, 97–98. So too Rohrbaugh, "Dysfunctional Family," 144–45; cf. Derrett, *Law*, 103; Brad Young observes that "the family problems in the parable are immense" (*Jewish Theologian*, 144).

22. Cf. Tolbert, "Prodigal Son," 11; Bailey, *Poet and Peasant*, 205; Snodgrass, *Stories*, 124.

23. Bailey argues that the fact the older son does not intervene to stop his brother's insulting behavior towards his father or to facilitate reconciliation between them, as would be expected in the cultural context, shows how poor the relationships were in the family (*Poet and Peasant*, 168–69); also Young, *Jewish Theologian*, 146–47.

dissimilar to his brother in virtue and considerably more ethical than his father in practice (vv. 28–30). Yet as the story unfolds, it emerges that the two boys are fundamentally alike in disposition and equally dislocated from their rightful place in the family. Both sons are lost to their father, though in different ways: one in a far country of self-indulgence, the other in a quagmire of self-pity and moral rectitude. Neither appreciates his father's love and neither loves his sibling. The parable could appropriately be titled, "the Tender-Hearted Father and His Two Difficult Sons," with the spotlight falling on the ruptured nature of their relationships and the restoring actions required to secure reconciliation.

This relational focus of the story is not simply a narrative deduction; it is also a cultural prerequisite for a tale that was, in Richard Rohrbaugh's words, "originally a Mediterranean story, told by a Mediterranean storyteller, for a Mediterranean audience."[24] Personal identity in ancient Mediterranean peasant society was essentially a relational, not an individualistic, construct. That is to say, an individual's sense of self—of who one is and where one belongs in the world—stemmed first of all from one's place in the family unit and secondly from participation in the village community. At the center of peasant psychology resided not the autonomous, self-sufficient ego of European modernity, but what anthropologists term a "dyadic" or group-oriented personality. This is where self-understanding and self-worth involve the internalizing and satisfying of the expectations of those to whom one is socially connected, especially those within one's immediate kin group.[25] Against such a backdrop, it is simply not possible to appreciate the significance of the actions of any of the characters in the parable without taking into account the ties of loyalty and identity that bound them together as a household unit and as a local community. Conformity to the values and role expectations of the wider collective was the *sine qua non* for maintaining social cohesion and preserving personal emotional and physical health.

This leads to a second reason why the parable has been so highly prized in the Western tradition: its penetrating insights into human psy-

24. Rohrbaugh, "Dysfunctional Family," 143.

25. See Malina, *New Testament World*, 63–89. It is possible to exaggerate the lack of individuality in antiquity (on which see Bauckham, *Eyewitnesses*, 172–74), but the socially embedded nature of personal identity was still more strongly apparent then than it is in Western society today.

chology. Although it aspires to be much more than a wisdom tale about the complexity of interpersonal relationships in general, and the emotional turmoil of parent-child conflict in particular, what makes this parable engrossing is the way it probes human psychology so profoundly. The story deals with universal themes of freedom and responsibility, leaving and returning, exile and homecoming, offending and forgiveness, estrangement and reconciliation, honor and shame, generosity and gracelessness, and of justice, jealousy, and joy. In particular, it explores the anatomy of moral change: what spawns it, what it requires in practice, what it achieves in effect, and how it may sometimes be resisted by those who consider themselves intrinsically more righteous than others.

Once again, it is the relational focus of the story that enables it to convey such mental and emotional intensity. There is an intentional parallelism between the two halves of the story that encourages hearers to draw comparisons between the personalities and motivations of the two sons. Both boys act high-handedly towards their father; both work in the fields; both experience a feeling of lack; both interact with servants; both travel to the house from some distance away; both are met outside by their father; both state their intentions directly; both assess their own moral condition; both are called "sons" by their father; and in both cases, the father has the final word. There is an intriguing pattern of similarities and differences between the two boys. At one level, they resemble each other profoundly in disposition and outlook, and to some extent in behavior. At another level, they differ sharply with respect to the things that matter most when relationships come under stress or have been fractured by selfishness. It is the remarkable sensitivity with which it portrays such relational and psychological dynamics that has enabled the parable, down through the centuries and across many cultures, to speak into multiple areas of human experience, including, as we will see, that of justice making.

THE GOSPEL WITHIN A GOSPEL

Beyond its literary artistry and its acute psychological perceptiveness, the parable has been cherished most of all for its theological value. The parable is unsurpassed in the biblical tradition in its depiction of the love and forgiveness of God. The story has frequently been dubbed an *evan-*

gelium in evangelio, a gospel within the Gospel.[26] Some balk at this label since the parable contains little or no Christology, no atonement theology, and no indication of the objective basis on which sins are forgiven and sinners restored.[27] In one sense this is true. But there is another sense in which the parable goes behind or beyond any mechanics of atonement to accentuate the fundamental driving force behind the good news of salvation proclaimed by Jesus in the Gospel tradition: the costly love and restoring justice of the reign of God.

Discerning the theological meaning of the story requires an appreciation of the metaphorical function of Jesus' parabolic discourse. As short metaphorical narratives, parables typically operate at two levels: a surface level and a referential level. Hearers are beckoned, often by the extravagance of what transpires in the story, to go beyond the surface value of the narrative to discern a deeper level of meaning being disclosed.[28] On the surface, the parable of the Prodigal Son is simply an account of everyday family dysfunction. It recounts the pernicious nature of sibling rivalry and the ultimate helplessness of parental love when children make bad decisions. But so unexpected or counterintuitive is its depiction of these everyday realities that there can be little doubt that what transpires in the story is intended to refer to something far more profound on Jesus' horizon, something to do with God and with the way God operates. This is not to invite fanciful or anachronistic allegorization of every detail of the account. It is simply to recognize the distinctive role

---

26. So, for example, Lenski, *Luke's Gospel*, 807; Farrer, *St. Luke*, 254; Plummer, *St. Luke*, 371 (citing Grotius); cf. Jeremias, *Parables*, 124; Donahue, *Gospel in Parable*, 146–62.

27. Bailey captures the problem succinctly: "The story appears to have no incarnation, no 'word that becomes flesh,' no cross, no crown, no suffering, no death, no resurrection, and no mediator between God and human beings. How can this be a 'gospel within the Gospel' when the gospel, as known throughout the New Testament, is apparently missing?" (Bailey, *Jacob*, 16). For an eminently sensible discussion of the theological and christological implications of the parable, see Snodgrass, *Stories*, 136–39. Snodgrass observes that the story is "a powerful presentation of the saving grace of God" (137), but thinks it is absurd to seek detailed insights from it on atonement theology or on the interplay between divine sovereignty and human responsibility. On a different note, Weaver sees a positively nonviolent atonement theology at work in the parable ("Forgiveness," 325–26).

28. The metaphorical quality of parables is not uniform throughout the collection (cf. Snodgrass, *Stories*, 1–35).

that Jesus' narrative parables play in his larger agenda of proclaiming and mediating the experience of God's kingdom to his audience.

In our parable, it is the father who exemplifies the character and actions of God.[29] Palestinian hearers would have been predisposed to take the father figure as a symbol for God (cf. Isa 63:16; Ps 103:3), just as they would have the images of king, master, bridegroom, landowner, and shepherd in Jesus' other parables. Not that the father is portrayed as a divine figure in any direct sense. He is an earthly father who is clearly differentiated from God or "Heaven" within the plotted narrative itself (vv. 18, 21). But he is an earthly father whose motivations and actions are so consistent with those of God that, as Jeremias puts it, "*in his love* he is an image of God." The father portrays with "touching simplicity what God is like, his goodness, his grace, his boundless mercy, his abounding love."[30] At the same time, he shows what those who know and worship this God ought to be like as well. They, too, should be full of goodness and grace, rich in mercy and abounding in love. This is the ethical consequence of the parabolic device of using human actors doing human things in a human world to represent God. Such parables do more than teach theology or ethics in the abstract; they bring God down to earth with a bump. They present God as a realistic model for listeners to emulate in their everyday lives. After all, if human actors within the story world can behave in ways that disclose the parental heart of God, so too can human hearers of the parable in the real world outside.[31]

Jesus himself, the one who tells the parable, is of course the supreme demonstration of this; he emulates and enacts the love and goodness of God. In Luke's presentation, this is precisely why Jesus tells the parable in the first place. It serves the apologetic function of defending his historical praxis as an outworking of the restorative compassion of

---

29. Some feminist scholars deny that the patriarchal figure of the father serves (or should serve) as an image for God, e.g., Schottroff, *Parables*, 149; Beavis, "'Making Up Stories'"; Durber, "Female Reader." But, as Bailey points out, Jesus does not use a standard Oriental patriarch as a model for God, but one who breaks "all the bounds of Middle Eastern patriarchy. . . . Jesus elevates the figure of father beyond its human limitations as he reshapes it into his primary metaphor for God" (*Jacob*, 101, 138-47). So, too, Donahue, *Gospel in Parable*, 160-62, cf. Scott, *Hear Then*, 117-18.

30. Jeremias, *Parables*, 128 (emphasis added), 131; so too Bailey, *Poet and Peasant*, 159; Fitzmyer, *Luke*, 1085; Green, *Luke*, 579.

31. On the role of biblical narratives (including this parable) that portray God as father in shaping the social construction of fatherhood, see Furrow, "Ideal Father."

God. The parable is the third in a trilogy of parables in Luke 15 that underscore God's determination to recover the lost and to celebrate their return with wild jubilation. That Luke intended all three stories to be read as a single unit is indicated by the use of the singular noun "parable" in v. 3 to introduce the collection and by the many common features that recur in the stories, such as the motifs of getting lost and being found, of eating meals and rejoicing, of individual effort and public proclamation. Together the stories serve as a rejoinder to the criticism of the scribes and Pharisees, who took strong exception to Jesus' habitual practice of welcoming sinners and eating with them (15:1–3).[32] Jesus justifies his odious conduct by reminding his critics parabolically of God's abiding love for outcasts, of God's concern to regather the lost, and of the pleasure God takes in the repentance of sinners. Such divine deportment is well attested in Jewish Scripture and tradition.[33] But it was lost sight of by Jesus' detractors, who preferred to emphasize those strands of sacred tradition that enjoin separation from the ungodly.[34] The overall message of Luke 15 is that in offering hospitality to sinners and tax collectors, Jesus was acting as God's representative. He was not simply conferring charity on the needy; he was actively embodying the

---

32. Young, *Jewish Theologian*, 145. Young flatly denies that the parable is an attack upon the Pharisees, but overlooks entirely its redactional setting in Luke 15 where it is part of a carefully crafted unit or *chreia* consisting of two short and one long parable with a single theme announced in vv. 1–3. Most scholars see a polemical dimension to the parable, for example: Manson, *Sayings*, 286; Fitzmyer, *Luke*, 1085; Hunter, *Parables*, 62; Dodd, *Parables*, 90. For a balanced discussion, see Snodgrass, *Stories*, 138–41.

33. God's concern for the outcast and mercy toward the penitent pervades the Old Testament (e.g., Isa 49:15; 55:7; Jer 3:12; 31:18–20; Ezek 33:11; 1 Kgs 8:47–51; Hos 11:1–9; 14:1–2; Ps 103:8–10, 12–13). Rabbinical tradition too stressed God's generosity toward the repentant (cf. Moore, *Judaism*, 157–58; Montefiore and Loewe, *Rabbinic Anthology*, 315–33). Jesus heightens this theme by depicting God's diligent searching out of the lost and his rejoicing over their restoration. "The virtues of repentance are gloriously praised in the Rabbinical literature, but this direct search for, and appeal to, the sinner, are new and moving notes of high import and significance" (Montefiore, *Synoptic Gospels*, 2:985; cf. Manson, *Sayings*, 284).

34. Note, for example, the repeated refrain in the Psalms, highlighted at the very beginning of the psalter, not to "take the path that sinners tread or sit in the seat of scoffers" (1:1). It seems probable that more rigorist Pharisees emphasized the need to avoid all contact with the ungodly lest they be defiled by their lawlessness. Manson points to the statement in the *Mekhilta* on Exod 18:1 perhaps typifying their attitude: "Let not a man associate with the wicked, not even to bring him nigh to the law" (*Sayings*, 283. Cf. Gal 2:12–13).

restoring love of God. By contrast, the complaining Pharisees were like the prodigal's law-abiding older brother, who was unable to appreciate the radical generosity and implicit justice of God's forgiving mercy.

As well as affording theological insight into the love and mercy of God, the parable also offers an invaluable theological perspective on the meaning of sin. Indeed, of all the major theological ideas the parable has been seen to epitomize—sin, repentance, grace, mercy, love, forgiveness, justice and reconciliation—only "sin" is explicitly mentioned in the text; twice the prodigal son declares, "I have sinned against heaven and against you" (vv. 18, 21). Luke's editorial placement of the story after the parables of the lost sheep and the lost coin (15:3–10) further underscores the prodigal's identity as a "sinner who repents" and who thereby ignites joy in heaven (vv. 7, 10, 18, 21). The parable may not articulate a full-fledged doctrine of atonement, but it certainly conveys a developed doctrine of sin.

It is for these three reasons, then, that the parable of the Prodigal Son has lodged itself so deeply in the Western imagination and attracted such scholarly attention: its superb literary qualities, its emotional intensity and psychological acuity, and its theological depth. It has not only furnished the subject matter of great literature, art, music, and theological reflection down through the generations but has also surfaced frequently in discussions of moral and social issues, including, from time to time, discussions of crime and punishment. The parable is mentioned briefly, for example, in the November 2000 statement by the US Conference of Catholic Bishops on criminal justice, where it is used to encourage acceptance of offenders who are contrite and change their way of life.[35] On a more radical note, legal scholar Thomas Shaffer uses the parable to commend what he calls a "jurisprudence of forgiveness" that necessarily opposes and disrupts "the legal order that serves the politics of coercive power."[36] Shaffer offers an imaginative or midrashic expansion of the dilemma faced by the older brother in the story as a way of crystallizing the subversive implications of factoring forgiveness into the theory of law, though other scholars have demurred at such oppositional thinking.[37]

35. United States Conference of Catholic Bishops, "Responsibility."
36. Shaffer, "Radical Reformation," 324.
37. For a critique of Shaffer, see J. Murphy, "Christianity and Criminal Punishment." Murphy judges Shaffer's opposition of forgiveness and law to be "confused and mistaken" (265), and his treatment of forgiveness to be "fundamentally mistaken" (267).

Picking up on these leads, in the discussion that follows I want to provide a more detailed analysis of the parable from a criminal justice perspective. For there is, I believe, still more blessing to be wrested from this extraordinary tale if we bring to its interpretation the analytical categories and insights of restorative justice theory and practice. Interestingly, in her staunch critique of restorative justice, to which I will return at the end of the book, legal scholar Annalise Acorn observes in passing that the depiction in Luke 15 of joy in heaven over one sinner who repents "describes the restorative justice dynamic to a tee."[38] That this is also true of the parable of the Prodigal Son will become apparent as we proceed.

A PARABLE OF RESTORING JUSTICE

There are two main reasons why reading the parable through a criminal justice lens is not an unreasonable thing to do. The first is that the main characters in the story occupy the roles of the three main parties to every incident of criminal wrongdoing—those of offender, victim, and the wider law-abiding community. The younger son is portrayed as a serious and serial *offender*, one who might even fall under the rubric of the "stubborn and rebellious son" of Deut 21:18–23 who is considered deserving of death. The father is the primary *victim* of his offending,[39] as

---

38. Acorn, *Compulsory Compassion*, 152.

39. A totally opposite interpretation is offered by Beavis, who sees the younger son as the victim of incest and the father as the perpetrator of homosexual abuse. Beavis is clear that her interpretation "does not purport to uncover the 'true' or 'original' meaning of the parable, the meaning intended by Jesus, or the meaning intended by Luke. Rather, informed by the skills of a professional biblical scholar, it attempts to read the parable from the perspective of an implied reader with the life experience of one of the runaways described above" ("Making Up Stories," 103, cf. 120–21). Reading against the grain is all very well for "professional biblical scholars" who are paid to play around with textual meaning for fun. But one wonders what controls—literary or ethical—such a mode of interpretation is subject to. If the teller and recorder of the parable intended the father to serve as a positive role model in the story, even as a metaphor for God, by what right can a professional biblical scholar *reverse* the referent of the story? Parables, by common consent, functioned to blow open existing worldviews and afford new ways of perceiving reality. But this, in turn, requires that the story had some given meaning, however open-ended, that could effectively subvert conventional wisdom. The parables lose their subversive power if their message is entirely subject to the whim of interpreters who feel free to play fast and loose with meaning in the name of larger ideological agendas.

well as someone who represents the demands of law and justice,[40] while the older brother is expressly depicted as an industrious and *law-abiding member of the household community* who is outraged at his father's judicial leniency. The interaction of these three characters is strongly conditioned by their differing reactions to an episode of willful and harmful offending, and, as Scott notes, "in describing the father-son relation, the story borrows heavily from a legal repertoire."[41]

This leads to the second reason why it is profitable to read the parable from a criminal justice angle: the older brother's reaction centers directly on the justice of his father's actions. Although the word "injustice" is not used in the text, there is no more appropriate term to capture the essence and tone of his angry complaint to his father. "Listen! For all these years I have been working like a slave for you, and I have never disobeyed your command; yet you have never given me even a young goat so that I might celebrate with my friends. But when this son of yours came back, who has devoured your property with prostitutes, you killed the fatted calf for him!" (vv. 29–30). Plainly it is the idea of justice that drives this final scene of the narrative, despite the absence of justice vocabulary, just as the ideas of repentance, love, forgiveness, and mercy propel earlier scenes in the story without the actual terminology being used. The parable reaches its climax, then, in a dispute about whether the father, in restoring his offending son to community without imposing retributive punishment, has acted justly or unjustly.

For these two reasons, then, it is legitimate to read the parable from a jurisprudential perspective. This is not to suggest that the parable provides normative guidelines for how we should go about constructing an ethics of criminal justice. It is, after all, just a parable, not a juridical or philosophical treatise. Moreover, it is a parable that deals with the dynamics of domestic life and family relations that, in a modern context, belong to the "private" sphere of life rather than the "public" sphere where justice norms usually prevail. There are, then, generic and hermeneutical limits that must be respected in moving from parable to practice. But it is precisely *as* a parable that the Prodigal Son is most relevant to Christian reflection on criminal justice issues. Like most of

---

40. "The father represents the demands of law. As a hierarchical figure in a patron-client society . . . he stands in judgment on the son's activity" (Scott, *Hear Then*, 116).

41. Ibid., 116.

Jesus' parables, it functions to break open existing frames of reference, to challenge or confound taken-for-granted assumptions about the world and its notions of justice, and to offer a radically different way of looking at reality for those who have the eyes to see it: one controlled by the in-breaking reign of God's justice and peace. Surely, if there is anything that makes Christian reflection on moral or legal matters "Christian," it is its attempt to develop workable ethical guidelines that are informed not just by the downward drag of normal human behavior but also by the radical possibilities of human transformation opened up by the manifestation of God's restorative righteousness in the mission of Jesus.

With that in mind, we turn now to the parable itself. My proposal is that the parable not only furnishes valuable insights into the nature of crime, it also mandates a response to serious wrongdoing that gives priority to the restoration and reintegration of offenders as an outworking of the discipline of forgiveness and in stark contradiction to the exclusionary conception of justice often favored by the law-keeping community. If, after pondering the parable's perspective on these matters, we are left with the feeling that "this couldn't possibly work in the real world," then perhaps we have begun to "hear" the parable in all its offensive glory.

8

Offending as Relational Rupture

The first half of the parable is devoted to describing in some detail the offending of the younger son. The boy is probably in his mid-to-late teens, since he is old enough to leave home but is not yet married.[1] It is ironic that whereas the boy comes to interpret his own conduct in the most serious of terms, as a case of sinning against heaven and against his own father (vv. 18, 21), modern readers often struggle to see wherein his transgression lay. True, he was a spendthrift who squandered his possessions in an intemperate lifestyle. That was certainly a foolish thing to do, even deeply shameful.[2] But to modern sensibilities it scarcely counts as dreadfully *sinful*. It is also not clear why the boy's wastefulness of his own inherited assets constituted a grievous sin against his father. In any event, living like there's no tomorrow is fairly typical teenage behavior, as even the ancients recognized,[3] and at least this lad ends up getting a job to support himself. This actually makes him quite a good role model for contemporary teenagers!

Later in the story, his older brother accuses the boy of having spent all his money on prostitutes (v. 30). This does perhaps up the sin-stakes a little further. Both Jewish and Hellenistic moralists disapproved strongly of prostitution, and the possibility of siring illegitimate offspring and contaminating the family's bloodline through consorting with harlots

---

1. Several commentators surmise the boy would have been around seventeen years of age, since marriage usually occurred between eighteen and twenty years. If the boy was already married at the time of his actions, the sinfulness of his deeds grows out of all proportion.

2. Ancient moralists in general considered prodigality to be shameful. See Holgate, *Prodigality*, 90–130; cf. Snodgrass, *Stories*, 120–22.

3. Moral teachers accepted that prodigality was more typical of young people than adults and often cured by maturation. See Holgate, *Prodigality*, 148.

was always a concern.[4] But the narrative description of the prodigal's behavior does *not* include him visiting brothels. The accusation that he did so could simply be prurient speculation on the part of a jealous sibling, aided by the common assumption that sexual and material indulgence often went hand in hand (cf. Luke 7:34). As for his initial act of asking for his slice of the inheritance in advance, several commentators can see no objection whatsoever to his request, nor to his decision to emigrate. Some even consider it to be a commendable sign of industriousness of the part of an ambitious young entrepreneur. According to A. E. Harvey, "The younger son's request was quite normal: the main part of the property would in any case go to his elder brother, and he could expect to do better by turning his share into cash and setting himself up in business among the Jews of the Dispersion in some foreign city, than by trying to live on a small-holding in the over-populated farmland of Palestine."[5]

But what appears to modern Western ears to be relatively innocent teenage behavior would have certainly struck Jesus' first-century Palestinian hearers, as it does many hearers in traditional societies today, as utterly repugnant and wholly blameworthy. They would have been appalled at the younger son's actions, which breached prevailing social and legal custom in a succession of ways, so that his offending actually compounds as the story advances. The boy's behavior is not merely irregular. It is offensive to such a severe degree that he might even have been reckoned for inclusion in the category of the "stubborn and rebellious son" of Deut 21:18–21 who is deemed worthy of public execution.[6] Defiance of parents was an extremely serious offence throughout the ancient world, and especially so in Judaism. His rebellion consisted in a thoroughgoing rejection of his relational connections with, and his responsibilities towards, his father, his brother, and his wider village community. The rebellious boy does not merely break biblical law at some technical level. He does something far worse: he wrecks bedrock relationships. His offending manifests a profound disrespect for the rights and needs of others,

---

4. Prostitution was frowned upon by both Jewish and Hellenist moralists; see ibid., 144 nn. 50, 51 for references.

5. Harvey, *Bible Companion*, 266. Similarly Via, *Parables*, 170; Linnemann, *Parables*, 75; Bovon, "First Reading," 53; Gnilka, *Jesus*, 99; Donahue, *Gospel in Parable*, 153.

6. Cf. Josephus, *Ant.* 4:264; Josephus, *Apion* 2.206; 11QTemple 64:2–6; *m. Sanh.* 7:4; 8.4–5.

something that, according to restorative justice thinking, constitutes the harmful essence of all crime.

THE INJURY OF DISRESPECT

The boy's first act of disrespect was to take the initiative of asking his father for a division of the family estate. The basics of Jewish inheritance laws are set out in Num 27:6–11 and 36:1–10. The precise application of these laws at the time of Jesus is not fully known, and scholars still disagree on the legal realities inferred in the account. But there is enough evidence in biblical and rabbinic tradition to get a reasonable understanding.[7] It appears that the owner of a property could pass on his estate to heirs either by a testamentary will that would take effect after his death, or by a deed of gift made during his lifetime. It is not clear how common the latter practice of gifting was. Some sages, like ben Sirach, considered it to be a highly imprudent thing to do and warned property owners against it.

> Hear me, you who are great among the people, and you leaders of the congregation, pay heed! To son or wife, to brother or friend, do not give power over yourself, as long as you live; and do not give your property to another, in case you change your mind and must ask for it. While you are still alive and have breath in you, do not let anyone take your place. For it is better that your children should ask from you than that you should look to the hand of your children. Excel in all that you do; bring no stain upon your honor. At the time when you end the days of your life, in the hour of death, distribute your inheritance. (Sir 33:19–24)

The basic concern here is that a benefactor who divides his property while he is still alive imperils his honor. He risks losing or diminishing the status, dignity, and material security associated with exercising absolute control over the family and its assets. A man's honor depended on his being embedded in his family, deriving support from the family, and functioning as the family's chief representative. If a property is divided,

---

7. In addition to standard commentaries, see Jeremias, *Parables*, 128–29; Manson, *Teaching*, 286–87; Derrett, *Law*, 102–12; Bailey, *Poet and Peasant*, 161–69; idem, *Cultural Keys*, 116–18; Malina and Rohrbaugh, *Social Science*, 372–73; Young, *Jewish Theologian*, 145–48; Forbes, "Repentance and Conflict," 214–16; Scott, *Hear Then*, 109–11. On Greco-Roman practice, see Holgate, *Prodigality*, 134.

therefore, both family integrity and patriarchal honor are at stake. On the positive side of the ledger, however, gifting could bring certain advantages. It was one way, for instance, of preventing future disputes between rival heirs. It was also a way of protecting the interests of the children born of a first marriage from any claimants from subsequent marriages. Gifting therefore probably occurred on many occasions, even if it was not the norm.[8]

For the deed of gift to be valid, it had to be an entirely voluntary decision on the part of the donor, not the result of being placed under any duress. Legal transfer of title took place at the time of donation, but full rights of disposition would come into effect only after the donor's death. In the meantime, the benefactor had a right to ongoing maintenance from the property and a good measure of control over its usage. He could continue to live off the produce of the land and would reinvest its income back into the enterprise. He could not, of course, sell the land to anyone else because his heir now held title, though he could lease it out on a temporary basis. The beneficiary also had no right to sell the land before his father's death. If he did so, the purchaser had no lawful claim on the land while the original owner was still alive.[9]

In our parable, the father opts to pass on his estate to his sons by deed of gift (cf. "give," *dos* v. 12). There was nothing improper about him doing so, except in one respect: the initiative for this arrangement came, not from the father himself, but from his youngest son ("give me"). Though not all commentators agree on this, it is probable that the parable's first hearers would have been horrified at the sheer arrogance and presumption of the boy's request, for a beneficiary had no legal or customary right to *demand* an inheritance.[10] According to Kenneth Bailey, it was unprecedented for a Jewish son to insist on a division of an estate while his father was still alive. Bailey writes, "the startling fact is that, to my knowledge, in all of Middle Eastern literature (aside from this parable), from ancient times to the present, there is no case of any son, older or younger, asking for his inheritance from a father who is still in good

---

8. According to Scott, the lack of Jewish case law on the situation envisaged in the parable indicates that, though not unknown, it was surely not the norm (*Hear Then*, 110–11).

9. *m. B. Bat.* 8:7.

10. So Derrett, *Law*, 104–5.

health."[11] Such a request was an extraordinary insult to the boy's father, for it was tantamount to wishing him dead.[12] It is one thing for an old man to anticipate the property implications of his own imminent decease and to make suitable arrangements in advance. It is quite another for a child to let his father know how much he coveted his possessions, itself a serious sin in biblical law,[13] and how eagerly he anticipated the financial benefits that would accrue to him once his father had the good grace to die. The youngest son in the parable had no qualms whatsoever about making his greedy impatience obvious to his father. This would have been as wounding to him as it was deeply dishonoring.

But it was even worse than that. The young son not only sought legal title to his inheritance, he planned to exercise full and immediate rights of disposition over his assigned share. Normally the donor would retain control over the land and its usufruct throughout his remaining life. Here the beneficiary plans to assume full control straightaway. Not content to wait for his father's death, the young man proceeds to act as though he were *already* dead. Tellingly, Luke describes the father's property as his "substance" (*ousia*) and his "life" (*bios*, vv. 12, 30): it was the source of his livelihood and of his very being. Given the inseparable connection between life, land, and identity in agrarian societies, the boy was, in effect, planning metaphorically to kill his father.[14] He was preparing to deprive him of the ground of his existence and belonging. It was an insolent and emotionally hurtful demand that manifested a profound distortion in a son's proper relationship to his father.

Though under no legal or customary obligation to do so, the father accedes to the request and apportions land to each son (v. 12). In so doing, he opened himself up potentially to severe criticism from his neighbors, both for jeopardizing his personal and family honor and for exposing other households to possible copycat offending. In parceling out the land, the father would have given his firstborn son a "double portion," that is twice the amount given to the younger son, as required by biblical law (Deut 21:17). The oldest son clearly did not claim the same powers of disposition over his portion that his brother did, for in the remainder of

---

11. Bailey, *Poet and Peasant*, 164. So too Rohrbaugh, "Dysfunctional Family," 150–51.
12. Bailey, *Poet and Peasant*, 163, and *Jacob*, 99; Young, *Jewish Theologian*, 145–46.
13. Exod 20:17, cf. Prov 21:26; 4 Macc 2:5–6; Rom 7:7; 13:9; Jas 4:2.
14. "The son's division of the property kills the father" (Scott, *Hear Then*, 111).

the story the father continues to act as master in charge of the estate and its workers (vv. 22–26, 29–30), even though he knows, in principle, the land now belongs to his successor ("all that is mine is yours," v. 31).

The younger boy, by shameless contrast, chooses to dispose of his share forthwith. The statement, "he gathered together all that he had" (*sunagagōn panta* v. 13) probably means he converted his inheritance into cash by putting it on the market, with the added implication that he did so out of greed.[15] The fact that he cashed up his share just "a few days after" gaining control of it (*met'ou pollas hēmeras* v. 13) reveals how eager he was to get away from his obligations at home. The fact that he sold "all" his inheritance shows he had no intention of ever coming back in the future. He was burning his bridges behind him. He was also leaving nothing behind for the support of his father in his declining years. This was to add injury to insult. It was also to defy the fifth commandment of the Decalogue, since honoring one's parents was understood to include sustaining them in their old age.[16] In all these ways, the boy was effectively "un-sonning" himself and "de-fathering" his father.[17]

When the old man agreed to distribute his land to his sons, he probably envisaged them marrying local village girls and setting up separate, though still interdependent, households nearby. He would never have dreamed that they would sell off their portion to outsiders. That was unconscionable. The customary ideal in peasant society was that family possessions were held in common for the benefit of the household as a whole, with the property of adult children being at the disposal of their parents and under the authority of the *paterfamilias*.[18] Certainly land

---

15. Arndt, Gingrich, and Bauer, *Lexicon*, 782; Moulton and Milligan, *Vocabulary*, 600. Snodgrass thinks that the boy was not given land as his inheritance but rather possessions of equivalent value to his portion of the land, Snodgrass, *Stories*, 131–32. On the implication of greed in the verb, see Holgate, *Prodigality*, 140–41.

16. Exod 20:12; Lev 19:3; Deut 6:13; Prov 3:9. The biblical command to honor one's parents was not merely an ethical rule but an economic responsibility that was in no way diminished by any discourtesy, unfairness, or favoritism on the part of the parent. See Derrett, *Law*, 109–11.

17. Volf, *Exclusion and Embrace*, 158.

18. According to Epictetus, in the area of possessions a son had an obligation, "to treat everything that is his own as belonging to his father, to be obedient to him in all things, never to speak ill of him to anyone else, nor to say or do anything that will harm him ... helping him as far as is within his power" (*Discourses*, 2.10.7), cited by Holgate, *Prodigality*, 190.

should never be allowed to slip permanently from family control if it could be avoided. This was especially important for Jewish peasants, who considered their land to be held on trust from God (Lev 25:23).[19]

Accordingly, for the younger son to sell the family patrimony to an outsider, presumably at a bargain basement price since the deal was struck so quickly,[20] was to express contempt for all that his father had accomplished during his lifetime. It was also to deprive the family enterprise of the land's future economic output. It is not without justification, then, that the older brother later complains to his father: "This son of yours has devoured *your living* with prostitutes" (v. 30). By his selfish actions, he had depleted the family's economic resources. He has also destroyed any chance of "dwelling together in unity" with his brother after their father's passing (Ps 133:1). This was the biblical ideal, even if in practice the goal of family solidarity sometimes foundered on fraternal rivalries and resentments.[21]

The younger son's action of shaming his father, alienating his brother, and flicking off his inheritance so glibly, would have provoked extreme hostility from other villagers. Although the village community is offstage until the final scene of the story, first-century hearers would have assumed their involvement in the drama from the outset.[22] The family home would probably have been located, not on the arable land of the estate, but on the streets of the tightly compacted village settlement nearby. Property owners rarely lived on their farms, as to do so would occupy precious acreage that could otherwise be cultivated. Isolated homesteads were also much too vulnerable to brigands. Assuming, then, the family lived in town, the son's insulting behavior and subsequent departure would soon be common knowledge. Eavesdropping, gossiping, and rumormongering are standard fare in all small-scale societies. Once they learnt of the boy's deeds, his neighbors would have been incensed. Their entire way of life was dependent on retaining control of the land and its output, for in peasant society land is life. Land tenure was based on family inheritance, and

---

19. Fiensy, *Social History*, 3–15; also Rohrbaugh, "Dysfunctional Family," 146, 148–49.

20. So Young, *Jewish Theologian*, 148; Bailey, *Poet and Peasant*, 169, and *Jacob*, 152–53. Bailey observes that property deals in the Middle East usually drag on for months. The rapidity of the deal in the parable implies an anxiety to get settlement as quickly as possible in view of communal displeasure.

21. Cf. Rohrbaugh, "Dysfunctional Family," 147–48.

22. So Bailey, *Jacob*, 100; Rohrbaugh, "Dysfunctional Family," 156–58.

everyone had a vested interest in keeping ancestral lands together under the jurisdiction of family heads. The boy's outrageous actions set a dangerous precedent that could imperil the welfare of the whole community.

Having liquidated his inheritance, the young man seals his alienation from kith and kin by departing for "a distant country" (*chōran makran*, v. 13). The distance he travels is emotional as well as physical. His outward separation manifests an inward detachment from his family duties. It is also a moral distance, for in this faraway land "he squandered his property in dissolute living" (v. 13). It is not uncommon for individuals suddenly freed from the constraints of tightly knit social networks to tip into hedonistic excess or sensual efforts at self-discovery that can quickly drain their economic resources. Jewish law forbade the selling of Jewish land to Gentiles, and anyone who did so faced being "cut off" from his people.[23] The prodigal does not sell his land directly to Gentiles, but he still ends up losing his Jewish inheritance in Gentile territory, even if conceivably it was among fellow Jewish profligates in Diaspora communities. His lack of care for the value of what his father had graciously bequeathed him is captured in the term "squandered" (*dieskorpisen*). The verb suggests throwing something into the air to be scattered by the four winds. The decadence of his lifestyle is conveyed by the adverb "dissolute" (*asōtōs*, literally "unsaving" or harmful), a term that suggests wildness and wastefulness, though not necessarily sexual license, even though promiscuity was considered to be a commonly related vice.[24]

The boy's reckless prodigality with his possessions was, according to the moral and cultural judgments of the time, thoroughly reprehensible.

---

23. "Do not give your inheritance to Gentiles . . . lest you be humiliated in their eyes, and foolish and they trample upon you for they will come to dwell among you and become your masters" (4Q542). The *kezazah* or "cutting off" ceremony dramatized this expulsion; any Jewish boy who gave his inheritance to Gentiles might, on returning to his community, be symbolically shunned by having a large earthen vessel with burned nuts and corn broken at his feet, with people shouting that he was now cut off from his people (Bailey, *Poet and Peasant*, 167–68, and *Jacob*, 102). Snodgrass considers it unlikely that this ceremony is anywhere in view in the parable (*Stories*, 132–33).

24. Foerster, *asōtos*, TDNT I: 506–7; Plummer, *St Luke*, 373. This is the only occurrence of the adverb *asōtos* in the New Testament, although the noun *asōtia* occurs in Eph 5:18; Titus 1:6; 1 Pet 4:4, cf. Prov 28:7; 2 Macc 6:4. Bailey notes that neither the Greek text nor the various Oriental versions indicate that the boy was guilty of sexual immorality (*Poet and Peasant*, 170). On the other hand, covetousness and immorality were frequently linked in Jewish, Greco-Roman, and early Christian literature (cf. Holgate, *Prodigality*, 142–48).

But what made it especially deplorable was that it thwarted his relational obligations to his father. Any inkling that he might have reserved some of his money to send home to sustain his father in his dotage is now gone forever.

Once he had lost everything, a severe famine breaks out in the boy's adopted homeland.[25] As an isolated sojourner in a foreign land, separated from supportive networks, the impoverished lad is unable to feed himself (v. 14). He now reaps what he has sown. He suffers what F. W. Farrer terms "retributive anguish" as the inevitable consequences of his choices come home to roost.[26] In desperation, he throws himself on the goodwill of "one of the citizens of that country" (v. 15). The citizen was presumably a member of the local urban elite whom peasants had good reason to fear and distrust.[27] The NRSV reads, "he hired himself out" to the citizen, but the Greek text speaks more graphically of him "clinging to" or "gluing himself to" the citizen (*ekollēthē*, v. 15). The radical dependency this implies is illustrated by the way the same verb is used elsewhere to portray sexual intimacy[28] and to depict exclusive religious devotion to God.[29] "Only someone who has lived in the Middle East," Bailey observes, "can fully appreciate this vocabulary. In the Middle East, the desperation of the indigent leads him to attach himself like glue to any potential benefactor."[30]

Jews did not look favorably on working for Gentiles or becoming dependent on them (cf. Acts 10:28, where the same verb occurs), and presumably the boy could have sought help from the nearest Jewish community.[31] But penniless, he is probably not alone in petitioning

---

25. Famines are frequent and deeply feared events in biblical literature; e.g., Gen 12:10; 26:1; 41:27-47; 42:5; 43:1; 47:4; Ruth 1:1; 1 Kgs 18:2; 2 Kgs 4:38; Luke 4:25; Acts 11:28.

26. Farrer, *St Luke*, 257. Early pagan, Jewish and Christian moralists differed on whether famines could be attributed to Providence (as a form of divine punishment) or were simply an inescapable part of life, cf. Holgate, *Prodigality*, 148-53. In the parable, the retribution is not the famine, but the boy's inability to cope with it due to his unwise choices.

27. Cf. Rohrbaugh, "Dysfunctional Family," 153-54. On the legal institution possibly evoked by the verb, see Harrill, "Indentured Labor," 714-17.

28. 1 Kgs 11:2; 1 Esd 4:20; Sir 19:2; Matt 19:5; 1 Cor 6:16.

29. Deut 6:13; 10:20; 2 Kgs 18:6; Pss 63:8; 119:31; 1 Cor. 6:17.

30. Bailey, *Poet and Peasant*, 170 n. 119.

31. Linnemann, *Parables*, 75-76; Donahue, *Gospel in Parable*, 153. There were well organized welfare systems in Diaspora communities for helping Jewish travellers and émigrés in need (cf. m. Pe'ah 8:7; Schürer, *History*, II:437).

the citizen for help. Ignoring the lad's religious scruples, the landowner assigns him a task that any good Jewish boy should have instinctively recoiled from: herding pigs.

Instead of turning for home at this point, the boy accepts the job and goes "into his fields to feed pigs" (v. 15). His dereliction is now total. Pigs were unclean animals to Jews. No fate could be more degrading to a Jew than to feed the pigs of a Gentile master on Gentile land. To do so would effectively require him to renounce the regular practice of his religion.[32] According to a Talmudic saying, "It is cursed for someone to raise pigs, and it is cursed for anyone to teach Greek learning to his son."[33] As Duncan Derrett wryly observes, "Pigs and Gentiles seem to have been held in equal esteem."[34] It is not surprising, then, that this particular Gentile employer is depicted as callous and tight-fisted, for he allows his Jewish swine herder to hover on the edge of starvation ("I am dying here of hunger," v. 17). Having acted unjustly himself towards his father and family, the prodigal son now learns what it is like to be treated unjustly by someone else.

So famished is the boy that "he longed to eat his fill of the carob pods the pigs were feeding on" (v. 16).[35] The syntax of v. 16 indicates that his desire remained unfulfilled.[36] This was either because he was too disgusted with the thought of scoffing down pigswill ever to attempt it,[37] or because the husks themselves were almost indigestible, so that no matter how many he ate he was never satisfied,[38] or because his pitiless master refused to permit him to eat the pig food he craved.[39] In any event, he is reduced to a condition lower even than his animals, since, unlike the pigs, "no one gave him anything to eat." For all his previous

---

32. Lev 11:7; 14:8; Deut 14:8, cf. 1 Macc 1:47; 2 Macc 6:18; 7:1; Luke 8:32. A number of Greco-Roman moralists also saw pigs as a symbol of moral degradation (Holgate, *Prodigality*, 157).

33. *b. B. Qam.* 82b.

34. Derrett, *Law*, 113.

35. A variant reading in the Western tradition reads "filled his belly with" in place of "to eat his fill of." Several scholars favor the Western reading, arguing that scribes would have preferred the more decorous *chortasthēnai* over the cruder alternative *gemisai tēn koilian autou*, including I. H. Marshall, *Luke*, 609, and Holgate, *Prodigality*, 41–43.

36. The imperfect *epethumei* + the infinitive *chortasthēnai* suggests ongoing action.

37. So Jeremias, *Parables*, 129; Derrett, *Law*, 113; Fitzmyer, *Luke*, 1088.

38. So Bailey, *Poet and Peasant*, 173.

39. Cf. Scott, *Hear Then*, 114–15.

lavishness, not a single friend remained as he slowly wastes away.[40] He is utterly destitute and forsaken, a social expendable for whom death is just a matter of time.

So then, the picture painted of the younger son's offending is something far worse than material extravagance or moral laxity. He has injured those closest to him in the gravest of ways. He has dishonored his father, acting as if he were as good as dead already and with no further claims upon him. He has also abandoned his brother and spurned his village community, selling off his heritage as quickly as possible so as to escape from the communal networks and obligations that furnished, what Maori in New Zealand would call his *turangawaewae*, his "place to stand." He has squandered his bequest, scattering it to the four winds in unbridled excess. Reduced to rags, he has attached himself to a Gentile patron, being prepared even to wallow among unclean animals and accept the religious compromises and ritual pollution that came from doing so. He is utterly degraded. In joining the swine, he has all but surrendered his humanity.[41]

He is, in short, a serious and serial offender who has so thoroughly covered himself in sin and shame that no place remained for him in regular society. He is utterly unclean, in every sense of the word, and utterly alone. But then, at absolute rock bottom, something shifts in him and his long trek to restoration commences.

THE OBLIGATION ON OFFENDERS

There is a rabbinic proverb that says: "When the Jew has to eat the fruit of the carob tree, then he repents."[42] When the bitter consequences of sinful behavior become sufficiently painful, penitence will follow. The Jewish concept of repentance centers on the notion of "returning" (*teshubah*), that is, a turning away from evil deeds and a returning to the path of doing good deeds. It involves a radical change of conduct and intention, and is the one indispensable condition for receiving God's forgiveness and restoration to divine favor. Neusner and Green summarize it as follows:

40. The present indicative middle *apollumai* (v. 17) implies, "I am slowly wasting away."

41. Scott, *Hear Then*, 115.

42. Montefiore and Loewe, *Rabbinic Anthology*, 95; Manson, *Teaching*, 288; Gnilka, *Jesus*, 100.

> Repentance entails confession of the sin before God and formulation of a resolve not to commit the same sin again. In the case of a sin against another person, repentance is possible only after full restitution or correction of the wrong deed has been made and a pardon from the other person has been obtained. In Scripture's system, repentance is followed by an expiatory offering. After the destruction of the Temple and the cessation of the sacrificial cult, the rabbis found a replacement for this offering in charitable deeds. Rabbinic authorities viewed repentance and charity together as a person's greatest advocates before God (*b.Shabbat* 32a).[43]

According to this description, repentance entails the key elements of contrition, confession, correction of life, and atonement or expiation. It is striking how each of these elements is present or implied in the description of the prodigal's transformation in the central section of the parable (vv. 17–21).[44] Admittedly, the terminology of repentance (*metanoia, metanoeō*) is not used in the text, and several interpreters think there is an enduring ambiguity throughout the narrative about the boy's true motivations.[45] Some even see his confession of sin as a clever ruse intended to secure his future economic security (cf. 16:1–9). But such cynicism is unwarranted. Luke's editorial placement of the parable after the parables of the good shepherd and the good woman (15:3–10) certainly indicates that he considered the boy's response to be emblematic of the "sinner who repents" and sparks joy in heaven, and there is no good reason to think otherwise.

---

43. Neusner and Green, *Dictionary*, 524. See also Moore, *Judaism*, 507-45. Cf. chapter 7, 190 n. 33 above.

44. Bailey, *Jacob*, 103-17, 162-63, and *Cultural Keys*, 129-94. Bailey argues that the story offers a radically new understanding of repentance as something that is spawned by the experience of grace rather than earned through penitential actions. He argues vigorously that the boy does not repent until later in the story when he encounters his father. But this view is forced and depends on denying the sincerity of the boy's confession in v. 18.

45. Ramsey says that although the preceding two parables predispose us to expect a repentant sinner in the third parable, it is possible that the narrator intends the third to be a contrast to the previous two. "Frequently, commentators find genuine repentance in the story; I propose that it is equally easy to discover a shrewd, calculating, self-seeking youngster" ("Plots, Gaps," 37-42 [at 40]).

Repentance as Contrition

On the edge of starvation, the boy finally decides to change his ways. In a lengthy soliloquy, he compares his own destitution with the circumstances of his father's hired hands, who not only have bread to eat in place of pigswill but have it in abundance (v. 17). He therefore hatches a plan to return home and throw himself on his father's mercy. Although some construe the boy's scheme as an exercise in self-centered expediency, there are several textual clues that genuine contrition is present.

To begin with, the entire soliloquy is predicated on the boy having "come to himself" (*eis heauton de elthōn*). This is an idiom used in several languages to denote a thoroughgoing change of heart.[46] Some commentators think the metaphor merely means he had a sudden brain wave and deny it implies moral change.[47] But the logic of the ensuing narrative strongly suggests otherwise. "'Coming to himself,'" Scott rightly comments, "is the first clue that the awaited restoration is beginning."[48] It may be true that the lad's change of heart was triggered by his hunger pangs more than by pangs of conscience. But what he ends up lamenting is not his own miserable situation, but his forfeited relationship with his father.[49] It is the recollection of his *father*, and of his father's generosity even to his hired servants, as much as it is his own material need, that evokes remorse. Twice in the soliloquy he uses the phrase "my father" (v. 17), and later he addresses him with the vocative "father" (v. 21), something his older sibling never does. The verbal confession he prepares in advance also centers on his father: on the wrong he has done to him and on his unworthiness to be called his son (v. 19). When the

---

46. So Jeremias, *Parables*, 130; Manson, *Teaching*, 288; Marshall, *Luke*, 609; Aus, "Luke 15:11-32," 457; cf. Holgate, *Prodigality*, 198-206.

47. The phrase is capable of carrying other shades of meaning besides repentance (cf. Snodgrass, *Stories*, 631 n. 251, cf. 138). Bailey thinks the term simply denotes the emergence of a face-saving plan (*Poet and Peasant*, 173-75, and *Cross*, 52-62). Sellew sees it as a literary device for introducing an interior debate ("Interior Monologue," 246-47); Via, *Parables*, 68, and Rohrbaugh, "Dysfunctional Family," 155, think it merely suggests the boy remembered where he had come from and who he actually was. Ramsey considers the phrase to be "tantalizingly ambiguous" intended to leave us unsure about what was going on in the boy's heart ("Luke 15," 38-41).

48. Scott, *Hear Then*, 115.

49. This is missed by James Breckenridge, who says the prodigal is "finally moved to repentance by making an honest but painful appraisal of his wretched state" ("Salvific Role," 79).

boy finally puts his plan into action by embarking on the return journey (itself a metaphor for repentance), the text touchingly says, "He went to his father." Not to his house, or to his village, or to his farm, but to "his very own father" (*ton patera heautou*).[50]

What caused the offender to confront his need for moral change, then, was the recollection that he is inescapably connected to the person of his father. As Volf comments, "There is no coming to oneself without the memory of belonging. The self is constructed in relation to others, and it can come to itself only through relationship to others. The first link with the other in a distant country of broken relationships is memory."[51] The boy's contrition was evinced by his remembering the bonds of belonging that grounded him in relationship to his paternal victim, and by his realization of the relational damage his behavior had caused. These, too, are the things that restorative justice seeks to place center-stage in its response to crime.

Repentance as Confession

Contrition, if it is sincere, will lead to confession and apology. In restorative justice theory, confession and apology play the important dual role of vindicating the victim and promoting healing in the offender. On the victim's side, confession serves to exonerate the victim of any blame or self-blame by clarifying where moral responsibility for the episode truly lies. On the offender's side, by naming and owning the wrongful behavior, confession enables the transgressor to begin recalibrating his moral compass and refocusing his desires on what is good and true. Confession externalizes or objectifies the inner change of heart that has occurred, and as such is a crucial component of accountability. What is remarkable in the parable is how the prodigal's confession crystallizes so succinctly what it means for offenders to assume genuine responsibility for their actions.

First it requires an *acceptance of moral blame*: "Father, I have sinned" (*hēmarton*). The boy makes no attempt to excuse or justify his offending as a mistake or an unfortunate lapse of judgment. He doesn't try to

---

50. Here I am construing *heatou* as emphatic, with Plummer, *St Luke*, 375. Bailey is mistaken when he claims that the prodigal plans "to go back to his village but not to his home" (*Poet and Peasant*, 205–6). The boy does not identify his goal as his village but as his father.

51. Volf, *Exclusion and Embrace*, 158.

shift the blame on to anyone else, whether his father, or brother, or his upbringing. No mitigation is offered. He confesses the wrong *he* has done, not what has happened *to* him, not what he has lost, or what he has suffered, or what he was hoping to achieve by his choices. He too has been a victim, first of a natural calamity (the famine), then of human exploitation (the oppressive citizen). But none of this is mentioned. All that the boy declares is the transgression he has committed and his personal liability for it: "I have sinned." Without this acknowledgement of blame, no basis for relational healing would exist.

In our exploration of the parable of the Good Samaritan, we encountered the longstanding debate in social psychology over the relative importance of "situational" versus "dispositional" variables in explaining pro-social or anti-social behavior. It is commonly assumed in society that disposition or personality traits have the greatest influence on human behavior. But experimental psychology has repeatedly shown that situation or social context is of far greater importance than most people realize. Seemingly small and subtle changes in someone's external situation can have far-reaching effects on their behavior. Furthermore, the stability of behavior or outlook that we tend to equate with someone's settled personality or fixed temperament arguably stems as much from the stability or predictability of their social circumstances as from the constancy of their moral character or disposition. Change their environment and their "personality" or "character" may change too, sometimes dramatically.

The implications of this for how society evaluates and responds to criminal wrongdoing are considerable. But, as Lee Ross and Donna Shestowsky point out, they are rarely discussed in legal theory and practice. Most agents in the criminal justice system, such as lawyers, judges, jurors, and police officers, mirror society's prevailing tendency to over-estimate the role of disposition or moral character in accounting for crime and underestimate the impact of situational forces. The legal system tends to perpetuate simplistic distinctions between good people and bad people. But if we possessed a more sophisticated and contextual understanding of behavioral causation, Ross and Shestowsky suggest, it would "compel us to treat transgressors with more compassion than they typically receive." It would force us to concede that our habitual resort to punitive rather than therapeutic or educational responses simply manifests a lack of insight into the complex drivers of social behavior. It would allow us to have "a more 'forgiving' response to transgressors who have been subjected to unusually strong situational pressures."[52]

Now the father's compassionate and forgiving response in the parable suggests that he would agree with the need for the "attributional charity" that Ross and Shestowsky call for. We will say more about this in due course. But what is noteworthy at this point is that the sinful son himself does not for one moment believe that his personal or environmental circumstances in any way diminish his moral culpability. He considers himself guilty. This is important. However understandable or excusable an offender's actions may appear to be to others due to circumstances, unless the wrongdoer himself accepts personal responsibility for causing harm, genuine change is not really possible.

The prodigal also acknowledges, secondly, that *his actions have injured others*: "I have sinned against heaven and against you." The prepositional phrase *eis ton ouranon* could mean "as high as the heaven," expressing the monstrous nature of his sin (cf. Ezra 9:6), but it more likely means "against heaven," in parallel with "against you" (both *eis* and *enōpion* have the same force here of "against"). The notion of sinning against heaven signals that when a sin is committed against another person, God too is the victim.[53] This is not just because God's law has been broken (in this case the fifth commandment, as well as a string of purity regulations). It is also because, in biblical tradition, God so identifies with innocent victims that when they are abused, God too is personally offended. To injure another person *is* to sin against God. They are not two separate offences. Sin, as a spiritual reality, usually has a social expression; sin, as a social reality, invariably has a spiritual dimension. Here the offender's social victim is his own father. He has rejected him emotionally, dishonored him publically, and deprived him materially of the land's output. In sinning against his father, the boy has spiritually offended against God. To put things right with God, the boy must also put things right with his father.

A third element in the boy's confession is an acknowledgement that his actions have *changed the nature of his relationship to the victim*. Once he stood in a relationship of filial duty and respect. Now, having betrayed his father's trust, he concedes, "I am no longer worthy to be called your

---

52. Ross and Shestowsky, "Psychology's Challenges," 1088, 1101; also Zimbardo, *Lucifer Effect*.

53. Num 5:6–7; Lev 6:1–7; Exod 10:16; Pss 32:5; 51:4.

son; treat me like one of your hired hands." In these words, the boy acknowledges two realities: the judgment of the law upon his conduct, and the impact of his conduct upon his relationships. In the patriarchal context of the time, his father represented the authority of law.[54] In surrendering any claim to filial standing, the prodigal is conceding the legitimacy of the law's condemnation of his deeds: "I am no longer worthy."

But more profoundly, the boy's words express a loss of relationship. "I am no longer worthy to be called *your* son." He renounces any inherent right he has to his father's affections, or forgiveness, or protection. Instead, he must adopt the place of a distant acquaintance, one whose connection with his father is that of a lowly day laborer (*misthios*). If this distance is ever to be lessened, if he is ever to be restored to a more intimate relationship with his father, if he is ever to be remade as a son, the initiative must come from the injured party. Relational renewal in the aftermath of victimization, if it is to occur at all, can only ever come as a *gift* from victim to offender. It is not a commodity that can be unilaterally purchased by confession or apology.[55]

The prodigal's confession, then, captures the three crucial elements of accountability: acceptance of moral blame, recognition of the impact of one's behavior on others, and acknowledgement that relationships have been damaged and can only be restored by an act of grace on the part of the victim. But still more is needed if restoration is to occur.

Repentance as Correction of Life

Repentance in Jewish understanding requires both desisting from the sinful acts of the past and resolving not to commit them again in the future. It also requires, where appropriate, restitution or compensation to the victims of one's offending. In biblical law, restitution is a prerequisite for offering a sacrifice of atonement to remit the sin before God (Num 5:6–7; Lev 6:1–7; cf. Matt 5:23–24). In the parable, the prodigal's remorse, his yearning for renewed contact with his father, his journeying home from a great distance, and his verbal confession of sin, all imply a commitment to a corrected lifestyle in the future, no longer marked by the selfishness and rebellion of the past. What about restitution? Is there

---

54. Cf. Scott, *Hear Then*, 116.
55. On the character of forgiveness, see Marshall, *Beyond Retribution*, 72–77, 263–84; Schriver, *Ethic for Enemies*, esp. 22–62.

any hint of his intention to make restitution for his crimes, as prescribed in biblical law and strongly affirmed in restorative justice theory?

A number of scholars think there is such a hint. They detect in the boy's request to become a day laborer rather than a household slave, an intention on his part to make eventual repayment to his father.[56] Knowing him to be a generous employer (v. 17), he asks him to contract him as a hired hand so that he can save enough money from his labors to restore his father's losses. Kenneth Bailey even surmises that what the prodigal really wanted was vocational training, so that he could boost his income as a skilled craftsman. As a paid worker, he would also retain a sense of personal dignity and a degree of financial independence from the village community, as well as from his older brother. It was only after making restitution that he planned to seek personal reconciliation with his father.[57]

Such a suggestion cannot be wholly discounted, given the importance of restitution in Jewish law. But at most it is a possible inference from the text, not the main point at issue. Day laborers were the lowest of the three classes of manual workers in the first-century world and were not considered part of the extended household.[58] In asking to be ranked among them, the prodigal was expressing his readiness to accept the most menial role available simply in order to be near to his father again and to render him service. It was not a means to some other laudable end, as Bailey implies. For the boy does not actually ask to be *made* a hired servant, but rather to be made *as* a hired servant (*poieson me hōs hena tōn misthiōn sou*, v. 19).[59] That is to say, he asks to be *treated* as someone of equivalent rank as a hired worker, even though his former status was that of a son. It is also worth noting that day laborers usually lived at a mere subsistence level since casual work was not always available. It is hard to believe that the prodigal, who himself had wasted away as a casual worker on a pig farm, imagined that by becoming a hireling of his father's he could generate enough surplus income to repay all his

---

56. So Derrett, *Law*, 110-16; Bailey, *Poet and Peasant*, 177-80, and *Jacob*, 103-7; Young, *Jewish Theologian*, 150; Cf. Forbes, "Repentance," 219; Keller speaks of the boy's "business plan for restitution," *Prodigal God*, 21-22.

57. Bailey, *Poet and Peasant*, 177-78, *Jacob*, 103-6, and *Cultural Keys*, 136-37.

58. Bock, *Luke*, 1313; Bovon, "Prodigal Son," 55.

59. In biblical Greek, *hōs* may serve to soften a statement to mean "as it were," "approximately," "perhaps" (Turner, *Grammar* III:320).

debts, even if his father was known to be generous. If restitution is in view, it is a restitution of willing and loyal service rather than a restitution of monetary losses.

Even so, the boy's offer to serve his father in this way has the same essential significance as financial reparation. In restorative justice theory, restitution is important for its symbolic power more than for its role in material recompense. As Howard Zehr explains: "Restitution symbolizes a restoration of equity, and it states implicitly that someone else—not the victim—is responsible. It is a way of denouncing the wrong, absolving the victim, and saying who is responsible. Accordingly, restitution is about responsibility and meaning as much as or more than actual repayment of losses."[60] In the parable, the boy's words of confession are matched by a willingness to behave henceforth in such a manner that his father's honor and dignity would be restored in the eyes of those who had witnessed his humiliation. It is in this sense that he makes symbolic restitution to him.

Repentance as Atonement and Reconciliation

The prodigal's pre-planning for repentance did not extend as far as arranging for ritual sacrifice, though in the religious and cultural setting of the time this would have been the concluding step in the boy's journey back to right standing in the community.[61] Because of his penitence, expressed through apology and restitutionary service to his victim, the boy knew he could count on God's forgiveness and mercy.[62] But he could be less certain of his father's pardon or his brother's acceptance. From the way he treated his hired hands, he knew his father to be a kind and gracious man (v. 17). But his own offending had been unusually grave, and he could not be sure his father's grace would extend that far. Certainly he did not anticipate full restoration to the bosom of the family, nor even to membership of the extended household. At best, he thought, he might be given the opportunity to perform casual tasks on the estate as one of the

---

60. Zehr, "Restoring Justice," 145.

61. Num 5:6–7; Lev 6:1–7; cf. Matt 5:23–24

62. "Repentance is the sole, but inexorable, condition of God's forgiveness and the restoration of his favor, and the divine forgiveness and favor are never refused to genuine repentance" (Moore, *Judaism*, 520).

laborers. As T. W. Manson observes, "Strict justice would disown him as a son; but perhaps mercy will accept him as a servant."[63]

What he experiences when he arrives home, however, is a merciful justice that confounds his expectations and restores him completely to the relationships he had so casually renounced. He discovers his father to be more graciously generous, and more genuinely just, than he could have ever imagined possible, though not, as we will see, to everyone's satisfaction!

SUMMARY

Modern readers are inclined to view the offending of the younger son as a relatively trifling episode of self-indulgent hedonism by a hormonally charged adolescent acting as though he were bullet proof in a cruel and unyielding world. Understood this way, the father's response to his son is much like what any enlightened parent would show to their misguided teenagers in such circumstances. But such a reading is far removed from how Jesus' first-century hearers would have interpreted events. They would have shared the prodigal's own assessment of his behavior as a case of sinning gravely against heaven and against his loving father (vv. 18, 21).

His sin was something much worse than material profligacy or moral laxity. It was a willful refusal to honor his father, as the law required, and to fulfill his relational obligations to his wider network of relationships. So severe was the boy's offending that he was, according to Deut 21:18–21, a candidate for the supreme penalty. Even if such a penalty was rarely, if ever, exacted for such transgression, its existence on the law books was a sign of just how seriously the crime of disrespecting parents was taken. As Josephus reasons: "God is displeased with those that are insolent towards their parents, because he is himself the Father of the whole race of mankind, and seems to bear part of that dishonor which falls upon those that have the same name . . . On such the law inflicts inexorable punishment, of which punishment may you never have the experience!"[64]

---

63. Manson, *Teaching*, 288.
64. Josephus, *Ant.* 4:262.

In the story of the parable, the youngest son dishonors his father in a whole sequence of ways. He covets his father's possessions, itself a dishonorable and unlawful thing to. He demands his share of his future inheritance now, an unprecedented effrontery. Once he has his hands on the property, he disposes of it immediately by putting it on the open market. He sells off his father's pride and joy, his "substance" and "life," to an outsider and leaves home with the proceeds. He thinks nothing of his father's future welfare. He treats him, in effect, as though he were already dead, with no further moral or emotional claims on him. In so doing, he piles dishonor upon dishonor on him. Once resident in foreign territory, he fritters away his entire legacy in dissolute living, and is reduced to rags. His inner moral bankruptcy is graphically displayed in his willingness to herd the swine of a brutal pagan overlord rather than confronting the reality of his sinful ways.

What fundamentally made the young man's sin so thoroughly sinful was its willful destruction of the mutuality and respect that ought to characterize human relationships. According to biblical tradition, humans are created as relational beings (Gen 1:27). Human identity resides fundamentally in our capacity for reciprocating relationships with one another and with God.[65] The prodigal son sinned by repudiating his reciprocal relationships with his father, his brother, his extended family, and his local community. He did not merely break some abstract moral or religious code. He did something far worse. He destroyed bedrock relationships by showing profound disrespect for the rights, needs, and dignity of those closest to him. His sin against others was simultaneously a sin against God, for it was a denial of the very meaning of his existence.

His subsequent experience shows that when a choice is made to sacrifice one's most foundational relationships in order to achieve some selfish form of autonomy, an almost dehumanizing vortex is created that sucks the sinner deeper into loneliness and despair. The prodigal abandoned the true source of his identity—the security of his father's love—in order to find freedom in a "distant country" (v. 13). But there is no freedom apart from the demands of love, and the prodigal ends up wallowing with unclean animals in servitude to the callous master, totally un-free and completely alone. The superficial friendships forged with his drinking buddies fail when needed most, for "no one gave him anything"

---

65. On this, see Marshall, *Crowned*, 54–63.

(v. 16). He is lost in relationlessness and gracelessness. The only solution is to retrace his steps back home and to rediscover what it means to be in intimate relationship again. For if sin is relational rupture, then the solution to sin is reconciliation and restoration.

But restoration, as restorative justice theory rightly emphasizes, is a costly undertaking. It is enormously costly for the victim, as we will see in the next chapter. But it is also acutely costly for the offender, who must accept the true price of accountability. The prodigal shows what accountability entails. It requires a genuine contrition of heart, evoked not merely by self-pity but by the memory of those who have been injured and by recollection of the value of the relationships that have been discarded. Contrition finds expression in verbal confession. This is critically important for clarifying where true responsibility for the injury lies and for beginning the process of recalibrating the offender's own moral compass towards virtuous commitment again. The prodigal's confession captures three crucial elements of accountability: acceptance of moral blame, recognition of the hurtful impact of one's behavior on others, and acknowledgement that one's relationships have been damaged and can only be restored by an act of unmerited grace on the part of the victim.

Equally important as verbal confession is the commitment to make good the losses the victim has endured. The prodigal's request to become a hired hand of his father's was a restitutionary gesture. Not because he intended to save money to make financial reparation, though this cannot be discounted. It was restitutionary because his willingness to serve as a laborer, rather than presume on his identity as a son, was a symbolic acknowledgement to others of his responsibility for humiliating his father in the past and of his desire in the present to restore honor to him through ungrudging service on his estate. But what the penitent boy did not reckon on was the sheer magnanimity of his father's love and the incorrigibility of his commitment to restorative justice.

9

A Better Justice

The father in the parable appears to be a relatively wealthy man. He owns herds of cattle and goats (vv. 27, 29), has numerous household servants to wait on him (v. 26), employs "many hired hands" whom he pays handsomely (v. 17), and owns fine robes, rings, and footwear (v. 22). He can afford to throw a huge party for his friends and neighbors, with red meat, not just chicken, on the menu (vv. 23, 27, cf. 5, 9), and with professional musicians brought in to entertain (v. 25). The fact that his oldest son, the future proprietor of the estate, still works manually in the fields (vv. 25, 31) may suggest that the family holdings are of moderate rather than very large size, particularly after the younger son had disposed of his share. Still, compared to most people, the father is clearly a man of means.

Typically in Luke's Gospel, and especially in the parables, the rich are targets of criticism and reproach for their greed and indifference to the needs of the poor.[1] Not in this case, however; the prodigal's father, though a prosperous landowner, proves himself to be a paragon of patient, merciful justice. In his role as family judge, he enacts that divine form of justice that is committed to reinstating penitent offenders to full participation in the life of the community they have spurned and even bestows honor on them for choosing again the path of freedom and life in place of alienation and death. He demonstrates the truth of Thomas Jay Oord's words that "righteousness rains like rivers when mercy reigns supreme."[2]

---

1. See Luke 1:51–53; 6:24–25; 12:15–21; 16:13–15, 19–31; 18:18–26; 19:1–10; 20:47, cf. 11:42–44; 21:1–2; 22:3–5. There is a vast literature on Luke's portrayal of the rich and poor. For useful brief overviews, see Donahue, "Two Decades," 129–44; Schmidt, *Hostility*, 135–62; Phillips, "Recent Readings," 231–69; Green, "Good News?," 59–74.

2. Oord, *Defining Love*, 197.

In his perceptive book *Rethinking Justice: Restoring Our Humanity*, philosopher Richard H. Bell observes that contemporary philosophical discussions on the topic of justice have become stuck. Post-Kantian discourse has been almost totally preoccupied with criticizing, defending, or amending liberalism's "thin" view of justice as a narrow political or legal principle. It has all but lost touch with the larger question of what it means to be a just human being, a topic that occupied many classical (and biblical) thinkers. What is needed, Bell urges, is recovery of a much "thicker" conception of justice as the practice of promoting or restoring human well-being in its totality, a justice that is "a testament to our humanity." Such a conception of justice may be more complicated to describe, since it strives to relate justice to the full panoply of human moral, spiritual, emotional, and aesthetic aspirations. But it is more consistent with the lived reality of human experience than are approaches that confine justice to technical considerations of laws, rights, and freedoms.[3]

One benefit of returning to a more textured view of justice is its capacity to hold justice and mercy together in the domain of corrective or criminal justice. Justice and mercy are often viewed there as contrasting concepts, with mercy serving to forestall or moderate or bypass the delivery of just deserts. But in a thicker conception of justice, mercy is not a substitute for justice, or merely some exterior check to prevent retribution from becoming excessive. It is an integral part of the meaning of justice itself, so that where mercy is absent, justice necessarily fails. Justice cannot stand as measured retribution alone; it must be joined at the hip with mercy in order to be truly just. In the words of legal philosopher Andrew Brien:

> Mercy provides sight to the moral agent; it enables her to perceive, be sensitive to, and understand the world, and to evaluate the salient moral properties of the people with whom she has contact. This virtue enables an actor to use power wisely. Without mercy, those dark passions that blind the framers and implementers of public policy to important facts about people, and lead them to focus instead only upon desert, are even more unchecked.[4]

3. See Bell, *Rethinking Justice*.

4. Brien, "Mercy," 104. Bell appeals to Brien's article, though without noting a significant difference in their positions. Bell argues for an expanded or thicker view of justice that incorporates mercy (*Rethinking Justice*, 45–65). Brien, however, argues

Unlike those legal thinkers who fear that any appeal to mercy threatens to undermine the rule of law, Brien insists that agents in a legal system stand under a positive obligation to cultivate a stance of mercy. Mercy entails the conscious refusal to remain indifferent to the defendant's individual circumstances and a determination to try to see things from their position. Insofar as the law vests discretionary power in judges, as it must in order to function properly, judges are morally obligated to engage the "gentle virtue of mercy" in exercising such discretion. Otherwise the law will be unable to achieve its goal of producing morally acceptable outcomes and promoting public well-being. Mercy also serves to disrupt "the incessant orgy of retribution" that would otherwise prevail without it, and contributes to promoting harmony, reconciliation, and human flourishing.

This truth—that there is no justice without mercy and mercy is essential to attaining justice in its thicker or restorative sense—is something that the father of the prodigal seems to understand intuitively. He knows that when mercy reigns supreme, righteousness, which in biblical understanding is the justice of right relationships, rains like rivers.[5]

THE MERCIFUL JUDGE

In the cultural setting of the day, the father's response to his returning son is nothing short of breathtaking. Indeed, it was so out of character for a wronged Palestinian *paterfamilias* to act as he does, and so unjustified by the particular circumstances of his son's offending, that his other son later vehemently accuses him of behaving unjustly (vv. 29–30). But from the father's perspective, no injustice transpires from allowing new life to trump former death, or recovery of the lost to cancel out former estrangement (v. 32, cf. v. 24). To display restorative love in place of punitive exclusion actually allows for a *better* justice to emerge, a justice that is fulfilled in personal reconciliation and reintegration in community. There are several dimensions to the father's response that help elucidate what is involved in this kind of restorative justice making.

---

against expanding the idea of justice to include all relevant moral considerations. Both, however, see justice and mercy as inseparable in operation. See also Rainbolt, "Mercy."

5. On biblical justice and righteousness, see Marshall, *Beyond Retribution*, esp. 35–95. On biblical justice and mercy, see Turner, "Justification and Justice," 510–23.

Respect for Personal Agency

The first notable feature is the respect the father shows for the personal agency of his two sons. When the younger son demands his share of the inheritance, the father accedes to his wishes. He thereby affords him the liberty to choose his own destiny and to experience the consequences of his choices. He does not try to deter him with threats or punishments but accepts his freedom of action. Kenneth Bailey explains that an Oriental patriarch would normally be expected to erupt in fury at such effrontery from one of his own children and to refuse to give ground. "It is difficult to imagine a more dramatic illustration of the quality of love, which grants freedom even to reject the lover, than that given in this opening scene."[6]

It is generally acknowledged that love cannot thrive apart from authentic freedom. Love is meaningless if individuals are not free to choose an alternative kind of response. Human freedom is never absolute, of course, and individual choices are always constrained by a range of external and dispositional factors. But there must still be some measure of genuine freedom for love to occur. As Oord explains in his analysis of the science of love, "To be free is to make choices that are not entirely dependent on external conditions that make it the case that one cannot do otherwise. Free choices entail that choosers are in some sense genuinely responsible for their actions. Coercion, in the sense of the unilateral determination of the chooser, is antithetical to love."[7] The freedom of the father's love is shown both by the way he freely loves his rebellious son despite his refusal to love him in return, and by the way he respects his right to self-determination, even when the choices he makes are hurtful and harmful.

The same is true with regard to his treatment of his other son. When, in defiance of social convention, the older boy refuses to participate in the family celebrations, the father employs the gentle art of persuasion rather than physical or emotional coercion to get him to change his mind ("he continually pleaded with him," *parekalei auton*, v. 28). This could be seen as contemptibly weak of the father. It would have been thought utterly demeaning for an old man to have to beg his son publicly to fulfill his wishes in this way. But, in reality, it turns out to be the father's greatest strength. For it is only through respecting his sons'

---

6. Bailey, *Poet and Peasant*, 165.
7. Oord, *Defining Love*, 17 (and passim).

personal agency that any hope exists for the emergence in the future of a relationship with them of mutuality, love, and respect. This happens with one son, but not with the other.

The father exhibits, then, a culturally exceptional deference to his sons' volitional freedom. He doesn't treat them as extensions of his own personality or surrogates for his own actions, but as autonomous moral agents. When humiliated by them, he resists asserting patriarchal authority to extract appropriate subservience. Instead of forcing them to bend to his will, he allows them full decision-making power, at considerable cost to his self. But in so doing, he furnishes the platform from which later restorative initiatives may occur.

None of this is to dispute the need for external coercion in some circumstances, particularly in the enforcement of justice. Coercion is one of the factors that is sometimes said to differentiate justice from love. Whereas love must of necessity be voluntary, justice often requires the exertion or threatened exertion of power to ensure that obligations are met and the weak are protected. Yet justice and love cannot be entirely sequestered from each other, since what ultimately distinguishes justice from tyranny is its respect for individual liberty. In this regard, justice and love require similar preconditions in order to prosper, and each needs the other in some measure to achieve its purpose. There is a legitimate place for external sanctions in the enactment of justice. But if justice relies wholly or predominantly on force, it can never achieve its ultimate goal of promoting human flourishing. It is revealing that what finally moved the prodigal to change his behavior and seek reconciliation was not fear of his father's power to punish him but recollection of his father's generosity of character (v. 17) and the regard he had shown for his moral autonomy, now expressed as a willingness to accept personal responsibility for his wrongful deeds ("Father, I have sinned," vv. 18, 21).

Hopeful Expectancy

A second notable feature of the father's restorative demeanor is his persistent expectancy. We are not told how long his younger son had been away from home at the point of his return, but it must have been for a considerable time. The older brother's complaint about having worked as a slave "all these years" (v. 29) probably refers to the period since the division of the property (v. 12). This would underscore his exceptional merit in continuing to work with his hands to provide for his father, even though he is now the legal owner of all that he surveyed (v. 31). In any event, the younger son clearly saw his initial departure as permanent. His cashing up of his inheritance—in its entirety—shows he had no intention of ever returning. Once he had gone, he was for all intents and purposes, in the eyes of others, as good as dead, never to be seen again (vv. 24, 32).

Yet the father never surrendered all hope. The fact that he saw his son approaching "while he was still far off" implies that he was regularly scanning the length of the road for any sign of his appearance (*eti de autou makran apechontos* is in the emphatic position in v. 20).[8] The father had never stopped waiting. His son had been long gone, lost in a "distant country." But his father continued to hope against hope that he might still be alive and would one day find his way back home. This is not to sentimentalize the narrative. Everything that happens subsequently is only explicable in light of a stubborn, passionate yearning on the part of the father to see his absent son restored. Miroslav Volf rightly sees this as the most amazing feature of the story.

> The most significant aspect of the story is . . . that the father who lets the son depart *does not let go of the relationship between them*. The eyes that searched for and finally caught sight of the son in "the distance" (v. 20) tell of a heart that was with the son in "the distant country" (v. 13). Away from home, the son still remained in the father's heart. Against the force of the wrongdoing suffered and the shame endured that sought to push the son out, he became a father of the "lost" son, of the "dead" son (v. 24). When the son's attempt to "un-son" himself changed the son's identity, the father had to renegotiate his own identity as a father.[9]

The father's stubborn refusal to "let go of his relationship" with his son is also shown in the emotional empathy he feels for his son's suffering.

Emotional Empathy

Catching sight of his emaciated son in the distance, the father is "filled with compassion" for him (v. 20). M. J. J. Menken uses statistical calculations to establish that this reference to compassion forms "the dramatic

---

8. So Bock, *Luke*, 2:1313 n. 21; Scott, *Hear Then*, 117; Bailey, *Cultural Keys*, 143.
9. Volf, *Exclusion and Embrace*, 159.

moment of the parable," the critical turning point in the drama, just as it does in the parable of the Good Samaritan.[10] The father had been deeply wronged by the boy's cruel actions, but there is nothing cold or calculating in his reactions when he sees him coming. He is overcome with emotion. He is stirred into action, not by the dictates of strict justice but by a compassionate craving to see his debilitated son restored to well-being and their relationship renewed. Later, a servant boy comments on the father's unbridled delight in having "received him back [into relationship], safe and sound [in body]" (*hugiainonta auton apelaben*, v. 27).

Kenneth Bailey suggests the father felt compassion for his son because he anticipated the rough reception that awaited him in the village square from indignant neighbors. He therefore rushes to provide him protection at the edge of town.[11] Richard Rohrbaugh agrees. He proposes that the verb used to depict the father's "running" (*dramōn*, v. 20) implies that he exerted himself to the limits of his ability in a desperate effort to reach the boy before others did.[12]

It is certainly possible that the father was worried about his boy falling victim to vigilante vengeance. We have already discussed the extent to which the entire village would have nursed a sense of grievance towards him. But in the text of the story, what elicited the father's pity was "seeing him" (*eiden auton*, v. 20), not contemplating the reactions of others to him. It was witnessing his son's distressed physical condition and human isolation that triggered pity in the father, just as the bereft state of the widow of Nain engendered compassion in Jesus (7:13), and the battered condition of the victim provoked compassion in the Samaritan (10:33).

10. Luke uses *splangchnizesthai* three times in his Gospel (7:13; 10:33; 15:20) and *splangchna* once (1:78). On each occasion, "Luke organizes his text in such a way that the word stands in the numerical middle of the pericope or of the part of the pericope in which it occurs, according to a count of words or syllables and/or according to a count of verbal forms or substantives. These numerical arrangements giving evidence of Luke's use of numerical literary techniques, confirm that in the passages in question 'compassion' is an important element or even the most important element." In Luke 15, the verb is preceded and followed by eleven verbal forms in the indicative. Menken, "Position," 112–13, cf. 108. See chapter 5 n. 31.

11. Bailey, *Poet and Peasant*, 181–82, and *Jacob*, 168.

12. Rohrbaugh, "Dysfunctional Family," 156–57. Rohrbaugh cites Arndt et al., *Lexicon*, 156 n. 56, for the meaning "to make an effort to advance, to exert oneself." It is worth noting, however, that in the third edition of the lexicon, Luke 15:20 is included in the meaning of "to make a rapid linear movement: run, rush, advance" rather than "to exert oneself" (1015).

What is most significant here is that this compassion welled up in the father's heart prior to any confession of guilt or any tangible evidence of behavioral change on the part of the wrongdoer. The father did not require rigorous proof of his son's penitence before leaping into action. It was enough to *see him* and know he was on the path home again, that his "return" was underway.

In the preceding parables of the lost sheep and the lost coin (15:4-10), the character who suffers the loss—the shepherd and the woman, respectively—actively goes in search of what has gone missing. At first sight, this does not happen in the parable of the Prodigal Son. Neither the father nor any agent on behalf of the father goes off to look for the lost boy in the distant country.[13] Instead, the father waits patiently at home for his son to *find himself* (v. 17) and return voluntarily.[14] This again underscores his respect for the boy's moral autonomy (something that sheep and coins lack), and his recognition that interior change cannot be cajoled from outside.

Yet there is also a sense in which the father *does* go in quest of his son. At the very moment the prodigal's decision for change becomes apparent to him, the father seizes the initiative and runs to embrace him. What he goes in search of is "this son of mine" (v. 24), the true relational identity behind the persona of sinful offender. In doing so, the father actually manifests a far greater dedication to recovery of the lost than either the shepherd or the searching woman showed. They acted as anyone else in their situation would be expected to act ("Which one of you . . . does not?"; "What woman . . . does not?" vv. 4, 8). The father, however, acts in a totally unexpected way and at considerable risk to himself. This brings us, then, to what is certainly the most striking feature of the father's behavior: his utter self-abnegation in the interest of reconciliation.

Heedless Humility

On catching sight of his boy, the father does not stand on ceremony, which decreed that he should wait at a dignified distance until his son

---

13. Keller suggests that the one who should have gone searching for the lost son was his older brother (*Prodigal God*, 79-84).

14. The reference to the prodigal "coming to himself" recalls the "going . . . finding . . . coming" of the shepherd in vv. 4-6 (*eis heauton de elthōn* v. 17, cf. *poreuetai . . . heurōn . . . elthōn*, vv. 4-6).

approached him and bowed reverently before him. Instead, "he ran and put his arms around him and kissed him" (v. 20). There is a fascinating parallel in the apocryphal book of Tobit that reinforces the father's impetuous delight. In the Tobit account, Anna is waiting for her son, Tobias, to return home, looking intently down the road on which he would travel. When she sees him, she tells her blind husband, Tobit, of the boy's approach and runs to embrace him, tearfully declaring, "Now that I have seen you, my child, I am ready to die" (11:5-15). The boy then approaches the father, who had stumbled out of his house into the courtyard at the commotion.

In our story, it is the *father* who runs down the road to greet the traveler. Dan Via proposes that, in Jungian terms, this could be seen as "an instance of 'the forgotten feminine in the Gospels,' an occasion of *eros*, the principle of relatedness, expressed by a man."[15] Be that as it may, commentators invariably point out that it was extremely undignified for an elderly gentleman to run in public. It involved a distinct lack of decorum because it required the runner to hike up his flowing robes and expose his legs to public view.[16] No ordinary Oriental father would have disgraced himself in this way. But here, as A. B. Bruce charmingly puts it, the father sprints towards his beloved boy "in the excitement and impatience of love, regardless of Eastern dignity and the pace safe for advancing years."[17]

His act of "falling on his neck and kissing him" was more than a simple gesture of greeting.[18] The repeated or ardent nature of the kissing, signaled by the compound form of the verb *katephilēsen*, implies that it

---

15. Via, "Prodigal Son," 37. Similarly Scott proposes that "the father combines in himself the maternal and paternal roles. As a father he is a failure, but as a mother he is a success," *Hear Then*, 116-17, 122. We should be cautious about gender stereotypes, however. In the story in Tobit, the father also expresses great tenderness towards his son. After being healed of his blindness, "Tobit saw his son and threw his arms around him, and he wept and said to him, 'I see you, my son, the light of my eyes!'" (11:13-14). Unlike the prodigal son, Tobias had not offended against his father.

16. Bailey, *Poet and Peasant*, 166, 181-82, *Cultural Keys*, 143-46, and *Jacob*, 166; Malina and Rohrbaugh, *Social-Science*, 372; Via, *Parables*, 172; Rohrbaugh, "Dysfunctional Family," 156; Snodgrass, *Stories*, 126 (who cites Sir 19:30; Aristotle, *Ethics*, 4.3.34); Burge, *Jesus*, 93.

17. Bruce, "Synoptic Gospels," 581.

18. Cf. Mark 14:45; Matt 26:49; Acts 20:37; 3 Macc 5:49.

was a gesture of reconciliation and offer of forgiveness.[19] It is striking, once more, that the father communicates his willingness to forgive even before the wrongdoer had uttered a single word of regret, or made any pledge of restitution, or expressed any kind of obeisance. In fact, by smothering the boy's neck with kisses, the father effectively prevents him from falling meekly at his feet and kissing his hand in deference, as would have been expected.[20] More important than receiving homage was conveying his eagerness to forgive his son and his desire to welcome him back into intimate relationship.

All this took place in full public view on the road into town. The household servants presumably saw what happened, as they were near the father at the time (v. 22). Other onlookers probably did so too. The father's flamboyant display of dashing toward his son and passionately embracing him would have quickly drawn spectators from the surrounding area, who become indirect participants in the event. Forgiveness may be a personal transaction between private individuals, but it can also have significant public ramifications.[21] It often spills over to affect others in the network of relationships the primary parties belong to, and thereby influences the mood and outlook of society at large.

Moral Integrity

The father's overwhelming generosity of spirit toward his offending son could easily be construed as a pathetic indulgence of his criminal profligacy. This is exactly how his older son will soon evaluate it (vv. 29–30). But for all his eagerness to forgive, the father still makes room for moral accountability, as he listens without objection to the prodigal confess his wrongdoing: "Father, I have sinned against heaven and against you; I am no longer worthy to be called your son" (v. 21). As we saw in the previous chapter, this confession discloses a profound level of self-awareness in the prodigal about the harmfulness of his offending and his culpability for it.

---

19. Jeremias, *Parables*, 130; Marshall, *Luke,* 610; Bailey, *Poet and Peasant*, 182. Cf. Gen 33:4; 45:14–15; 2 Sam 14:33; Luke 7:38.

20. Linnemann, *Parables*, 77.

21. On the public, even political, aspects of forgiveness, see Schriver, *Ethic*; idem, *Honest Patriots*.

Interestingly, the boy omits the third part of his prearranged confession: "Treat me like one of your hired servants" (cf. vv. 18–19).[22] Exegetes differ over the significance of this omission. Many suggest that the father cuts short the boy's confession because he wants to spare him further public humiliation or because he is eager to commence the celebration of his homecoming (cf. "quickly," v. 22).[23] Others attribute the omission to a change of heart in the boy himself. His initial intention had been to offer his father financial compensation through his labors. Yet on witnessing his father's unrestrained delight at his arrival, the boy realizes that the real issue is not the lost money but the broken relationship. Unable to see past the damage done to his relationship with his father, he focuses only on his unworthiness to be his son.[24]

The former explanation seems more probable. But in either case, what is telling is that the father does not challenge the accuracy of his boy's confession or deny the reality of his own victimization at his hands. He receives his confession without protest or contradiction. He does so not least because, as we have seen, confession plays an important dual role in restoration: it clarifies where responsibility for wrongdoing lies, thus vindicating the victim, and it helps recalibrate the offender's own moral compass, and thus promotes inward renewal.[25] The father may or may not have felt any personal need for public vindication of his own innocence. But he would certainly have been anxious to affirm his penitent son's commitment to a new level of moral performance, and at least for that reason does not discount his confession.

But no sooner is the confession out than the father "quickly" (*tachu*, v. 22) sets about to reverse the damage done by restoring to the offender the very thing he had spurned: his rights of sonship in the household. No verbal declaration of forgiveness is uttered, but it is implicit in all that

---

22. The words are included in several good manuscripts, but the shorter reading is preferred by most commentators and followed in Nestle-Aland. Holgate, *Prodigality*, 43–44, however, argues for the longer reading. He attributes the omission to homoioteleuton and argues that the longer reading is important for the moral meaning of the story.

23. Lenski, *Interpretation*, 816; Farrer, *St. Luke*, 183; Fitzmyer, *Luke*, 1089–90.

24. Bailey, *Poet and Peasant*, 183–84, 187; Forbes, "Repentance," 220; Via, *Parables*, 173–74.

25. In a wonderfully insightful essay, Aristotle Papanikolaou explores the moral, emotional, and therapeutic power of the act of confession, in addition to its juridical and sacramental significance ("Liberating Eros," 115–36).

happens. What Henri Nouwen calls "this mysterious event of reconciliation, forgiveness, and inner healing" then culminates in several concrete steps of restoration.[26]

Reintegrative Honor

Turning to his slaves, the father issues a flurry of instructions. Every detail underscores his commitment to secure the full rehabilitation of his offending son. He orders the slaves to fetch clothing and dress the boy, just as they would the lord of the house. Their act of clothing him would reestablish the appropriate relationship between them as household slaves and him as reinstated son and master.[27] At the same time, it symbolizes the change of moral commitment in the offender on which his new filial standing is founded. Clothing is a common biblical metaphor for inner moral character, and the changing of clothes an image for moral and spiritual transformation.[28] The penitent boy is clothed with new garments because he is now considered morally and spiritually worthy to wear them.

Each item of clothing manifests the respected status being accorded him. First the servants are to bring him "the best robe" (v. 22).[29] This presumably was the garment that the father himself wore on festal occasions. In the ancient world, clothing was a crucial indicator of social standing.[30] The impoverished majority of the population wore short, unbleached tunics of poor quality. Those of higher rank and wealth wore full, richly colored garments, with the length, color, quality of fabric, and degree of ornamentation being markers of social location (cf. Luke 20:46). If a king or nobleman wished to honor a deserving official, he would present him with a costly and ornate robe. This is exactly what the father does for his disgraced son. The boy expected to be relegated to the class of a manual laborer; instead, he is fêted as an honored dignitary.

Next the servants are told to "put a ring on his hand" (v. 22). The word for ring (*daktulios*) probably denotes a signet ring that served as a

---

26. Nouwen, *Return*, 9.

27. Cf. Isa 61:10; Zech 3:1–10; Rev 3:18.

28. Resseguie, *Spiritual Landscape*, 89–100.

29. The phrase *stolen ten prōten* could be translated "former robe," and some have argued it refers to the garment the boy formerly wore. Such a meaning, however, would usually require *autou*, "his." The phrase is best taken as a reference to the father's finest garment.

30. Generally on clothing in antiquity, see Batten, "Clothing."

symbol of gravitas and authority (cf. Gen 41:42; Esth 3:10; 8:2; 1 Macc 6:15). It was not simply a gift handed over to a visitor, it was "an emblem of power."[31] Instead of becoming a casual worker under orders, the prodigal is entrusted with a share in his father's authority. From a condition of irresponsibility, he assumes a position of influence and control. It is also a position of freedom, for the servants are next instructed to put "sandals on his feet." Slaves went about barefooted (cf. 10:4); only freedmen wore shoes, and only the master wore footwear inside the house.[32] The boy's calloused feet are shod with the shoes of shared sovereignty.

It is impossible, then, to miss the message implied by the father's actions. He does not merely supply his son's bare physical necessities; *he makes him an object of honor.*[33] He confers upon him the full dignity of sonship, notwithstanding his past offenses. The warm embrace, the kisses, the robes, the ring, and the sandals are together emblematic of honorable restoration to the family he had snubbed and the privileges he had renounced.

This emphasis on the bestowing of honor makes good sense in the context of a Mediterranean social order in which honor and shame were pivotal values in public life. In such a context, to offend against social and legal convention incurred social shame as well as moral blame. Forgiveness, accordingly, was as much about restoring honor as assuaging guilt.[34] While honor and shame play a less significant public role in contemporary Western society, the experience of being humiliated or honored by others still carries immense psychological potency. Honor and shame are universal, primal human realities. Tellingly, Howard Zehr has argued that much criminal offending is rooted in an offender's sense of shame and in his drive to remove or transform that shame by exerting power over others. We might speculate that the prodigal's downward spiral in a faraway land was a matter of him "acting out" the shame he knew he had incurred and internalized through his treatment of his father and family. Certainly his confession of sin fairly drips with feelings of worthlessness ("I am not worthy," vv. 19, 21). The father's symbolic reaffirmation of his

---

31. Bovon, "First Reading," 57. Scott, *Hear Then,* 118. Otherwise, Marshall, *Luke,* 583 n. 245.

32. Marshall, *Luke,* 610–11.

33. Plummer, *St. Luke,* 376; Scott, *Hear Then,* 118.

34. For an introduction to these categories, see Malina, *New Testament World,* 28–62; Moxnes, "Honor and Shame."

worthiness by attiring him as a son to be proud of would thus function to discharge him from the shame of his offending, as well as to rehabilitate him in the eyes of others.

By contrast, in our criminal justice system, prosecution and punishment usually serve to exacerbate the offender's sense of shame rather than alleviate it. As Zehr observes:

> If it is true . . . that shame and the desire to remove it motivates much crime, then our prescription for crime is bizarre: we impose more shame, stigmatizing offenders in ways that begin to define their identities and encourages them to join other "outsiders" in delinquent subcultures. Guilt and shame become a self-perpetuating cycle, feeding one another. In fact, psychiatrist Gilligan argues that punishment decreases the sense of guilt while at the same time accentuating shame, the very motor which drives offending behavior.[35]

It is noteworthy in the parable that the one who is instrumental in lifting the boy's shame was the primary *victim* of his offending, one who himself had been profoundly shamed by his actions. The father's restorative gestures actually entailed a remarkable interchange of honor and shame between victim and offender. Just as the boy's admission of wrongdoing restored honor to his humiliated father, so the father's acknowledgement of his son's repentance ended his humiliation and restored his dignity.

Punishment, it should be noted, plays no role whatsoever in this exchange. As John Caputo observes, "the father does not sit down and calculate just how much suffering he should inflict on his errant son for his prodigality but is prodigal with forgiveness; indeed, the idea that seeing the son suffer would in some way constitute a payback to the father would clearly be abhorrent to the sort of father portrayed in this story."[36] The transaction between the two characters is not based on an economy of equivalence, with punitive suffering the currency of exchange; it is based on an economy of gift, with forgiveness the coin of the realm. Punishment may play a number of valuable roles in social life,[37] but by itself punishment is not empowered to exorcise shame or re-create

---

35. Zehr, "Journey," 27.
36. Caputo, *Weakness*, 232–33.
37. See Marshall, *Beyond Retribution*, 97–144; Redekop, *Changing Paradigms*.

relationship. The replacement of shame and humiliation with honor and respect requires something far more potent than punishment. It requires confession, compassion, and forgiveness, and these in turn usually require some kind of personal encounter between victim and offender.

Perhaps the profoundest insight of restorative justice theory, and the secret to the power of its simple mechanism of bringing victims and offenders together to talk about what has happened, is its recognition that offenders and victims are on parallel journeys of dealing with the crushing impact of shame—for one, the shame of *doing* harm, for the other, the shame of *being* harmed—and that each party, paradoxically, holds the key to the other's healing. This key, moreover, is the mutual conferral of honor; it is the respect and dignity that each accords to the other through their voluntary participation in the process. Some criminal justice theorists advocate the use of "reintegrative shaming" or "shaming with compassion" as a restorative justice mechanism. This is where wrongdoing is dealt with in ways that ensure appropriate shame attaches to the offender's *behavior* rather than to their *person*, so that their willingness to disown their antisocial behavior becomes the basis for their reintegration in society.[38] One problem with such a concept is that it implies that shaming does the heavy lifting in the process of restoration. But this is not really the case. As the parable of the Prodigal Son indicates, it is the positive bestowal of honor on the shamed party, not the reinforcement or clarification of their shame, that makes the critical difference. And the person best equipped to confer such honor on the wrongdoer is the victim of their offense.

Public Acknowledgement

Shame has both interior and exterior dimensions. Inwardly it is an emotional feeling of disgrace. Outwardly it is a reproach in the eyes of others, a social stigma that needs to be publicly removed if the bearer of shame is to be rehabilitated. That is why the father caps off his restorative gestures by going public and throwing a lavish party. Feasts were not a common occurrence in village life, and few could afford to eat meat. So when the father orders the slaughtering of "the" calf that had

---

38. The seminal work on shaming is Braithwaite, *Crime, Shame*. But see also Maxwell and Morris, "Place of Shame," 133–42. See also the several studies on shame in *Restorative Justice*, edited by Hoyle, 3:379–415, 4:139–218.

been fattened up for a special occasion (*ton moschon ton siteuton*), he confers a massive honor on his son.

The festal gathering envisaged is obviously very large. A fattened calf could feed hundreds, and the presence of an orchestra and dancers at the event (v. 25) also implies a village-wide gathering of friends and neighbors (cf. vv. 5, 9). Bailey surmises that the feast was intended to draw public attention to the father's success in peacemaking, as well as to build bridges of reconciliation to the alienated village community.[39] We have already observed that the boy's neighbors probably nursed a deep sense of grievance towards him, and perhaps also his father. But the principal goal of the feast was not to placate them; it was to lift the cloak of shame from his son's shoulders and underscore his reinstatement as an esteemed member of the family. Just as both the shepherd who found his lost sheep and the woman who found her lost coin summoned their friends and neighbors to "rejoice with me" at their good fortune (vv. 6, 9), so the father invites his friends and neighbors to "celebrate and rejoice" (v. 32) with him that he had found his lost son.

For the father, such a sumptuous celebration was nothing short of a necessity ("we *must* celebrate," *edei* v. 32).[40] Of course, there can be no greater cause for parental happiness than having a child given up for dead found to be alive and well again (vv. 24, 32, cf. 27). But the father's words suggest more than just huge relief at his son's physical survival. They also express delight at the recovery of the lost *relationship* with him. The young lad had disowned his father by selling up and leaving forever. But the father had never forgotten his absent son; he may have been "lost" to him, and even "dead" to him, but he was never disowned. For all his wrongful deeds, for all the emotional pain he had caused, when the prodigal returned to the father, he embraced him as "this son of mine" (v. 24, cf. 30). He refused to exclude him from family membership and would not let his brother exclude him either ("this brother of yours," v. 32). Moreover, he ensured that the whole village community knew that he was home again, absolved of all wrongdoing and reinstalled as a fully functioning son. "Let us eat and celebrate," he declares, "and they began to celebrate" (vv. 23–24).

---

39. Bailey, *Jacob*, 112–15, 178–81; Rohrbaugh, "Dysfunctional Family," 157–58, 61.

40. The impersonal verb *dei* is one of Luke's favorite terms for expressing divine necessity (e.g., 2:49; 4:43; 9:22; 12:12; 13:14, 16; 17:25; 18:1; 19:5; 22:37; 24:7, 26).

All this stands in stark contrast to what usually prevails with ex-offenders in the modern criminal justice system. A former prison inmate in New Zealand made the following comment after his release:

> In the eyes of society, I am condemned forever to the underclass, to sub-citizenship. I will carry the stigma of a convicted career criminal for the rest of my life—never to be accepted by society as a person worthy of any meaningful degree of respect or dignity. The weight of shame and guilt is too great a burden to carry with me forever. Slowly the depth of my punishment became clear to me and I realized that certain elements of my punishment and stigmatization will follow me back into society and remain in place as long as I live. There will be no forgiveness.[41]

Not so with the prodigal son; the father's forgiveness was without reserve. The boy deserved reprimand and punishment. At the very least, he merited a long period of probation to demonstrate the genuineness of his reform. Instead, the father moves with lightening speed and in a flood of symbolic gestures to restore him to full belonging.

The sheer magnanimity of the father's response is intended, we have seen, to characterize the restoring love of God—a God who is also filled with compassion at the distressed state of his children and who longs to heal, forgive, and restore them (Ps 103:6–18). But Jesus' intention in portraying God in this way, and Luke's intention in locating the parable where he does in chapter 15, is not merely to say something about God; it is also to say something about the people of God. It is intended to furnish a viable model for how believers are to treat those whom the wider community judges to be treacherous offenders worthy only of punishment. They are to emulate the graciousness of God towards them—which means inviting their repentance, receiving their confession without objection, and restoring them to full participation in community. To do this is to imitate the compassion of God. But it is equally to imitate the *justice* of God, for in the final scene of the parable, the father must confront the accusation of having perpetrated a palpable injustice in forgiving his son. He is forced to defend his own thicker conception of restorative justice against the narrow, rules-based notion of justice advocated by his law-abiding son.

---

41. Cahill, "Victimisation," 2.

RESTORATION AND THE RESISTANCE OF THE LAW-ABIDING COMMUNITY

The role of the older brother in the parable brings a note of stark realism to the episode. Characterizing himself as an industrious ("all these years I have slaved for you") and a thoroughly law-abiding ("and never disobeyed your command") member of the household community (v. 29), he recoils in disgust at the sheer inequity of his father's showing mercy to such a serious and serial offender.[42] He complains that his years of dedicated toil have never been rewarded with even the smallest of parties, yet no expense has been spared in welcoming home his sinful sibling (v. 30, cf. 27). As Plummer infers of the grumbling son, "He is jealous, and regards his father as utterly weak in his treatment of the prodigal; but what specially moves him is *the injustice of it all.* His own unflagging service and propriety have never been recognized in any way, while the spendthrift has only to show himself in order to receive a handsome recognition."[43]

It is not hard to feel sympathy for the older son. On the face of it, he has a valid complaint, and his father does not contest the legitimacy of his feelings. But the instant rage (*ōrgisthē* v. 28) he experiences at the news of his father's actions—and anger is the only active emotion credited to him—indicates that behind the facade of a conscientious, law-abiding individual who wants simple justice to prevail lies a range of attitudes and personality traits that blind him to the essential justness of his father's restorative actions. These attitudes and attributes are present in everybody to some degree. But they are magnified out of all proportion in the psyche of collective society, which so often greets efforts to rehabilitate or reintegrate criminal offenders with indignation and disgust.

Harsh Judgmentalism

One such attribute is a tendency towards haughty judgmentalism. The parable makes it clear that the older son was "in the field" (v. 25) when his brother returned and had no idea why music and dancing were emanating from the house. He had to call over one of the passing servants to ask what

---

42. Many commentators take this reference to law-keeping as a polemical allusion to the Pharisees, cf. Plummer, *Luke*, 378; Green, *Luke*, 586. Otherwise, Scott, "Prodigal Son."

43. Plummer, *Luke*, 378 (emphasis added); so too Holgate, *Prodigality*, 185.

was going on (v. 26).⁴⁴ When told of his brother's return and his father's joy, he explodes in anger (v. 28). He does not inquire into his brother's state of mind. He doesn't ask about what transpired when he encountered his father on the road. The possibility that his brother might have changed never enters his head. He simply recalls his past identity as someone who has defrauded his family and consorted with prostitutes, someone beyond the pale who ought to be excluded from communal gatherings, not fed the fattened calf. There is a revealing parallelism between the three-part narrative description of the prodigal's actions in v. 13 and his brother's cynical summation of his behavior in v. 30.⁴⁵

| v. 13 | "... he squandered *dieskorpisen* | his property *tēn ousian autou* | in dissolute living" *zōn asōtōs* |
| v. 30 | "... he devoured *kataphagōn* | your property *sou ton bion* | with prostitutes" *meta porneōn* |

It is clear from this comparison that the older brother puts the worst possible construction on his sibling's behavior. His careless wastefulness (*dieskorpisen*) is construed as greedy consumption (*kataphagōn*); his disregard for his own property (*tēn ousian autou*) is rendered as a despoiling of his father's livelihood (*sou ton bion*); and his loose living is given explicitly sexual overtones (*meta porneōn*).

The reference to prostitutes is particularly scurrilous. There is no mention of prostitutes in the earlier part of the story, so the older son was presumably making this lurid deduction on the basis of what he considered to be his brother's fixed character. It is a classic example of "deviance labeling," a commonplace in the criminal justice domain. This is where attaching an abnormal label to certain people functions to stigmatize them in the public eye and even to prescribe matching behaviors from them in the future. Call someone a criminal and he is more likely to *behave* like a criminal.⁴⁶ This is because our sense of identity is largely

44. Most commentators take *paidion* to refer to a household servant. Bailey prefers to see it as a village youth, because he speaks to the older brother of "your father" rather than "the master" (*Poet and Peasant*, 194).

45. I am indebted to George Ramsey for noting this parallel (Ramsey, "Plots, Gaps" 36–37).

46. The extent to which labeling of criminals encourages further offending is disputed by the experts (see Wellford, "Labeling Theory").

conferred upon us by the way other people treat us and by the manner in which they speak of us. The labels used can easily become self-fulfilling prophecies. We start to act in ways that confirm the beliefs that others have of us, whether for good or for ill.[47]

Deviance labeling appears to be less pronounced in smaller-scale societies than in larger, more complex groupings. The interdependence and relative equality of people in small, tightly knit communities fosters a higher degree of tolerance for eccentric behavior and a general reluctance to label such actors as deviants. The exception is where their behavior is considered to be a positive threat to the integrity or security of the larger unit.[48] Perhaps this is why the older brother alleges promiscuity. As Richard Rohrbaugh explains, "If he can make the promiscuous label stick he can destroy the younger brother's place in the family and probably in the village as well. The fear would be that down the road 'sons' of the prodigal might show up claiming family and village rights and chaos would ensue. If the older son's label sticks, therefore, the younger son would have to leave the village for good and no progeny of his could ever return."[49]

It is obvious, then, that the law-abiding older brother views his younger sibling in the darkest of terms. He makes no allowance for the possibility that, as a result of bitter experience or advancing maturity, he might have changed. His persona as transgressor is fixed forever and eclipses all else in his character. He is simply a bad apple who should be ostracized from respectable society, not welcomed back into the family bosom.

Cold Self-Righteousness

Such exclusionary judgmentalism in the older son is paired, secondly, with an exaggerated sense of his own virtue. "For all these years I have slaved for you and I have never disobeyed your command" (v. 29). There are two tragic ironies here. The first is that he views himself as a slave

---

47. "Our sense of identity is in large measure conferred on us by others in the ways they treat or mistreat us, recognize or ignore us, praise us or punish us . . . . We come to live up to or down to the expectations that others have of us. The expectations of others often become self-fulfilling prophecies. Without realizing it, we often behave in ways that confirm the beliefs others have about us. Those subjective beliefs can create new realities for us. We often become who other people think we are, in their eyes and in our behavior" (Zimbardo, *Lucifer Effect*, 321).

48. Raybeck, "Anthropology and Labeling Theory."

49. Rohrbaugh, "Dysfunctional Family," 161.

(*douleuō soi*) when, in fact, he is the firstborn son. His work on the estate is performed out of a sterile sense of duty, not out of loving devotion.[50] He has no conception of what it means to be a caring son, and so cannot appreciate what it must be like to be a rejected parent. Though his father addresses him affectionately as "dear child" (*teknon*, v. 31),[51] the boy never once calls him "father." Although his father delights in his companionship as one who is "always with me" (v. 31), the boy's emotional ties lie elsewhere, for what he most wants to do is to "celebrate with my friends" (v. 29), not be with his father. He takes no pleasure in his relationship with him; there is no joy or delight or tenderness. He treats him as a master to be obeyed, not as a father to be cherished, and he considers this to be a sign of virtue. But his virtue is only skin-deep, an exterior conformity to social convention rather than an inner fidelity to what is true and good.

The second irony is that, at the very point of appealing to his unstinting obedience to his father, the young man is actually standing in defiance of him. Custom required that he should be present at family banquets, where he would serve jointly as host with his father, greeting important guests and ensuring that they were properly provided for. His stubborn refusal to do so, despite his father's continual pleading (*parakalei*, v. 28), together with the bitter tirade he launches against him (*idou*, "Listen to me!" v. 29), would have counted as profoundly insulting.[52] As Joel Green observes, it was "a symbolic act of gargantuan proportions in a culture where kinship boundaries are secured through the sharing of food."[53] The older son was knowingly humiliating his father. He was inflicting on him an injury every bit as deep as that caused by his younger brother. Most Oriental patriarchs would have reacted with violent fury to such insolence.[54] But the long-suffering father "goes out" (*exelthōn*) from the

---

50. Some exegetes, it should be said, take *doulein* to signal filial piety rather than a servile obedience (e.g., Bovon, "First Reading," 60; Linnemann, *Parables*, 79).

51. The Greek term *teknon*, "child," is more intimate than *huie*, "son," and the addition of the grammatically unnecessary pronoun *su* underscores the intended intimacy of the expression in this context.

52. Bailey, *Poet and Peasant*, 195. Derrett sees it as tantamount to breaking the fifth commandment, *Law*, 115.

53. Green, *Luke*, 584-85; also Rohrbaugh, "Dysfunctional Family," 158-60.

54. According to Bailey, a typical Middle Eastern father would be expected to lock up such a son, finish the banquet, and have him beaten (*Poet and Peasant*, 196, and *Cultural Keys*, 163).

banquet to find his missing son and reassure him of his affection (v. 28). For the second time in the story, the father lays aside his own dignity to move benevolently towards his wayward children, and for the second time he expresses no recrimination at the wrongs they have done to him.

It is because the non-prodigal son exaggerates his own virtue and magnifies his brother's vice that he fails to see their common kinship. When the servant refers to him as "your brother" (v. 27), he grows sullen; he prefers to think of him contemptuously as his father's "so-called son" (*ho huios sou houtos,* v. 30). He considers himself to be morally superior to his sinful brother, but in fact he resembles him in many ways. Both sons are equally prepared to dishonor their father for personal ends, one by selling off his livelihood, the other by refusing to join him at the table. Both are thoroughly self-centered, preoccupied in different ways with money and pleasure. The younger one demands that his father "give me" (*dos moi,* v. 12) his inheritance so that he can live the high life now; the older son complains that his father has "never given me" anything (*emoi oudepote edōkas,* v. 29), and perhaps feels envious of his brother's imagined frolicking with hookers (v. 30). Both are indifferent to their father's feelings. The younger son demands his inheritance immediately without any concern for the impact of his words on his father. The older son is similarly insensitive. He remains impassive when his father is affronted by his youngest son and makes no effort to heal the rift that emerges between them.[55] Both sons misconstrue the kind of relationship their father wants of them. The returning son imagines that his father would be content to relate to him as a hired servant (v. 19); the remaining son boasts that he has "slaved" for his father for countless years (v. 29). Both sons view him as a lord to be placated, not as a father to be treasured.

Most importantly, both sons offend against their father, though in different ways. One does so as a law-breaker, the other as a law-keeper. In both cases, their transgression entails a violation of relationship. One breaks the relationship by failing to fulfill the obligations of a dutiful and devoted son. The other does so by claiming to fulfill those expectations,

---

55. "Breaks in relationships are always healed through a third party among Middle Easterners. The third party is selected on the basis of the closeness of the relationship to each side. In this case, the role of reconciler is thrust upon the older son by all the pressures of custom and community. His silence means refusal" (Bailey, *Poet and Peasant,* cf. 168, and *Jacob,* 154; Young, *Jewish Theologian,* 146–47; Rohrbaugh, "Dysfunctional Family," 151).

though in a niggardly, self-centered, and ultimately fragile way. But whereas the prodigal comes to acknowledge his sin and confess his unworthiness, his older brother can only profess his superior virtue and bemoan his unrewarded rectitude. Refusing to view himself as part of the common stream of sinful humanity, he is trapped in his own bitterness. He is unable to understand his father's forgiveness because he feels no need of forgiveness himself.

Structures of exclusion and stigmatization, of which the fantastically misnamed "Corrections System" is the most hideous and violent example, are invariably sustained by a similar refusal on the part of the "righteous" to admit their common, flawed humanity with those they deem to be intractable sinners and criminals. Because "we" are not like "them," "they" can be treated in ways that we would never consider appropriate for ourselves. And if they are, it only leads to a displaced feeling of victimization.

Embittered Victimhood and Distrust

A third attribute that precludes the older son from understanding his father's actions is his acute sense of victimhood. On the one hand, he encourages his father to dwell on his own victimization at the hands of his youngest offspring, who "devoured *your* property with prostitutes" (v. 30). As an innocent victim, his father ought to demand satisfaction, not offer absolution. On the other hand, the son casts himself as a victim of his father's callous neglect in the past and blatant favoritism in the present: "*You* have never given *me* even a young goat so that *I* might celebrate with *my* friends; but when this son of yours came back . . . *you* killed the fattened calf for *him*!" (vv. 29–30). His sense of victimhood runs so deep that he assumes that the celebration thrown for his brother somehow detracts from his own virtue and devalues his standing in his father's eyes.

This entrenched sense of personal victimhood explains a fourth attribute observable in the older brother: his instinctive distrust of judicial leniency. He is angered by his father's apparent indulgence of his brother's wrongdoing, and contests the justness of throwing a party for someone so unsuitable. The father repudiates this charge of injustice in two important ways. First, he rejects the implication that love is a limited commodity—that the love shown to the delinquent son must somehow be deducted from the love available to his other son. "Dear child," the father says with tenderness, "you are always with me, and all that is mine is yours" (v. 31). The firstborn son loses nothing from the love directed at his brother; his standing is in no way diminished. If anything it is enhanced, for the offending brother's return to right relationship only serves to vindicate the first son's choice of remaining always with his father. Love is not a zero-sum game. The father continues to love his "good" son even while pouring abundant love on his "bad" son. For all the delight he feels at the return of his lost boy, the father still notices the absence of his other boy from the party and goes in search of him. Rejoicing with one son, he remains ever vigilant to the needs of the other. He loves them both equally, and wants them to love each other as "this brother of yours" (v. 32).

What about the older son's complaint of past neglect by the father? Why had the father "never" (*oudepote*) rewarded his fidelity and hard work with a celebratory meal? It is impossible to say. Some think the boy's accusation is simply erroneous. The father had continually acknowledged his son's contribution ("always . . . everything," v. 31), but the self-absorbed grumbler was incapable of recognizing it.[56] Or perhaps he was such a misery that his father never thought he wanted to party in the first place! According to T. W. Manson, "the chief reason why he never got so much as a kid to make merry with his friends was that he would not know how to make merry had he got it."[57] Still others suggest the father didn't give him a kid because he thought he did not need his permission to take one. Since "all that is mine is yours," the boy could have organized his own social gatherings whenever it suited him. The fact that he never did so simply reveals how little he appreciated his filial status. For John Dominic Crossan, this "clear and unsolved paradox" in the parable is an intentional literary device that "invites, permeates, and relativizes each and every reading."[58]

Whatever the explanation, more important for our purposes is the second defense the father offers for his actions. The complaining son assumed that the banquet in full swing was simply a celebration of his brother's homecoming, since all he had been told by the passing servant was that "your brother has come" (v. 27). Such merriment he deemed to be a breach of natural justice, given his brother's disgraceful behavior. But

---

56. Plummer, *Luke*, 379; Morris, *St. Luke*, 244.
57. Manson, *Sayings*, 290.
58. Crossan, "Metamodel," 138–39.

for the father, the feast was a celebration, not of his son's simple return, but of his transformation. "We had to celebrate and rejoice," he explains, "*because* [*hoti*] this brother of yours was dead and has come to life; he was lost and has been found" (v. 32). It was not merely the *fact* of his return but the *condition* of his return that was the occasion for rejoicing. The word pairs "dead-alive" and "lost-found" are plainly metaphorical for the boy's moral transformation. As David Holgate observes, "The father's words express a recognition that the son has gone through a life-changing experience. What is celebrated is not the son's restoration to his former state (which was one of moral death leading to physical death, v. 17c), but a celebration of his new state, which is one of moral life. There is also the implication that part of this recovery of life is a recovery of relationship."[59]

That is why no injustice had occurred. What made the lavish feast entirely just and equitable was that it marked the prodigal's renewed commitment to right living, in parallel with his brother's alleged commitment. The essential "justice" of restorative justice, in other words, depends on factoring in repentance. Genuine repentance induces a transformation of identity, so that the contrite sinner becomes a different person than he was before. He thus becomes a candidate not merely for a suspension of punishment but for a whole new beginning. No injustice transpires when the lost are recovered, when the dead are restored to life, when sinners are forgiven. Justice is vindicated in such transformations, for things are returned to how they ought to be and righteousness prevails once more.

This, however, is not how the law-abiding son construes the nature of justice. He employs a thin, rules-based notion of retributive justice that gives priority to just deserts and the stringent enforcement of moral rules. There is nothing inappropriate in the rules of natural justice themselves. By any measure, hard work merits greater reward than profligacy, obedience to the law deserves better treatment than disobedience, and meeting one's obligations is more commendable than flouting them. The problem is not with the rules but the brother's insistence on strictly enforcing them irrespective of individual circumstance. He prefers the simplicity of punitive ostracism to the complexity of wrestling with the ambiguities that always surround situations of human offending and the corresponding obligation to employ Brien's "gentle virtue of mercy" in the interests of achieving moral outcomes.

59. Holgate, *Prodigality*, 167.

By contrast, his father employs a relational conception of justice that acknowledges the radical implications of repentance and prioritizes the need for relational recovery. This is evident in the way he construes the offending and its consequences in entirely relational terms ("this son of mine," "dear child," "you are always with me," "this brother of yours," "he was dead and is alive again," "he was lost and is found"). The father still recognizes the importance of moral principles and just rules for the proper functioning of the household community: he pays his workers well (v. 17), expects his servants to follow his instructions (v. 22–23), and honors the principles of hospitality (vv. 24–25). But he knows that human community is constituted by something far deeper than any set of moral or social rules. It is comprised of relationships.

Moral performance may affect the quality and character of these relationships. But the relationships exist independently of the way people behave, for relationships are what constitute us as human beings. No one has expressed this better than John Donne: "No man is an island entire of itself, every man is a piece of the continent. . . . [A]ny man's death diminishes me, because I am involved in mankind; and therefore never send to know for whom the bell tolls; it tolls for thee."[60] Human beings are inescapably interconnected with one another; the plight of one affects the plight of all. It follows, then, that in the quest for justice, it is not moral or legal rules that should have the only say; it is the objectivity and irreducibility of human relationship. Certainly there is a "must" to observing shared moral and legal codes. But there is also a "must" to receiving back into fellowship those who have broken the rules and who want to return to right standing.[61] For justice is finally fulfilled only when relationships are restored.

SUMMARY

I have proposed that what distinguishes the father's response from that of the law-abiding older son is how each construes the meaning of justice and the place each gives to mercy in the enactment of justice. The father employs a "thick" conception of justice that focuses on reconciliation and is salted with compassion. The son operates with a "thin," morality-based

---

60. Donne, Meditation XVII, *Emergent Occasions*.
61. Volf, *Exclusion and Embrace*, 164.

notion of justice that prioritizes just deserts and strict application of the law of equivalence. One practices *restorative* justice; the other favors *retributive* justice.[62]

The father's more holistic approach to justice rests, initially, on a profound respect for the personal agency of his two sons. He acknowledges their freedom of choice that brings with it moral accountability. This in turn rests on an even more fundamental respect for the inherent relationality or sociality of human beings. It is this fact that gives rise to the familial and communal groupings to which we all belong, as well as to the moral, legal, and cultural codes we all observe. These codes are important, but they are secondary to the ontological reality of human relatedness. It is only because we exist in reciprocating relationships that issues of justice arise in the first place, and justice is essentially the making right of relationships.

It is this appreciation of his enduring interconnection with his son that enabled the father of the prodigal to remain confident of his son's capacity for change, even after he had violated one of his most foundational relationships. It is also what freed him to be filled with compassion and forgiveness rather than simmering resentment when the boy finally turned up. Forgiveness, by definition, is a gift freely given to the guilty party, otherwise it is not forgiveness. But it is not given cheaply, for it occurs in the moral space created by remorse, repentance, confession, and accountability, and demands moral effort on the part of both giver and receiver. But when it occurs, it lifts the shame of offending (and, indeed, the shame of victimhood) from the heads of those affected.

The father silently acknowledges the prodigal's expression of shame ("I am not worthy"), but he does not accentuate the shame. He does not use it as an instrument for reintegrating the offender back into society. On the contrary, he uses *honor*. For all his wrongful actions, the prodigal was still "this son of mine," and the moment he chose to act like an honorable son by returning in penitence to his father, the father confers on him all the dignities that belonged to a true son—the best robe, the signet ring, the sandals, the celebratory banquet, the fattened calf. He restores him to right relationship in every way, and justice prevails. Punishment is not involved. Whatever else punishment may achieve, it cannot give life to the dead or bring joy, music, and dancing into the experience of

---

62. This is not to say that restorative and retributive conceptions of justice are mutually exclusive. See, for example, Roche, "Retribution"; Walgrave, "Restorative Justice?"

former victims (vv. 23, 25, 32). Only repentance, confession, compassion, and forgiveness—the "gentle virtue of mercy"—can satisfy justice in its thickest sense.

This is not, however, how the economically productive, law-abiding member of the family understands justice. For him, justice is a matter of delivering just deserts and upholding moral standards, and because his younger brother is a promiscuous, profligate good-for-nothing, he does not deserve redemption. To throw a party in his honor is to perpetrate an injustice. It is, in effect, to revictimize the innocent. What justice requires is to take the celebration away from his offending brother and redirect the resources to the more deserving one. It is a zero-sum game: what is given to the offender must be deducted from the victim, so what is given to the victim should be taken from the offender.

In reply, the father defends the essential justness of his actions in two significant ways: he challenges the notion that love is a limited commodity, to be divided up between recipients according to their moral worth, and he underlines the crucial importance of factoring repentance into the equation. Repentance generates a change of identity in the offender, so that he or she becomes a candidate for a fresh start. When true repentance is present, that which was lost through the offending is found again; what has died is raised to new life. "We *had to* celebrate and rejoice *because* this brother of yours was dead and has come to life; he was lost and has been found" (v. 32).

The father's final words to his oldest son contain a double challenge. Would he recognize the returned prodigal as "this brother of yours," someone to whom he owed fraternal love as a fellow, flawed human being, or would he continue to despise him as an outcast? And would he join in the celebration of his restoration, or would he keep his distance on the strict principle of retributive justice? The impersonal verb "must" (*edei*) lacks a stated subject. Most modern translations supply a plural subject—"*we* must celebrate." But given the predominance of singular pronouns in the immediate context, it is equally possible to read a singular subject—"*you* must celebrate." You, the righteous son, stand under a bounden duty to rejoice because your offending brother has been restored to relationship and righteousness prevails.

One last point needs to be made, though it is rarely noticed. For the older son to relinquish his objections and join in the feast of forgiveness would be costly for him. It could require of him a willingness to share his possessions with his penniless brother. The prodigal had lost everything through his reckless living, and while his father could confer on him the symbols of forgiveness and familial esteem, he could not give him any more land, for what remained had already been gifted to his other son (vv. 12, 31). The prodigal's inheritance had gone for good—*unless* his upright brother should graciously choose to give him a stake in what he possessed.[63] The father's remission of the offender's guilt and shame presented the law-abiding son with a mandate and an invitation: a mandate to endorse the offender's forgiveness, and an invitation to accept the costs of providing him with the wherewithal to become a fully functioning member of the estate.

This, then, is the final challenge of this parable of restorative justice: a challenge to contemplate not only the restoration and reintegration of offenders as an outworking of the discipline of forgiveness, but also to display towards them an open-handed hospitality, a readiness to share with them what the parable calls our "living" (*bios*) and "substance" (*ousia*), so that they may again participate as equals in the social and economic life of society. Nothing less than this qualifies, finally, as restorative justice. Nothing less accords with the graciousness of God, who "makes his sun to rise on the evil and on the good, and sends rain on the righteous and on the unrighteous" (Matt 5:45).

We are not told how the resentful young man responded to the summons of the forgiving father. It is this that gives the story its endlessly searching power. But from the narrative point of view, there is little doubt how he *ought* to have responded. Obligated by the logic of the offender's repentance and the victim's compassionate forgiveness, he should rise above his own sense of grievance and fear of personal loss to celebrate the restoration of his brother to right standing and to give freely to him from what he himself had been graciously given by his father (v. 12). For "righteousness rains like rivers, when mercy reigns supreme."

---

63. Luise Schottroff argues that the father must have promised his son another share in the inheritance, though the story fails to give any details about the legal implications of such a promise (*Parables*, 140, 143). Rohrbaugh also recognizes the dilemma. "The prodigal's loss of the money means the older brother will be the sole support of the father in his old age and *likely of the prodigal as well*. His interests have been damaged. Yet a reconciliation between the brothers is essential to the well-being of *all* members of the family and indeed to its relations with the larger community" ("Dysfunctional Family," 159 [my emphasis]).

PART 3

Just Compassion

10

Public Compassion

In both the parables we have been discussing, the turning point is reached when the central character is "moved with compassion" (10:33; 15:20) at the suffering he witnesses and responds with a clear-sighted determination to restore the subject to physical, social, and material wellbeing. Both stories, I have proposed, may be understood as episodes of restorative justice, since both deal with serious wrongdoing and its consequences and both recount restorative responses. In the Good Samaritan, the innocent *victim* of criminal violence is restored to health and safety by the extraordinary actions of a compassionate stranger, who, in acting this way, is said to have fulfilled the true meaning of God's law (10:36). In the Prodigal Son, the contrite *offender* is reinstated to an honored position in the household community by the actions of his compassionate father, who considered such a response to be a "necessity" (15:32) in view of the boy's repentance. In both episodes, justice entails a compassionate commitment to restoration. Justice and mercy are not arraigned in opposition to each other; on the contrary, it is only through the mercy-full actions of key participants in the drama that justice is effected for those caught up in the tragedy of criminal wrongdoing. Justice encompasses mercy, and mercy evinces justice.

Such a proposition becomes controversial, however, once we intend it as a general truth about the pursuit of justice in a complex society. It is one thing to derive personal inspiration from the way two fictional characters in two ancient folktales respond mercifully to the predicaments they encounter; it is quite another to draw normative conclusions about the nature of justice or to advocate an alternative paradigm for the operation of the criminal justice system on the basis of such accounts. There are major complications entailed in moving from the imaginative world of Jesus' parables to the world of normative ethics or the world of institutional practice today, and any attempt to bridge the gap must grapple with the peculiar characteristics and theological intent of Jesus' parabolic discourse. That does not mean that the message of the parables should be restricted to purely private religious or existential concerns alone, as has often been the case in the history of interpretation, especially in the modern era. The stories themselves mirror the social and political realities of everyday life in first-century Palestine, and their subject matter ought to be allowed to inform reflection on everyday issues of social and political life today as well, including issues of crime and punishment.

Importantly, the relevance of the parables to this end lies precisely in their character as *parables*. Parables should not to be treated as repositories of normative rules, juridical principles, or procedural guidelines that may be translated directly into justice theory or political policy in general society today. Instead, their value lies in the distinctive worldview or hierarchy of values they depict, the universe of meanings they portray, by means of which hearers are invited to fashion the way they live at every level of their existence: personal and public, private and social.[1] Jesus used the parables as tools for breaking open existing frames of reference, for challenging or confounding taken-for-granted assumptions about the world and its notions of justice, and for offering a radically different way of conceiving reality, a way conditioned by the restoring and liberating justice of God now at work in the present.

What these parables afford us, then, is not so much a set of conceptual ideas or speculative principles for transposing directly into social theory or political policy, but imaginative examples of what is possible in human affairs if we can but grasp—or be grasped by—the restorative reality of God's justice, a justice that now confronts us most directly in the teaching and career of Jesus. This means that in extrapolating from the narrative world of the parables to the task of judicial reflection today, it is important to factor in both sides of that "striking mix of realism and unrealism" I have drawn attention to in the exegesis.

---

1. "There is no direct route from our parable to an ideology of social ethics," writes McDonald. The parable instead embodies a "narrative concept of morality" that subverts the values operating in conventional society and, by intersecting creatively with the life stories of its hearers, creates an "effective moral community" that is receptive to the meanings implied by the story and willing to act on them ("View," 36–37).

On the one hand, both stories deal with the most realistic situations imaginable—an act of criminal violence and a breakdown in family relationships—and both commend practicable ways of resisting the common downward drag of human behavior toward selfishness and retributive resentment. The compassion they depict is also a commonplace phenomenon. Most people exhibit some level of compassionate concern for others in their day-to-day living, without which life would indeed be nasty, brutish, and short. Every hearer of the parables is capable, therefore, of choosing to emulate the self-giving Samaritan or the forgiving father, in preference to the preoccupied priests or the censorious older brother. To that extent, both accounts offer realistic moral instruction for everyone. This applies at an institutional level as well. It is perfectly feasible for the criminal justice system to strive to exhibit a compassionate concern for the welfare of victims and a commitment to the reintegration of offenders in a manner that corresponds to the priorities evident in the parables, and it should be encouraged to do so.

At the same time, however, the stark *unreality* of the response of the Samaritan and the forgiving father also needs to be factored in. Both characters display a depth and devotedness of compassion that surpasses anything that is normally seen or naturally attainable. Each exhibits a level of moral excellence that few persons in this life attain to, not least because of the enormous self-discipline required to achieve it.[2] In depicting such an extraordinary expression of sacrificial and extensive love, the parables implicitly summon their listeners to open their hearts to the eschatological power of God's kingdom at work in their midst in order to inspire, empower, and sustain a similar, all-surpassing generosity of spirit in their own lives as well.

Put simply, the parables operate on two dimensions—a common ethical dimension and an eschatological "plus" dimension—and both need to be given full weight in their interpretation and application. It is precisely at the intersection of these two dimensions—the natural and the unnatural, the expected and the unexpected, the possible and the impossible—that the interpretive challenge lies. The stories simultaneously enjoin a universal moral obligation to pursue restorative or transformative justice in this world ("Go you and do likewise") and underscore the need for divine empowerment to fulfill this obligation to the unlimited

---

2. Cf. Reilly, "Compassion as Justice," 21.

extent envisaged. Every individual, and every social institution, is capable of "going and doing" to a morally significant degree, and is summoned by the parable to move in this direction. But they can only truly "do likewise" by appropriating the transforming power and restorative priorities of God's eschatological presence manifested uniquely in the person and work of Jesus. Such appropriation requires both divine grace and human response—the grace of encountering the compassion of God made eschatologically available in Jesus, and the moral commitment to work assiduously at broadening and deepening one's own compassionate responsiveness to the sufferings of others in light of that grace.[3]

In this final section of our study, I want to explore in more abstract terms the connection between compassion and justice. If the style of justice portrayed in the parables may fairly be described as a *restorative justice*, as I have argued, and if such justice is expressly understood as the outworking of *compassion*, which in both accounts it plainly is, then restorative justice may be characterized, from a Gospel perspective, as a *compassionate justice*. It is a justice that is enriched, informed, and empowered by the space it gives to compassion. But is this a meaningful or philosophically coherent way to construe justice? Is it possible to envisage some kind of marriage between justice and compassion? Or does any attempt to reconcile two apparently divergent impulses end up degrading both? This is an important question to consider at a theoretical level. It is also important at a practical level, and it is precisely in this regard that legal scholar Annalise Acorn has subjected restorative justice to its most searing recent critique in her exquisitely written book *Compulsory Compassion*. In the following chapter, I will explore the place of compassion specifically in the justice system and offer a response to Acorn's remorseless assault on restorative justice as an illegitimate attempt to coerce compassion from vulnerable victims. This chapter prepares the ground for that discussion by clarifying what is meant by compassion and how it pertains to both personal and institutional behavior.

---

3. "'Go and do thou likewise' is not a pious exhortation to be kindly and considerate. It is a startling invitation to re-examine our life-style in the light of the transcendent moral reality that addresses us and to act upon it in our own life situation" (McDonald, "View," 32).

THE MEANING OF COMPASSION

There are three main terms for compassion in the New Testament: *splangchna*, *eleos*, and *oiktirmos*, together with their derivatives. The corresponding verbs in the passive voice highlight the *emotional* experience of sorrow at another person's plight, while in the active voice they designate the *outward expression* of such feelings, especially in deeds of helpfulness. This distinction is evident in the story of the Good Samaritan. The reference to the Samaritan being "moved with compassion" (*esplangchnisthē*) in verse 33 refers to the affective distress he felt, in the very pit of his belly, when he saw the victim's miserable condition. Only after he has carried out concrete deeds of deliverance is he described in verse 37 as "the one who performed mercy" (*ho poiēsas to eleos*). "Having compassion" designates the emotional reality and "doing mercy" its practical outworking, and it is the combination of the affective and the ethical that signals the Samaritan's exemplary character.

But what precisely is this emotional reality? And how is it related to the constellation of other concepts that orbit around it, such as sympathy, empathy, and pity? Some researchers use these terms interchangeably, while others assign varying shades of meaning to each.[4] For our purposes, all four terms will be taken as roughly equivalent in meaning, even though in current usage "pity" has acquired unfortunate overtones of superiority and condescension toward the sufferer, "empathy" lacks the emotional tenderness and urgency implied in compassion, and "sympathy" increasingly connotes a kind of polite commiseration with, or a pathetic indulgence of, someone's sense of personal grievance. But used here as equivalents for compassion, none of these nuances applies. While each term could be given greater semantic precision if we so wished, nothing is lost for our analysis by treating them synonymously.

Defining Compassion

Compassion may be defined as *an experience of emotional pain and moral concern occasioned by the awareness of, and identification with, another subject's suffering or unhappiness*. Several features of this definition require elaboration. To begin with, the "emotional pain" of compassion

---

4. On terminological distinctions, see Feigenson, "Sympathy," 4–12; Henderson, "Legality," 1578–87; Nussbaum, *Upheavals*, 301–3, 327–42.

is a vicarious pain. That is to say, it is not the pain caused by the triggering of painful memories in the observer's own past but by a sympathetic participation in the painful predicament of the one who is suffering. As the Latin etymology of the English term implies, compassion is a "suffering with" another individual, a sharing in *their* emotional distress, a comprehending of their pain as gravely painful and being pained oneself in consequence of it.

For this "experience" or "awareness" to happen, it is not enough simply to witness the painful event. It is necessary to dwell mentally upon the condition of the sufferer, to enter imaginatively into his or her inner world, as best one can, so that an experiential "identification" takes place with the person's subjective feelings. This makes compassion a costly undertaking. It requires the spectator, in the words of Costa Avgoustinos, to stand "open-faced and wide-eyed to the suffering" encountered, willing to appreciate the sufferer's experience in detail, being determined not to turn away, no matter how much the scene of suffering will pain or haunt the observer.[5] The recently labeled phenomenon of compassion fatigue—whereby caring professionals who confront human suffering on a daily basis begin to exhibit the symptoms of secondary traumatic stress disorder as a result—is testament to just how excruciating compassion can be. Obviously, there is a limit to how fully or accurately someone can identify with the inner experience of another person. But it is only by making the effort to do so, however difficult or disturbing it may be, that one can begin to grasp the other person's needs and try to meet them.

This is where the element of "moral concern" in our definition comes into play. Compassion is principally an emotional feeling, but it is also a moral and cognitive commitment to discerning the needs of this particular sufferer at this particular time. It remains focused on the welfare of the sufferer, not on one's own empathetic discomfort, and it is concerned with attending to the sufferer's anguish in some appropriate way. Compassion is more than a vague *caring about* human suffering in general; it is a positive response of *caring for* concrete instances of pain and misery.[6]

The emotive nature of compassion is both its power and its weakness—its power because emotions move us to action and bind us in

---

5. Avgoustinos, "Compassionate Judge," 13, 35.

6. I borrow this useful distinction between "caring about" and "caring for" from Elisabeth Porter (who in turn takes it from Nell Noddings), "Can Politics?," 102–3.

solidarity to other people, its weakness because feelings are notoriously fickle and fleeting and are often considered to be a serious impediment to rational thought and objective analysis. Nowhere is this reserve toward emotion more evident in public life than in the judicial system, where processes have been carefully designed to eliminate or minimize emotional influence on legal reasoning and where justice is measured by its evident imperviousness to emotional manipulation. It is because emotion per se is thought to be detrimental to rational analysis that the particular emotion of compassion has ended up being corralled off from the public sphere and, a bit like religion in liberal society, confined to the private sphere of personal sentiment and individual benevolence.

But is it really feasible or desirable to exclude emotion from moral, legal, and political deliberation? Is emotional experience at best irrelevant to public culture, at worst a positive threat to achieving procedural and substantive justice? In her imposing book *Upheavals of Thought*, American philosopher Martha Nussbaum explores the positive contribution that emotions can and do make to ethical deliberation, both personal and public. Normative moral judgments can never rest solely on emotional considerations, to be sure. But emotion still plays a critical role in guiding moral discernment, creating moral community, and motivating moral performance. The emotion that is most important in all these respects, Nussbaum proposes, is "the basic social emotion" of compassion.[7]

Nussbaum mounts a compelling case for the indispensable role of compassion in moral and political deliberation and is able to appeal to an array of Western thinkers in support of her claim, from Aristotle to Jean Jacques Rousseau (universally regarded as the father of the modern political virtue of compassion underpinning the welfare state).[8] But the dominant voice in Western thought, Nussbaum discovers, has been "the anti-compassion tradition," flowing from Socrates and the ancient Stoics through Descartes and Spinoza to Immanuel Kant, Adam Smith, and Freidrich Nietzsche. Philosophers in this stream have raised strong objections to any calculated attempt to base moral or political judgment on emotional considerations, including compassion, because to do so

---

7. Nussbaum, *Upheavals*, esp. 297–454, and "Compassion."

8. "That Rousseau is the source of modern liberal political compassion, which has come to be embodied especially in the welfare state with its vast bureaucracy of help-giving, seems so widely agreed as to be beyond serious dispute" (Ward, *Enlightenment*, 171).

threatens the primacy of pure reason, limits the freedom of individual actors, opens the floodgates to arbitrary and unpredictable impulses, and misjudges the importance of external goods to human flourishing. Nussbaum responds ably to each of these objections, challenging in particular their underlying ontology of competitive, individualistic autonomy, while still working herself within the basic framework of liberal secular humanism (she gives little attention, for example, to the contribution of biblical or Christian thought to elaborating the duty of compassion).

Nussbaum is not alone in her emphasis. She is representative of a wider, recent multidisciplinary interest in the cultural and political significance of the emotions, especially amongst feminist scholars. From one angle, her extended apologia for compassion may seem somewhat superfluous in our age of the welfare state and socialized care, an age in which even the conservative critics of welfarism still lay claim to compassionate motivations.[9] Indeed, compassion could well be seen as the sole remaining moral absolute in the sea of relativism and moral neutrality that characterizes the modern liberal political order. But from another angle, there is little ground for complacency. The state-sponsored experts who deliver institutionalized care today usually focus on the "how" rather than the "why" of compassion, as they juggle conflicting priorities on limited budgets, and even professional ethicists are rarely able to give a clear rationale for why compassion is a crucial moral imperative.[10] The reservoirs of compassion in contemporary society may not be as bounteous or self-sustaining as sometimes assumed. One need only look at the deepening social inequities that have accompanied the ascendancy of free market economics in recent decades, or the dreadful excesses of Fallujah, Guantanamo Bay, and Abu Ghraib in the so-called War on Terror, or the "new punitiveness" that has distorted the criminal justice practices of so many Western jurisdictions in the past generation, to appreciate just how vulnerable compassion can be during times of social stress, moral panic, or economic recession. Compassion is ever in need of its articulate defenders, and Christians have more reason than most to champion its cause.

---

9. For an analysis and critique of compassionate conservatism, see Woodward, "Calculating Compassion."

10. Ward, *Enlightenment*, 155–56.

Nussbaum goes a long way to offering a persuasive secular defense of compassion's centrality to moral and political deliberation, and in what follows I draw gratefully on many of her insights, as well as those of other "scholars of sentiment."[11] Whether secularism itself, however, has the necessary resources to stimulate and sustain the deep-rooted culture of compassion that these thinkers call for is open to debate. Their fine analysis of the personal and political dimensions of compassion needs to be complemented, I suggest, with religious or theological insights that ground compassion in ultimate reality and that offer a motivation and enablement for compassionate living that surpasses anything the secular philosophical tradition can engender.

In his piercing analysis of the development of the Western intellectual tradition, David Bentley Hart comments that values like compassion and respect for human dignity are not given in nature but are contingent cultural convictions that need never have arisen.[12] In the West, these values assumed preeminence as a direct result of the impact of the Christian gospel on social existence. As Christianity slowly permeated the pagan civilization into which it was born, it brought about "a truly massive and epochal revision of humanity's prevailing vision of reality, so pervasive in its influence and so vast in its consequences as actually to have created a new conception of the world, of history, of human nature, of time, and of the moral good."[13] Arguably Christianity's most important cultural achievement, Hart suggests, was "the strange, impractical, altogether unworldly tenderness of the moral intuitions it succeeded in sowing in human consciences."[14] Its belief in a God of omnipotent love, made visible in the historical life of Jesus, gave rise to the novel idea that there is an absolute moral and religious duty to care for the wretched of the earth, for the mentally ill and disabled, for refugees and exiles, for the hungry and homeless, for criminals and reprobates. Only someone woefully ignorant of history could possibly view such moral sensibilities as the accidental product of nature; rather, they are the fruit of the Christian revolution in our history.

---

11. I borrow this term from Woodward, "Calculating Compassion," 241.
12. Hart, *Atheist Delusions*.
13. Ibid., x.
14. Ibid., 213.

Yet we deceive ourselves, Hart continues, if we fail to understand the fragility of this compassion-filled vision of reality when divorced from its theological moorings. "For every ethical theory developed apart from some account of transcendent truth—of, that is, the spiritual or metaphysical foundation of reality—is a fragile fiction, credible only to those sufficiently obstinate in their willing suspension of disbelief. If one does not wish to be convinced, however, a simple 'I disagree' or 'I refuse' is enough to exhaust the persuasive resources of any purely worldly ethics."[15] As the plausibility of the Christian vision of reality recedes in the West, a question mark hangs over the future of our moral culture: will its "gentler ethical prejudices," such as compassion for the weak and service of the indigent, persist once the faith that gave them meaning has withered away? Hart, like Nietzsche before him, is doubtful they will. Love may be eternal and endure all things, he remarks, but love still needs a reason to be counted as preeminent among the virtues. As the Christian rationale for love's supremacy ceases to be self-evident to our society, only time will tell whether the compassionate habits it has fostered will retain their grip for long on our collective hearts and minds.

The Cognitive Structure of Compassion

Those who oppose the use of compassion as a reference point for moral or political deliberation typically posit a sharp dichotomy between reason and emotion. Intellect and affect are considered mutually exclusive realities, with the unruly emotions having nothing useful to contribute to cognitive thought. Strictly rational deliberation, it is said, requires the conscientious exclusion of emotional interference so that truth can be established objectively and reliably. The full force of this assumption, as we will see in the next chapter, is particularly evident in the criminal justice sphere, where standard legal theory and practice persist in the belief that reason and emotion stand in polar opposition to each other.

Such a belief, however, cannot be reasonably sustained. It flies in the face of the evidence amassed by philosophers, cognitive psychologists, and neuroscientists. Notwithstanding the enormous complexity surrounding the study of the emotions, recent scholarship is virtually unanimous on one key finding: cognition and emotion cannot be viewed in splendid

15. Ibid., 15.

isolation from each other. They act in concert in shaping human perceptions and reactions. Emotions have a cognitive aspect (there are *reasons* why we feel as we do), and reasoning has an emotive aspect (including its *passion* for logic, order, and coherence). Different emotions also have different cognitive characteristics. This is certainly true for compassion. Far from being an impulsive reaction to irrational stimuli, compassion is a distinctive mode of reasoning, with its own cognitive structure. Drawing principally on Aristotle's *Rhetoric*, Nussbaum proposes that compassion involves three distinct cognitive judgments about the nature of suffering, each of which must be present for this upheaval of emotion to occur.[16]

First, compassion requires the belief that *the suffering in question is serious rather than trivial*. As Nussbaum observes, we don't go around pitying those who have lost a paper clip or a toothbrush, or even an important item that is readily replaceable.[17] We reserve compassion for situations of substantial loss or significant harm. Elisabeth Porter similarly explains that "what marks the subject of compassion is the graveness of the situation in which persons experience serious pain, anguish, torture, misery, grief, despair, hardship, destitution, agony, affliction, hardship, and suffering."[18] Most often it is the central disasters that touch all of human life—such as accidents, disease, birth defects, disability, isolation from friends, destitution, and bereavement—that evoke compassion in us.

Second, compassion requires the belief that *the suffering in view is unmerited or excessive rather than richly deserved*. When people come to grief through their own irresponsible or immoral actions, we tend to feel blame, reproach, or smug satisfaction rather than pity. But when they are *not* at fault for their condition, when their suffering is a result of a cruel twist of fate or unjust victimization, compassion more readily arises. We may still feel some level of compassion in instances where personal wrongdoing is involved. But usually it is only because there are mitigating factors present in the perpetrator's background or circumstances, or where their actions seem oddly out of character, or where the consequences they have suffered greatly exceed the gravity of their offending. Otherwise we

---

16. Acorn is critical of Nussbaum, however, for turning Aristotle's descriptive account of compassion, elaborated in the context of discussing rhetorical strategies speakers may use to garner a spontaneous emotional endorsement for their position, into one that carries normative freight (*Compulsory Compassion*, 122–35).

17. Nussbaum, *Upheavals*, 307.

18. Porter, "Politics?," 100.

reserve compassion for innocent persons who have fallen on hard times, while withholding it from evildoers who are architects of their own undoing. It is this feature that brings compassion into close connection with justice. If injustice is understood as the undeserved imposition of suffering on another person, it is our capacity for compassion that enables us to register its occurrence and do something about it.

The third cognitive requirement for compassion is a sense of *commonality or solidarity with the suffering of the victim*. In Nussbaum's words: "The point . . . seems to be that the pain of another will be the object of my concern, a part of my sense of my own well-being, only if I acknowledge some sort of community between myself and the other, understanding what it might be for me to face such pain."[19] This sense of community requires an awareness of possessing some degree of similarity to the victim, especially in terms of a common susceptibility to suffering. We make sense of their pain by imagining what it would be like to have a similar experience ourselves, which presupposes a sense of shared vulnerability to life's misfortunes. But something further is needed as well. Compassion arises only when I choose to include the suffering of the other party within my personal sphere of concern, such that their condition affects my sense of well-being or flourishing. The suffering remains *their* suffering, not mine, which is to acknowledge the validity of their separate existence, their alterity or otherness, their distance from me. Yet their pain now also affects *my* sense of thriving as a human being, which is to acknowledge our interconnectedness, our similarity, even our fundamental equality. Cognitively speaking, then, compassion requires an awareness of a common but distinctive participation in the precariousness of life.

This third facet of compassion affords a valuable perspective on God's unwavering compassion for the human race in the biblical story. The compassion that God feels, of course, is not rooted in God's subjective awareness of possessing a similar susceptibility to weakness, failure, or misfortune. In these respects, God is utterly dissimilar to us. But God chooses to enter into a relationship of loving solidarity with his human creatures, so that God becomes, so to speak, emotionally vulnerable to their pain, and their plight becomes integral to God's own interior experience. "As a father has compassion for his children, so the LORD has

---

19. Nussbaum, *Upheavals*, 317.

compassion for those who fear him. For he knows how we were made; he remembers that we are dust" (Ps 103:13–14).

These, then, are the three epistemological components of compassion: an assessment of seriousness, a judgment about culpability, and a consciousness of common participation in the frailties of the human condition. Compassion does *not* arise where we consider the losses to be trivial, the suffering to be justly deserved, or the victim to be utterly unlike us in essential humanity. (This final observation explains why those who engage in systematic violence against entire ethnic groups usually portray their targets as subhuman vermin, utterly unworthy of fellow feeling. It is also why we rarely feel compassion for the flies we swat or the ants we spray.) Compassion only figures where we perceive in the suffering of others that same defenselessness before the vicissitudes of life to which we, too—as finite, embodied, sentient beings—are exposed. Accordingly, to experience compassion for another being is already a "significant quasi-ethical achievement,"[20] because it involves a valuing of the distressed victim as part of one's own universe of meaning and concern. Compassion is an emotion that registers the intrinsic human or creaturely worth of the one who suffers and the moral significance of their pain, and hence it is highly relevant to moral deliberation.[21] It cannot be deprecated as some distorting, irrational intrusion into the realms of higher rationality and moral perception.

Of these three cognitive requirements for compassion, the most equivocal, to my mind, is that of blamelessness. Admittedly it is a more *difficult* task to feel compassion for hardened criminals than for faultless victims of misfortune. But it is not clear why compassion should be deemed cognitively or morally *inappropriate* in such situations. Even when we believe an offender's predicament is self-inflicted and that he fully deserves to be punished for his crimes, we can still feel pity for the wretchedness of what he has become as a human being or for the bleakness of what lies ahead of him. Indeed, it is only by enlisting compassion that we can avoid self-righteousness or vindictiveness. It is only compassion that enables us

---

20. Ibid., 336.

21. Our focus here is on compassion for other human beings, but it is both possible and morally desirable to feel compassion for animals as well. Such compassion bespeaks consciousness of our common creaturely susceptibility to suffering. For a moving example of a dawning awareness of animal suffering and its moral significance, see Jackson, *Priority of Love*, xii–xv.

to take into account all the genetic, circumstantial, and social influences that have limited his freedom of action and abetted his offending. It is only compassion that spares us from demonizing wrongdoers as somehow less than fully human or less intrinsically valuable than we ourselves are.

Nussbaum endorses such a discerning and solicitous attitude towards guilty offenders as well. But in company with other social theorists, she prefers to speak of this stance as one of mercy rather than compassion. Mercy and compassion have a great deal in common, she concedes. Both involve a sympathetic and imaginative engagement with the painful experience of others, and both seek to alleviate human distress. But whereas compassion is a reaction to unmerited suffering and implies innocence, mercy is a response to deliberate wrongdoing that confirms guilt, yet moderates punishment.[22]

Such a terminological distinction may be analytically useful for philosophers. But it is difficult to apply in the real world. Human behavior is too complex a mixture of volitional freedom and circumstantial constraint to know at what point compassion (for situational forces) should give way to mercy (for culpable choices). Naturally, the intensity of our feelings of sympathy will fluctuate from case to case depending on a host of variables, including the degree of personal fault involved, itself a somewhat arbitrary and subjective judgment. But surely there is no experience of human suffering, however morally corrupted it is, that does not warrant some effort at compassionate understanding from others. Rather than distinguishing between mercy and compassion on the basis of blameworthiness, it is better, along with the New Testament writers, to understand mercy as the active expression of the underlying response of compassion, in any situation where authority or power may be exercised or withheld to another person's detriment (cf. Mark 10:47).

PROBLEMS WITH COMPASSION

Compassion, then, as Nussbaum dissects it, is not simply an irrational sensation. It has a cognitive character and a relational focus that makes

---

22. See Nussbaum, *Upheavals*, 397–98; cf. 365–66, 441–53. See also Rainbolt, "Mercy," 226–41. Andrew Brien makes a useful distinction between *mercy as an action*, which in a legal setting entails mitigating punishment, and *mercy as a virtue*, which designates a character trait involving an ongoing stance of benevolent care and concern for others that issues in merciful actions ("Mercy," 83–110).

it intrinsically significant to morality. That does not mean, of course, that compassion is always a reliable or adequate guide to ethical discernment. The emotional response needs to be scrutinized, disciplined, and developed in a variety of ways. This cognitive and moral conditioning is necessary because there are several pitfalls associated with giving normative space to compassion. Contrary to what is sometimes said, however, none of these problems, properly conceived, discredits the importance of allowing compassion to inform and guide moral, political, and judicial decision-making.

The Problem of Mistaken Priorities

One such pitfall is the danger of investing too much value in people's exterior circumstances rather than in their inward character and commitment to moral virtue. There is a significant strand in post-Enlightenment philosophy that grounds human worth and equality in possession of autonomous reason and volition. These faculties are not dependent on the ups and downs of everyday life but are given in our essential humanity. Accordingly, our capacity to flourish as human beings is not dependent on external goods or the shifting tides of fortune but on how we exercise our freedom of will. To evince compassion at life's misfortunes, therefore, is to insinuate that what really matters in life are outward circumstances and material possessions rather than inner freedom and virtue. It also diminishes the sufferer's status as an autonomous moral agent. What we really owe those who suffer is respect for their human dignity, not pity for their losses.[23]

Now perhaps it is true that the compassionate heart does sometimes run the risk of exaggerating the importance of the temporal fluctuations of fate and fortune and of undervaluing virtuous character. But we should beware of creating a false dichotomy between respecting human dignity and lamenting circumstantial suffering. There is no reason why both cannot be operative at the same time. The Stoic proposition that attachment to external goods is irrelevant to human flourishing must be rejected as false. It is false both because the richness of human identity cannot be reduced to rational and volitional freedom alone, and because the great character virtues of courage, justice, temperance, humility, wisdom, and

---

23. For a more detailed analysis of this argument, see Nussbaum, *Upheavals*, 356–400.

patience can only be developed in response to exterior circumstances. Indeed, the turbulence of compassion is arguably a more reliable indicator of what is truly valuable in human life than is some dogmatic valorizing of individual moral autonomy. For the sufferings that most readily evince feelings of compassion in us are those that assail the most basic human goods of all, such as life itself, good health, freedom, physical vigor, and sustaining relationships. These are precisely the goods the psalmist lists as benefits bestowed by the Creator on his human creatures, the loss of which evokes God's own tender compassion (Ps 103:1–5, 13–15).

The Problem of Diverted Energy

Another potential problem with compassion is that it may sap the energies of the stronger members of society and divert their focus from pursuit of personal success and achievement. As is well known, Friedrich Nietzsche saw all human behavior as manifestations of the "will to power." Compassion for the poor, he thought, functions only to frustrate the resolve of the strong and drag them down to the miserable condition of the weak. Compassion permits the poor paradoxically to exercise too much influence in society by distracting the attention of the powerful, so that society comes to esteem suffering and weakness more highly than their opposites. As Bruce Ward summarizes this view, "The higher human beings, instead of marshalling their energies for an upward fight, are obliged to dissipate them in downward movements of compassion, in response to the perpetual chorus of complaint that characterizes modern culture."[24] Nor does becoming objects of compassion necessarily help the poor. The shame of their plight is merely compounded by such pity, and they are as likely to end up feeling envy and resentment towards those who commiserate with them as to find incentive to escape their predicament.

Although rarely expressed with such pungency today, it is not hard to detect neo-Nietzschean strains behind the oft-heard complaint of economic rationalists that demands for greater equity in society, or for the redistribution of wealth through the taxation system, are simply exercises in the "politics of envy." Compassion may be justified in certain cases, they allow, but not on a society-wide scale and certainly not at significant cost to the most productive members of the marketplace.

---

24. Ward, *Enlightenment*, 176.

Instead of being envied for their success, these high achievers should be emulated by the rest of us.

Once again, there may be some validity to this fear that an exaggerated emphasis on compassion for the needy only multiplies the amount of misery in the world, unless it is accompanied by action to create a more prosperous social order in which personal success is rewarded and the poor are induced to improve their lot by dint of effort. It may also be true that those who concentrate on sharing vicariously in the pain of the poor and oppressed run the risk of deriving such a sense of virtue from doing so that, instead of being impelled to work for structural change, they will withdraw ever more deeply into the world of private sentiment and spiritual self-satisfaction. As we noted in our discussion of the Good Samaritan, there is no automatic link between empathetic experience and altruistic behavior. A whole array of contingent factors, including moral smugness, can decouple the link between affect and action. But normally the two are closely related: strong empathizers are usually highly inclined to altruism. Those who *feel* the suffering of the needy most keenly are the ones most disposed to *act* ethically on their behalf and in service of the common good. Their emotional experience compels and energizes, rather than impedes or derails, their social engagement.

What about the worry that an undue emphasis on compassion may distract the strong from pursuit of their own self-fulfillment? Indeed it may. But that is precisely why it is so important. Striving for individual achievement is a worthy goal and not to be discounted. But it is compassion, not ambition, that reminds us of our co-humanity and mutual responsibilities. As the biblical writers continually stress, we cannot truly flourish as human beings by entertaining a callous indifference to the suffering of others or living selfishly at their expense. It is only by means of loving our neighbors as ourselves that we "find" ourselves and become more truly free. Self-realization, oddly enough, comes from forgetting our sectional interests and attending benevolently to the needs of others (cf. Mark 8:35 pars).

In an astute discussion, Nussbaum proposes that the differences between the pro-compassion and anti-compassion strands in Western philosophy come down, in the end, to divergent visions of political community and human integrity.[25] In one vision, community is forged

---

25. Nussbaum's words are worth quoting in full: "The debate over compassion constructs, in effect, two visions of political community and of the good citizen and

through emotions, and human beings are understood to be both aspiring and vulnerable, both noble and weak. The central task of the political order is to ensure that the basic needs of all citizens are met and that all are supported through times of common weakness and risk. According to the other vision, based on the sequestering of emotional influence and the prioritizing of individual liberty, human beings are esteemed solely for their moral autonomy and rationality, and the central task of the body politic is to remove the barriers to self-realization and freedom of choice. One vision accepts human weakness as the condition of human sociality; the other considers weakness to be a hindrance to the creation of a community of self-sufficient persons. Both visions have advocates in Western intellectual history, as Nussbaum documents. But only one of these visions bears any resemblance whatsoever to the worldview expressed in the Bible and reflected, not least, in the parables of Jesus we have examined.

> judge within it. One vision is based upon the emotions; the other urges their removal. One sees the human being as both aspiring and vulnerable, both worthy and insecure; the other focuses on dignity alone, seeing in reason a boundless and indestructible worth. One sees the central task of community as the provision of support for basic needs; bringing human beings together through their common weakness and risk, it constructs a moral emotion that is suited to supporting efforts to raise the worst off. The other sees a community as a kingdom of free responsible beings, held together by the awe that they feel for the worth of reason in one another; the function of their association will be to assist the moral development of each by judgments purified of passion. Each vision, in its own way, pursues both equality and freedom. The former aims of equal support for basic needs and hopes through this to promote equal opportunities for free choice and self-realization; the other starts from the fact of internal freedom—a fact that no misfortune can remove—and finds in this fact a source of political equality. One sees freedom of choice as something that needs to be built up for people through worldly arrangements that make them capable of functioning in a fully human way; the other takes freedom to be an inalienable given, independent of all material arrangements. One aims to defeat the selfish and grasping passions through the imagination of suffering, and through a gradual broadening of concern; the other aims to remove these passions completely, overcoming retaliation with self-command and mercy. One attempts to achieve benevolence through soft-heartedness; the other holds, with Kant, that this soft-heartedness 'should not be at all among human beings.' One holds that 'it is the weakness of the human being that makes it sociable.' The other holds that weakness is an impediment to community, that only the truly self-sufficient person can be a true friend. We see that the debate between the friends and enemies of compassion is no merely formal debate concerning the type of thought process or the type of faculty that should influence choice in public life. Nor is it a debate between partisans of reason and partisans of some mindless cognitive force. It is a substantive debate about ethical value" (Nussbaum, *Upheavals*, 367–68; more briefly in "Compassion," 44).

The Problem of Negative Emotions

This brings us to a third potential pitfall with compassion. The same circumstances that induce compassion can also open the door to other, more objectionable emotions, such as anger, resentment, hatred, and bigotry. Instead of compassion, observers may be consumed with retributive rage, or may feel intense fury alongside compassion. Such destructive emotions need to be held in check, however, if a peaceful social order is to be preserved. This is much harder to do in the wake of the emotional release occasioned by indulging compassionate sentiments.

There may be some truth to this concern. Emotions are rarely unadulterated, and it is not uncommon to have a range of emotional reactions to stressful situations. But that does not mitigate the value of compassion itself, nor does it mean that compassion is invariably contaminated with destructive urges. Many of the occurrences that elicit compassion in us, such as sickness or disability or bereavement, entail little or no personal fault, and so do not occasion fantasies of revenge. They may trigger feelings of anger, since anger is a close ally of grief and often accompanies it. But anger is a morally neutral emotion. It all depends on what we do with our anger and how we express it. Anger is also a morally valuable emotion. To seek to avoid all anger would be to shun a major force for social justice in the world. It is true that anger, when provoked by witnessing social injustice or criminal victimization, can easily spill over into vengeful intentions towards the perpetrator, as the flip side of intense sympathy for the victim. But here too the solution is not to deny or suppress the anger but rather to channel its energy in a more constructive direction, while actively nourishing empathy for the victim.

Compassion is actually a powerful tool for preventing anger from tipping into hatred and retaliation. Nussbaum notes that compassionate agents are more likely to eschew personal retribution in favor of formal legal remedies because they understand that personal revenge usually means the exchange of damages will perpetuate itself without limit and its pain will be unending.[26] Compassion inclines them to alleviate rather than perpetuate pain. One of the recognized functions of the criminal justice system is to forestall personal vendettas fuelled by vengeful emotions. What is often overlooked is the positive role of compassion in achieving this goal.

26. Nussbaum, *Upheavals*, 396.

The Problem of Partiality

This brings us to the fourth and most significant problem with letting compassion serve as a moral guide. It is a problem that relates to the inherent psychology of this particular emotion. As we have seen, feelings of compassion are only triggered as we become personally aware of concrete instances of serious suffering. Usually, these are instances that occur within our own immediate circle of contacts or sphere of interest. This is hardly surprising. Psychologists tell us that our facility for empathy arises initially from our experience of intense attachment to our parents and first caregivers. Although our circle of natural empathy widens as we mature, it remains ever easier for us to empathize with people who are personally connected to us, or who are similar to us in terms of background, class, nationality, race, language, culture, or religion. If we heed the dictates of compassion, then, in deciding upon our moral responsibilities, we will end up with a very parochial sense of obligation. Instead of acknowledging the equal claims of all people to our concern, we will favor those who are closest to us physically or who most closely resemble us in other ways. Compassion may even end up reinforcing group rivalries, unjust power structures, and hierarchies of race, class, and gender.

Now this is a serious concern. In our discussion of the moral significance of distance in the duty of rescue, we noted that human beings are not equipped psychologically to feel equal levels of care for everyone on the planet, and any attempt to do so would soon destroy us as finite agents. We also found that there is something about personal encounter, about seeing actual, embodied human suffering with our own eyes, that functions to overcome the affective tyranny of distance and to translate some vague duty of benevolence into a specific duty of care to *this* person, at *this* time, in *this* situation. This psychological dynamic, however, inevitably creates a bias towards the limited number of souls whom we happen to encounter in our daily lives or whose needs we choose to expose ourselves to.

So the problem of partiality is a sizeable one. But it is fatal only if we assume that the feeling of compassion alone is an adequate guide to determining our moral duties. Plainly it is not. Subjective emotional engagement needs to be combined with an objective ethical theory that clarifies how far our compassionate concern ought to extend and how purposefully it ought to be managed. It is here that Nussbaum thinks a program of education that works at progressively expanding the boundaries of compassion beyond our immediate circle of contacts to the larger human community is essential. "The right solution to its partiality problems is to work on compassion's developmental history . . . through appropriate education and institutional design."[27] Rather than dispensing with compassion as a moral guide, the answer is to unite it with an ethical code that educates and extends the emotional response beyond its initially narrow focus, and to forge a set of institutional mechanisms that compensate for the partisan nature of personal sentiment and ensure that compassionate outcomes are delivered in a comprehensive and just manner. This brings us, at last, to the role of compassion in the public arena, including in the operation of the criminal justice system.

THE PLACE OF COMPASSION IN PUBLIC LIFE

Compassion is a fundamentally *social* emotion because it entails a "suffering with" other persons or other creatures. It reminds us of our essential interdependence; it attests to the fact that, whether we like it or not, we are our brother's and sister's keeper and that our own well-being is necessarily bound up with theirs. Compassion is part of the emotional glue that cements us together in social solidarity. Relationships mediated through emotional empathy and moral commitments are much more satisfying, and much less fragile, than those based purely on formal arrangements or coercive rules. For this reason alone, the level of compassion that exists in society has political implications. A stable and secure political order requires more than a rational system of laws and public institutions to enact them. It also requires a network of compassionate relationships between citizens and the appropriate involvement of compassion in the way that the various institutions of collective life operate. Both aspects are important and mutually reinforcing. As Nussbaum explains, "The relationship between compassion and social institutions is and should be a two-way street: compassionate individuals construct institutions that embody what they imagine; and institutions, in turn, influence the development of compassion in individuals."[28]

27. Ibid., 392.
28. Ibid., 405.

Educating for Compassion

How, then, is compassion to be fostered in individual citizens and their social networks? Nussbaum stresses the importance of moral and civic education for cultivating people's imaginative capacity to participate sympathetically in the lives of others. Such training of the imagination begins in the home, with the simple nursery rhymes and bedtime stories taught to small children. These stories evoke in children a sense of wonder in the surrounding world and elicit empathy by attributing an emotional inwardness to the characters and objects described. As children grow, they need to be progressively exposed to stories that display the contingencies, disappointments, and calamities of life, so that they learn to sympathize with the sorrows as well as the joys of others. Moving into adolescence and beyond, literary and artistic works that promote engagement across social and cultural barriers become increasingly important. Especially useful in evoking compassion, Nussbaum believes, is exposure to tragic drama and related narrative literature. "Tragedies acquaint young people with the bad things that may happen in a human life, long before human life itself does so: they thus enable concern for others who are suffering what the spectator has not suffered."[29]

The value of a broad education in the liberal arts and humanities cannot be stressed too highly, claims Nussbaum. It makes a vital contribution to citizenship by nourishing the imaginative abilities that are central to political life. Without such capacities, "we will very likely have an obtuse and emotionally dead citizenry, prey to the aggressive wishes that so often accompany an inner world dead to the images of others."[30] The goal of such an education is not erudition, she stresses, but empathy and the enlargement of the boundaries of compassion beyond its parochial default setting. An education in compassion must therefore be a multicultural education, exposing learners to worlds quite unlike their own but in which they still encounter familiar human fears and foibles.

The curriculum also needs to include training in ethical theory, especially relating to the three cognitive judgments mentioned before—judgments about seriousness, about moral deserts, and about the proper boundaries of responsibility. The third area is the trickiest. People have different views about how far their compassionate responsibilities extend

---

29. Nussbaum, "Compassion," 39, and *Upheavals*, 351–53.
30. Nussbaum, *Upheavals*, 426.

across the spectrum of social groups they belong to, from their immediate families, to members of the same political community, to humanity at large. But moral theorists are agreed that our prevailing tendency is to be too restrictive in our sympathies. Thus moral instruction is needed to explain *why* we should reach across the barriers of race, class, and comfort that otherwise confine and restrict us.

For Nussbaum, then, an education that develops "the muscles of the imagination" is a major tool for fostering compassion in society. There is no need to contest this claim. The potential for compassion seems to be innate in human beings, but its cognitive and moral features still need to be developed and practiced through learning and experience.[31] Like any virtue, compassion can be taught and learned to some degree, even if, as with most forms of moral education, as much is learned informally through observation and osmosis as is acquired through formal instruction. Education (in its most inclusive sense) in compassion is therefore essential. But education also has its limits. Education cannot generate compassion *ex nihilo*, nor is moral training alone sufficient to overcome what Ward terms that "obstinate resistance to altruistic compassion that seems so deeply imbedded in human nature," certainly not as far as St. Paul is concerned (Rom 7:7–25).[32] Schooling in compassion and its practices is best thought of as a second-order exercise that depends upon the prior existence of compassion in the human heart, and it is

---

31. Philosophers and social scientists have long discussed the origins of altruism, empathy, sympathy, and compassion, but only recently have neuroscientists examined this question. For a review of such research, see Singer and Lamm, "Social Neuroscience," 81–96. On the possible evolutionary origins of altruism, see Fehr and Fischbacher, "Human Altruism," 6–47. Nussbaum rightly observes that recent work on the evolutionary basis for compassion needs to be handled with caution because "there is a great tendency in the surrounding culture to over read the data, and to draw from them normative implications that they do not have." Such work does confirm, however, that humans have inbuilt psychological mechanisms that tend in the direction of compassion and altruism (*Upheavals*, 338).

32. Ward, *Enlightenment*, 160. Timothy Jackson calls this the "perversity problem." He notes that whereas Plato saw the cause of human weakness as an ignorance that could be remedied through more information, the biblical writers, especially Paul, see it as a willful disobedience that can only be cured through conversion of the heart and deliverance from the power of sin (Jackson, *Priority of Love*, 37–38). As H. R. Mackintosh once observed: "To lead an ethical life men need light; but primarily they need not so much higher ideals as triumphant power to give effect to the ideals they in point of fact revere; the worst know more than the best practise" (*Originality*, 144).

crucial that society attends to the origins of compassion as well as to its secondary formation.

The proximate source of compassion is the experience of attachment and nurture in infancy. But this too comes from somewhere prior. Our first caregivers lovingly nurture us only because they were first nurtured themselves. They pass on to us what they have in turn received; they love us because they have first been loved themselves. This cycle of human nurture and empathy, of giving and receiving, reveals something important about compassion. Our facility for compassion, and our continued development in the skills of compassion, stems principally from our involvement in the mystery of love that undergirds all existence,[33] an involvement that, in biblical perspective, is nothing less than a participation in divinity, for "God is love" (1 John 4:8, 16). It follows that the more we are exposed to love, the more conscious we become of love, and the more we choose to align ourselves with love, the more loving and compassionate we will be to others.

Call this an education if you will. But compassion's growth comes not principally from the stimulation of our imaginative faculties through narrative literature or tragic drama, but from participation in loving relationships, and supremely from our relationship to God, whose compassion is most perfectly displayed in the person of Christ. Paul tells his hearers to "clothe yourselves with compassion" (Col 3:12) as a practical ethical discipline, but the compassion in question is the "compassion of Christ" that comes from "sharing in the Spirit" (Phil 1:8; 2:1). As always in Pauline teaching, demand and gift are held together. Believers are to show compassion because they have first received compassion, and the more they appreciate what they have received, the better equipped they are to extend this gratuity to others.

At the beginning of this study, we noted how stories are uniquely efficacious in social and moral formation, much more so than abstract rules or philosophical principles. This makes the stories we choose to tell and retell critically important for how we understand our collective identity and hone our values. Western civilization has been decisively shaped by narratives drawn from two main sources—classical antiquity and the Bible—which together have provided the raw materials for almost all the

---

33. For a wide-ranging discussion of the extent to which interdependence and other-regard permeates physical and biological reality, see Barasch, *Compassionate Life*.

great works of European literature. Nussbaum accents the importance of classical sources, especially Greek tragedy, for nourishing the compassionate imagination.[34] But she gives scant attention to the potential of that other great source of Western consciousness, the Bible, for doing the same. Here it is worth recalling, once more, David Bentley Hart's emphasis on the role of early Christianity in transforming pagan culture, with its wanton depravity and its "pervasive, relentless, and polymorphous cruelty," into a culture that prized compassion as a supreme moral and religious obligation.[35]

> Pagan culture was never more tolerant than in its tolerance—without any qualms of conscience—of poverty, disease, starvation, and homelessness; of gladiatorial spectacle, crucifixion, the exposure of unwanted infants, or the public slaughter of war captives or criminals on festive occasions; of, indeed, almost every imaginable form of tyranny, injustice, depravity, or cruelty. The indigenous sects of the Roman world simply made no connection between religious piety and anything resembling a developed social morality . . . anything like a religious obligation to care for the suffering, feed the hungry, or visit prisoners. Nor did the authority of the sacred, in pagan society, serve in any way to mitigate the brutality of the larger society—quite the contrary, really—and it would be difficult to exaggerate that brutality. . . .
>
> The old gods did not—and by their nature could not—inspire the building of hospitals and almshouses, or make feeding the hungry and clothing the naked a path to spiritual enlightenment, or foster any coherent concept of a dignity intrinsic to every human soul; they could never have taught their human charges to think of charity as the highest of virtues or as the way to union with the divine.[36]

These convictions were derived, not from the classical tradition, nor from some immanent evolutionary progression in human nature, but from the Christian story of a God of absolute love made most fully known in the self-giving life, death, and resurrection of the human person, Jesus Christ. As a direct consequence of this story, from its very inception the church developed a system of social assistance that no civic or religious

---

34. Nussbaum, *Upheavals*, 426–33.
35. Hart, *Atheist Delusions*, 122.
36. Ibid., 121–22, 124.

office in the pagan world had ever provided. After Constantine, the church became the first organized institution of large-scale public welfare in Western history, a great repository and redistributor of goods, alms, state moneys, and bequests that funded hospitals, orphanages, hostels, and asylums. The church often failed to live up to its own compassionate ideals, as is frequently pointed out these days. But even in its failures, the church achieved far more than the Roman gods had ever inspired.[37]

The tide is now turning again. Christianity is fading rapidly from our collective cultural memory, and with it is receding the potential of the Bible's master narratives to shape public sentiment and clarify moral commitment at a grassroots level. There is, of course, no loss of appetite for narrative experience as such. If anything, popular storytelling is an even more pervasive feature in today's entertainment-bloated, mass media culture than it ever was in previous times. But while the cacophony of popular stories that fill the airwaves may sometimes offer profound insights into human behavior, what these stories lack, as do the literary classics taught in schools and universities, is that unique blend of simplicity, moral profundity, popular accessibility, and, most of all, spiritual authority characteristic of biblical stories in general, and the Gospel stories in particular. The stories of Jesus, like the Good Samaritan, the Prodigal Son, and the Unforgiving Servant, have done more historically to inspire and democratize compassion in Western society than was ever achieved by exposure to classical literature.

There is another reason too why attending to the spiritual roots of compassion is vital. Any attempt to engineer social compassion through pedagogical or institutional mechanisms alone, cut adrift from an independent source of spiritual motivation and prophetic insight, runs the risk of the state disguising efforts to control and subjugate its citizens in the name of implementing compassion. The awful history of institutional abuse of prisoners, orphans, geriatrics, and mental health patients is a salutary warning of this danger. So too is the political capture of compassion language in recent political discourse. In her analysis of the phenomenon of "compassionate conservatism" in American politics, Kathleen Woodward finds that the terminology of compassion in the movement's discourse no longer refers to an emotional feeling or a moral concern; it is simply a rhetorical cipher for signaling a particular

---

37. Ibid., 163–64.

package of conservative economic policies. Rather than focusing on actual narratives of human distress, emphasis tends to fall on the possibility of a bright economic future for the poor if they are willing to identify their economic goals and work hard to achieve them. The language of compassion, in other words, effectively conceals an ideology of radical economic individualism. But in fact, there is little place in such an ideology for genuine compassion. For if the poor remain poor by choice rather than by systemic constraint, they are in some measure to blame for their own situation, hence undeserving of compassion.[38]

This returns us to the libertarian objections to compassion discussed earlier. The more radical our conception of human free will, the less place there is for compassion. By contrast, the Pauline understanding of sin as a systemically embedded bondage to which all human beings are subject, and of saving grace as both liberation from this bondage and divine enablement to bear its continuing legacy in the overlap of the ages, provides a normative grounding for both freedom and compassion. What in Romans 8 Paul calls "the glorious liberty of the children of God" is a genuine liberty, a deliverance from the compulsions and condemnation of sin that brings actual existential change. But it is not an unfettered freedom. For we yet have only the "first fruits" of salvation, lived out in the midst of the "sufferings of this present age" and accompanied with an "inward groaning" and an enduring sense of "weakness" as we await "the redemption of our bodies." This continuing subjection of even redeemed humanity to the afflictions of the old age—"whether tribulation or distress or persecution or famine or nakedness or peril or sword"—gives ample room for compassion, a compassion that even God's Spirit feels as the Spirit intercedes for us with "sighs too deep for words" (Rom 8:18–30).

Institutionalizing Compassion

If moral and civic education is one major means of nurturing compassion in society, the other is the incorporation of compassionate values and priorities into the way public institutions operate. Of course, there is an important sense in which compassion can never be institutionalized. Compassion is an emotion, and soulless institutions do not have

---

38. Woodward, "Calculating Compassion," esp. 237–43.

emotions. Compassion's power, furthermore, lies in its free and voluntary character. It cannot be compelled on demand nor delivered in prepackaged amounts on the basis of encoded rights.[39] Pure compassion is a transaction between free persons in particular contexts; it is not the product of impersonal systems or faceless bureaucracies. This means that individual agency and contextual sensitivity will always be of paramount importance in the quest to promote a more compassionate society.

But private philanthropy can never do the whole job. Compassion is a costly undertaking, human beings are imperfect creatures, and even the best among us often look for excuses not to act compassionately. It is essential, therefore, to fashion political and institutional mechanisms that will compensate for the unevenness of individual sentiment and the parochialism of personal judgment to deliver compassionate outcomes in a predictable and equitable manner across the entire community. It is perfectly intelligible to speak of institutions exercising compassion. If institutions can be cruel, as few would deny, they can also be compassionate, not by *feeling* compassion as an emotion, but by observing the principles of compassion in the way they operate. Cognizant of the precariousness of human existence and of the vulnerability of every citizen to the arbitrary twists of fortune and fate, compassionate institutions seek to embody compassionate insights into their processes, to encourage compassionate sensitivity amongst their staff, and to strive always to take the full humanity of their clients into account.

Yet the concept of compassionate institutions is by no means commonplace in current political discourse. This is primarily because in mainstream political thought, the governing norm for public life is understood to be that of justice, not compassion. Love and justice are differentiated in liberal political theory in much the same way as are reason and emotion: one is allocated to the private sphere, the other to the public realm. But such a sharp dichotomy between personal compassion and public justice cannot stand, for several interlocking reasons.

---

39. In New Zealand, some people have campaigned for inclusion of "the right to be treated with compassion" in the Code of Health and Disability Consumers' Rights (1996). But there are significant losses when morality is transposed entirely into the language of rights and obligations, as is our wont today. See the moving reflection by Charlotte Paul, "Question," 33–34. For a more general call to universal compassion as a means of religious peacemaking, see "Charter for Compassion," available at http://charterforcompassion.org.

To begin with, institutional life has an inescapably personal and moral dimension. While social institutions are structurally more than a collection of individual actors, they still operate at a cultural level through individual human agency and have direct impact on actual human experience. I have repeatedly stressed in this study that human beings are irreducibly relational creatures. All of human life, both private and public, comprises of personal relationships and attachments, for there is no other way to be human. If compassion is essential to relationships in the private sphere, it must be essential to relationships in the public and institutional sphere as well. As Elisabeth Porter comments, compassion is not too personal for politics, for politics too is personal.[40]

Nor can emotion be excluded from how institutions function in practice. Politicians and corporate executives often claim to be governed solely by rational argument and empirical evidence in reaching their conclusions. But that is far from the case. Countless studies of decision-making processes have shown that emotional forces and personal prejudices affect deliberations in a multitude of ways. These subterranean emotional realities are all the more dangerous for being concealed behind a façade of rational neutrality and objectivity. Much safer to acknowledge the influence of hidden drives and motivations and make appropriate allowances for them than to pretend they do not exist or are easily sidelined. The question is not *whether* institutional life is affected by emotional considerations, but in *what way* it is and *how* this affects institutional performance.

The reverse is also true. Individual emotional experience is shaped by the systems and institutional structures people work within. Medical students, for example, are more inclined to express compassion for patients if the hospital system allows them to invest significant time in the cases they are involved in. The overall shape of the medical environment, Gregory Pence argues, is far more important for teaching students compassion than are courses on medical ethics or even exposure to heroic role models.[41] To use the language of social psychology again, contextual "situation" and individual "disposition" are intricately connected in generating compassion.

Along the same lines, it is a mistake to try to unhook love and justice from one another and assign each to a different sphere. Although they

---

40. Porter, "Politics?," 109.
41. Pence, "Can Compassion," 189–91.

are not the same thing and should not be conflated in political theory, love and justice cannot be neatly separated. They are interdependent realities. Love delivers more than justice can demand, but it never delivers less. Justice, in turn, is never threatened by love. Indeed, justice can be seen to be a derivative of love. As Timothy Jackson convincingly argues, love precedes justice both chronologically and axiologically. That is to say, love comes first in human experience and has absolute priority; it is the root of all other virtues, including justice, the metavalue without which we have no access to any other goods.

This is not only a theological claim, though on this point the New Testament writers could scarcely be any clearer;[42] it is also an empirical claim. Human beings are created for love, and without first being formed in love, they cannot know what justice means or learn how to act justly. Our adult capacity for justice, even narrowly defined as the fair distribution of goods on the basis of merit and the honoring of contracts, can only emerge *after* we have received unconditional love from others as infants and children and been formed into persons by it. As Jackson puts it, we rely on the kindness of strangers to nurture us into personhood, and without this experience of love, however minimal it might be, we do not have the conditions in which justice matters.[43]

It is significant that the cry for justice, both distributive justice and retributive justice, often originates in the care-full witnessing of injustice around us and in a primal craving to see it remedied. If social, political, and judicial institutions are to service justice, therefore, as political theory says they should, they must strive also to be compassionate. "Love never falls below justice, never gives less than is due," Jackson writes, "but if history has taught us anything it is that a reciprocal 'justice' without love is itself volatile and destructive."[44] Certainly there is more to justice than compassion, for compassion has a distinctive focus on human suffering, whereas justice embraces a wider regime of rights and freedoms as well. But there is no justice without compassion and no compassion that is indifferent to justice. "Compassion is not the entirety of justice," Nussbaum explains, "but it contains a powerful, if partial, vision of just

---

42. See, e.g., Mark 12:28–34 pars.; 1 Cor 13:13; 2 Cor 13:11; 1 John 4:8.
43. Jackson, *Priority of Love*, 29, 57.
44. Ibid., 18–19.

distribution and provides imperfect citizens with an essential bridge from self-interest to just conduct."[45]

Taken together, these considerations all support the legitimacy of seeking to institutionalize compassion. The modern welfare state is probably the most obvious example of such an effort. Though not without its problems and ambiguities, the welfare system represents a remarkable attempt to build compassionate values into the functions of the collective state by ensuring that every citizen's basic needs are met when they suffer as a result of sickness, accidents, poverty, unemployment, homelessness, and old age. Compassion has a vital role to play in other spheres of institutional life as well: in the taxation system, the education system, the public health system, in the mass media (which has immense power both to humanize and to dehumanize the suffering of its subjects),[46] in foreign policy, and in the immigration system, especially with respect to refugees.

Refugee policy is, in fact, a particularly striking illustration of the importance of institutional compassion. At one level, the entire enterprise of refugee selection and settlement is an exercise in compassion, with the host country going out of its way to assist displaced inhabitants of other nations, despite those persons being of no official interest or benefit to it. But the concrete practice of refugee acceptance is often brutally lacking in the kind of compassionate attentiveness to human suffering that is called for. In the current political environment, Western governments have been guilty of ramping up the fear of outsiders as a means of strengthening domestic borders.[47] Australia's draconian response to boat people is an especially conspicuous example of a stubborn refusal on the part of politicians and public officials to try to imagine just what it must be like to be so desperate as to resort to such extreme measures in the first place.

Even refugees who apply for sanctuary in more conventional ways often face unsympathetic treatment from front-line staff in the receiving

---

45. Nussbaum, "Compassion," 57.

46. The role of the media in cultivating public compassion is deeply ambiguous. On the one hand, the media trades in stories of human interest and deliberately elicits feelings of vicarious anger, disgust, sympathy, and compassion. On the other hand, because these sentiments are not based in actual human relationships, they lack mutuality, complexity, and duration. The media itself is keenly aware of the limited shelf life of emotional arousal in the public, and quickly replaces one object of attention with another, with the result that the compassion induced is extremely fleeting and volatile.

47. On the "ecology of fear" surrounding migration and a Christian response, see Snyder, "Asylum Seekers," and Cruz, "Toward an Ethic of Risk."

country. The problem is not so much with the laws and rules that govern admission processes; it is more to do with reluctance on the part of those who apply the rules to enter imaginatively and empathetically into the lived reality of applicants' previous experience. Often the only evidence applicants have of the incidence of torture, rape, abuse, persecution, or confiscations needed to support their claim to refugee status are their personal narratives. Listening sympathetically, and in detail, to these stories of suffering is incredibly important, not only for gathering relevant information but also for affirming the dignity of the victims and humanizing their plight. But officials often greet the stories with an ingrained suspicion and skepticism, sometimes to the point of subjecting victims to an additional form of abuse. It is necessary, of course, to assess the credibility of applicants' testimonies, since dishonest claims are made. But the predisposition to disbelief and the demand for unrealistic proof of claim sometimes reflects a simple failure of imagination on the part of immigration staff. It is only by engaging in "the thought experimentation of compassion"[48]—with its determination to enter imaginatively into the sufferer's unique experience and to understand its human complexity—that a true picture of the situation can begin to emerge.

Refugee policy often vests discretionary power in senior officials or government ministers to exercise compassion when prescribed standards cannot be met. This is a wholly commendable example of institutionalized compassion. But compassion will ever remain in short supply unless those officials are prepared to practice the slow and costly task of entering imaginatively into the bitter experience of persons who are quite unlike themselves and who come from worlds quite foreign to their own. Without that commitment, the system will fail to deliver the compassionate outcomes it provides for. This same commitment to compassionate deliberation is sorely needed in another sphere of institutional life as well: the criminal justice system. We turn to this institution in the next chapter.

SUMMARY

In this chapter we have examined the cognitive and affective character of compassion, and argued that it has an essential role to play in both personal and public moral deliberation. Compassion is the experience of

---

48. Avgoustinos, "Compassionate Judge," 26–32.

sharing emotionally in the suffering of another sentient being, an experience that is rooted in the facility we have to imagine what it must be like to stand in the shoes of one who is suffering and to allow ourselves to be profoundly affected by such contemplation.

Human beings, it appears, have an innate capacity for compassion. This capacity stems, according to the Bible, from our creation in the image of a compassionate God, made for relationships of mutual dependence and love. This compassionate potential is "released," so to speak, through our earliest experiences of attachment, vulnerability, and nurture in infancy. Thereafter, it is refined and developed through multiple kinds of experience and learning, including the learning that comes through civic and moral education. The fostering of a compassionate society requires the growth and development of compassionate citizens, and education, broadly defined, is an important tool for achieving this outcome. Among the chief tasks of such education, we have seen, is to overcome the partiality that so naturally attends the emotional experience of compassion by encouraging us to broaden the boundaries of our concern to include those who are dissimilar to us and those who are geographically distant from us.

Exposure to narrative literature, especially literature that carries us imaginatively into foreign cultural worlds where we witness human tragedy and suffering that is every bit as real and intense as in our own familiar world, is one crucial means of cultivating a more inclusive and extensive type of compassion in citizens. But something more is needed as well, something that connects compassion with ultimate reality and that compels and empowers compassionate behavior in individuals at a deeply personal and spiritual level. It is here that Christian faith has had such an important role to play historically in obligating and democratizing compassion, so much so that the failure of modern secular proponents of compassion to acknowledge its role is astonishing. And among the most potent of Christianity's means of achieving this have been the parables of compassion taught by Jesus, in particular the Good Samaritan and the Prodigal Son.

As well as educating for compassion, there is also a need to fashion public institutions and political structures that embody, as best they can, the insights and priorities of compassion and that are staffed by agents who seek to engage all their imaginative and empathetic skills in dealing with clients. Social-welfare services and refugee-selection agencies are two very clear examples of how institutional compassion requires both well-designed systems and well-trained, compassionate individuals if they are to succeed in delivering social outcomes that are simultaneously just and compassionate.

The same applies to the criminal justice system. More than any other institution in society, the legal system has doggedly resisted the well-founded truth that reason and emotion cannot be surgically separated from each other. It has failed to recognize that it is far wiser to acknowledge and accommodate the role of emotions than to pretend they can conveniently be switched off like a light bulb in the search for the truth, the whole truth, and nothing but the truth. With that in mind, we turn now to consider the contested place of compassion in the justice arena, and in particular the distinctive contribution restorative justice can make to the fostering of an emotionally satisfying experience of justice.

11

Compassion and the Criminal Justice System

If there is any institution where the need for the insights and instincts of compassion appears to be self-evident, yet where its appropriate role is fraught with uncertainty and unease, it is the criminal justice system. The need for compassion seems obvious because much crime involves personal injury and suffering, and the pursuit of justice necessarily entails attending to the human wreckage that has ensued and the amplitude of emotional reactions that accompany it.[1] We defined compassion as "the experience of emotional pain and moral concern occasioned by the awareness of, and identification with, another person's suffering or unhappiness." Inasmuch as the criminal justice system exists to express moral concern at the suffering or unhappiness caused by criminal behavior, and does so by providing a platform for participants to recount their experiences in detail, compassion seems plainly relevant to its work. Skillful trial attorneys understand this fact. They often consciously try to get the best possible outcomes for their clients by eliciting feelings of sympathy for them from judges and jurors.

Yet the proper role of compassion in the justice system is also hugely contested. There is a pervasive belief in the legal world that strong emotions serve only to cloud rational judgment and create confusion. Probably the single greatest influence on the evolution of modern criminal procedure has been the desire to preclude or moderate the distorting influence of emotion on legal discovery and judgment. This has resulted in a legal culture that prizes rationality, logic, predictability, universality,

---

1. For an overview of the extent to which "emotions pervade penal law and the criminal justice system," see Karstedt, "Emotions."

and formalism, and that downplays or marginalizes the language of feeling and imagination. Legal reasoning aims to be an emotionless endeavor that transcends the passions and prejudices of individual sentiment. The ideal judge applies the rule of law dispassionately in a manner untouched by subjective considerations. Compassion may well be an essential constituent of a healthy society, but its cultivation is best left to institutions other than the law. Legal institutions are duty-bound to follow formal rules and procedures that rise above the disruptive influences of emotion and to deliver objective, untrammeled justice.

This ambivalence towards the place of compassion in the justice system is well illustrated by a recent court case in New Zealand.[2] In October 2010, an eighteen-year-old youth, Ashley Austin, appeared before the Christchurch District Court for sentencing on a charge of dangerous driving causing death and injury. The teenager had not been speeding and was not intoxicated. But he had lost control of his powerful car, which had been illegally modified and was uncertified for public roads, on a wet suburban street. He careered off the road and mounted the curb, where he struck a four-year-old child, Nayan Woods, who was walking along the footpath with his mother and six-year-old brother. The little boy was killed and his mother and brother injured. Incredibly, in the weeks and months that followed the accident, the grieving parents found it in their hearts to forgive Ashley. They met with him several times in a restorative justice setting to talk about what had happened. They accepted his remorse as genuine. They acknowledged that everyone is capable of making foolish decisions with devastating consequences. They also expressed gratitude to him for remaining at the scene of the accident and taking over CPR from the mother as she fought to save her little boy's life.

At his sentencing, the teenager was too distraught to speak in court, so his mother read a statement on his behalf. It reiterated Ashley's profound regret for what had happened and thanked Nayan's parents for "their compassion and empathy despite their pain and tragedy." For their part, the bereaved parents asked the judge not to send Ashley to prison. They said he could not be punished any more than by having the weight of a dead child on his conscience for the rest of his life. The judge agreed. In sentencing the teen to six months community detention, two hundred hours of community work, and disqualification from driving for

2. Anonymous, "Driver."

three years, he told Ashley that Nayan's family had forgiven him—now he needed to learn to forgive himself.

This stunning display of compassion, first from the victims and then from the judge, was not universally applauded, however. Conservative newspaper columnist Michael Laws acknowledged the parents had been far more compassionate than he could ever be in such circumstances. But he suggested that their "curious combination of fatalism and forgiveness" was simply a coping mechanism following their bereavement. He also expressed skepticism at the genuineness of the offender's remorse and tears. His main criticism, however, was directed at the court for allowing the victims' attitude to have such an impact. To tolerate a justice system in which victims hold sway over sentencing is inherently wrong, Laws fumed, for it inevitably leads to dissimilar sentences for similar crimes depending on the attitude of the aggrieved party. Justice comes down to whether you have the luck to encounter "foolishly compassionate" victims, such as Nayan's parents, or the misfortune to strike some "vengeful bastard" intent on retribution. Laws concluded his column by referring to the parents' comment about the young driver having the child's death on his conscience for the remainder of his life. "Well, gee, I should hope so," Laws scoffed. "But that does not preclude proper punishment." To allow him to walk free from court sends the worst possible message to the criminal fraternity.[3]

In this heart-wrenching case, as far as the victims were concerned, and as far as the judge determined, justice was served through exercising appropriate compassion. As far as the newspaper columnist was concerned, compassion got in the way of justice and heightened the danger for everyone else in the community. Yet behind his bleak assessment lies a simple failure of compassionate effort on his part, a resolute determination *not* to enter imaginatively into the painful experience of all the parties caught up in the tragedy. In a published reply the following week to his disdainful criticism, the mother of the dead child, Emma Woods, explained the rationale for their allegedly "foolish compassion." She mentioned the driver's good character and lack of intent, the uncertainty about whether the modifications to his vehicle contributed to the accident, and the inappropriateness of prison for someone who was neither a threat to anyone else nor in need of rehabilitation. She also pointed out

---

3. Laws, "Forgiving Killers."

that the judge, far from being swayed by irrational emotion, spent thirty minutes in court explaining the reasons for his sentence.[4] Compassion was certainly operative in his judgment, in a variety of ways, but not at the expense of the rule of law. Rather the law was applied in a manner that was consistent with *both* the judgment of compassion *and* the principles of legality.

THE CALCULUS OF COMPASSION

Building on the core insight that all forms of intellectual activity, including legal reasoning, are inevitably influenced by emotional variables, several scholars have mounted cogent arguments for the value of empathy or sympathy or compassion (terms I am using synonymously) in judicial discovery and decision-making.[5] They contend that mainstream legal theory and practice, in attempting to banish the language of emotion and sentiment from view, effectively dehumanizes the parties involved. Lynne Henderson, for example, in a highly influential article decries the tendency of "legality"—by which she means the prevailing legal culture based on the rule of law and the primacy of disembodied reason—to "abstract the problem of persons to the point of denying persons altogether." Legal decisions and lawmaking, she complains, "frequently have nothing to do with understanding human experiences, affect, suffering—how people *do* live. And *feeling* is denied recognition and legitimacy under the guise of the 'rationality' of the Rule of Law."[6]

She calls it a "guise" because emotional influences cannot be magically disappeared by a simple wave of the legal wand. Even if gentler emotions and personal moral preferences may be consciously bracketed out of legal deliberation, other passions rumble beneath the surface, hidden from view. These include the passion for precision, precedent, logic, order, security, predictability, individual responsibility, and the zeal to prosecute. Susan Bandes similarly observes that "legal reasoning, although often portrayed as rational, does not—indeed, cannot—transcend passion or emotion. Instead, it is driven by a different set of emotional variables, albeit an ancient set so ingrained in the law that its contingent

4. Woods, "Amazing Grace."
5. See above, chapter 10, 249–82.
6. Henderson, "Legality," 1574–75.

nature has become invisible."[7] Emotion, then, is an inextricable part of all legal discourse. The issue is not *whether* emotion plays a role, but *which* emotions are at work, how self-consciously they are handled, and how well they enable the legal system to do its job.

It is in this connection that the particular emotion of empathy or compassion has a valuable contribution to make. Judges and jurors are normally expected to arrive at their decisions on the basis of hard evidence alone, without heed to personal sympathies or biases. "In judicial inquiry," a US federal court judge once intoned, "the cold clear truth is to be sought and dispassionately analyzed under the colorless lenses of the law."[8] Yet a strong argument can be mounted that it is *compassionate* judges and jurors, not *dispassionate* ones, who have the greater claim to judicial impartiality. Those who cultivate a heightened awareness of the unique experiences, sufferings, and dignity of the persons with whom they have to do—which is the essence of compassion—are better equipped to render fair and just decisions than are those who strive to avoid the discomfort and moral ambiguities that inevitably attend empathetic engagement. Just as the priest and the Levite in the parable took refuge in role morality and professional ethics to avoid dealing with actual human suffering at their feet, so it is possible for legal professionals today to do the same in the name of preserving the artifice of judicial impartiality and the rule of law. Only a commitment to compassionate listening and care-filled deliberation can prevent this from happening.

The Competencies of Judicial Compassion

It stands to reason that the more knowledge one has of a complex situation, the better one's decision-making will be. Good decisions require good information. Compassion, we saw earlier, is a distinctive form of knowing with its own identifiable cognitive structure. Conceivably, it is a form of knowing that enables judges and jurors to gain better understanding of the cases before them—whether criminal or civil—and thus promotes normatively better legal outcomes. It does so in at least four interrelated ways.

---

7. Bandes, "Empathy," 369.
8. In F. W. Woolworth Co. v. Wilson, quoted in Feigenson, "Sympathy," 15.

First, compassion permits a fuller *appreciation of the humanity of the people involved.* Emotion is intrinsic to human experience and fundamental to understanding human behavior. Humans are not just reasonable beings; they are also passionate beings. The only way to appreciate the passions or feelings of another person is by drawing upon one's own feelings or emotions. A dispassionate stance—one that conscientiously shuns emotional connection—impedes our ability to understand the subjective experiences of the other. It thereby diminishes our mindfulness of their humanity. Compassion, we have seen, is a response that acknowledges both the similarity of the sufferer to oneself, as well as their distance or difference. Dispassionate judgment heightens the element of distance by sanctioning emotional disengagement, while discounting the element of similarity. A compassionate mindset, by contrast, gives equal recognition to both dimensions. It views the other person as a vulnerable equal, with an inner world and an outer world paralleling one's own. Except in one crucial respect: her inner world has been rocked with a calamity that ours has not, and the only way we can begin to fathom her discomposure is by a focused act of empathetic identification.

This leads to the second point. A compassionate stance gives *experiential insight into the sufferings of others.* Crime almost invariably involves personal suffering. It is only by utilizing empathy that judicial agents can hope to comprehend the physical, emotional, mental, and spiritual anguish experienced by both victims and victimizers. To favor dispassionate analysis is actually to forego a valuable means of judicial discovery. It allows decision-makers to avoid facing the full extent of the suffering that has transpired, perhaps through fear of being overwhelmed by its misery or haunted by its memory. But evading this deeper level of affective engagement can lead to an oversimplification of the facts and produce poor or callous decisions.

A compassionate orientation is particularly vital for disclosing more covert or abstract forms of suffering. It is relatively easy to observe physical wounds and material losses of a victim and to determine what is required in way of redress. It is much harder to grasp emotional, mental, spiritual, or psychological wounds that, though invisible to the eye, are every bit as real and painful. It is only through an act of compassionate, imaginative reconstruction, that this hidden level of suffering can be accessed. This is particularly important in cases of sexual violence, which involve an assault on every level of the victim's experience: body, mind, and spirit. The same applies to what might be termed "foreign" suffering, that is, forms of suffering, such as torture, or religious persecution, or extreme cruelty, that fall outside anything the legal decision-makers have personally experienced or are ever likely to face. It is only by engaging the imaginative and humanizing tools of compassion that they can hope to do any justice at all to such remote yet psychologically crippling kinds of affliction.[9]

Third, compassion encourages a more *careful and comprehensive consideration of all the information relevant to justice*. We have noted how compassion acknowledges the intrinsic value of human suffering, registering in particular its level of severity and its unmerited nature. These are aspects that bring it into close association with the discernment of injustice. We have also seen that compassion is not infallible and is often partial. It therefore requires filtering and cognitive extension in order to serve appropriately as a moral guide. The point to be added now is that such cognitive development comes readily to a compassionate observer.

This is because of compassion's distinctive focus on the personhood of the subject facing hard times. As an expression of personal care and commitment, compassion takes a genuine interest in the perspective of the particular sufferer. It is not content with superficial explanations or rushed judgments. By its very nature, compassion slows analysis down; it strives for greater knowledge and clarity about the object of its concern. Compassionate observers care about getting it right and are attuned to extraneous influences that interfere with that goal. In these ways, compassion enhances the key task of gathering and processing all the information relevant to just judgments.[10]

Finally, compassion can aid judges in *interpreting legislation and developing the law*. Good law is fundamentally about what is appropriate and attainable in social relationships. Compassion provides the necessary framework for determining how particular laws can be applied in specific contexts in a manner that is both just and humane. Compassion also helps judicial interpreters humanize the technical language of the law. It reminds them that legal language is but shorthand for flesh-and-blood realities that must always be kept in view in deciphering legislation. Judges have a professional responsibility to attend to the express

---

9. For these points, see Avgoustinos, "Compassionate Judge," 16–22.

10. Cf. Avgoustinos, "Compassionate Judge," 13–14, 39–40; Feigenson, "Sympathy," 23–40.

provisions of statutes and to legal precedent. Compassion teaches them to attend also to the distinctive narratives of those persons upon whom the law bears down most heavily. Only thus can they dispense true justice, not merely administer legal writ.[11]

This dual accountability to inscribed law and contextual meaning is important to emphasize. To say that compassion has a crucial role in legal decision-making is not to say that it has the only role or that it can replace the standard tools of legal interpretation. The greatest anxiety critics have about giving place to compassion in the legal process, whether criminal or civil, is that decision-makers will be guided by compassion *despite* what the law says or will allow feelings of sympathy to compromise appropriate impartiality. But, as Lynne Henderson argues at length, empathy and legality are not mutually exclusive commitments; they belong together. Judges are accountable finally to the law, but empathy alerts them to the human meanings encoded therein. It safeguards them from an unreflective or mechanical reliance on technical details or established doctrine at the expense of human understanding. It was empathy, Henderson explains, that led the federal courts in America to strike down segregation; empathy enabled them to recognize that no matter how much it could be rationalized and defended in theoretical terms, segregation caused untold misery to actual human beings and stripped them of their human dignity, and therefore had to be dismantled.[12]

In all these interlocking ways, then, compassion enhances the work of the judiciary. Of course, the relationship of judges and jurors to defendants and plaintiffs is not normatively a therapeutic one. Judges are there to pass judgment, not provide treatment, even if the resulting sentence may include therapeutic provisions, such as anger management, counseling, or alcohol and drug treatment. This role imposes a restriction on the style and substance of the personal connection they can have with the parties. It also conditions the kind of language they can use. Many judges conscientiously avoid using emotive terms in their judgments, not least to avoid the appearance of bias. Some think judges should be encouraged to incorporate more affective vocabulary into their judicial language to help them better cope with "the burden and pain of judging."[13] But the

11. Kimmel, "Compulsory Compassion."

12. Henderson, "Legality," passim. See also the defense of the compatibility of acting mercifully and acting lawfully in Brien, "Mercy."

13. Bandes, "Empathy," 379.

careful and precise use of language is intrinsic to legal analysis and essential for legal precedent, so legal speech needs always to be measured and meticulous. Fortunately, compassionate discourse does not require highly emotive language or fulsome rhetorical flourish. It can take the form of restrained, matter-of-fact description that nonetheless discloses real attentiveness to the personal narratives and human sufferings of those involved, not just to the abstract legal principles at stake.[14]

The Limits of Legal Compassion

In the preceding chapter, we reviewed some of the pitfalls associated with giving compassion a significant role in moral valuation. These include the problems of mistaken priorities, of dissipated energy, and of unwarranted partiality. A parallel set of problems arises in the legal arena. In fact, the problems with respect to the legal system are so pronounced that even some of those who concede the positive benefits of compassionate deliberation—its sensitivity to undeserved suffering, its proclivity towards information gathering, its attention to actual human need—also warn of its attendant dangers. Neal Feigenson, for example, is clear on all these benefits of legal sympathy. He is equally clear that emotional deliberation is no more arbitrary or subjective than nonemotional deliberation, which is equally affected by a range of subconscious influences, such as cultural scripts, intuitive knowledge structures, and pre-understandings of various kinds. He also points out that "soft" emotions, like compassion, have less of an impact on the complex information processing functions of the brain than do more intense emotions, like anger, while the slow, time-consuming nature of legal processes moderates even further the disruptive impact of emotional arousal. Yet for all this, Feigenson thinks there are still peculiarities to the psychology of compassion that complicate its function in a courtroom setting and counsel against any deliberate expansion of its role.[15]

One such complication is the problem of *perspective or projection*. There is a marked tendency for us to project our own mental, emotional, or moral perspective on to persons we feel sympathy for. We interpret their experience through the lens of our own personalities and egos. We presume that they have experienced what we are now experiencing

14. See Henderson, "Legality," 1650–52.
15. Feigenson, "Sympathy," passim.

on their behalf, that they have reacted just as we would in such circumstances. This raises the question of empathetic accuracy. Compassionate observers may be *wrong* in how they interpret what the sufferer is feeling or thinking, especially if the person comes from a different culture or subculture, and this can result in mistaken legal conclusions.

Another complication is compassion's *predisposition to partiality or bias*, which we have discussed at length already. Research shows that the greater the similarity between sufferer and observer, the more readily compassion is evinced. This is partly because we find it easier to identify with those who resemble us in important ways. We also find it easier to feel sympathy for those whom we find physically attractive. But neither similarity nor likeability is a legally relevant consideration. Fellow feeling for the sufferer may result in us being captured by the sufferer's point of view. This "dark underbelly of empathy," as Susan Bandes calls it, is particularly worrisome in cases of rape or domestic violence. Male judges and jurors may find it easier to identify with male defendants than with female victims and misconstrue the evidence accordingly.[16] Or they may allow their assessment of criminal liability to be determined by speculations about the likely consequences of an acquittal or a conviction on the accused rather than in terms of the evidence.

This leads to yet another complication with compassion: the problem of *proportionality or balance*. There is no necessary correlation between the emotional intensity of the compassion experienced by decision-makers and the legal seriousness of the issues at stake. Emotional feelings are affected by a range of extralegal considerations, such as the physical appearance of the victim, the presence or absence of key parties in the courtroom, whether or not the event occurred under exceptional circumstances, and the physical severity of the victim's pain. Not only may the depth of compassion evoked be disproportionate to the legal description of the injury, it may encourage an unfair allocation of responsibility. Research shows that the greater the sympathy jurors have for victims, the more likely they are to blame defendants. They are also less willing to entertain the possibility of shared culpability for the event and to concede the mitigating influence of situational influences. The more they pity one party, the more they heap blame on the other.[17]

16. Bandes, "Empathy," 376–77.
17. Feigenson, "Sympathy," 57–60. According to Ross and Shestowsky, research shows that people, especially in individualistic cultures, are prone to underestimate the

This is where the increasingly common practice of reading victim impact statements in court hearings is laced with danger. The argument in favor of such statements is that they bring silenced narrative voices into the legal arena and enable the court to empathize firsthand with the suffering of victims. In that sense, they represent a laudable attempt to institutionalize compassion. But the practice carries great risks as well. Susan Bandes speaks positively of the growing emphasis on storytelling and empathetic engagement in the legal process. But neither feature should be regarded as an unmitigated good in every circumstance, she insists. Normative criteria are needed to determine which narrative voices should be heard in court and what emotions should be encouraged. Despite the claim that they promote compassionate engagement with sufferers, Bandes argues that victim impact statements should be suppressed in court hearings, especially if heard prior to the determination of guilt and sentencing, as happens in some jurisdictions, and particularly in capital cases.[18]

The principal reason for this is that victim impact statements trigger the wrong emotions. They evoke empathy for the victim, to be sure, but often in a way that stirs up hatred, fear, anger, and disgust towards the defendant. Richard Bell describes the good judge as one who attends to the accused person's silent cry "to be read differently," to be seen as more than what appears before him in the dock.[19] Victim impact statements push public sentiment in the opposite direction. To the extent that they feed feelings of disgust for the defendant, they diminish our ability to see him in his totality as a unique human being. They may instead fuel a primitive urge for revenge in the public mind by depicting the accused as a monster wholly and solely responsible for the evil perpetrated.[20] This frequently leads to criticism of judges for failing to impose punishments commensurate with the level of public loathing felt for the offender, which in turn places pressure on legislators to ramp up levels of punitive severity.

Bandes is also concerned that victim impact statements can skew the pitch unfairly against the party in the legal process who is already at

---

role of situational factors and overestimate the importance of dispositional factors in explaining past behavior or predicting future behavior, and to presuppose simplistic distinctions between good and bad characters ("Psychology's Challenges").

18. Bandes, "Empathy."
19. Bell, *Rethinking Justice*, 48–49.
20. Nussbaum, *Upheavals*, 448–53.

a distinct disadvantage. It is usually not too difficult for judges and jurors to establish an empathetic connection with victims; it is much more difficult to do so with defendants. "We do not need elaborate structures to assist us in feeling fear, pain, and grief for those like us who have suffered violence at the hands of the other. This is already the dominant narrative of the criminal trial. The difficult challenge lies in making possible the decision-maker's identification with the other."[21] This doesn't mean minimizing or excusing their wrongdoing. But it does mean striving to comprehend the larger societal context of their behavior. It means acknowledging all the historical, political, racial, and economic realities that consistently disadvantage certain groups in society and propel them toward lawbreaking.

It is also questionable whether victim impact statements encourage genuine or lasting empathetic connection with victims. As a brief snapshot in time, and in language sometimes constrained by court protocol, victim statements can never do justice to the complexity and variability of the subject's experience. Nor do they allow the victim's unique identity and particularity to emerge. Instead, by using stock victim imagery and categories, the statements may pander to stereotyped distinctions between "good" victims and "bad" offenders. But reality is more complex than this. Victimhood is not a proxy for virtuousness. For every good, decent, law-abiding victim, there are also corrupt, violent, and lawbreaking victims—and endless shades in between. Most offenders, furthermore, have first been victims themselves. It is also dangerous to extrapolate from a victim's immediate experience to what all victims really want or need or what is best for them or society. There is a tendency for onlookers to misinterpret the anger and pain victims express as an intense desire for retribution and to assume that harsher penalties are the way to satisfy their wants. As a result, victims' deeper needs for counseling and understanding, for long-term support and financial restitution, often get lost in the mix. Meanwhile, law-and-order lobbyists expropriate their stories for ulterior political and ideological agendas.[22]

The argument against reading victim impact statements in open court, then, is not that they appeal to emotion instead of reason or that

---

21. Bandes, "Empathy," 409–10.

22. Bandes, "Empathy," 406–7, 410; Henderson, "Legality," 1652–53. See also Strang, "Victim Movement."

they give undue emphasis to storytelling over legislative prescription. It is that, in some cases in particular, they encourage an incomplete, one-sided, and unreflective empathy that disadvantages and dehumanizes the person in the trial process, the accused, who requires the greatest effort at empathetic understanding. In seeking to express compassion for victims, they can also encourage vindictiveness towards offenders. They may enlist empathy in service of exclusion rather than genuine understanding. The problem is not so much their direct impact on legal decision-makers, for whom victim impact statements are only a small part of the information available to inform their deliberations. More worrying is the effect they have on public sentiment, especially in particularly graphic, high-profile cases that attract media attention. An exaggerated emphasis on selected aspects of victim statements cumulatively has a coarsening effect on public civility and a deleterious downstream impact in sentencing practices.

It is also problematic that defendants are not given any opportunity to respond to what is said in an appropriate way. They must remain silent, an involuntary silence often construed by onlookers, and experienced by victims, as added confirmation of their lack of remorse and basic human decency. Certainly there is a need for victims' stories to be heard in the course of proceedings and for their suffering to be acknowledged. But restorative justice mechanisms arguably provide a more constructive way for this to happen. In place of the lopsided public theatre currently employed, it would be better to adjourn hearings after conviction to allow victims, if they so choose, to meet directly with the defendant in closed session to recount the impact of the crime on their lives and to provide an opportunity for the defendant to respond appropriately. Dialogue is nearly always preferable to monologue, especially when addressing emotional injury.

Reflective Compassion

Undoubtedly, then, there are complicating factors to the psychology of compassion in a courtroom setting. It is vulnerable to projection, to bias, and to prejudicial resolutions of blame. This does not vitiate its value, however. It only shows that compassionate analysis takes time, effort, and practice. It is commonly accepted that justice is an achievement, often a slow and arduous achievement, and there is no reason why compassionate justice should be any different.[23] Unreflective compassion can be dangerous and distorting. But it is not spontaneous or unreflective empathy that is being commended as a judicial virtue but rather a thoughtful, reflective, and informed empathy. There is no institution in society better equipped to promote such educated compassion than the judicial system. It is futile to expect judicial agents to aspire to Martian-like emotional detachment and neutrality in their work. Even if such a standpoint were possible, it would be undesirable. Instead, judges and jurors should be encouraged to appreciate both the epistemological value of affective and imaginative involvement in helping them discern where and how injustice has lodged, and, at the same time, the fallibility of such emotional responses and the need for external testing against normative criteria.

Individuals differ, of course, in their levels of self-awareness and emotional intelligence. But a high level of sophistication is not required in this instance. If ordinary people can be taught how to regulate powerful emotions like anger and envy, and to monitor the factors that contribute to their incidence, they can also be taught to understand the potential pitfalls of gentler instincts like compassion, and what is needed to compensate for its propensity towards projection, partiality, and proneness to blaming. Such self-consciousness can certainly be expected of the professional players in the system, such as lawyers and adjudicators. But even laypersons recruited to jury service are capable of being sensitive to the dangers of bias and projection and of compensating for them. When made aware of the stakes, most mature adults readily acknowledge that subjective emotional judgments need to yield to rules of evidence, standards of proof, and the requirements of natural justice. They also accept the need to incorporate the values of consistency, integrity, and impartiality into their decision-making. Most psychologically healthy individuals are capable of combining compassionate judgment with consideration of wider moral, social, and legal norms. Unreflective compassion is indeed dangerous. But so, too, is uncompassionate reflection. The goal to pursue is a *reflective* or *informed* compassionate deliberation, which is not as alien to ordinary people as sometimes assumed.

23. Duncan Forrester explains that classical (and biblical) conceptions of justice always assume that justice is objectively real, has absolute priority, and requires a kind of *ascesis* to achieve—that is, a rigorous and lifelong engagement with the social and psychic forces that obstruct our grasping and implementation of justice. Postmodern ideological talk of justice is often defective in all these respects (*Christian Justice*, esp. 38–60).

Education and Design for Judicial Compassion

In the preceding chapter, we discussed the twin roles of institutional design and public education in promoting compassion in society. Both apply to the criminal justice system. Embedding compassionate priorities in the judicial system requires attending to its structural design, on the one hand, and to the education of judges and future judges, on the other. Neither is simple or straightforward. There are major hurdles to overcome, especially relating to the psychology of compassion. But the benefits of creating a more compassionate justice system are worth the effort.

With respect to *institutional structure*, a compassionate justice system is one that affords judges sufficient flexibility to deal with the nuances of any given case. One disturbing feature of recent developments in criminal justice policy has been the drive to reduce judicial discretion in sentencing, often reflecting the fear that judges won't be tough enough if left to their own devices. Consistency in sentencing is a legitimate concern and an essential feature of the rule of law. But discretion is an indispensable requirement for exercising compassion in any setting, for no rigid system of rules can cover every exigency or anticipate every consideration. Some measure of discretion is therefore essential if the law is to achieve the moral outcomes it aims for. The institutionalizing of discretionary powers, within set guidelines, in turn requires competently compassionate judges who use their judgment wisely after having gained as much insight as possible into the persons they are dealing with.

Another important design feature is restraint on the use of punishment. "Love only resorts to punishment," Timothy Jackson explains, "when there has been a proven offence and when retributive steps will likely benefit all concerned; punishment is not a proper means of indoctrination, or conversion, or crowd control."[24] Our ingrained recourse to punitive over therapeutic, educational, or preventative interventions, even when punishment so patently fails to achieve the purposes we claim for it, is a telling indication of how reluctant we really are to confront the actual social drivers of human behavior. This constitutes a collective failure of compassionate imagination. When penalties are imposed, the corrections system needs to be shaped by compassionate commitments, such as rehabilitation of offenders and their preparation for successful

---

24. Jackson, *Priority of Love*, 15. For a fuller discussion of the ethics of punishment, see Marshall, *Beyond Retribution*, esp. 97–143.

reintegration in society. Also required is a greater responsiveness to the needs and vulnerabilities of victims. Historically victims have been the missing party in the justice process, mainly because the state has assumed the mantle of victimhood on their behalf, reducing the role of the actual victims to little more than being witnesses for the prosecution.

With respect to *legal education*, it is vital that members of the judiciary acquire not only technical mastery of the law and of legal process but also the ability to enter imaginatively, yet critically, into the inner worlds and life ways of the varied individuals that come before them. In Martha Nussbaum's words, "we need judges who are appropriately emotional."[25] This requires an education of both heart and mind. Reflecting on the necessary attributes of judges in society, social thinker Simone Weil advised: "[They should be] drawn from very different social circles; be naturally gifted with wide, clear, and exact intelligence; and be trained in a school where they receive not just a legal education but above all a *spiritual* one; and only secondarily an intellectual one. They must be accustomed to love truth."[26]

A "spiritual" education is needed to help judges understand that all human beings are fallible, that everyone, including themselves, is capable of great evil in certain circumstances, and that those on whom they must sit in judgment have been formed by personal and social forces often beyond their control. A "love of truth" ensures that judges will hold the guilty accountable. But it also guarantees that they will take into consideration all the contextual factors that have contributed to their offending. Modern psychology has highlighted the extent to which genetic and environmental factors play a significant role in determining human behavior. In discussing the implications of this finding for the criminal justice system, Ross and Shestowsky suggest that a more "logically coherent account of behavioral causation would compel us to treat transgressors with more compassion than they typically receive."[27]

The chief virtue of judicial compassion, according to its proponents, is that it enriches and extends judicial processes of discovery, analysis, and decision-making. Compassionate judges are better judges than their dispassionate counterparts because they are committed to hearing the

---

25. Nussbaum, *Upheavals*, 446.
26. Weil, *Need*, 40 (emphasis added); cited in Bell, *Rethinking Justice*, 48–49.
27. Ross and Shestowsky, "Psychology's Challenges," 1088, cf. 1101.

whole story and to facing squarely the full human and moral dimensions of their role. Their task is to adjudicate, not to offer psychotherapy, as previously observed, but that does not mean that they must stand at a lofty distance from the human realities involved. Compassionate judges exhibit their compassion, not simply by feeling the pain of the parties, but by taking into reckoning all the cognitive variables of compassion that Nussbaum identifies, such as the seriousness of the suffering endured, the degree of personal fault involved, and the common vulnerability to damage that is the universal lot of us all. In these ways, the judge's capacity for compassion is "a vital part of his judicial equipment and of his judicial rationality."[28]

Employing the considerations of compassion is not without its dangers, as we have repeatedly acknowledged. But equally dangerous is a refusal to employ empathetic sensitivity. Lynne Henderson ends her discussion of empathy and legality with these words: "Empathy cannot tell us what to do or how to accomplish something, but it does alert us to moral choice and responsibility. It also reminds us of our common humanity and responsibility to one another. We could do worse—indeed we have done worse—than to employ the knowledge empathy imparts."[29]

Compassion's Currents

Recent debate on the place of empathy or compassion in the justice system has focused almost entirely on its usefulness to decision-makers in the system, particularly judges and jurors. Advocates of empathetic deliberation argue that it produces better legal outcomes; critics contend that putting too much emphasis on sympathy or compassion heightens the risk of bias, stereotyping, and disproportionate allocation of blame. What has been largely missing from the debate is any recognition of the value of reciprocal empathy between the principal participants in the criminal event itself, that is, between victims and offenders. The currents of compassion have been assumed to flow in a unilateral and hierarchical direction, from judges, jurors, and judicial officials down to defendants or plaintiffs. Little thought has been given to the desirability of a horizontal exchange of compassion between the persons most affected by the matter at hand.

28. Nussbaum, "Compassion," 55–56.
29. Henderson, "Legality," 1653.

This is where restorative justice has something distinctive to offer the quest for a more compassionate justice system. Restorative justice is a process that brings together victims and offenders, and their relational networks, to deliberate on the suffering that has been unleashed by the wrongdoing and to reflect on ways that repair can be achieved. Through its central procedure of facilitated encounter between victims and offenders, restorative justice furnishes the practical means by which compassion can flow in multiple directions in the work of justice. In her discussion of the politics of compassion, Elisabeth Porter proposes that a compassionate political system has three characteristics: attentiveness to the suffering of the most vulnerable people in the community, active listening to their voices in order to discern what they need most, and wise and appropriate responses to alleviate their distress.[30] This is precisely what restorative justice seeks to provide in the justice system: a forum where attention is given to the sufferings of victims and victimizers, where time is given to listening to their narratives and discerning their needs, and where agreements are forged between the parties to address those needs in a way that entails mutual encounter and understanding. And the tools of compassion are relevant to every step in the process.

At the beginning of this chapter, I recounted the death of four-year-old Nayan Woods and the criticism leveled at the judge for allowing irrational compassion to dictate his sentencing of the young man responsible. Nayan's family defended the judge's actions and were supportive of the court's compassionate dealing with the offender. But what was more significant for them was their experience of meeting directly with the offender, Ashley Austin, and his family in a restorative justice setting. Nayan's mother, Emma Woods, explained their reason for doing so.

> We met Ashley and his family to get a better idea of them. We wanted to get first-hand experience of the person responsible for Nayan's death. We didn't do this out of weakness or naivety; we did it to acquire knowledge. We also wanted to honor Nayan by having them learn more about him through photos and stories. We wanted the little body Ashley saw on the footpath to become a real person. We wanted him to hear how much we love Nayan and how much our lives have changed without him. It is one thing to feel the impact when you care very little about the person who has been at the cause, or the effect, but quite another

30. Porter, "Politics," 113–17.

when you see them as real people. It would have been much easier for Ashley and his family to keep us at a distance. [Michael] Laws seems to consider all that weak and foolish. He has no idea of the strength needed on both sides to make those meetings happen, and to acknowledge the humanity in each other.[31]

There is no more insightful description of the essence of compassionate engagement than this one. Emma Woods goes on in the article to explain that their decision to deal with their loss as they did was not intended to be a precedent for anyone else, nor necessarily the right way for others to respond. "We approached it in the way that was right for us, based on the facts of the case." But not everyone would agree on the rightness of the choice she made even for herself. There are some critics who claim that restorative justice trades in a coercive form of compassion that exploits the vulnerability of victims and permits offenders to evade proper accountability. Is such criticism justified? Or is restorative justice possibly the most significant experiment in compassionate justice yet to emerge?

RESTORATIVE COMPASSION

From modest Mennonite beginnings in the early 1970s, restorative justice has burgeoned into one of the most prolific and innovative fields of justice thought and practice in the world today. It has been described as the current "big idea" in justice theory and possibly the most significant development in criminal justice since the emergence of the nation-state.[32] Different scholars trace the roots of restorative justice to different sources. Some appeal to biblical theology, others to aboriginal conceptions of justice, some to the feminist ethics of care, others to communitarian political thought. Proponents tend to characterize restorative justice in contrastive terms to traditional justice. It is relational, not impersonal; curative, not punitive; community-based, not state-dominated; empowering of participants, not professionally controlled; forward-looking, not preoccupied with past infractions; contextual, not rules-governed.

The chief concern of restorative justice is to enable victims and offenders, and their supporters, to work collaboratively at repairing the

31. Woods, "Amazing Grace."
32. Archibald, "Restorative Justice," 941; Thorburn, "Impossible Dreams," at 866; Karstedt calls restorative justice currently "the most successful reform movement in criminal justice world-wide" ("Emotions," 302).

damage caused by wrongdoing through respectful dialogue, acceptance of responsibility, reparation of losses, and reconciliation. This goal makes restorative justice both much simpler than traditional justice and more ambitious. It is simpler because the focus is on facilitating personal encounter rather than enacting a formalized process of investigation and adjudication. It is more ambitious because its aim is not merely to denounce wrongdoing and punish the guilty party but to promote good relationships in society and to address wider social problems.

As it has flourished and diversified, restorative justice has also drawn mounting criticism. Two main kinds of criticism have been advanced. One comes from those with an interest in the design of criminal justice institutions, such as legal scholars, criminologists, lawyers, and senior public servants. They complain that the *ad hoc* nature of restorative processes rides roughshod over long-established judicial principles of fairness, precision, impartiality, consistency, transparency, universality, and proportionality. Some detect in restorative justice a worrying desire to dismantle the apparatus of state-controlled justice in favor of a return to a purely private system of conflict resolution, in which it is left to the interested parties to deal with events as they see fit.

The other kind of criticism is more philosophical in nature. It contests the wisdom or adequacy of redefining justice in terms of relational renewal, emotional healing, reciprocal respect, or mutual regard rather than in more traditional terms of just deserts or retributive balance. By favoring impossibly "thick" conceptions of justice, critics contend, restorative justice slides into conceptual vagueness and idealism.[33]

Nowhere has this latter argument been made with greater vigor and eloquence than by Canadian legal scholar Annalise Acorn, in her crusading book *Compulsory Compassion: A Critique of Restorative Justice*.[34] John Braithwaite, a world authority on the subject, describes it as "the

33. Thorburn claims that restorative justice "does not really provide a substantive theory of justice at all, but a sort of anti-theory. Rather than setting out a new way of structuring the state apparatus of criminal justice, it suggests that we dismantle that apparatus and leave it largely up to the interested parties to deal with the aftermath of crime as they see fit" ("Impossible Dreams," 870). This is a misleading assertion that underestimates the theoretical coherence of restorative justice (see, for example, Bell, *Rethinking Justice*, 95–116) and misconstrues its goals. Closer to the truth is John Braithwaite, who describes restorative justice as a "radical re-theorizing of the justice field" in the pragmatist tradition ("Narrative," 427).

34. Acorn, *Compulsory Compassion*.

most beautifully written of the now countless books on restorative justice" and "the most foundational critique yet to appear."[35] We will have cause to reject Acorn's critique as overstated and seriously misleading. But *Compulsory Compassion* touches on many of the themes we have been exploring throughout this study, so there is good reason to conclude our investigation with a careful consideration of this book.

Before turning to Acorn's substantive arguments, two ironies are worth noting at the outset. The first is that, in the process of excoriating restorative justice root and branch, Acorn ends up providing one of the most perceptive accounts of the distinguishing features of restorative justice theory yet produced. She crystallizes the defining values and ethos of the restorative justice vision with remarkable perception and precision. This makes her analysis invaluable for anyone interested in the field. At the same time, as will soon become clear, she is guilty of badly misconstruing the practice of restorative justice and relying on crudely drawn stereotypes for ammunition.

The second irony relates to the tension that exists between the book's autobiographical starting point and the author's repeated attack on restorative justice for its excessive reliance on personal testimonies and stories of success to bolster its claims. Acorn speaks of "wincing with embarrassment" at the sentimentality of the tales of cathartic encounters between victims and offenders that circulate in restorative justice circles.[36] In an effort to break away from such mawkish anecdotes, she turns to the world of literary fiction for counter-narratives that contradict restorative justice fancies. Great novels tell stories that ring more true to human experience, she claims, than do the simplistic narratives that come out of the restorative justice movement.[37]

Now, one might question this odd preference for the truth of art over the truth of firsthand testimony of those who have actually been through painful events. One reviewer comments on the curious methodological spectacle of mounting a critique of restorative justice, not on the basis of empirical evidence, but by means of "ambiguous notions of love and justice culled from utterances of fictional characters, many struggling in a world of hideous Victorian values that, one hopes, the postmodern era

---

35. Braithwaite, "Narrative," 425.
36. Acorn, *Compulsory Compassion*, 78–98.
37. Ibid., 24.

may be in the process of transcending."[38] Another considers it brazen of Acorn "to advance a condemnation of restorative justice based primarily on an argument that giving the perpetrator a chance at reform didn't work with Pap in *Huckleberry Finn*."[39] But the deeper incongruity concerns the exception Acorn makes for her own personal testimony and experience in presenting her case.

She begins the book by describing her initial enthusiasm for restorative justice, at both a theoretical and an emotional level. One of the things that drew her to it was the way it challenges "our cultural obsession with punishment as a satisfying proxy for justice."[40] It debunks the age-old idea that the only way to rectify the imbalance caused by wrongdoing is by the imposition of proportionate suffering on the wrongdoer. Rather than inflicting retaliatory pain on the criminal or casting him out of society, the best way to restore social equilibrium is by involving the offender in the project of repairing the harm he has caused. But the attraction was short-lived; over time Acorn began to experience "twinges of doubt" about the viability of restorative justice, with its "rhetorical platitudes of right-relation, mutuality, equality, and respect."[41] She found herself unable to let go of her "moral intuition" that justice sometimes means throwing the book at wrongdoers rather than bending over backwards to be nice to them. She also felt troubled by her own hypocrisy. "Restorative justice seemed just fine for other people, for harms I had not suffered, but when it came to *me*, restorative justice wasn't what I wanted. I did not feel competent as an advocate for restorative justice because I doubted both my ability to repair relationships marred by wrongdoing and my commitment to doing so."[42] Acorn reached the conclusion that her early zeal for restorative justice stemmed in part from a psychological need not to miss out on the fantasy of right-relations that everyone else was talking about. But that's all it was, she concluded: a romantic, starry-eyed fantasy.

This sense of letdown and loss of faith pervades the discussion that follows. It also perhaps accounts for the emotive language and name-calling Acorn often engages in. She concedes that her skepticism about restorative justice may simply reflect her own moral failings. But if the

38. Archibald, "Restorative Justice," 944.
39. Ribet, "Emotion," 119.
40. Acorn, *Compulsory Compassion*, 1.
41. Ibid., 6.
42. Ibid., 7.

success of restorative justice depends on its participants being uncommonly patient and virtuous, and even more committed to peace, harmony, and healing than she is, then it is in deep trouble. For the justice system has to work for people who are morally run-of-the-mill, not just for those inclined to sainthood. We should therefore be concerned about any system that depends for its success on a commitment to supererogatory virtue on the part of its participants.[43]

We will return to this charge presently, and to the erroneous insinuation that restorative justice aims to supplant the current justice system with an alternative model that every run-of-the-mill citizen should find usable. But the thing to observe at this point is simply its anecdotal basis. Acorn derides restorative justice's "skilful deployment—through theory and story—of cheerful fantasies of happy endings in the victim-offender relation, emotional healing, closure, right-relation, and respectful community."[44] Yet it is her own cheerless story of disappointment and disenchantment that provides the launching pad and principal justification for her intransigent opposition to restorative justice. Her repeated refrain that it is "seductive," "enticing," "sentimental," "naïve," "idealistic," "trendy," "utopian," "vague," "romantic," and so forth, could simply be seen as self-flagellation for her past gullibility rather than an informed assessment of restorative justice's true character and potential.

"Dewy-Eyed Justice"

A recurring theme in Acorn's book is that restorative justice's aspiration to promote relationships of mutuality, equality, and respect is an "optimistic fantasy" that is "staggeringly vague," "culpably sentimental," and "dangerously naïve."[45] It is a sensibility drawn from a whitewashing modern culture and informed by Californian new age thinking, self-help therapies, pop psychology, and a "soft religion" that substitutes repentance and forgiveness for punishment and condemnation.[46] Its "dewy-eyed" approach to justice is "emotionally grounded in fear of criminals and a craven hope

43. Ibid., 12.
44. Ibid., 16.
45. Ibid., 16, 19.
46. Ibid., 160. John Braithwaite, a secular proponent of restorative justice, speaks of how he has found that conservative, right-wing Christians in the United States are often willing to give restorative justice a hearing because they preferred Tutu and Mandela to the militarism of George Bush ("Narrative," 430).

that they will be nicer to us if we don't offend them with punishment."⁴⁷ Its "devout practitioners" proffer a beguiling mix of emotional healing for victims, moral transformation of offenders, and the creation of respectful community for everyone else, all based on "an extraordinary amount of faith" in the "magically transformative power" of restorative encounters. "Yet, as with all seductions, the fantasies that lure us tend to be very different from the realities that unfold."⁴⁸

Interestingly, Acorn traces the source of this alluring belief in human transformability to the spiritual or religious ideals that underpin much restorative justice thinking.

> Such is the case, in part, because so many of the philosophical roots of restorative justice are theological. Pulls toward and away from institutions of restorative justice are bound up with our feelings about a relationship to the divine. The more we are emotionally drawn to a religious ethic of love, the more we will be motivated to make restorative justice work. The more we have both a longing for some conflation of love or compassion and justice (and some theoretical framework within which to situate the possibility of that conflation), the more we will be motivated to persist in the project of justice-as-repair. The more we are committed to an ethic of nonviolence, the more we suffer at the thought of inflicting suffering on others. The more we are drawn to the value of harmony, the more the aspirations of restorative institutions will appear worthwhile to us.⁴⁹

There is truth in this observation. The restorative justice vision probably does owe more to the influence of religious, and specifically Christian, theological and moral understandings than some of its secular protagonists recognize. But to dismiss any talk of love, forgiveness, and reconciliation in the context of justice as simplistic and seductive, or to disparage it as "soft religion" of a piece with the TV talk show mentality of confession and disclosure, is mere vilification. Acorn exaggerates the role of emotional catharsis in restorative processes, claiming it produces momentary illusions of dramatic change. At the same time, she relies heavily in her own critique on emotionally loaded assertions based on nothing

---

47. Acorn, *Compulsory Compassion*, 164.
48. Ibid., 18–19, cf. 86.
49. Ibid., 19.

more than personal opinion. Her analysis is neither academically rigorous nor empirically grounded. She fails entirely to engage with the growing body of empirical research on the issues she discusses, relying instead on a string of intuitive judgments and psychological speculations about the feelings and motivations of participants. A good part of her argument, brilliantly articulated though it is, comes down to the simple contention that she knows best what human nature is like. She understands what is *really* going on behind the surface of restorative encounters, whatever the participants might say to the contrary.[50]

Perhaps the most troubling aspect of Acorn's analysis is her gross caricaturing of victims and offenders. She speaks of both groups in totalizing terms. She makes no allowances for the diversity and complexity that characterizes each category, and never acknowledges that victims and offenders often have much in common. She presumes, for example, that most offenders belong to lower socioeconomic groups in society than their victims.[51] But that is not true. Most crime victims come from the same marginalized communities that most offenders come from.[52] The poor are more frequently victims of crime than are the middle classes. Acorn frequently reminds us of just how bad offenders really are, and she is deeply skeptical about the transformability of their character.[53] She claims that restorative justice is committed to the belief that bringing victims and offenders together can have a powerfully transformative impact on offenders, implying, wrongly, that changing offenders is the overriding goal of the process. Victims are encouraged to view offenders,

50. So, correctly, Ribet, "Emotion," 118.

51. Acorn, *Compulsory Compassion*, 145–46.

52. *The New Zealand Crime and Safety Survey* (NZCASS) 2006 reports that the risk of victimization is highest for young people, sole parents, those who are unemployed or on a benefit, and those living in rented property or in the most deprived areas of the country (at 46). Tony Paine, the CEO of the New Zealand organization Victim Support, rightly comments: "It is very easy to talk about victims and offenders as if they were two quite separate groups (both demographically and morally). Of course the world is not that black and white . . . 50% of all victimizations are experienced by only 6% of New Zealanders and . . . the social and demographic indicators that identify those who are most likely to be victimized are identical to the markers for those likely to be offenders. The life stories and cultural contexts that weave victims and offenders together (often within the same person) make any artificial separation between offenders and victims just that: an artifice that oversimplifies our complex world" (Paine, "Victim Support," 157).

53. Acorn, *Compulsory Compassion*, 60–69.

she says, not simply as criminals but as rounded human beings who are just as worthy of respect as are their own family or friends. It is by exhibiting such respect for offenders that moral change may be triggered.

Acorn is scornful of this "complicated request" for respect.[54] It is merely a rhetorical device to encourage a false sense of optimism about the perpetrator's capacity to change. The idea that a loving connection with the wrongdoer has the power to induce radical change in him is a soothing idea, and often part of a larger "spiritual mythology," but it is entirely lacking in empirical foundation. "Both personal experience and the teachings of literature affirm the intuition that, for the most part, people remain 'in character.'"[55] Restorative optimism flies in the face of our instinctive "commonsensical cynicism" about people's capacity to change.[56]

As well as typecasting most offenders as nasty and devious and disputing their potential for change, Acorn objects to the alleged power that perpetrators have over the success or failure of the restorative encounter. Restorative justice is perhaps the ideal solution where offenders have the "capacity for serious critical self-reflection, the resources and ability to repair the damage caused, and the *bona fide* desire, along with sufficient self-command, to behave respectfully in their relations with the victims and their communities in the future."[57] But most offenders simply aren't like that.

> However, one brush with a perpetrator whose inner life truly is inaccessible to us, whose conscience is beyond our reach, who is either smugly self-excusing and self-justifying or, more likely, smugly (if secretly) aware that his self-interest is promoted by performances of contrition, and the lure of restorative justice fades; the reasonableness of the position of detached disengagement resurfaces. Restorative justice provides no protection against the offender who has pegged us as suckers for performances of contrition and remorse. To promise relational healing with such an offender seems to be culpably naïve and unconcerned with the interests of the victim.[58]

---

54. Ibid., 63.
55. Ibid., 67.
56. Ibid., 61.
57. Ibid., 18.
58. Ibid., 76.

Acorn claims to be concerned for the welfare of victims. But her treatment of victims is similarly undifferentiated, and even more patronizing, than her treatment of offenders. The ability of victims to transcend pain and loss, she asserts, is strictly limited. Those victims who participate in restorative meetings in the hope of doing so are dupes who have been taken in by fake promises of healing. "Healing" is probably the most emotively powerful word in the restorative vocabulary, she suggests. "No punitive system would presume to offer 'healing' to victims. Yet restorative justice entices victims with precisely such hopes."[59] Acorn slams all talk of justice as healing as "suspiciously sentimental," a studied denial of "the complexity of human relations, the concrete reality of some offenders' delight in violating others, and the permanence of the loss suffered by many victims of crime."[60] It is also profoundly unethical to promise something that is so difficult to achieve or to assess. Healing is a prohibitively mysterious process over which we ultimately have little control, and it is morally wrong to imply otherwise.

It is also unethical, Acorn charges, to use the hope of healing to entice victims to try to reconnect emotionally with their abusers. She is fiercely critical of the confidence restorative justice places in the strategies of apology and forgiveness to promote recovery in victims, comparing it to the way perpetrators of domestic violence manipulate their victims. "The lure of apology and forgiveness saps the victim's energy and resolve to move toward some more radical transformation of, or break with, the relationship."[61] Restorative practitioners, she alleges, usually frown on the idea of a permanent break in the relationship between victims and offenders because they subscribe to the romantic but misguided belief that justice consists in the achievement of right-relationship. This brings us to one of the most important insights of Acorn's analysis, though one she characteristically spins in the wrong direction.

Justice as Right-Relation

Acorn proposes that the sole distinguishing feature of restorative justice theory—the key idea that sets it apart from retributivist or utilitarian

---

59. Ibid., 69.
60. Ibid., 70–71, 76.
61. Ibid., 74.

theories of justice—is its notion of justice as right-relation.[62] Restorative justice shares with retributivism a concern to rectify the imbalance created by crime, and it resembles utilitarianism in its rejection of avoidable suffering. Where it departs from both is in its conception of wrongdoing as wrong-relation and justice-doing as the restoration of right-relation. Justice is not to be located in any second-order token, such as retributive punishment, nor is it to be equated with any one of the procedural steps in the restorative justice process, such as personal encounter, mutual truth telling, repentance, confession, restitution, or forgiveness. Justice inheres rather in the establishment of right-relationship between the parties. "The justice to be restored is the experience of relationships of mutuality, equality, and respect in community. And it is this extravagant ambition—this understanding of justice in terms of an idealized conception of right-relation—that is the single distinguishing element of restorative justice."[63]

In my view, Acorn correctly pinpoints the importance of right-relations in restorative theory and practice, though not all experts agree. Braithwaite, for example, claims that only a minority of theorists conceive of justice as right-relation and concedes that he himself is unsure of what the phrase means.[64] Malcolm Thorburn considers the concept altogether too grandiose and suggests that the distinctiveness of restorative justice lies in two much humbler directions: its recognition of the importance of attending to the emotional needs of participants in the criminal justice process and its plea for restraint in the use of penal sanctions. He is persuaded by Acorn's claim that the idealistic notion of right-relations is largely a product of our unwillingness to accept some grim facts about human experience.[65] Wayne Northey regards right-relation as a significant idea but prefers the notion of peacemaking as the salient feature of restorative theory.[66] Bruce Archibald, on the other hand, agrees with Acorn on the foundational significance of right-relation, though he disputes the undercurrent of eroticism she detects in it.[67]

---

62. Ibid., 20–26.
63. Ibid., 22; cf. 48.
64. Braithwaite, "Narrative," 437–38.
65. Thorburn, "Impossible Dreams," 881–82.
66. Northey, "Review," 7–8.
67. Archibald, "Restorative Justice," 947.

Perhaps the notion of justice as right-relation is more common among those thinkers who have engaged with the biblical tradition than it is among secular theorists and practitioners (though the idea may still be present, even if the terminology is avoided). If so, then perhaps a more precise appreciation of the biblical notion of justification could help to answer Acorn's chief criticism of justice as right-relation or as reciprocal respect.

Acorn objects to the conception of right-relation because it sets the bar impossibly high. It requires of victims a supererogatory devotion to forgiveness and reconciliation, while denying them their right to seek a total disconnection from their offender. It also opens the door to offenders faking contrition and feigning respect in order to evade severe punishment.[68] She is particularly sensitive to these dangers in the context of intimate violence. What victims of sexual or domestic violence usually want, she maintains, and what they have a right to receive as a matter of justice, is freedom from any further unwanted interference by the offender. They want to exclude the wrongdoer entirely from their field of vision and circle of concern. "They don't want right-relation. They want no relation. And they want to be able to look to a powerful and trustworthy state capable of prohibiting relation."[69] If we think of justice as right-relation, Acorn worries, a battered woman loses her right to demand, as a matter of justice, the right to be rid of her violent spouse. If we assume right-relation as the core of justice, "unless we say that right-relation sometimes means no relation, which is basically to strip the idea of right-relation of any meaning whatsoever, breaking relations is always counter to justice."[70]

Such a worry may be alleviated, however, if we conceive of justice, not so much as right-relation, which for Acorn evokes implications of newfound intimacy and mutuality between the parties, but as *righted-relation*. This term captures more precisely the idea of the relationship between the parties being rectified or "right-wised" by having the wrongs that have distorted it removed, as in the biblical conception of justification by faith. On this analogy, the relationship between victim and offender is made right by having the wrongs exposed and dealt with, not by

---

68. Acorn, *Compulsory Compassion*, 55–60.
69. Ibid., 116.
70. Ibid., 117.

the securing of new depths of intimacy and trust between them, which often may not happen or even be appropriate. The relationship is righted because the damage caused to it by the offending party has been addressed. It is therefore a healthier relationship than it was before and, in that sense, a "right" relationship. But it is not necessarily a closer or ongoing relationship, which may not be the *right* kind of relationship for the parties to have anyway. This notion of righted-relations is a more modest and realistic understanding of relational justice than Acorn allows. It by no means requires the supererogatory commitment to unilateral forgiveness and reconciliation she imagines.

Justice and Compassion

This brings us, at last, to Acorn's major theme and most valuable contribution. The restorative justice understanding of justice as right-relation, she proposes, furnishes it with the means to pursue its ultimate goal of bringing about a convergence between the presumptively conflicting values of love or compassion, on the one hand, and justice or accountability, on the other. Restorative justice places "an extraordinary amount of faith in the idea that compassion itself, when extended toward and effected between victims and wrongdoers, will have an overwhelming and magically transformative power in the direction of justice."[71] Universal love is seen to be an "explosive force powerful enough to demolish our moral intuition that justice demands the infliction of a painful comeuppance upon the wrongdoer."[72]

Acorn raises several objections to this attempt to surmount the "radical disproportionality" between love and justice.[73] To begin with, she notes that rhetorical efforts to reconcile love and justice in situations of injustice often serve to preserve unjust hierarchical structures of oppression. "Love-talk in the context of injustice tends toward conservatism inasmuch as it argues against angry agitation or resistance and in favor of cheerful acquiescence in the status quo. People in positions of power preach brotherly love as a means of condemning resistance."[74]

71. Ibid., 18–19.
72. Ibid., 27.
73. Ibid., 31.
74. Ibid., 70.

In the criminal justice setting, this conservatism expresses itself as an attempt to quell the victim's legitimate desire for vengeance by summoning a response of forgiveness and a relinquishment of the desire for punishment. Acorn speaks approvingly of the way Mohandas Gandhi and Martin Luther King allowed love to "render assistance to justice" in their struggles for social change. But their examples of nonviolent resistance to political oppressors, she insists, cannot be transferred to the domestic criminal justice sphere.[75] To appeal to love in a restorative justice context is more akin to indulging wrongdoers than resisting them. Moreover, whereas Jesus, Gandhi, and King all anticipated martyrdom as the price to pay for their commitment to enemy love, restorative justice blithely believes that the victim's turning of the other cheek will mysteriously transform the wrongdoer and secure genuine justice.

Counseling people to respond to victimization with reconciling love is also arrogant and naïve because most people lack the capacity for self-sacrificing goodwill towards their opponents. Whence comes the motivation and empowerment for such unsolicited goodness, especially in the absence of religious devotion? The hubris and naïveté of restorative justice is that it encourages people to disrupt the normal reciprocity and equivalences that govern everyday life without reliance on "that great otherworldly insurer who will indemnify worldly losses with supreme concessions in the hereafter."[76] Even if we understand enemy love to be a volitional commitment rather than an emotional experience, the enormous difficulty of mastering such a commitment cannot be overestimated. We should therefore be cautious about any theory of justice grounded in the teachability of a loving disposition on the part of victims toward their abusers. "By falling for the rhetoric of universal love here, we lull ourselves and others into misguided reliance on the false but easy comfort of a love we are almost certain to be woefully unable to deliver. The mind reels at the host of betrayals, disappointments, and power plays that a system of justice based on optimism about our shared capacity for such love will yield."[77]

Seeking to reconcile love and justice in the criminal justice sphere is also highly dangerous. It is dangerous "both because it renders us

---

75. Ibid., 34–40.
76. Ibid., 38.
77. Ibid., 45.

vulnerable to the threats of those who will never be constrained by anything but violent coercion, and because it fosters the expectation and desire for frictionless harmonies that will never be achieved."[78] No viable conception of justice can be founded on a repudiation of one's rightful entitlements and interests. Stories of victims turning the other cheek may fascinate, amaze, or horrify us, but we cannot design our justice institutions to set the stage for such self-sacrificial play. To do so would simply create a breeding ground for anger, resentment, and violence arising from a frustrated sense of justice.[79]

Striving to fuse justice and compassion not only subverts justice, but it also corrupts compassion. Here Acorn provides a superb and highly suggestive analysis of the distinctive way compassion operates in restorative justice. In the conventional justice system, as we have seen, if compassion is operative at all, it flows in a unilateral direction from judges to defendants and victims (no one, of course, envisages it flowing in the opposite direction). In restorative justice, by contrast, because justice is construed as right-relations, compassion may be elicited from every participant in the process. This emphasis on engaging multilateral or reciprocal compassion in the justice process is, I suggest, a significant advance on the standard discussions of legal empathy. Also an advance is the way restorative justice provides the procedural mechanisms for directing and educating compassion so that it becomes a more powerful moral instrument than is spontaneous or unreflective compassion. As Acorn explains:

> Restorative justice does not attempt to rely on a descriptive account of compassion as an emotional reflex. Rather, it seeks to encourage a discipline of compassion as an ethical achievement characterized by an acknowledgement of: (a) the complexity and concreteness of the inner life of the other; (b) the paradigmatic mutuality of compassion; and (c) the necessity that compassion be grounded in an ethic of humility such that one sees both oneself and others as shared participants in a human condition of vulnerability to loss and a human capacity for renewal and repair.[80]

78. Ibid., 34.
79. Ibid., 117–18.
80. Ibid., 122.

Here Acorn identifies three normative conditions for restorative compassion to flourish. The first is a cognitive and affective awareness of the complexity and concreteness of the inner lives of other participants and their experience of suffering. Restorative justice enables this awareness to emerge through its practices of face-to-face encounter, respectful dialogue, self-disclosure, and truth telling. The second condition is mutuality. Restorative justice is a nonhierarchical process where compassion is extended and received by all the parties involved. This avoids the element of condescension involved where compassion is passed down gratuitously from judges or jurors to defendants and complainants. It also overcomes the limitation of tying compassion to blamelessness. "The good, the bad, and the guilty are all seen as standing in shared need of each other's compassion."[81] The third condition is humility. This entails an acknowledgement that we are all ontologically implicated in the human condition of suffering and vulnerability to loss. We are never merely spectators of the pain of others but actual participants in it. Therefore, we are also potential sources of mutual flourishing and renewal. Humility is thus paired with a sense of hopefulness in our shared capacity to be agents that effect healing and repair in each other's lives.

So Acorn provides a wonderfully rich account of the role of compassion in the restorative justice vision. But there remains for her a fundamental problem to all this: *compassion cannot be compelled without destroying the thing itself*. "Compulsory compassion is an oxymoron."[82] To construct a justice process, therefore, in which compassion is a necessary ingredient is highly problematic. The problem is compounded by the fact that many offenders are ill disposed to feel compassion for their victims, especially if they consider them to be from more privileged backgrounds than themselves. Even more troublesome is the way restorative justice functions to elicit greater compassion for offenders than for victims. "Curiously, as soon as the restorative momentum is in play, spontaneous compassion for the offender becomes the dominant energetic force in the encounter. Further, the compassion we feel for the offender—in its moral and emotional complexity—often upstages the compassion we feel for the victim."[83]

81. Ibid., 140.
82. Ibid., 137.
83. Ibid., 150.

The reason for this dynamic, Acorn suggests, is that the encounter process places the perpetrator's feelings of shame and humiliation at the center of attention. The gist of every offender's speech in such encounters, Acorn maintains, is the same: "I feel so miserable . . . if you knew how miserable I am, you would feel sorry for me."[84] This causes acute discomfort for those who witness it and creates an irresistible urge to release the offender from the pain and shame of contrition through pardon. Compassion for the suffering of the offender thus soon eclipses compassion for the suffering of the victim.

> The offender's suffering ends up counting for more, first, because of the possibility of it actually being the most despairing suffering produced by the recognition of one's unjustness; second, because it marks a breakthrough, a conversion, an epiphany; third, as such, it holds out optimistic promise for positive change; fourth, because it appears to be more immediate than the past suffering of the victim; and, finally, because it is the only suffering to which we have the power to put an end. It is suffering that holds within it the possibility of a collective experience of release from discomfort and despair.[85]

To draw these threads together: Acorn considers the distinctive notion of right-relation to be the conceptual means by which restorative justice seeks to realize "the age-old human hope for the convergence of love and justice."[86] Not all advocates agree that this is the leading goal of restorative justice. John Braithwaite thinks that only a minority of theorists, among whom he counts himself, speaks of love at all in connection with restorative justice.[87] But even if the language of love is not always used, the concept may still be present, and I am inclined to agree with Acorn's assertion that restorative justice aims to reconcile justice with love. What makes restorative justice significant in this respect is not simply that it accents the crucial role of compassion in the quest for justice, but that it offers the additional insight that compassion can be reciprocal, and it provides the procedural mechanisms for such shared compassion to emerge and to be enlarged or educated. To my mind, this represents a

---

84. Ibid., 156.
85. Ibid., 157–58.
86. Ibid., 22.
87. Braithwaite, "Narrative," 440–41.

substantial contribution to the existing discussion on empathetic justice, at both a theoretical and procedural level.

Yet, for all this, Acorn remains stubbornly opposed to any attempt to reconcile justice and compassion. Compassion, she urges, is "an unreliable guide toward justice inasmuch as it tends to spring from arbitrary and irrational forces."[88] It is too capricious to be a dependable tool in the justice process. It introduces a wild card by requiring participants to cultivate emotional states of understanding and forgiveness when confronting wrongdoing rather than seeking appropriate retributive balance.

Once again, Acorn works with starkly totalizing alternatives. Participants are either compelled by the process to be compassionate or they are free to seek justice; they cannot do both. Moreover, her contention that restorative praxis *requires* victims to be forgiving and reconciling as a necessary component of the encounter is a serious misrepresentation of what the vast majority of theorists and practitioners contend. It may happen that some participants sometimes feel compelled to exhibit a greater level of compassion or forgiveness than they want to. But that is neither normal nor normative to the approach.[89] Acorn repeatedly slides from envisaging potentially harmful dynamics in the victim-offender encounter to presuming that this is commonly what takes place. She does concede that there is a difference between nurturing or encouraging compassionate sensitivity and coercing or compelling it.[90] But her critique proceeds as though this distinction does not count for much. In fact, the distinction is crucial. Restorative justice *does* seek to provide the venue and tools that allow for compassion to emerge and to condition the doing of justice. But it does *not* coerce anyone to do or to feel anything, other than to listen.

One final comment is in order. Perhaps revealingly, Acorn's disavowal of the place of compassion in the pursuit of justice is accompanied by a troubling complacency towards the current penal justice system. She explains how she was initially seduced by the restorative critique of punitive justice. She then came to see that the victim's central intuition—that the perpetrator deserves to suffer for what he has done—cannot be ignored, and that the attempt to eschew tokens of justice, such as punishment,

---

88. Acorn, *Compulsory Compassion*, 81.
89. See, for example, Zehr, *Little Book*, esp. 8–13.
90. Acorn, *Compulsory Compassion*, 137.

in favor of experiential justice is a dangerously retrograde maneuver. Retributive punishment, far from being a crude and destructive proxy for justice, she decided, actually functions to protect both victims and offenders from more severe forms of harm. Perpetrators are protected from the nastiest extremes of the victim's sense of indignation. "Our institutions of retributive punishment put forward measured, state-administered punishment *precisely as a token* in order to prevent outraged victims and communities from going for what they *really* want. Retribution is a means of limiting the potentially limitless desire for revenge."[91]

Punishment also protects victims from further abuse by the offenders, who are removed from regular society. In restorative justice processes, by contrast, victims are exposed to the possibility, even the likelihood, of contrived expressions of contrition and respect by manipulative offenders, and thus remain vulnerable to further injury. For this reason, Acorn says, any attempt to displace the current regime of punitive justice with restorative alternatives must be firmly rejected.

Acorn's desire to protect victims from self-serving offenders, not to mention from their own credulity, may be commendable. But she is again guilty of hugely exaggerating the dangers she conjures up in her mind and of misreading the intentions of the restorative justice movement. She implies that advocates of restorative justice view it as a model that can replace the conventional criminal justice system and bring about an end to any social use of punishment. But this is far from the case. Most proponents see restorative justice as a parallel system of justice that offers those who freely choose to participate in it a level of satisfaction beyond anything the mainstream system can deliver. It is not a substitute for the established system but a complement to it. At the same time, it is a critique of, and corrective to, the retributive excesses of the current system.

Acorn is highly critical of restorative justice, labeling it as dangerous and delusional. But rather than urging it to improve its practices or to broaden its agenda to embrace a more comprehensive social transformation,[92] she uses its putative weaknesses to defend the continu-

---

91. Ibid., 51.

92. Several critics point out that Acorn only discusses restorative justice in the criminal sphere and fails to consider its role in other spheres of life, such as education or politics or business. She has little appreciation of restorative justice as a social movement, which often works with a broader agenda of social transformation.

ation of a punitive system that will ensure that the bad guys are properly skewered. She fails entirely to acknowledge the enormous damage done to the most vulnerable groups in society by the large-scale enterprise of incarceration that characterizes the present system.[93] She claims a concern for victims, but she is evidently untouched by the fact that the retributive system she defends has a brutalizing and victimizing impact on the most deprived groups in society, especially indigenous communities.[94] Acorn professes a deep anxiety about restorative justice's alleged propensity to *compulsory compassion*. But it is a manufactured concern. Surely a greater cause of concern, and a much greater threat to social well-being, is our mammoth reliance on *compassionless compulsion* as the most effective way to redress criminal offending.

SUMMARY AND CONCLUSION

Annalise Acorn has written one of the most fluent and interesting critiques of restorative justice yet to appear. Her exploration of the topic is a disconcerting combination of remarkable insight and profound distortion. The book's greatest strength, apart from its literary virtuosity, is its analysis of the distinctive role played by the concept of right-relation in restorative thought. It is this concept, Acorn suggests, that enables restorative justice to attempt to bring about the reconciliation, at both a theoretical and practical level, of the values of love and justice.

Though not all experts agree, I think Acorn is correct about this. Restorative justice does strive for a uniquely compassionate or loving style of doing justice. It not only affirms the principle that compassion is integral to the work of justice; it also provides the procedural mechanisms by which such compassion can be engaged and enlarged in the process. Most significantly, it conceives of compassion as a horizontal or bilateral reality that flows in both directions between victims and offenders, between the guilty and the innocent, between the hurters and the hurting. Acorn's analysis of this distinctive conception of compassionate justice is richly perceptive. Yet ultimately she rejects the validity and practicability of such a vision. She ends the book by declaring: "I have

---

93. For a superb analysis, see Logan, *Good Punishment?*
94. So, rightly, Ribet, "Emotion," 126, 129, 138.

come to the conclusion that the vision restorative justice offers us is not a vision . . . of anything genuinely desirable."[95]

The reason it is not desirable is quite simple: Acorn seems to believe that there are good people and there are bad people, and bad people don't usually change. Any justice process that seeks to change bad people, rather than to control them and to protect others from them, is therefore dangerous and delusional. Acorn's attack on restorative justice is essentially a reiteration of the standard "realist" critique of nonviolence: it can't possibly work because there are some people against whom violence is an absolute necessity. Yet, as is typical of so-called realists, she conveniently ignores the reality of the crushing failure of our institutions of violent coercion to achieve their stated goals of deterrence, protection, rehabilitation, or correction. Claiming to take the dark side of human nature seriously as the reason for repudiating restorative justice, she ends up allowing darkness to have the final say.

Such an option is not available to those who take seriously the conception of justice commended in the parable of the Good Samaritan and the parable of the Prodigal Son. Both stories, we have seen, are utterly realistic in the circumstances they portray: an act of criminal violence on an unsuspecting traveler and a display of appalling indifference towards one's family and social responsibilities. Both also evidently regard restorative responses to such criminal actions to be a thoroughly realistic way of dealing with the needs of victims and offenders—not only realistic but a moral "necessity," in fact (Luke 15:32, cf. 10:25, 28, 37).

Certainly there is also an *unreality* to the episodes depicted, and I have argued that this unreality—this "eschatological plus dimension"— must be given full weight in our interpretation of these parables. What is unreal, however, is not the emphasis they give to compassion in the task of doing justice, but the sheer bounty of the compassion they portray. This bounty beckons us to seek a source of compassion beyond our own natural strength, to align ourselves with the divine, creative compassion that resides at the center of the universe and permeates all things, a compassion made historically visible and available in the life, death, and resurrection of Jesus Christ. Participation in God's love alone can empower the full measure of compassion enacted by the merciful Samaritan and the forgiving father. But in whatever measure it is known, the parables

---

95. Acorn, *Compulsory Compassion*, 160.

unmistakably enjoin upon all hearers, as a universal moral obligation, the conscientious cultivation of compassion in response to the needs of victims and contrite offenders. This is considered a realistic, achievable goal and an essential requisite for doing justice: "Go you and do likewise" (10:37). This is the enduring challenge of both parables. They summon a commitment to just compassion for victims and compassionate justice for offenders as the heart of God's law, the centerpiece of God's will, and the key to life itself—life in this present world, with all its tragedies and unavoidable suffering, and life in the eternal world to come. "Do this," Jesus says, "and you will live" (10:28).

In his absorbing story-rich book, *The Compassionate Life: Walking the Path of Kindness,* Marc Barasch, a journalist, social activist, and Buddhist practitioner, speaks of the emergence of the restorative justice movement all around the world, with its distinctive emphasis on justice as healing, as a development of historic significance. A tension always exists, he notes, between those who counsel restoration, restitution, and absolution in response to wrongdoing, and those who favor some variation of retaliation. But in the rise of restorative justice, we may be witnessing the "prefigurations of an age when the binding of wounds takes precedence over the binding of captives, the beginning of a new covenant to heal the damage done by not caring passionately enough what happens to one another." Barasch even wonders whether future historians will look back at our age as the time when, after eras of assuming that only saints could ever get the hang of it, the doctrine of forgiveness finally took hold—a doctrine epitomized, he says, in the "radical experiment" Jesus proposed when he told Peter to forgive, not seven times, but seventy-seven times.[96]

Restorative justice is not, strictly speaking, a doctrine of forgiveness, since forgiveness is a voluntary affair of the heart, not a predetermined facet of a formalized process. But by placing the healing of hurts, the renewal of relationships, and the re-creation of community at the center of its agenda, restorative justice paves the way for forgiveness to occur.[97] And when, by grace, it does occur, the ship of justice reaches homeport. If Barasch's dream ever does come true, and restorative justice finally takes hold of our collective hearts and minds, it will not only be

---

96. Barasch, *Compassionate Life,* 213–15.
97. Marshall, *Beyond Retribution,* 255–84.

consistent with Jesus' call to radical forgiveness. It will also be the social realization of the two most powerful narrative examples of compassionate justice ever invoked: the figure of the enemy-loving, wound-binding, caregiving, compassionate Samaritan, and the figure of the patient, forgiving, banquet-throwing, compassionate father of the prodigal son.

Bibliography

Acorn, Annalise E. *Compulsory Compassion: A Critique of Restorative Justice.* Law and Society Series. Vancouver: University of British Columbia Press, 2004.
Allison, Dale C. *Resurrecting Jesus: The Earliest Christian Tradition and Its Interpreters.* London: T. & T. Clark, 2005.
Ames, James B. "Law and Morals." In *The Good Samaritan and the Law,* edited by James M. Ratcliffe, 1–22. Garden City, NY: Anchor, 1966.
Anderson, Robert T., and Terry Giles. *The Keepers: An Introduction to the History and Culture of the Samaritans.* Peabody, MA: Hendrickson, 2002.
Angier, Natalie. "The Pathological Altruist Gives Till Someone Hurts." *The New York Times,* October 3, 2011.
Anonymous. "Driver Who Hit and Killed Boy Avoids Jail." *The Dominion Post,* October 28, 2010, A3.
Antoine, Gerald. "The Three Parables of Mercy: Exposition of Luke 15:1–32." In *Exegesis: Problems of Method and Exercises in Reading,* edited by F. Bovon and G. Rouiller, 197–210. Pittsburgh Theological Monograph Series 21. Translated by Donald G. Miller. Pittsburgh: Pickwick, 1978.
Archibald, Bruce. "Why Restorative Justice Is Not Compulsory Compassion: Annalise Acorn's Labour of Lost Love." *Alberta Law Review* 42 (2005) 941–52.
Arndt, William, F. W. Gingrich, and Walter Bauer. *A Greek-English Lexicon of the New Testament and Other Early Christian Literature.* Chicago: University of Chicago Press, 1957.
Arneson, Richard J. "Moral Limits on the Demands of Beneficence?" In *The Ethics of Assistance: Morality and the Distant Needy,* edited by Deen K. Chatterjee, 33–58. Cambridge Studies in Philosophy and Public Policy. Cambridge: Cambridge University Press, 2004.
Aus, Roger David. "Luke 15:11–32 and R. Eliezer Ben Hyrcanus's Rise to Fame." *Journal of Biblical Literature* 104 (1985) 443–69.
Avery-Peck, Alan J., and Jacob Neusner. "Altruism in Classical Judaism." In *Altruism in World Religions,* edited by Jacob Neusner and Bruce Chilton, 31–52. Washington, DC: Georgetown University Press, 2005.
Avgoustinos, Costa. "The Compassionate Judge." *Public Space: The Journal of Law and Social Justice* 1 (2007) 1–41.
Bailey, Kenneth E. *The Cross and the Prodigal: Luke 15 through the Eyes of Middle Eastern Peasants.* 2nd ed. Downers Grove, IL: InterVarsity, 2005.
———. *Finding the Lost Cultural Keys to Luke 15.* Saint Louis: Concordia, 1992.
———. *Jacob and the Prodigal: How Jesus Retold Israel's Story.* Downers Grove, IL: InterVarsity, 2003.
———. *Poet and Peasant and Through Peasant Eyes: A Literary-Cultural Approach to the Parables in Luke.* Grand Rapids: Eerdmans, 1983.

Bandes, Susan. "Empathy, Narrative, and Victim Impact Statements." *University of Chicago Law Review* 63 (1996) 361–412.

Banks, Robert. *Jesus and the Law in the Synoptic Tradition*. Society for New Testament Studies Monograph Series 28. Cambridge: Cambridge University Press, 1975.

Barasch, Marc Ian. *The Compassionate Life: Walking the Path of Kindness*. San Francisco: Berrett-Koehler, 2009.

Barth, Alan. "The Vanishing Samaritan." In *The Good Samaritan and the Law*, edited by James M. Ratcliffe, 159–70. Garden City, NY: Anchor, 1966.

Batson, C. Daniel. "Attribution as a Mediator of Bias in Helping." *Journal of Personality and Social Psychology* 32:3 (1975) 455–66.

———. "Good Samaritans—or Priests and Levites? Using William James as a Guide in the Study of Prosocial Motivation." *Personality and Social Psychology Bulletin* 16 (1990) 758–68.

——— "Prosocial Motivation: Why Do We Help Others?" In *Advanced Social Psychology*, edited by A. Tesser, 333–81. New York: McGraw-Hill, 1995.

Batson, C. Daniel, et al. "'And Who Is My Neighbor?': Intrinsic Religion as a Source of Universal Compassion." *Journal for the Scientific Study of Religion* 38 (1999) 445–57.

Batson, C. Daniel, et al. "Failure to Help When in a Hurry: Callousness or Conflict?" *Personality and Social Psychology Bulletin* 4 (1978) 97–101.

Batten, Alicia J. "Clothing and Adornment." *Biblical Theology Bulletin* 40 (2010) 148–59.

Bauckham, Richard. *Jesus and the Eyewitnesses: The Gospels as Eyewitness Testimony*. Grand Rapids: Eerdmans, 2006.

———. "The Scrupulous Priest and the Good Samaritan: Jesus' Parabolic Interpretation of the Law of Moses." *New Testament Studies* 44 (1998) 475–89.

Beasley-Murray, George R. *Jesus and the Kingdom of God*. Grand Rapids: Eerdmans, 1986.

Beavis, Mary Ann. "'Making Up Stories': A Feminist Reading of the Parable of the Prodigal Son (Luke 15.11b–32)." In *The Lost Coin: Parables of Women, Work, and Wisdom*, edited by Mary Ann Beavis, 98–122. Biblical Seminar 86. Sheffield: Sheffield Academic, 2002.

Beck, Elizabeth, Nancy P. Kropf, and Pamela Blume Leonard, editors. *Social Work and Restorative Justice: Skills for Dialogue, Peacemaking, and Reconciliation*. Oxford: Oxford University Press, 2011.

Bedggood, Margaret. "Who Then Is My Neighbour? Ethical Decision Making around Our International Obligations—the Contribution of Human Rights Theory and Practice." In *Ethics and Public Policy: Contemporary Issues*, edited by Jonathan Boston, Andrew Bradstock, and David Eng, 75–97. Wellington: Victoria University Press, 2011.

Beirmaert, Louis. "The Parable of the Prodigal Son Read by an Analyst." In *Exegesis: Problems of Method and Exercises in Reading*, edited by F. Bovon and G. Rouiller. Pittsburgh: Pickwick, 1978.

Bell, Richard H. *Rethinking Justice: Restoring Our Humanity*. Lanham, MD: Lexington, 2007.

Berchman, Robert M. "Altruism in Greco-Roman Philosophy." In *Altruism in World Religions*, edited by Jacob Neusner and Bruce Chilton, 1–30. Washington, DC: Georgetown University Press, 2005.

Berkman, John, and Michael Cartwright, editors. *The Hauerwas Reader*. Durham: Duke University Press, 2003.

Besser, Anne Cucchiara, and Kalman J. Kaplan. "The Good Samaritan: Jewish and American Legal Perspectives." *Journal of Law and Religion* 10 (1993) 193–219.

Biggar, Nigel. "The New Testament and Violence: Round Two." *Studies in Christian Ethics* 23 (2010) 73–80.

———. "Specify and Distinguish! Interpreting the New Testament on 'Non-violence.'" *Studies in Christian Ethics* 22 (2009) 164–84.

Blomberg, Craig L. *Interpreting the Parables*. Leicester, UK: Apollos, 1990.

Bock, Darrell L. *Luke*. Vol. 2, 9:51—24:53. Baker Exegetical Commentary on the New Testament. Grand Rapids: Baker, 1997.

———. *Luke: The NIV Application Commentary*. Grand Rapids: Zondervan, 1996.

Boff, Leonardo. *When Theology Listens to the Poor*. Translated by Robert R. Barr. New York: Harper & Row, 1988.

Bornkamm, Günther. *Jesus of Nazareth*. Translated by Irene and Fraser McLuskey, with James M. Robinson. London: Hodder & Stoughton, 1960.

Bovon, Francois. "The Parable of the Prodigal Son, Luke 15:11–32, First Reading." In *Exegesis: Problems of Method and Exercises in Reading*, edited by F. Bovon and G. Rouiller, 43–74. Pittsburgh: Pickwick, 1978.

———. "The Parable of the Prodigal Son, Second Reading." In *Exegesis: Problems of Method and Exercises in Reading*, edited by F. Bovon and G. Rouiller, 441–66. Pittsburgh: Pickwick, 1978.

Boyack, James, et al. "How Does Restorative Justice Ensure Good Practice? A Values-Based Approach." In *Critical Issues in Restorative Justice*, edited by Howard Zehr and Barb Toews, 265–76. Palisades, NY: Criminal Justice Press, 2004.

Braithwaite, John. *Crime, Shame, and Reintegration*. Cambridge: Cambridge University Press, 1989.

———. "Narrative and 'Compulsory Compassion.'" *Law and Social Inquiry* 31 (2006) 425–46.

Breckenridge, James. "The Salvific Role of Knowledge in a Buddhist and a Christian Context: A Comparative Study of Two Parables." *Buddhist-Christian Studies* 11 (1991) 75–84.

Brien, Andrew. "Mercy within Legal Justice." *Social Theory and Practice* 24 (1998) 83–110.

Broughton, Geoff. "Restorative Justice: Opportunities for Christian Engagement." *International Journal of Public Theology* 3 (2009) 299–318.

Brown, Robert McAfee. "The Holocaust as a Problem in Moral Choice." In *A Peace Reader: Essential Readings on War, Justice, Non-violence, and World Order*, edited by Joseph J. Fahey and Richard Armstrong, 223–39. New York: Paulist, 1992.

Bruce, A. B. "The Synoptic Gospels." In vol. 1 of *The Expositor's Greek Testament*, edited by W. Robertson Nicoll. London: Hodder & Stoughton, 1903.

Brysk, Alison. *Global Good Samaritans: Human Rights as Foreign Policy*. Oxford: Oxford University Press, 2009.

Bultmann, Rudolf. *The History of the Synoptic Tradition*. Translated by John Marsh. Oxford: Blackwell, 1972.

Burge, Gary M. *Jesus, the Middle Eastern Storyteller*. Grand Rapids: Zondervan, 2009.

Burridge, Richard A. *Imitating Jesus: An Inclusive Approach to New Testament Ethics*. Grand Rapids: Eerdmans, 2007.

Cahill, Dan. "Victimisation." *Movement for Alternatives to Prison* 98 (2006) 2–3.

Caird, G. B. *Saint Luke*. Harmondsworth, UK: Penguin, 1963.

Caputo, John D. *The Weakness of God: A Theology of the Event*. Bloomington: Indiana University Press, 2006.

Carlston, Charles E. "Reminiscence and Redaction in Luke 15:11–32." *Journal of Biblical Literature* 94 (1975) 368–90.

Carroll R., M. Daniel. *Christians at the Border: Immigration, the Church, and the Bible.* Grand Rapids: Baker Academic, 2008.

Chang, Ha-Joon. *Bad Samaritans: The Myth of Free Trade and the Secret History of Capitalism.* New York: Bloomsbury, 2008.

Chatterjee, Deen K. "Introduction." In *The Ethics of Assistance: Morality and the Distant Needy*, edited by Deen K. Chatterjee, 1–10. Cambridge: Cambridge University Press, 2004.

Chilton, Bruce. "Altruism in Christianity." In *Altruism in World Religions*, edited by Jacob Neusner and Bruce Chilton, 53–66. Washington, DC: Georgetown University Press, 2005.

Clements, Kevin. "Enlarging the Boundaries of Compassion: Opportunities and Challenges for Peace Research in the Twenty-First Century." Unpublished inaugural professorial lecture. Dunedin: University of Otago, 2009.

Corrigan, John, editor. *The Oxford Handbook of Religion and Emotion.* Oxford: Oxford University Press, 2008.

Cowley, A. E., Joseph Jacobs, and Henry Minor Huxley. "Samaritans." Online: http://www.jewishencyclopedia.com/articles/13059-samaritans.

Craddock, Fred B. *Luke.* Interpretation. Louisville: Westminster John Knox, 1990.

Cranfield, C. E. B. "The Good Samaritan (Luke 10:25–37)." *Theology Today* 11 (1954) 368–72.

Creed, J. M. *The Gospel according to Saint Luke.* London: Macmillan, 1942.

Crespy, Georges. "The Good Samaritan: An Essay in Structural Research." *Semeia* 2 (1974) 27–50.

Crossan, John Dominic. *In Parables: The Challenge of the Historical Jesus.* San Francisco: Harper & Row, 1985.

———. "A Metamodel for Polyvalent Narration." *Semeia* 9 (1977) 105–47.

———. "Parable and Example in the Teaching of Jesus." *New Testament Studies* 18 (1972) 285–307.

———. "Parable and Example in the Teaching of Jesus." *Semeia* 1 (1974) 63–104.

Cruz, Gemma Tulud. "Toward an Ethic of Risk: Catholic Social Teaching and Immigration Reform." *Studies in Christian Ethics* 24 (2011) 294–310.

Dagan, Hanoch. "In Defense of the Good Samaritan." *Michigan Law Review* 97 (1999) 1152–1200.

Danker, Frederick W., et al. *A Greek-English Lexicon of the New Testament and Other Early Christian Literature.* 3rd ed. Chicago: University of Chicago Press, 2000.

Darley, John M., and C. Daniel Batson. "'From Jerusalem to Jericho': A Study of Situational and Dispositional Variables in Helping Behavior." *Journal of Personality and Social Psychology* 27 (1973) 100–108.

Darley, John M., and Bibb Latané. "Bystander Intervention in Emergencies: Diffusion of Responsibility." *Journal of Personality and Social Psychology* 8 (1968) 377–83.

Daube, David. *The New Testament and Rabbinic Judaism.* Jordan Lectures in Comparative Religion 2. 1956. Reprinted, Eugene, OR: Wipf & Stock, 2011.

Davies, W. D., and Dale C. Allison Jr. *A Critical and Exegetical Commentary on the Gospel according to Saint Matthew.* 3 vols. International Critical Commentary. Edinburgh: T. & T. Clark, 1988–1997.

Davis, Michael. "How Much Punishment Does a Bad Samaritan Deserve?" *Law and Philosophy* 15 (1996) 93–116.

Dawson, John P. "Rewards for the Rescue of Human Life?" In *The Good Samaritan and the Law*, edited by James M. Ratcliffe, 63–90. Garden City, NY: Anchor, 1966.
Department of Corrections. *Over-representation of Māori in the Criminal Justice System: An Exploratory Report*. Policy, Strategy and Research Group, Department of Corrections (September 2007). Online: www.rethinking.org.nz.
Derrett, J. Duncan M. *Law in the New Testament*. 1970. Reprinted,
Devlin, Patrick. *Samples of Lawmaking*. London: Oxford University Press, 1962.
Dodd, C. H. *Gospel and Law*. Cambridge: Cambridge University Press, 1951.
———. *The Parables of the Kingdom*. Rev. ed. New York: Scribner, 1961.
Donahue, John R. *The Gospel in Parable: Metaphor, Narrative, and Theology in the Synoptic Gospels*. Philadelphia: Fortress, 1988.
———. "Tax Collectors and Sinners: An Attempt at Identification." *Catholic Biblical Quarterly* 33 (1971) 39–61.
———. "Two Decades of Research on the Rich and the Poor in Luke-Acts." In *Justice and the Holy: Essays in Honor of Walter Harrelson*, edited by Douglas A. Knight and Peter J. Paris, 129–44. Scholars Press Homage Series 12. Atlanta: Scholars, 1989.
———. "Who Is My Enemy? The Parable of the Good Samaritan and the Love of Enemies." In *The Love of Enemy and Nonretaliation in the New Testament*, edited by Willard M. Swartley, 137–52. Louisville: Westminster John Knox, 1992.
Donne, John. *Devotions upon Emergent Occasions and Death's Duel*. New York: Vintage Spiritual Classics, 1999.
Drapkin, I. *Crime and Punishment in the Ancient World*. Lexington, MA: Lexington, 1989.
Driver, Julia. "The Ethics of Intervention." *Philosophy and Phenomenological Research* 57 (1997) 851–70.
Dunn, James D. G. *Jesus Remembered*. Christianity in the Making 1. Grand Rapids: Eerdmans, 2003.
Durber, Susan. "The Female Reader of the Parables of the Lost." *Journal for the Study of the New Testament* 45 (1992) 59–78.
Elliott, John H. "Temple Versus Household in Luke-Acts: A Contrast in Social Institutions." In *The Social World of Luke-Acts: Models for Interpretation*, edited by Jerome H. Neyrey, 211–40. Peabody, MA: Hendrickson, 1991.
Ellis, E. Earl. *The Gospel of Luke*. 3rd ed. New Century Bible Commentary. Grand Rapids: Eerdmans, 1974.
Elwell, Walter A., and Philip Wesley Comfort. *Tyndale Bible Dictionary*. Wheaton, IL: Tyndale, 2001.
Esler, Philip F. "Jesus and the Reduction of Intergroup Conflict: The Parable of the Good Samaritan in the Light of Social Identity Theory." *Biblical Interpretation* 8 (2000) 325–57.
Farrer, F. W. *The Gospel according to St. Luke*. Cambridge: Cambridge University Press, 1905.
Fehr, Ernst, and Urs Fischbacher. "Human Altruism: Proximate Patterns and Evolutionary Origins." *Analyse and Kritik* 27 (2005) 6–47.
Feigenson, Neal R. "Sympathy and Legal Judgment: A Psychological Analysis." *Tennessee Law Review* 65 (1997–98) 1–78.
Feldbrugge, F. J. M. "Good and Bad Samaritans: A Comparative Survey of Criminal Law Provisions Concerning Failure to Rescue." *The American Journal of Comparative Law* 14 (1965) 630–57.

Ferguson, Everett. *Backgrounds of Early Christianity*. 3rd ed. Grand Rapids: Eerdmans, 2003.

Fichtner, Johannes, and Heinrich Greeven. "Πλησίον." In *Theological Dictionary of the New Testament*, edited by Gerhard Kittel and Gerhard Friedrich, translated by Geoffrey W. Bromiley, 4:311–18. Grand Rapids: Eerdmans, 1964–76.

Fiensy, David A. *The Social History of Palestine in the Herodian Period: The Land Is Mine*. Studies in the Bible and Early Christianity 20. Lewiston, NY: Edwin Mellen, 1991.

Fingarette, Herbert. "Some Moral Aspects of Good Samaritanship." In *The Good Samaritan and the Law*, edited by James M. Ratcliffe, 213–24. Garden City, NY: Anchor, 1966.

Fitzmyer, Joseph A. *The Gospel according to Luke*. 2 vols. Anchor Bible 28–28A. Garden City, NY: Doubleday, 1985.

Foerster, Werner. "αόσωτοβ, αόσωτια," *TDNT* 1:506–7.

Forbes, Greg. *The God of Old: The Role of the Lukan Parables in the Purpose of Luke's Gospel*. Journal for the Study of the New Testament Supplement Series 198. Sheffield: Sheffield Academic, 2000.

———. "Repentance and Conflict in the Parable of the Lost Son (Luke 15:11–32)." *Journal of the Evangelical Theological Society* 42:2 (1999) 211–29.

Ford, J. Massyngberde. "Reconciliation and Forgiveness in Luke's Gospel." In *Political Issues in Luke-Acts*, edited by Richard J. Cassidy and Philip J. Scharper. Maryknoll, NY: Orbis, 1983.

Forrester, Duncan B. *Christian Justice and Public Policy*. Cambridge Studies in Ideology and Religion. Cambridge: Cambridge University Press, 1997.

Freedman, Zelic Lawrence. "No Responses to the Cry for Help." In *The Good Samaritan and the Law*, edited by James M. Ratcliffe, 171–82. Garden City, NY: Anchor, 1966.

Fuchs, Ernst. *Studies of the Historical Jesus*. London: SCM, 1964.

Funk, Robert W. "The Good Samaritan as Metaphor." *Semeia* 2 (1974) 74–81.

Furrow, James L. "The Ideal Father: Religious Narratives and the Role of Fatherhood." *Journal of Men's Studies* 7 (1998) 17–32.

Gagnon, Robert A. J. "A Second Look at Two Lukan Parables: Reflections on the Unjust Steward and the Good Samaritan." *Horizons in Biblical Theology* 20 (1998) 1–11.

Geldenhuys, Norval. *Commentary on the Gospel of Luke*. New International Commentary on the New Testament. Grand Rapids: Eerdmans, 1952.

Gerhardsson, Birger. *The Good Samaritan—The Good Shepherd?* Coniectanea Neotestamentica 16. Lund: Gleerup, 1958.

Giles, Terry. "Samaritans." In *Encyclopedia of the Historical Jesus*, edited by Craig A. Evans, 539–42. London: Routledge, 2008.

Gnanavaram, M. "'Dalit Theology' and the Parable of the Good Samaritan." *Journal for the Study of the New Testament* 50 (1993) 59–83.

Gnilka, Joachim. *Jesus of Nazareth: Message and History*. Translated by Siegfried S. Schatzmann. Peabody, MA: Hendrickson, 1997.

Goldstein, Herman. "Citizen Cooperation: The Perspective of the Police." In *The Good Samaritan and the Law*, edited by James M. Ratcliffe, 199–208. Garden City, NY: Anchor, 1966.

Gopin, Marc. *To Make the Earth Whole: The Art of Citizen Diplomacy in an Age of Religious Militancy*. Lanham, MD: Rowman & Littlefield, 2009.

Goulder, Michael D. *Luke: A New Paradigm*. Journal for the Study of the New Testament Supplement Series 20. Sheffield: JSOT, 1989.

Gourgues, Michel. "The Priest, the Levite, and the Samaritan Revisited: A Critical Note on Luke 10:31-35." *Journal of Biblical Literature* 117 (1998) 709-13.

Graves, Mike. "Luke 10:25-37: The Moral of the 'Good Samaritan' Story?" *Review and Expositor* 94 (1997) 269-75.

Green, Joel B. "Good News to Whom? Jesus and the 'Poor' in the Gospel of Luke." In *Jesus of Nazareth: Lord and Christ: Essays on the Historical Jesus and New Testament Christology*, edited by Joel B. Green and Max Turner, 59-74. Grand Rapids: Eerdmans, 1994.

―――. *The Gospel of Luke*. New International Commentary on the New Testament. Grand Rapids: Eerdmans, 1997.

Green, Joel B., and Max Turner, editors. *Jesus of Nazareth: Lord and Christ: Essays on the Historical Jesus and New Testament Christology*. Grand Rapids: Eerdmans, 1994.

Green, William Scott. "Altruism and the Study of Religion." In *Altruism in World Religions*, edited by Jacob Neusner and Bruce Chilton, ix-xiv. Washington, DC: Georgetown University Press, 2005.

Gregory, Charles O. "The Good Samaritan and the Bad: The Anglo-American Law." In *The Good Samaritan and the Law*, edited by James M. Ratcliffe, 23-42. Garden City, NY: Anchor, 1966.

Grieb, Katherine. "The Real Prodigal: 2 Corinthians 5:16-21; Luke 15:1-3, 11b-32." *The Christian Century*, March 18, 2004.

Gusfield, Joseph. "Social Sources of Levites and Samaritans." In *The Good Samaritan and the Law*, edited by James M. Ratcliffe, 183-98. Garden City, NY: Anchor, 1966.

Gushee, David P. "Christians as Rescuers During the Holocaust." In *Must Christianity Be Violent? Reflections on History, Practice and Theology*, edited by Kenneth R. Chase and Alan Jacobs, 69-78. Grand Rapids: Brazos, 2003.

Gutbrod, W. "νόμος κτλ." In *Theological Dictionary of the New Testament*, edited by Gerhard Kittel and Gerhard Friedrich, translated by Geoffrey W. Bromiley, 4:1022-91. Grand Rapids: Eerdmans, 1964-76.

Haacker, Klaus. "'What Must I Do to Inherit Eternal Life?' Implicit Christology in Jesus' Sayings about Life and the Kingdom." In *Jesus Research: An International Perspective*, edited by James H. Charlesworth and Petr Pokorny, 140-53. Grand Rapids: Eerdmans, 2009.

Hanfling, Oswald. "Loving My Neighbour, Loving Myself." *Philosophy* 68 (1993) 145-57.

Harries, Jill. "Courts and the Judicial System." In *The Oxford Handbook of Jewish Daily Life in Roman Palestine*, edited by Catherine Hezser, 85-101. Oxford: Oxford University Press, 2010.

Harrill, J. Albert. "The Indentured Labor of the Prodigal Son (Luke 15:15)." *Journal of Biblical Literature* 115 (1996) 714-17.

Hart, David Bentley. *Atheist Delusions: The Christian Revolution and Its Fashionable Enemies*. New Haven: Yale University Press, 2009.

Harvey, A. E. *The New English Bible, Companion to the New Testament*. Oxford: Oxford University Press, 1970.

Hauerwas, Stanley. "Politics of Charity." *Interpretation* 31 (1977) 251-62.

Hays, Richard B. "Narrate and Embody: A Response to Nigel Biggar, 'Specify and Distinguish.'" *Studies in Christian Ethics* 22 (2009) 185-98.

―――. "The Thorny Task of Reconciliation: Another Response to Nigel Biggar." *Studies in Christian Ethics* 23 (2010) 81-86.

Henderson, Lynne N. "Legality and Empathy." *Michigan Law Review* 85 (1987) 1574-1653.

Herzog, William R., III. *Jesus, Justice, and the Reign of God: A Ministry of Liberation*. Louisville: Westminster John Knox, 2000.

Higton, Mike. "Boldness and Reserve: A Lesson from St. Augustine." *Anglican Theological Review* 85 (2003) 447–56.

Hjelm, Ingrid. "What Do Samaritans and Jews Have in Common? Recent Trends in Samaritan Studies." *Currents in Biblical Research* 3 (2004) 9–59.

Hoffmeier, James K. *The Immigration Crisis: Immigrants, Aliens and the Bible*. Wheaton, IL: Crossway, 2009.

Holgate, David A. *Prodigality, Liberality and Meanness: The Prodigal Son in Greco-Roman Perspective*. Sheffield: Sheffield Academic, 1999.

Honoré, Antony M. "Law, Morals, and Rescue." In *The Good Samaritan and the Law*, edited by James M. Ratcliffe, 225–42. Garden City, NY: Anchor, 1966.

Hoyle, Carolyn, editor. *Restorative Justice: Critical Concepts in Criminology*. 4 vols. London: Routledge, 2010.

Hultgren, Arland J. *The Parables of Jesus: A Commentary*. Grand Rapids: Eerdmans, 2000.

———. "Salvation: Its Forms and Dynamics in the New Testament." *Dialog: A Journal of Theology* 45 (2006) 215–22.

Hunter, A. M. *Interpreting the Parables*. London: SCM, 1964.

Jackson, Timothy P. *The Priority of Love: Christian Charity and Social Justice*. New Forum Books. Princeton: Princeton University Press, 2003.

Jeremias, Joachim. *Jerusalem in the Time of Jesus*. Translated by F. H. and C. H. Cave. 3rd ed. London: SCM, 1969.

———. *New Testament Theology*. Edited by John Bowden. Vol. 1. London: SCM, 1971.

———. *The Parables of Jesus*. Rev. ed. Translated by S. H. Hooke. London: SCM, 1972.

Johnson, Luke Timothy. *The Gospel of Luke*. Sacra Pagina 3. Collegeville, MN: Michael Glazier, 1991.

———. *The Literary Function of Possessions in Luke-Acts*. SBL Dissertation Series. Missoula, MT: Scholars Press for the Society of Biblical Literature, 1977.

Jones, Mark. *Criminals of the Bible: Twenty-Five Case Studies of Biblical Crimes and Outlaws*. Grand Haven, MI: FaithWalk, 2006.

Jones, Peter Rhea. "The Love Command in Parable." *Perspectives in Religious Studies* 6 (1979) 224–42.

Jülicher, Adolf. *Die Gleichnisreden Jesu. Zweiter Teil. Auslegung der Gleichnisreden der Drei Ersten Evangelien*. Freiburg: Mohr, 1899.

Just, Arthur A., Jr. *Ancient Christian Commentary on Scripture: Luke*. Edited by Thomas C. Oden. Downers Grove, IL: InterVarsity, 2003.

Kamm, F. M. "The New Problem of Distance in Morality." In *The Ethics of Assistance: Morality and the Distant Needy*, edited by Deen K. Chatterjee, 59–74. Cambridge: Cambridge University Press, 2004.

Karstedt, Susanne. "Emotions and Criminal Justice." *Theoretical Criminology* 6 (2002) 299–317.

Keener, Craig S. *The IVP Bible Background Commentary: New Testament*. Downers Grove, IL: InterVarsity, 1993.

Keizer, Kees. "The Spreading of Disorder." *Science* 322 (2008) 1681–85.

Kelber, Werner H. *The Oral and the Written Gospel: The Hermeneutics of Speaking and Writing in the Synoptic Tradition, Mark, Paul, and Q*. Philadelphia: Fortress, 1983.

Keller, Timothy. *The Prodigal God: Recovering the Heart of the Christian Faith*. New York: Dutton, 2008.

Kimmel, Eyal. "Compulsory Compassion: A Critique of Restorative Justice." *Ottawa Law Review/Revue de Droit D'Ottawa* 37 (2005–6) 360–63.

King, Martin Luther, Jr. "Beyond Vietnam: A Time to Break Silence." Delivered April 4, 1967. Online http://www.americanrhetoric.com/speeches/mlkatimetobreak silence.htm.
———. "I Have Been to the Mountaintop." Delivered April 3, 1968. Online: http://www.afscme.org/union/history/mlk/ive-been-to-the-mountaintop-by-dr-martin-luther-king-jr.
———. *Strength to Love*. Philadelphia: Fortress, 1963.
Kistemaker, Simon. *The Parables of Jesus*. Grand Rapids: Baker, 1980.
———. *The Parables: Understanding the Stories Jesus Told*. Grand Rapids: Baker, 2002.
Kleinig, John. "Good Samaritanism." *Philosophy and Public Affairs* 5 (1976) 382–407.
Knowles, Michael P. "What Was the Victim Wearing? Literary, Economic, and Social Contexts for the Parable of the Good Samaritan." *Biblical Interpretation* 12 (2004) 145–74.
Lampman, Lisa Barnes, and Michelle D. Shattuck, editors. *God and the Victim: Theological Reflections on Evil, Victimization, Justice, and Forgiveness*. Grand Rapids: Eerdmans, 1999.
Laws, Michael. "The Children Who Survive." *Sunday Star Times*, November 23, 2008, B5.
———. "Forgiving Killers Revs Up Danger." *Sunday Star Times*, October 31, 2010.
Lenski, R. H. C. *The Interpretation of St Luke's Gospel*. Minneapolis: Augsburg, 1946.
Lichtenberg, Judith. "Absence and the Unfond Heart: Why People Are Less Giving than They Might Be." In *The Ethics of Assistance: Morality and the Distant Needy*, edited by Deen K. Chatterjee, 75–97. Cambridge: Cambridge University Press, 2004.
Liefeld, Walter L. "Luke." In *The Expositor's Bible Commentary*, edited by Frank E. Gaebelein, 8:796–1059. Grand Rapids: Zondervan Regency, 1984.
Lindberg, Tod. *The Political Teachings of Jesus*. New York: HarperCollins, 2007.
Linden, Allen M. "Rescuers and Good Samaritans." *The Modern Law Review* 34 (1971) 241–59.
Linnemann, Eta. *Parables of Jesus: Introduction and Exposition*. Translated by John Sturdy. London: SPCK, 1966.
Loader, William R. G. *Jesus' Attitude towards the Law: A Study of the Gospels*. Grand Rapids: Eerdmans, 2002.
Logan, Samuel. *Good Punishment? Christian Moral Practice and U. S. Imprisonment*. Grand Rapids: Eerdmans, 2008.
Macaulay, Thomas Babington. "Indian Penal Code." In *The Works of Lord Macaulay*, edited by Lady Trevelyan, 7:415–558. London: Longmans, Green, 1866.
Maccoby, Hyam. *Ritual and Morality: The Ritual Purity System and Its Place in Judaism*. New York: Cambridge University Press, 1999.
Mackintosh, H. R. *The Originality of the Christian Message*. London: Duckworth, 1920.
MacMullen, Ramsay. *Roman Social Relations, 50 BC to AD 284*. New Haven: Yale University Press, 1974.
Malina, Bruce J. "Is There a Circum-Mediterranean Person? Looking for Stereotypes." *Biblical Theology Bulletin* 22 (1992) 66–87.
———. *The New Testament World: Insights from Cultural Anthropology*. wnd ed. Louisville: Westminster John Knox, 1993.
———. "Understanding New Testament Persons." In *The Social Sciences and New Testament Interpretation*, edited by Richard L. Rohrbaugh, 41–61. Peabody, MA: Hendrickson, 1996.

Malina, Bruce J., and Jerome H. Neyrey. "First-Century Personality: Dyadic, Not Individualistic." In *The Social World of Luke-Acts: Models for Interpretation*, edited by Jerome H. Neyrey, 67–96. Peabody, MA: Hendrickson, 1991.

———. "Honor and Shame in Luke-Acts: Pivotal Values of the Mediterranean World." In *The Social World of Luke-Acts: Models for Interpretation*, edited by Jerome H. Neyrey, 25–66. Peabody, MA: Hendrickson, 1991.

Malina, Bruce J., and Richard L. Rohrbaugh. *Social-Science Commentary on the Synoptic Gospels*. Minneapolis: Augsburg Fortress, 1992.

Malm, H. M. "Bad Samaritan Laws: Harm, Help, or Hype? The Moral and Legal Limits of Samaritan Duties." *Law and Philosophy* 19 (2000) 707–50.

———. "Liberalism, Bad Samaritan Law, and Legal Paternalism." *Ethics* 106 (1995) 4–31.

Mann, Jacob. "Jesus and the Sadducean Priests: Luke 10. 25–37." *The Jewish Quarterly Review, New Series* 6 (1916) 415–22.

Manning, Rachel. "The Kitty Genovese Murder and the Social Psychology of Helping: The Parable of the 38 Witnesses." *American Psychologist* 62 (2007) 555–62.

Manson, Thomas W. *The Sayings of Jesus*. London: SCM, 1957.

———. *The Teaching of Jesus: Studies of Its Form and Content*. 2nd ed. Cambridge: Cambridge University Press, 1935.

Mantouvalou, Virginia. "N v UK: No Duty to Rescue the Nearby Needy?" *Modern Law Review* 72 (2009) 815–43.

Marshall, Christopher D. *Beyond Retribution: A New Testament Vision for Justice, Crime and Punishment*. Grand Rapids: Eerdmans, 2001.

———. *Crowned with Glory and Honor: Human Rights in the Biblical Tradition*. Telford, PA: Pandora, 2001.

———. *Faith as a Theme in Mark's Narrative*. Society for New Testament Studies Monograph Series 64. Cambridge: Cambridge University Press, 1989.

———. "'Go and Do Likewise': The Parable of the Good Samaritan and the Challenge of Public Ethics." In *Ethics and Public Policy: Contemporary Issues*, edited by Jonathan Boston, Andrew Bradstock, and David Ong, 49–74. Wellington: Victoria University Press, 2011.

———. "'I Have Sinned Against Heaven and Against You': Sin as Relational Rupture in the Teaching of Jesus." In *A Thinker's Guide to Sin: Talking About Sin Today*, edited by Neil Darragh, 65–73. Auckland: Accent, 2010.

———. *The Little Book of Biblical Justice: A Fresh Approach to the Bible's Teachings on Justice*. Edited by Howard Zehr. Little Books on Justice and Peacemaking. Intercourse, PA: Good Books, 2005.

———. "The Meaning of Justice: Insights from the Biblical Tradition." In *Justice as a Basic Human Need*, edited by A. J. W. Taylor, 25–38. Huntington, NY: Nova Science Publishers, 2006.

———. "Offending, Restoration and the Law-Abiding Community: Restorative Justice in the New Testament and in the New Zealand Experience." *Journal of the Society for Christian Ethics* 27 (2007) 3–30.

———. "Prison, Prisoners and the Bible." *Restorative Directions Journal* (2006) 118–31.

———. "A Prophet of God's Justice: Reclaiming the Political Jesus." *Justice Reflections* 14 (2007) 1–26.

———. "Reflections on the Spirit of Justice." In *Restorative Justice and Practices in New Zealand: Towards a Restorative Society*, edited by Gabrielle Maxwell and James H. Liu, 311–20. Wellington: Victoria University Institute of Policy Studies, 2007.

———. "Religious Violence, Terrorism and Restorative Justice." In *Handbook of Restorative Justice*, edited by Daniel Van Ness and Gerry Johnstone, 372–94. Cullompton: Willan, 2007.

———. "Satisfying Justice: Victims, Justice and the Grain of the Universe." *Interface: A Forum for Theology in the World* 8 (2005) 35–51.

———. "What Language Shall I Borrow? The Bilingual Dilemma of Public Theology." *Stimulus* (2005) 11–18.

Marshall, I. Howard. *The Gospel of Luke: A Commentary on the Greek Text*. New International Greek Testament Commentary. Exeter, UK: Paternoster, 1978.

———. *Luke: Historian and Theologian*. Grand Rapids: Zondervan, 1971.

Martin, Nancy M., and Joseph Runzo. "Love." In *The Oxford Handbook of Religion and Emotion*, edited by John Corrigan, 311–32. Oxford: Oxford University Press, 2008.

Matera, Frank J. *New Testament Ethics: The Legacies of Jesus and Paul*. Louisville: Westminster John Knox, 1996.

Matthews, Victor H. "Conversation and Identity: Jesus and the Samaritan Woman." *Biblical Theology Bulletin* 40 (2010) 215–26.

Mayhew, Pat, and James Reilly. *New Zealand Crime and Safety Survey 2006*. Wellington: Ministry of Justice, 2007.

Maxwell, Gabrielle, and Allison Morris. "What Is the Place of Shame in Restorative Justice?" In *Critical Issues in Restorative Justice*, edited by Howard Zehr and Barb Toews, 133–41. Monsey, NY: Criminal Justice Press, 2004.

Maxwell, Gabrielle, and James H. Liu, editors. *Restorative Justice and Practices in New Zealand: Towards a Restorative Society*. Wellington: Victoria University Institute of Policy Studies, 2007.

McArthur, Harvey K., and Robert M. Johnston. *They Also Taught in Parables: Rabbinic Parables from the First Centuries of the Christian Era*. Grand Rapids: Zondervan, 1990.

McDonald, J. Ian H. "Alien Grace (Luke 10:30–36)." In *Jesus and His Parables: Interpreting the Parables of Jesus Today*, edited by George V. Shillington, 35–54. Edinburgh: T. & T. Clark, 1997.

———. "The View from the Ditch—and Other Angles: Interpreting the Parable of the Good Samaritan" *Scottish Journal of Theology* 49 (1996) 21–37.

McFarland, Ian A. "Who Is My Neighbor? The Good Samaritan as a Source for Theological Anthropology." *Modern Theology* 17 (2001) 57–66.

McIntyre, Alison. "Guilty Bystanders? On the Legitimacy of Duty to Rescue Statutes." *Philosophy and Public Affairs* 23 (1994) 157–91.

McKnight, Scot. *The Jesus Creed: Loving God, Loving Others*. Brewster, MA: Paraclete, 2004.

McLeod, Rosemary. "Hear No Evil, See No Evil, Speak No Evil—What a Sick Society." *Sunday Star Times*, November 23, 2008, A7.

Meier, John P. *A Marginal Jew: Rethinking the Historical Jesus*. Vol. 3, *Companions and Competitors*. New Haven: Yale University Press, 2001.

———. *A Marginal Jew: Rethinking the Historical Jesus*. Vol. 4, *Law and Love*. New Haven: Yale University Press, 2009.

Menken, M. J. J. "The Position of Σπλαγχνίζεσθαι and Σπλάγχνα in the Gospel of Luke." *Novum Testamentum* 30 (1988) 107–14.

Mika, Harry et al. *The Listening Project: Taking Victims and Their Advocates Seriously*. Akron, PA: Mennonite Central Committee Office in Crime and Justice, 2002.

Miller, Richard W. "Moral Closeness and World Community." In *The Ethics of Assistance: Morality and the Distant Needy*, edited by Deen K. Chatterjee, 101–22. Cambridge: Cambridge University Press, 2004.

Miller, Warren P., and Michael Zimmerman. "The Good Samaritan Act of 1966: A Proposal." In *The Good Samaritan and the Law*, edited by James M. Ratcliffe, 279–300. Garden City, NY: Anchor, 1966.

Montefiore, C. G. *Rabbinic Literature and Gospel Teachings*. London: Macmillan, 1930.

———. *The Synoptic Gospels: Edited with an Introduction and a Commentary*. 2 vols. London: Macmillan, 1909.

Montefiore, C. G., and H. Loewe. *A Rabbinic Anthology: Selected and Arranged with Comments and Introductions*. London: Macmillan, 1938.

Montefiore, Hugh. "Thou Shalt Love the Neighbour as Thyself." *Novum Testamentum* 5 (1962) 157–70.

Moore, George Foot. *Judaism in the First Centuries of the Christian Era: The Age of the Tannaim*. 1927. Reprint, Peabody, MA: Hendrickson, 1960.

Morris, Leon. *The Gospel according to St. Luke*. Leicester: InterVarsity, 1974.

Morris, Norval. "Compensation and the Good Samaritan." In *The Good Samaritan and the Law*, edited by James M. Ratcliffe, 135–40. Garden City, NY: Anchor, 1966.

Morrison, Bronwyn, Melissa Smith, and Lisa Gregg. *New Zealand Crime and Safety Survey 2009*. Wellington: Ministry of Justice, 2010.

Moulton, James Hope, and George Milligan. *The Vocabulary of the Greek New Testament*. Grand Rapids: Eerdmans, 1963.

Moulton, James Hope, and Nigel Turner. *A Grammar of New Testament Greek*. Edinburgh: T. & T. Clark, 1906.

Moxnes, Halvor. *The Economy of the Kingdom: Social Conflict and Economic Relations in Luke's Gospel*. 1988. Reprinted, Eugene, OR: Wipf & Stock, 2004.

———. "Honor and Shame." In *The Social Sciences and New Testament Interpretation*, edited by Richard L. Rohrbaugh, 19–40. Peabody, MA: Hendrickson, 1996.

———. "Patron-Client Relations and the New Community in Luke-Acts." In *The Social World of Luke-Acts*, edited by Jerome H. Neyrey, 241–68. Peabody, MA: Hendrickson, 1991.

———. Review of *Jacob the Prodigal: How Jesus Retold Israel's Story*, by Kenneth E. Bailey. *Scottish Journal of Theology* 58 (2005) 354–56.

Muddiman, John, and John Barton. *The Oxford Bible Commentary on the Gospels*. Oxford: Oxford University Press, 2001.

Murphy, Jeffrie G. "Christianity and Criminal Punishment." *Punishment and Society* 5 (2003) 261–77.

Murphy, Liam. "Beneficence, Law and Liberty: The Case of Required Rescue." *Georgetown Law Journal* 89 (2000) 605–50.

Myers, Ched, and Elaine Enns. *Ambassadors of Reconciliation*. Vol. 1, *New Testament Reflections on Restorative Justice and Peacemaking*. Maryknoll, NY: Orbis, 2009.

Neusner, Jacob. *The Mishnah: A New Translation*. New Haven: Yale University Press, 1988.

Neusner, Jacob, and Alan J. Avery-Peck. "Altruism in Classical Judaism." In *Altruism in World Religions*, edited by Jacob Neusner and Bruce Chilton. Washington, DC: Georgetown University Press, 2005.

Neusner, Jacob, and Bruce Chilton, editors. *Altruism in World Religions*. Washington, DC: Georgetown University Press, 2005.

Neusner, Jacob, and William Scott Green, editors. *Dictionary of Judaism in the Biblical Period: 450 BCE to 600 CE*. Peabody, MA: Hendrickson, 1996.

New Zealand Ministry of Justice. *The New Zealand Crime and Safety Survey*. Online: http://www.justice.govt.nz/publications/crime/crime-and-safety-survey.

Neyrey, Jerome H. "Ceremonies in Luke-Acts: The Case of Meals and Table-Fellowship." In *The Social World of Luke-Acts: Models for Interpretation*, edited by Jerome H. Neyrey, 361–88. Peabody, MA: Hendrickson, 1991.

———, editor. *The Social World of Luke-Acts: Models for Interpretation*. Peabody, MA: Hendrickson, 1991.

Nolland, John. *Luke 9:21–18:34*. Word Biblical Commentary 35B. Dallas: Word, 1993.

Northey, Wayne. Review of *Compulsory Compassion: A Critique of Restorative Justice*, by Annalise Acorn. *Justice Reflections* 19 (2008) 1–20.

Nouwen, Henri J. M. *The Return of the Prodigal Son: A Story of Homecoming*. New York: Doubleday, 1992.

Nussbaum, Martha C. "Compassion: The Basic Social Emotion." *Social Philosophy and Policy* 13 (1996) 27–58.

———. *Upheavals of Thought: The Intelligence of Emotions*. Cambridge: Cambridge University Press, 2001.

Oliner, Samuel O., and Pearl M. Oliner. *The Altruistic Personality: Rescuers of Jews in Nazi Europe*. New York: Maxwell Macmillan International, 1988.

Oakman, Douglas E. "Was Jesus a Peasant? Implications for Reading the Samaritan Story (Luke 10:30–35)." *Biblical Theology Bulletin* 22 (1992) 117–25.

Oord, Thomas Jay. *Defining Love: A Philosophical, Scientific, and Theological Engagement*. Grand Rapids: Brazos, 2010.

Paine, Tony. "Victim Support, Victims Rights: An Agenda for Prevention." In *Addressing the Causes of Offending: What Is the Evidence?*, edited by Gabrielle Maxwell, 157–61. Wellington: Victoria University Institute of Policy Studies, 2009.

Papanikolaou, Aristotle. "Liberating Eros: Confession and Desire." *Journal of the Society of Christian Ethics* 26 (2006) 115–36.

Pardun, John T. "Good Samaritan Laws: A Global Perspective." *Loyola of Los Angeles International and Comparative Law Journal* 20 (1997) 591–613.

Patrick, M. W. "Understanding the 'Understanding Distance' Today: The Love Command of Jesus." In *Interpreting Disciples: Practical Theology in the Disciples of Christ*, edited by L. D. Richesin and L. D. Bouchard, 101–29. Fort Worth: Texas Christian University Press, 1987.

Paul, Charlotte. "A Question of Compassion." *New Zealand Listener*, August 15, 2009. Online http://www.listener.co.nz/commentary/a-question-of-compassion.

Pence, Gregory E. "Can Compassion Be Taught?" *Journal of Medical Ethics* 9 (1983) 189–91.

Perkins, Pheme. *Love Commands in the New Testament*. New York: Paulist, 1982.

Phillips, Thomas E. "Reading Recent Readings of Issues of Wealth and Poverty in Luke and Acts." *Currents in Biblical Research* 1 (2003) 231–69.

Pilch, John J., and Bruce J. Malina, editors. *Biblical Social Values and Their Meaning: A Handbook*. Peabody, MA: Hendrickson, 1993.

Plummer, Alfred. *A Critical and Exegetical Commentary on the Gospel according to St. Luke*. International Critical Commentary. Edinburgh: T. & T. Clark, 1901.

Pokorny, Petr, and James H. Charlesworth, editors. *Jesus Research: An International Perspective*. Grand Rapids: Eerdmans, 2009.

Pope, Stephen J. "'Equal Regard' versus 'Special Relations'? Reaffirming the Inclusiveness of Agapé." *Journal of Religion* 77 (1997) 353–79.

Porter, Elisabeth. "Can Politics Practice Compassion?" *Hypatia* 21 (2006) 97–123.

Powell, Mark Allan. "The Religious Leaders in Luke: A Literary-Critical Study." *Journal of Biblical Literature* 109 (1990) 93–110.
Pranis, Kay. "Restorative Values." In *Handbook of Restorative Justice*, edited by Gerry Johnstone and Daniel W. Van Ness, 59–74. Cullompton: Willan, 2006.
Radcliffe, Dana M. "Hanfling on Neighbour Love." *Philosophy* 69 (1994) 497–502.
Rainbolt, George. "Mercy: In Defense of Caprice." *Noûs* 31 (1997) 226–41.
Ramsey, George W. "Plots, Gaps, Repetitions, and Ambiguity in Luke 15." *Perspectives in Religious Studies* 17 (1990) 33–42.
Ratcliffe, James M., editor. *The Good Samaritan and the Law: The Morality—and the Problems—of Aiding Those in Peril*. Garden City, NY: Anchor, 1966.
Raybeck, Douglas. "Anthropology and Labeling Theory: A Constructive Critique." *Ethos* 16 (1988) 371–97.
Redekop, Paul. *Changing Paradigms: Punishment and Restorative Discipline*. Scottdale, PA: Herald, 2007.
Reilly, Richard. "Compassion as Justice." *Buddhist-Christian Studies* 26 (2006) 21.
Reiser, Marius. "Love of Enemies in the Context of Antiquity." *New Testament Studies* 47 (2001) 411–27.
Resseguie, James L. *Spiritual Landscape: Images of the Spiritual Life in the Gospel of Luke*. Peabody, MA: Hendrickson, 2004.
Ribet, Beth. "Emotion, Power Relations, and Restorative Justice: A Review of Compulsory Compassion by Annalise Acorn." *UCLA Women's Law Journal* 115 (2006) 115–38.
Rigby, Paul, and Paul O'Grady. "Agape and Altruism: Debates in Theology and Social Psychology." *Journal of the American Academy of Religion* 57 (1989) 719–37.
Ringe, Sharon H. *Luke*. Westminster Bible Companion. Louisville: Westminster John Knox, 1995.
Roberts, Robert C. "Emotions Research and Religious Experience." In *The Oxford Handbook of Religion and Emotion*, edited by John Corrigan, 490–506. Oxford: Oxford University Press, 2008.
Roche, Declan. "Retribution and Restorative Justice." In *Handbook of Restorative Justice*, edited by Gerry Johnstone and Daniel W. Van Ness, 75–90. Cullompton: Willan, 2007.
Rohrbaugh, Richard L. "A Dysfunctional Family and Its Neighbours." In *Jesus and His Parables: Interpreting the Parables of Jesus Today*, edited by V. George Shillington, 141–64. Edinburgh: T. & T. Clark, 1997.
Ross, Lee, and Donna Shestowsky. "Contemporary Psychology's Challenges to Legal Theory and Practice." *Northwestern University Law Review* 97 (2003) 1081–114.
Roukema, Riemer. "The Good Samaritan in Ancient Christianity." *Vigiliae Christianne* 58 (2004) 56–74.
Rowe, Mary, Linda Wilcox, and Howard Gadlin. "Dealing with—or Reporting—'Unacceptable' Behavior." *Journal of the International Ombudsman Association* 2 (2009) 52–64.
Rudolph, Wallace M. "The Duty to Act: A Proposed Rule." In *The Good Samaritan and the Law*, edited by James M. Ratcliffe, 243–78. Garden City, NY: Anchor, 1966.
Rudzunski, Alexander W. "The Duty to Rescue: A Comparative Analysis." In *The Good Samaritan and the Law*, edited by James M. Ratcliffe, 91–134. Garden City, NY: Anchor, 1966.

Safrai, Shemuel, and M. Stern. *The Jewish People in the First Century: Historical Geography, Political History, Social, Cultural and Religious Life and Institutions*. Compendia Rerum Iudaicarum ad Novum Testamentum. Assen: Van Gorcum, 1974.
Saiman, Chaim. "Jesus' Legal Theory—A Rabbinic Interpretation." *Journal of Law and Religion* 23 (2007) 97–130.
Sanders, E. P. *Judaism: Practice and Belief, 63 BCE–66 CE*. London: SCM, 1992.
Schaab, Gloria L. "Which of These Was Neighbor? Spiritual Dimensions of the U.S. Immigration Question." *International Journal of Public Theology* 2 (2008) 182–202.
Schmidt, Thomas E. *Hostility to Wealth in the Synoptic Gospels*. Sheffield: JSOT, 1987.
Schnelle, Udo. *Theology of the New Testament*. Translated by M. Eugene Boring. Grand Rapids: Baker Academic, 2009.
Schottroff, Luise. *The Parables of Jesus*. Translated by Linda M. Maloney. Minneapolis: Fortress, 2006.
Schrage, Wolfgang. *The Ethics of the New Testament*. Translated by David E. Green. Edinburgh: T. & T. Clark, 1988.
Schriver, Donald W. *An Ethic for Enemies: Forgiveness in Politics*. Oxford: Oxford University Press, 1995.
———. *Honest Patriots: Loving a Country Enough to Remember Its Misdeeds*. Oxford: Oxford University Press, 2005.
Schroeder, David A., Rose Penner, John Dovido, Mary Elizabeth Allyn, and Horace Warren Allyn. *The Psychology of Helping and Altruism: Problems and Puzzles*. McGraw-Hill Series in Social Psychology. New York: McGraw-Hill, 1995.
Schürer, Emil. *The History of the Jewish People in the Age of Jesus Christ (175 BC–AD 135)*. Edited by Geza Vermes, Fergus Millar, and Matthew Black. 3 vols. Edinburgh: T. & T. Clark, 1979.
Scott, Bernard B. *Hear Then the Parable: A Commentary on the Parables of Jesus*. Minneapolis: Fortress, 1989.
———. "The Prodigal Son: A Structuralist Interpretation." *Semeia* 9 (1977) 45–73.
Sellew, Philip. "Interior Monologue as a Narrative Device in the Parables of Luke." *Journal of Biblical Literature* 111 (1992) 239–53.
Sellin, Gerhard. "Lukas Als Gleichniserzähler: Die Erzählung Vom Barmherzigen Samariter (Luke 10:25–37)." *Zeitschrift fur die neutestamentliche Wissenschaft und die Kunde* 65 (1974) 166–89.
———. "Lukas Als Gleichniserzähler: Die Erzählung Vom Barmherzigen Samariter (Luke 10:25–37)." *Zeitschrift fur die neutestamentliche Wissenschaft und die Kunde* 66 (1975) 19–60.
Shaffer, Thomas L. "The Radical Reformation and the Jurisprudence of Forgiveness." In *Christian Perspectives on Legal Thought*, edited by Robert F. Chochran Jr. et al., 321–40. New Haven: Yale University Press, 2001.
Shaw, Perry W. H. "Jesus: Oriental Teacher Par Excellence." *Christian Education Journal* 1NS (1997) 83–94.
Shen, Peidong et al. "Reconstruction of Patrilineages and Matrilineages of Samaritans and Other Israeli Populations From Y-Chromosome and Mitochondrial DNA Sequence Variation." *Human Mutation* 24 (2004) 248–60.
Sherson, Venetia. "Caring Till It Hurts." *Your Weekend*, March 13, 2010, 7–11.
Siebald, Manfried, and Leland Ryken. "Prodigal Son." In *A Dictionary of Biblical Tradition in English Literature*, edited by Jeffrey David Lyle, 640–44. Grand Rapids: Eerdmans, 1992.
Singer, Peter. *The Life You Can Save: Acting Now to End World Poverty*. New York: Random House, 2009.

———. "Outsiders: Our Obligations to Those Beyond Our Borders." In *The Ethics of Assistance: Morality and the Distant Needy*, edited by Deen K. Chatterjee, 11–32. Cambridge: Cambridge University Press, 2004.

Singer, Tania, and Claus Lamm. "The Social Neuroscience of Empathy." *Annals of the New York City Academy of Science* 1156 (2009) 81–96.

Skillen, James W. *A Covenant to Keep: Meditations on the Biblical Theme of Justice*. Grand Rapids: CRC, 2000.

Smith, Lewis. "Britain 'Knows Little About Bible.'" Online: http://www.independent.co.uk/arts-entertainment/books/news/britain-knows-little-about-bible-1722933.html.

Snodgrass, Klyne. "From Allegorizing to Allegorizing: A History of the Interpretation of the Parables of Jesus." In *The Challenge of Jesus' Parables*, edited by Richard N. Longenecker, 3–29. Grand Rapids: Eerdmans, 2000.

———. "Modern Approaches to the Parables." In *The Face of New Testament Studies: A Survey of Recent Research*, edited by Scot McKnight and Grant R. Osborne, 177–90. Grand Rapids: Baker Acadmic, 2004.

———. *Stories with Intent: A Comprehensive Guide to the Parables of Jesus*. Grand Rapids: Eerdmans, 2008.

Snyder, Susanna. "Encountering Asylum Seekers: An Ethic of Fear or Faith?" *Studies in Christian Ethics* 24 (2011) 350–66.

Soares, Theodore Gerald. "Some Psychological Aspects of Regeneration." *The Biblical World* 37 (1911) 78–88.

Soerens, Matthew, and Jenny Hwang. *Welcoming the Stranger: Justice, Compassion and Truth in the Immigration Debate*. Downers Grove, IL: InterVarsity, 2009.

Soloveichik, Rabbi Meir Y. "Torah and Incarnation: Torah Learning Bridges the Gap between Man and God." *First Things* (October, 2010) 44–49.

Stassen, Glen H., and David P. Gushee. *Kingdom Ethics: Following Jesus in Contemporary Context*. Downers Grove, IL: InterVarsity, 2003.

Steger, Michael F., Todd B. Kashdan, and Oishi Shigehiro. "Being Good by Doing Good: Daily Eudaimonic Activity and Well-Being." *Journal of Research in Personality* 42 (2008) 22–42.

Stein, Robert H. "The Interpretation of the Parable of the Good Samaritan." In *Scripture, Tradition, and Interpretation*, edited by W. Ward Gasque and William Sanford LaSor. Grand Rapids: Eerdmans, 1978.

Story, J. Lyle. "The Spirit-Filled Servant's Agenda of 'Becoming the Neighbor.'" *Pax Pneuma* 5 (2009) 21–33.

Strack, H. L., and P. Billerbeck. *Kommentar zum Neuen Testament aus Talmud und Midrash*. 6 vols. Munich: Beck, 1922–61.

Strang, Heather. "The Crime Victim Movement as a Force in Civil Society." In *Restorative Justice and Civil Society*, edited by Heather Strang and John Braithwaite, 69–82. Cambridge: Cambridge University Press, 2001.

Strang, Heather, and John Braithwaite. *Restorative Justice and Civil Society*. Cambridge: Cambridge University Press, 2001.

Staub, Ervin. "Helping a Distressed Person: Social, Personality, and Stimulus Determinants." In *Advances in Experimental Social Psychology*, edited by L. Berkowitz, 293–341. New York: Academic Press, 1974.

Talbert, Charles H. *Reading Luke: A Literary and Theological Commentary on the Third Gospel*. Reading the New Testament Series. New York: Crossroad, 1982.

Tallon, Andrew. "Christianity." In *The Oxford Handbook of Religion and Emotion*, edited by John Corrigan, 111–24. Oxford: Oxford University Press, 2008.

Thorburn, Malcolm. "The Impossible Dreams and Modest Reality of Restorative Justice." *Queens Law Journal* 30 (2005) 863–82.

Tissot, Y. "Patristic Allegories of the Lukan Parable of the Two Sons." In *Exegesis: Problems of Method and Exercises in Reading*, edited by F. Bovon and G. Rouiller, 362–409. Pittsburgh: Pickwick, 1978.

Tolbert, Mary Anne. "The Prodigal Son: An Essay in Literary Criticism from a Psychoanalytic Perspective." *Semeia* 9 (1977) 1–20.

Tucker, Jeffrey. *Example Stories: Perspectives on Four Parables in the Gospel of Luke*. Journal for the Study of the New Testament Supplement Series 162. Sheffield: Sheffield Academic, 1998.

Tunc, André. "The Volunteer and the Good Samaritan." In *The Good Samaritan and the Law*, edited by James M. Ratcliffe, 43–62. Garden City, NY: Anchor, 1966.

Turner, Kathryn. "Justification and Justice in a Theology of Grace." *Theology Today* 55 (1999) 510–23.

Turner, Nigel A. *A Grammar of New Testament Greek*. Vol. 3. Edinburgh: T. & T. Clark, 1965.

Umbreit, Mark, and Marilyn Peterson Armour. *Restorative Justice Dialogue: An Essential Guide for Research and Practice*. New York: Springer, 2010.

United Kingdom. House of Lords. Donaghue v Stevenson, [1932] AC 562.

United Kingdom. House of Lords. Mitchell v Glasgow City Council, [2009] UKHL 11. Online: www.publications.parliament.uk/pa/ld200809/ldjudgmt/jd090218/mitche-1.htm.

United Nations Office on Drugs and Crime. *Compendium of United Nations Standards and Norms in Crime Prevention and Criminal Justice*. Vienna: United Nations, 2006.

United States Conference of Catholic Bishops. "Responsibility, Rehabilitation, and Restoration: A Catholic Perspective on Crime and Criminal Justice." *A Statement of the Catholic Bishops of the United States* (2000). Online: http://www.usccb.org/issues-and-action/human-life-and-dignity/criminal-justice-restorative-justice/crime-and-criminal-justice.cfm.

Van Ness, Daniel W. "Restorative Terminology: A Modest Proposal." Online: http://www.restorativejustice.org/RJOB/restorative-terminology-a-modest-proposal#1309431821.

Van Ness, Daniel W., and Karen Heetderks Strong. *Restoring Justice: An Introduction to Restorative Justice*. 3rd ed. Cincinnati, OH: LexisNexis/Anderson, 2006.

Van Ness, Daniel W., and Gerry Johnstone, editors. *Handbook of Restorative Justice*. Cullompton: Willan, 2007.

Varah, Chad. "Why Samaritans Started." Online: www.samaritans.org/about_samaritans/governance_and_history/why_samaritans_started.aspx.

Vass, Beck. "Good Samaritan, Best New Zealander." *The New Zealand Herald*, Dec 6, 2008.

Via, Dan Otto, Jr. "Parable and Example Story: A Literary-Structuralist Approach." *Semeia* 1 (1974) 105–33.

———. *The Parables: Their Literary and Existential Dimension*. 1967. Reprinted, Eugene, OR: Wipf & Stock, 2007.

———. "The Prodigal Son: A Jungian Reading." *Semeia* 9 (1977) 21–43.

Volf, Miroslav. *Exclusion and Embrace: A Theological Exploration of Identity, Otherness, and Reconciliation*. Nashville: Abingdon, 1996.

———. "Forgiveness, Reconciliation, and Justice: A Christian Contribution to a More Peaceful Social Environment." Online: http://livedtheology.org/pdfs/Volf.pdf.

———. "God Is Love: Biblical and Theological Reflections on a Foundational Christian Claim." In *A Common Wor: Muslims and Christians on Loving God and Neighbor*, edited by Miroslav Volf, Ghazi bin Muhammad, and Melissa Yarrington, 88–109. Grand Rapids: Eerdmans, 2010.

———. "Original Crime, Primal Care." In *God and the Victim: Theological Reflections on Evil, Victimization, Justice, and Forgiveness*, edited by Lisa Barnes Lampman and Michelle D. Shattuck, 17–35. Grand Rapids: Eerdmans, 1999.

Wailes, Stephen L. *Medieval Allegories of Jesus' Parables*. Berkeley: University of California Press, 1987.

Walgrave, Lode. "Has Restorative Justice Appropriately Responded to Retribution Theory and Impulses?" In *Critical Issues in Restorative Justice*, edited by Howard Zehr and Barb Toews, 47–60. Monsey, NY: Criminal Justice Press, 2004.

Waller, Louis. "Rescue and the Common Law: England and Australia." In *The Good Samaritan and the Law*, edited by James M. Ratcliffe, 141–58. Garden City, NY: Anchor, 1966.

Ward, Bruce K. *Redeeming the Enlightenment: Christianity and the Liberal Virtues*. Grand Rapids: Eerdmans, 2010.

Weaver, J. Denny. "Forgiveness and (Non) Violence: The Atonement Connections." *Mennonite Quarterly Review* 83 (April 2009) 319–47.

———. *The Nonviolent Atonement*. Grand Rapids: Eerdmans, 2001.

Weil, Simone. *The Need for Roots*. New York: Harper Colliphon, 1971.

Wellford, Charles. "Labeling Theory and Criminology: An Assessment." *Social Problems* 22 (1975) 332–45.

Wells, Samuel. "The Jericho Affair." *The Christian Century*, June 29, 2004, 1.

Wilkinson, John. "The Way from Jerusalem to Jericho." *Biblical Archaeologist* 38 (1975) 10–24.

Williams, Carol J. "Good Samaritans Get No Aid from High Court." *Los Angeles Times*, Dec 19, 2008. Online: http://articles.latimes.com/2008/dec/19/local/me-good-samaritan19?pg=1.

Willis, S. "The Good Samaritan: Another View." *Expository Times* 112 (2000) 92.

Wilson, Stephen G. *Luke and the Law*. Society for New Testament Studies Monograph Series 50. Cambridge: Cambridge University Press, 1983.

Wink, Walter. "The Parable of the Compassionate Samaritan: A Communal Exegesis Approach." *Review and Expositor* 76 (1979) 199–217.

Witherington, Ben, III. *Jesus the Sage: The Pilgrimage of Wisdom*. Minneapolis: Fortress, 1994.

Wittig, Susan. "A Theory of Multiple Meanings." *Semeia* 9 (1977) 75–103.

Woods, Emma. "Family's Amazing Grace Honours Son's Memory." *Sunday Star Times*, November 7, 2010, A3.

Woodward, Kathleen. "Calculating Compassion." *Indiana Law Journal* 77 (2002) 223–45.

Woozley, A. D. "A Duty to Rescue: Some Thoughts on Criminal Liability." *Virginia Law Review* 69 (1983) 1273–1300.

Wright, N. T. *Jesus and the Victory of God*. Christian Origins and the Question of God 2. London: SPCK, 1996.

———. *The New Testament and the People of God*. Christian Origins and the Question of God 1. Minneapolis: Fortress, 1992.

Young, Brad H. *Jesus the Jewish Theologian*. Peabody, MA: Hendrickson, 1995.

Zehr, Howard. *Changing Lenses: A New Focus for Crime and Justice*. 3rd ed. Scottdale, PA: Herald, 2005.

———. "Journey to Belonging." In *Restorative Justice: Theoretical Foundations*, edited by Elmar G. M. Weitekamp and Hans-Jürgen Kerner, 21–31. Cullompton: Willan, 2002.

———. *The Little Book of Restorative Justice*. Intercourse, PA: Good Books, 2002.

———. "Restoring Justice." In *God and the Victim: Theological Reflections on Evil, Victimization, Justice, and Forgiveness*, edited by Lisa Barnes Lampman and Michelle D. Shattuck, 131–59. Grand Rapids: Eerdmans, 1999.

———. "Ten Ways to Live Restoratively." Online: http://emu.edu/now/restorative-justice/2009/.

Zehr, Howard, and Barb Toews. *Critical Issues in Restorative Justice*. Monsey, NY: Criminal Justice Press, 2004.

Zeisel, Hans. "An International Experiment on the Effects of a Good Samaritan Law." In *The Good Samaritan and the Law*, edited by James M. Ratcliffe, 209–12. Garden City, NY: Anchor, 1966.

Zimbardo, Philip. *The Lucifer Effect: Understanding How Good People Turn Evil*. New York: Random House, 2007.

Scripture and Ancient Sources Index

Old Testament

Genesis
1:27	215
3:21	121n34
4:12	229
12:10	203n25
18:1	121n34
25:11	121n34
26:1	203n25
28:4	55n1
29:34	89n13
33:4	226n19
37–50	182n3
41:27–47	203n25
41:42	229
42:5	203n25
43:1	203n25
45:14–15	226n19
47:4	203n25

Exodus
10:16	210n53
18:1	190n34
20:12	200n16
20:17	199n13
21:35	117n22
22:21–27	90n17
23:4	91n24
23:4–5	97
23:6–12	90n17

Leviticus
6:1–7	210n53, 211, 213n61
11:7	204n32
14:8	204n32
17–26	64
18:5	44, 62
19	66
19:3	200n16
19:9–18	90n17
19:16	97, 99
19:16–19	76
19:17	92, 97
19:17–18	40
19:18	8, 24, 31, 34, 46, 50, 64, 65, 66, 67, 76, 78–79, 80, 130, 148
19:33–34	90n17
19:34	65, 77
21:1–3	99
21:1–4	94
21:11	94
22:4–7	94
23:13	123
23:22	90n17
25:18	44, 62
25:23	201

Numbers
5:2	94
5:6–7	210n53, 211, 213n61
6:6–12	94
15:37–41	64n23
19:11–16	94

27:6–11	197		30:15–20	44, 62, 109, 149
36:1–10	197		30:16	65
			34:6	121n34

Deuteronomy

1:8	55n1		Joshua	
2:12	55n1		15:7	82n2
4:1	55n1		18:17	82n2
4:22	55n1		22:5	65
4:24	121n34		23:11	65
4:26	55n1			
4:29	109		Ruth	
5:33	44, 62		1:1	203n25
6	66			
6:4–5	31, 63, 66, 67		2 Samuel	
6:5	64, 65, 73n43		14:33	226n19
6:6–9	64n23			
6:7	64n23		1 Kings	
6:13	200n16, 203n29		8:47–51	190n33
6:16	56n5		11:2	203n28
6:24	44, 62		18:2	203n25
8:2	56n5, 109			
8:16	56n5		2 Kings	
10:12	121		4:38	203n25
10:16	109		17:24–41	115
10:19	77		18:6	203n29
10:20	203n29			
11:1	65		1 Chronicles	
11:13–21	64n23, 65		15:4–12	89
11:18	109		24:1–19	89
11:29	114			
13:5	121		2 Chronicles	
14:8	204n32		19:2	92n25
15:7	90n17		28:5–15	39
19:9	65			
21:17	199		Ezra	
21:18–21	214, 196		7:6	43
21:18–23	192		9:6	210
22:2	97; 97n42			
22:4	90n17		Nehemiah	
24:11–21	90n17		10:37–38	89n13
27:12	114			
28:9	121		Esther	
29:9–15	90n17		3:10	229
30:6	44, 62, 109		8:2	229

Psalms

1:1	190n34
5:5	92n25
15:2–5	62n19
24:3–6	62n19
26:5	92n25
32:5	210n52
37:9	55n1
37:11	55n1
37:22	55n1
37:29	55n1
37:34	55n1
51:4	210n53
63:8	203n29
68:1	92n25
78:18 [LXX 77:18]	56n5
89:23	92n25
103:1–5	264
103:3	189
103:6–18	233
103:8–10	190n33
103:12–13	190n33
103:13–14	261
103:13–15	264
119:31	03n29
133:1	201
139:21–22	92

Proverbs

3:9	200n16
8:17	92
21:26	199n13
25:21–22	97
24:17–18	97
28:7	202n24

Isaiah

1:6	123
29:13	109
40:4	18
49:15	190n33
55:7	190n33
58:5–9	124n40, 130
58:7	90
60:21	55n1, 58n12
61:10	228n27
63:16	189
66:2	62n19

Jeremiah

3:12	190n33
22:3–4	62n19
30:17	123
31:18–20	190n33
31:33	109
32:40	109

Ezekiel

33:11	190n33
44:25–27	94

Daniel

12:2 (LXX)	44, 55n1

Hosea

2:19–20	62n19
6:6	45, 124n40, 130
11:1–9	190n33

Micah

6:7–8	124n40, 130
6:8	45, 62n19, 130

Zechariah

3:1–10	228n27
7:9	viii
7:9–10	62n19
8:16–17	62n19

Malachi

4:4–5	44n41

New Testament

Matthew

4:7	56n5
5:17–48	61
5:23–24	211, 213n61

5:43	51, 78	2:27	144, 145
5:44	80n52	3:1–6	66n30
5:44–45	51	6:13	123
5:45	245	6:34	27n21, 120n32
5:45–48	80	6:56	85n10
5:46–47	51	7:1–7	60
7:12	68, 69	7:3	60
9:36	27n21, 120n32	7:13	27n21
10	117	7:1–14	146
10:5	116	7:1–23	66n30
10:5–6	115, 118	8:2	27n21, 120n32
12:1–8	144	8:34–38	164
12:7	145	8:35	265
14:14	27n21, 120n32	9:22	27n21
15:1–20	146	10:17	32, 56n2
15:32	27n21, 120n32	10:17–22	63n21
18:27	120n32	10:30	57
18:23–25	126	10:36	27n21
19:5	203n28	10:47	262
19:16	32, 56n2	12	31, 68
19:16–22	63n21	12:28–29	68
19:29	57	12:28–34	30, 31, 63n21, 66, 278n42
20:34	120n32		
21:28–31	185	12:31	68
22	31, 68	12:32	67
22:34–40	30, 63n21	12:33	66n30, 68
22:35	42n33	12:34	67
22:38	68	12:40	42n32
22:39	68	13:1	93
22:40	68	14:43	46n48
23:1–36	60	14:45	225n18
23:5	85n10		
23:6	42n32	**Luke**	
23:23	63n21, 124n40	1:1–4	29
23:34–40	63n21	1:5–25	93
24:1–2	93	1:8	89
25:1–13	185	1:50	27, 121
25:46	57	1:51–53	217
26:47	46n48	1:52–53	217n1
26:49	225n18	1:54	27
		1:76	37
Mark		1:78	27, 121, 223n10
1:41	27n21	1:79	37
2:23–28	144	2:49	232n40

Scripture and Ancient Sources Index 347

3:3–5	37	7:13	27; 27n21, 120n32, 121, 223
3:5	18	7:25	57n7, 83n6, 85
3:11	85	7:27	37
4:2	56	7:29–30	45, 57
4:12	56n5	7:30	42
4:24–30	57n7	7:33–34	57n7
4:25	203n25	7:34	196
4:29	78	7:35–50	57n7
4:40–41	57n7	7:38	226n19
4:43	232n40	7:39	45
5:12–13	48	7:41–42	185
5:12–15	57n7	8:26–39	57n7
5:13	27n21, 96	8:32	204n32
5:14	93	8:40–56	57n7
5:17	42, 42n33, 45, 96	8:43–48	96
5:21	42, 45	8:54	96
5:27–28	57n7	9:3	85
5:29–30	96	9:13	27n21
5:29–32	57n7	9:22	42n34, 232n40
5:30	42n34, 45	9:38	27n21
5:32	56	9:41	27n21
5:33	57n7	9:51–55	51
5:33–34	48	9:52–53	118
5:33–38	44n42	9:52–56	57
6:1–6	144	9:53	37
6:1–11	48, 96	9:57	37
6:3	44n42	9:60	48
6:6	44n42	10	31, 42, 54, 56n5
6:6–11	57n7, 96	10:2	27n21
6:7	42n34; 45	10:4	37, 229
6:11	45	10:7–8	96
6:19	57n778	10:15	223n12
6:22	78	10:25	8, 31, 41, 42n33, 43, 44, 56n5, 67, 96, 131, 321
6:24–25	217n1	10:25–26	48, 129
6:27	78	10:25–27	41n30
6:27–31	51	10:25–29	21, 30, 55
6:27–36	68n32	10:25–37	1, 14, 18, 31n9, 49
6:29	85	10:26	8, 41, 44, 63
6:31	38	10:27	31, 41, 74, 41n30
6:32–34	51	10:27–36	31
6:35–36	51, 80	10:28	31, 39, 41, 41n30, 44, 71, 131, 321
6:38	164		
7:11–17	57n7		

10:29	31, 41, 41n30, 77, 129, 138, 147	15:5	217, 232
		15:6	232
10:30	8, 37	15:7	191
10:30–35	129	15:8	224
10:30–36	41	15:9	217, 232
10:31	86	15:10	191
10:32	107	15:11–32	1, 178, 182n3,
10:33	10, 27, 37, 73, 112, 118, 120n32, 131, 223, 249, 253	15:12	198, 199, 221, 238, 245
		15:13	200, 202, 215, 222, 235
		15:13b–19	185
10:34	37, 118, 126	15:14	203
10:35	37, 36n22, 118, 126, 128n55	15:15	203, 204
		15:16	204, 216
10:36	27n21, 31, 37, 38, 39, 41n30, 137, 249	15:17	204, 206n40, 207, 212, 213, 217, 221, 224, 241, 242
10:36–37	30, 108		
10:37	31, 33, 39, 40, 41, 41n30, 123, 124, 131, 137, 138, 145, 253, 321	15:17–19	185
		15:17–21	206
		15:18	189, 191, 195, 205n44, 214, 221
11:37–38	96		
11:41	48	15:18–19	227
11:42	48, 57, 63n21, 130	15:19	207, 212, 229, 238
11:42–44	217n1	15:20	10, 27, 120n32, 121, 222, 223, 225
11:45	42		
11:53	42n34	15:21	189, 191, 195, 207, 214, 221, 226, 229
12:12	232n40		
12:15–21	217n1	15:22	83n6, 85, 85n10, 226, 227, 228
12:22–23	85		
12:27	85	15:22–26	200
12:33	83	15:22–23	242
12:39	83	15:23	217, 244
13:10–17	48	15:23–24	232
13:14	232n40	15:24	219, 222, 224, 232
13:16	232n40	15:24–25	242
14:1–6	48, 66n30	15:25	217, 232, 234, 244
15	190, 190, 192, 223n10, 233	15:26	217, 235
		15:27	217, 223, 232, 234, 238, 240
15:1–3	184, 190		
15:2	42n34	15:28	220, 234, 235, 237, 238
15:3	190	15:28–30	186
15:3–10	191, 206	15:29	217, 221, 234, 236, 237, 238
15:4	224		
15:4–6	224n14	15:29–30	193, 200, 219, 239
15:4–10	224		

15:30	195, 199, 201, 232, 234, 235, 238, 239	22:37	232n40
		22:47	46
15:31	200, 217, 222, 237, 240, 245	22:52	37
		22:63	85
15:32	219, 222, 232, 240, 241, 244, 249, 321	22:63–65	37
		22:66	42n34
16:1–9	206	23:10	42n34
16:13–14	57	23:11	37
16:13–15	217n1	23:16	37
16:14	42n32	23:18–25	37
16:15	56	23:32	37
16:16	33, 48	23:34	37
16:16–18	33n16	23:46–49	37
16:18	48	24:6	49n59
16:19	83n6, 85	24:7	232n40
16:19–31	217n1	24:26	232n40
16:29	48	23:57	37
17:13	27n21	24:53	37, 93
17:14	93		
17:18	51, 115	**John**	
17:25	232n40	4	115, 116
18:1	232n40	4:8–9	116
18:9–14	34n17, 185	4:20	114
18:10–12	56	4:22	51, 115
18:18	32, 48, 56n2, 63n21	5:2–18	66n30
18:18–19	48	6:6	56n5
18:18–23	48, 63n27	8	118
18:18–26	217n1	8:48	22
18:30	57	8:48–49	118
18:38	27n21	12:6	83
19:1–10	217n1	12:25	164
19:5	232n40	17:15	7
19:45–46	96	18:3	46n48
19:47	42n34	18:12	46n48
20:1	42n34		
20:19	42n34	**Acts**	
20:20	56	1:1	29
20:39	42n34	2:46	93
20:46	42n34, 83n6, 85, 228	3:1	93
20:47	42n32, 57, 217n1	5:12	93
21:1–2	217n1	5:25	93
21:5–6	93	5:34	42
22:2	42n34	6:7	93
22:3–5	217n1	7:5	55n1
		10:28	203

11:28	203n25
12:21	83n6
12:85	83n6
13:46	56n2
13:48	56n2
16:14	83n6, 85
16:22–23	85
16:23	84
16:27	85
20:37	225n18
23:24	118n25
24:6	49n59

Romans
3:21	146
3:31	146
5:5	75
7	146
7:7	199n13
7:7–25	271
8:1–4	75, 146
8:18–30	275
13:8–10	75
13:9	65n28, 199n13
13:14	75
15:30	75

1 Corinthians
6:16	203n28
6:17	203n29
10:9	56n5
13:13	278n42

2 Corinthians
6:5	84
11:23	84
13:5	56n5
13:11	278n42

Galatians
2:12–13	190n34
5:14	65n28, 75
5:24–26	75
6:10	51n63

Ephesians
5:18	202n24
6:21	v

Philippians
1:8	27n21, 272
2:1	27n21, 272

Colossians
3:12	272

1 Timothy
1:2	27n21
1:7	42n33

2 Timothy
1:2	27n21

Titus
1:6	202n24
3:9	42n33

James
2:8	65n28
4:2	199n13
4:17	24
5:14	123

1 Peter
4:4	202n24

1 John
2:6	75
3:16	75
3:23	133
4:7	18
4:7–12	80
4:8	272, 278n42
4:16	272
4:19	35n19
4:20	71

2 John
3	27n21

Revelation

2:2	56n5
3:18	228
6:6	123

Apocrypha

1 Esdras
4:20	203n28

1 Maccabees
1:47	204n32
6:15	229

2 Maccabees
2:14	97
6:4	202n24
6:18	204n32
7:1	204n32

3 Maccabees
5:49	225n18

4 Maccabees
2:5–6	199n13
4:11	84n7
5:4	43
7:6–7	43

Sirach
7:21	64n25
7:30–36	64n25
12:1–7	91
19:2	203n28
19:30	225n16
25:21	91
33:19–24	197
50:25–26	115

Tobit
1:17–19	98
11:5–15	225
11:13–14	225n15

Pseudepigrapha

1 Enoch
40:9	55n1

Jubilees
	61
7:20	64n25
30:21–22	58n12
36:4–8	65n27
36:78	64n25

Psalms of Solomon
14:10	55n1

Testament of Abraham [B]
12	120n32

Testament of Dan
5:3	65n27

Testament of Issachar
5:2; 7:6	65n27

Testament of Job
18	55n1

Testament of Zebulun
8:1–2	120n32

Qumran Documents

1QM
1:1	77n47

1QS
1.1–3	65n27
1:3–4	92n25
1:9–10	65n27, 77n47, 92n25
2:24	77n47
5:25	77n47

4Q542
	202n23

11QTemple
64:2–6	196n6

Rabbinic Sources

Babylonian Talmud

Abodah Zarah
15a	114n9
26a–b	77n47

Baba Mesi'a
32a	91n24
30a	91n23
32a–b	91n23
32a–33a	97n40
33a	91n23

Baba Qamma
47b	64n25
82b	204n33

Berakot
21b	64n23
28b	56n3
47b	64n23

Gittin
10a, 10b	114n8

Ketubbot
36b	64n25

Megillah
3b	98n47

Nazir
47b–49a	98n47

Niddah
16b	64n25
31b	116n1
56b	116n14

Pesahim
74a	64n25

Qiddushin
41a	64n25

Sanhedrin
10a	64n25
52a	64n25
52b	64n25
57a	117n22
73a	97n42
84b	64n25

Shabbat
32a	206

Sotah
43a	64n25
14a	121n34
43b–44a	100n55

Zebahim
100a	98n47

Jerusalem Talmud

Abodah Zarah
5:4	117n22

Mishnah

Abodah Zarah
1:1	77n47
2:1	98n44, 125n46
2:1–2	77n47
4:9–10	77n47
26a–b	77n47

Abot
1:13	42n32
4:5	42n32
5:22	58n12

Baba Batra
8:7	198n9

Baba Mesi'a
2:10	97n40

Berakot
1:1–4	64n23

3:1 98n46
4:6 42n32

Nazir
7:1 98n47

Niddah
4:1 116n16
7:1 116n16
7:4–5 116n14

Pe'ah
8:7 203n31

Rosh HaShanah
2:2 117n22

Shabbat
7:11 63n20

Sanhedrin
7:4 196n6
8.4–5 196n6
10:1 58n12

Shebi'it
8:10 116n17

Tamid
5:1 64n23

Christian Literature

Barnabas
19:25 65n28

Didache
1:2 65n28

Justin, *Dialogue with Trypho*
93:2–3 65n28

Martyrdom of Polycarp
3:3 65n28

Other Ancient Writings

Epictetus, *Discourses*
2.10.7 200n18

Josephus, *Jewish Antiquities*
4.8.13 §212–13, 64n23
4:262 214n64
4:264 196n6
13:275–81 117n18
18:29–30 117n19
20:118–26 117n21
20:181 93n30
20:207 93n30

Josephus, *Against Apion*
2.206 196n6

Josephus, *The Life*
1:1 93n31

Josephus, *Jewish War*
1:311 83n3
2.124 83n5
2:139 77n47
2.228 83n5
2.232–46 117n21

Juvenal, *Satires*
14:103–4 90n18

P. Amherst II
141:13 84n7

Philo, *On the Special Laws*
1:299–300 65n27
2:63 65n27
4:141 64n23

Tacitus, *Histories*
5:5 90n18

Author Index

Acorn, Annalise, 10–11, 192, 252, 259n16, 302–20
Allison, Dale, 65n27, 66n30, 68n33
Anderson, Robert T., 112n3, 114n9, 114n10
Angier, Natalie, 127n51
Archibald, Bruce, 301n32, 304n38, 310
Aristotle, 225n16, 255
Armour, Marilyn P., 5n5
Arndt, William, 200n15, 223n12
Atkin, Lord, 147–48
Aus, Roger D., 182n3, 207n46
Avery-Peck, Alan J., 97n44
Avgoustinos, Costa, 254, 280n48, 289nn9–10

Bailey, Kenneth, 51, 52n64, 58n11, 63n22, 77n49, 85n8, 91n24, 93n29, 95n36, 99n50, 100n55, 107n71, 118n23, 118n25, 124, 182, 184n17, 185nn22–23, 188n27, 189n29, 189n30, 196n7, 198, 199nn11–12, 201n20, n22, 202nn23–24, 203, 204n38, 206n44, 207n47, 208n50, 212, 220, 222n8, 223, 225n16, 226n19, 227n24, 232, 235n44, 237n52, n54, 238n55
Bandes, Susan, 286, 287n7, 290n13, 292–293, 294n22
Banks, Robert, 31n11, 48n53, 70n35
Barasch, Marc I., 163n37, 272n33, 321, 322n95
Batson, C. Daniel, 103nn63–64, 104n66, 105n67

Batten, Alicia, 228n30
Bauckham, Richard, 30n4, 31n9, 37n24, 93n30, 95n36, 96n38, 98n48, 99n50, 106n70, 185n20, 186n25
Bauer, Walter, 200n15
Beasley-Murray, George R., 184n17
Beavis, Mary Ann, 189n29, 192n39
Beck, Elizabeth, 5n4
Bell, Richard H., 218, 293, 298n26, 302n33
Bentham, Jeremy, 155n17
Besser, Anne C., 91n24, 97, 98n45, 99n52, 127n53, 152n10
Billerbeck, P., 64n23, 77n47
Blomberg, Craig, 41n30
Bock, Darrell L., 212n58, 222n8
Boff, Leonardo, 80n52
Bornkamm, Günther, 37n24
Bovon, François, 181n2, 184n16, 196n5, 212n58, 229n31, 237n50
Boyack, James, 6n7
Braithwaite, John, 6n8, 231n38, 302, 303n35, 305n46, 310, 316
Breckenridge, James, 207n49
Brien, Andrew, 218–19, 262n22, 290n12
Bridges, Robert M., 183n6
Brown, Robert McAfee, 120n31
Brysk, Alison, 22n8
Bultmann, Rudolph, 185n20
Burge, Gary, 42n35, 225n16
Burridge, Richard, 32n12, 48, 48n57, 50n62

Cahill, Dan, 233n41
Caputo, John, 184n15, 230
Carlston, Charles, 185n20
Carroll R., M. Daniel, 22n9
Chang, H.-J., 22n8
Chaterjee, Deen K., 159n27
Columella, 125
Cover, Robert, 108n73
Cowley, A., 116n15
Cranfield, C. E. B., 31n11, 37n23, 77n49
Creed, J. M., 29n2, 31n7, 32n12, 77n49, 82n2, 107n71, 130n57
Crossan, John Dominic, 31, 33, 112n2, 183n8, 240
Cruz, Gemma T., 279n47

Dagan, Hanoch, 155n19, 162n35, 165n41
Darley, John M., 102n61, 103nn63–64
Daube, David, 63n22
Davies, W. D., 66n30, 68n33
Davis, Michael, 158n24
Derrett, Duncan M., 31n9, 44, 63n22, 95n36, 100n55, 106, 118n25, 119, 123n39, 126n49, 127n54, 142, 182n3, 185n21, 197n7, 198n10, 200n16, 204, 212n56, 237n52
Devlin, Lord, 155–56
Dodd, C. H., 72n41, 190n32
Donahue, John R, 50, 99n50, 121, 181n1, 184, 188n26, 189n29, 196n5, 203n31, 217n1
Donne, John, 242
Driver, Julia, 127n52, 161n33
Dunn, J. D. G., 30n4
Durber, Susan, 189n29

Ellis, E. E., 58n11, 77n49
Elwell, Walter, 125n45
Epictetus, 200n18
Esler, Philip, 29n2, 47, 49, 57n9, 112n3, 117, 132n63

Farrer, F. W., 90n19, 130n57, 188n26, 203, 227n23
Fehr, Ernst, 271n31
Feigenson, Neal, 253n4, 287n8, 289n10, 291, 292n17
Feldbrugge, F. J. M., 99n49, 155n18, 167n46
Fichtner, Johannes, 76
Fiensy, D. A., 201n19
Fischbacher, Urs, 271n31
Fitzmyer, J. A., 25n17, 31n11, 56n5, 73n43, 77n49, 181n1, 182n3, 184, 185n20, 189n30, 190n32, 204n37, 227n23
Foerster, W., 202n24
Forbes, Gregory, 24n15, 26 n20, 29n2, 31n11, 37n24, 56n5, 185n20, 197n7, 212n56, 227n24
Forrester, Duncan, 296n23
Freedman, Zelic, 92n26
Fuchs, Ernst, 184
Funk, Robert W., 37, 123n39
Furrow, James L., 189n31

Gagnon, Robert A., 37n24, 38
Geldenhuys, Norval, 34n18
Gerhardsson, Birger, 25n17, 26n18, 27, 29n2, 31n9, 36, 42n35, 65n26
Giles, Terry, 112n3, 114n9, 114n10
Gingrich, F. W., 200n15
Gnanavaram, M., 112n2
Gnilka, Joachim, 31n7, 32n12, 50n62, 66n30, 93n32, 96n37, 185, 196n5, 205n42
Gopin, Marc, 53n66, 109
Goulder, Michael D., 29n2
Gourgues, Michel, 96n37, 112n2
Graves, Mike, 37n23, 57n10
Green, Joel, 41n30, 56n5, 77n49, 91n23, 96n37, 184n11, 189n30, 217n1, 234n42, 237
Green, W. Scott, 60n13, 205, 206n43
Gregory, Charles O., 152n11
Gusfield, Joseph, 21n6

Gushee, David P., 92n28, 123n38, 126n48
Gutbrod, W., 42n33

Haacker, Klaus, 32n14
Hanfling, Oswald, 72n36
Hart, David Bentley, 20n3, 149n8, 257–258, 273n35
Harvey, A. E., 196
Hauerwas, Stanley, 20n4
Hays, Richard B., 135
Heetderks Strong, Karen, 5n3
Henderson, Lynne N., 108n73, 253n4, 286, 290, 291n14, 295n22, 299
Higton, Mike, 25n17
Hjelm, Ingrid, 113n5
Hoffmeier, James K., 22n9
Holgate, David A., 182n3, 183n7, 184n13, 195nn2–3, 196n4, 197n7, 200n15, 200n18, 202n24, 203n26, 204n32, 204n35, 207n46, 227n22, 234n43, 241
Honoré, Antony, 158, 163n36
Hoyle, Carolyn, 5n3, 87n12, 231n38
Hultgren, Arland J., 126n48
Hunter, A. M., 183n6, 184n16, 190n32
Hwang, J., 22n9

Jackson, Timothy, ix, 160n31, 164, 261n21, 271n32, 278, 297
Jeremias, Joachim, 34n18, 43n37, 46n48, 63n22, 77n47, n49, 85n8, 89n13, 96n37, 112nn2, 3, 118nn24–25, 129n56, 130n57, 184, 188n26, 189, 197n7, 204n37, 207n46, 226n19
Johnson, Luke Timothy, 90n19, 185n20
Johnston, R. M., 40n29
Johnstone, Gerry, 5n3
Jones, Mark, 130n57
Jones, Peter, 22n10, 27n22, 92n27, 125n45, 133

Josephus, Flavius, 45, 63n20, 64n23, 77n47, 83, 93nn30–31, 112n3, 115, 117nn18–19, 21, 196n6, 214
Just, A. A., Jr., 25n17, 182n4
Juvenal, 90n18

Kaplan, Kalman J., 91n24, 97, 98n45, 99n52, 127n53, 152n10
Karstedt, Susanne, 283n1, 301n32
Kashdan, Todd B., 163n37
Keizer, Kees, 175n57
Kelber, Werner H., 183n8
Keller, Timothy, 184, 212n56, 224n13
Kimmel, Eyal, 290n11
King, Martin Luther, Jr., 8, 15–21 passim, 90n20, 131, 133, 134n66, 139, 176, 313
Kistemaker, Simon, 34n18
Kleinig, John, 155n17, 162, 167, 168n47
Knowles, Michael P., 40, 89n14, 118nn25–26
Kropf, Nancy P., 5n4

Lamm, Claus, 271n31
Lampman, Lisa B., 36n20
Latané, Bibb, 102n61
Laws, Michael, 154n15, 285
Lenski, R. H. C., 34n18, 58n11, 77n49, 90n20, 126n48, 188n26, 227n23
Leonard, Pamela B., 5n4
Liefeld, Walter, 96n37
Lindberg, Tod, 45n45
Linnemann, Eta, 196n5, 203n31, 226n20, 237n50
Liu, James H., 5n5
Loader, William R. G., 48n55, 49nn58–59, 56n5
Loewe, H., 190n33, 205n42
Logan, Samuel, 319n93

Macaulay, Thomas B., 165, 166n42
Mackintosh, H. R., 271n32
MacMullen, Ramsay, 125n47

Malina, Bruce J., 57nn8–9, 77n49, 83n4, 96n39, 119n27, 126n48, 186n25, 197n7, 225n16, 229n34
Malm, H. M., 155n16, 167, 169n49, 171n52, 172, 175nn56–57
Mann, Jacob, 42n35
Manning, Rachel, 101n57
Manson, T. W., 31n11, 32, 56n4, 64n24, 66n30, 74, 184, 185n20, 190nn32–34, 197n7, 205n42, 207n46, 214, 240
Mantouvalou, Virginia, 160n29, 170
Marshall, Chris D., 3n1, 30n3, 145n4, 146n5, 149n8, 175n57, 211n55, 215n65, 219n5, 230n37, 297n24, 322n96
Marshall, I. H., 31n8, n11, 56n4, 63n22, 73n43, 77n49, 107n71, 123n39, 130n57, 185n20, 204n35, 207n46, 226n19, 229nn31–32
Martin, Nancy, 18n2, 73n44
Matera, Frank J., 50n62
Maxwell, Gabrielle, 5n5, 231n38
McArthur, H. K., 40n29
McDonald, Ian, 26, 27n22, 37n24, 50n62, 92n28, 250n1, 252n3
McFarland, Ian A., 77
McIntyre, Alison, 153n12, 155n16
McLeod, Rosemary, 154n14
Meier, John, 22n12, 30n6, 32n12, 44, 48n53, 50n62, 61–62, 63n20, 66–67, 68n32, 69n34, 70n35, 72, 73n43, 78–79, 91n24, 112n3, 113, 114n6, 115n12, 124n41, 131n61
Menken, M. J. J., 73n42, 222, 223n10
Mika, Harry, 87n11
Miller, Richard, 160
Milligan, G., 84, 200n15
Montefiore, C. G., 31n7, 50n62, 51n63, 190n33, 205n42
Moore, G. F., 190n33, 206n43, 213n62
Morris, Allison, 231n38
Morris, Leon, 58n11, 77n49, 126n48, 240n56
Moulton, J. H., 84, 200n15

Moxnes, Halvor, 182n3, 229n34
Murphy, Jeffrie G., 191n37
Murphy, Liam, 155n17, 158n24, n26, 166n43, 168n48, 171, 175n55

Neusner, Jacob, 60n13, 97n44, 205, 206n43
Neyrey, Jerome H., 57n9, 77n49
Nietzsche, Friedrich, 264
Nolland, John, 26, 29n2, 31nn9–10, 56n4, 65nn26–27, 119, 126n48, 131n59
Northey, Wayne, 310
Nouwen, Henri, 228
Nussbaum, Martha, 101n56, 131n58, 161, 253n4, 255–59, 260n19, 262, 263n23, 265–71, 273, 278, 279n45, 293n20, 298n25, 299

Oakman, Douglas E., 83n4, 119nn28–29, 126n50
O'Grady, Paul, 104n67
Oliner, Samuel and Pearl, 105, 136n69
Oord, T. J., 18n2, 35n19, 80n51, 105n68, 160n31, 217, 220

Paine, Tony, 307n52
Papanikolaou, A., 227n25
Pardun, John, 155n18, 172
Patrick, M. W., 66n30
Paul, Charlotte, 276n39
Pence, Gregory, 277
Perkins, Pheme, 47, 48n53, 50n62, 52
Phillips, Thomas, 217n1
Philo, 63n20, 64n23, 65n27
Plummer, Alfred, 34n18, 56n4, 58n11, 77n49, 107n71, 130n57, 188n26, 202n24, 208n50, 229n33, 234, 240n56
Porter, Elisabeth, 254n6, 259, 277, 300
Powell, Mark A., 57n6
Pranis, Kay, 6n7

Radcliffe, Dana, 72n37
Rainbolt, George, 218n4, 262n22

Author Index

Ramsey, G. W., 183n7, 184n12, 206n45, 207n47, 235n45
Ratcliffe, James M., 101n59
Raybeck, Douglas, 236n48
Redekop, Paul, 230n37
Reilly, Richard, 251n2
Reiser, Marius, 50n62
Resseguie, James, 288n28
Ribet, Beth, 304n39, 307n50, 319n94
Rigby, Paul, 104n67
Ringe, Sharon H., 77n49, 83n4, 90n20, 96n37, 119n27
Robertson, A. T., 22n10
Rohrbaugh, R. L., 57nn8–9, 83n4, 96n39, 119n27, 185n21, 186, 197n7, 199n11, 201n19, n21, n22, 203n27, 207n47, 223, 225n16, 232n39, 236, 237n53, 238n55, 245n63
Ross, Lee, 209, 210, 292n17, 298
Roukema, Riemer, 25n17, 37n24
Rowe, Mary, 101n58
Rudzunski, A. W., 155n18
Runzo, Joseph, 18n2, 73n44
Ryken, Leland, 181n1

Safrai, Shemuel, 43, 89
Saiman, Chaim, 47n50, 142–44
Sanders, E. P., 42n31, 43n37, 46n46, n49, 66n29, 72, 89n13, 90n16
Schaab, G. L., 22n9, 26n20, 37n23
Schmidt, Thomas, 217n1
Schnelle, Udo, 33n16
Schottroff, Luise, 43n40, 50n62, 93n32, 96n37, 121n34, 185n20, 189n29, 245n63
Schrage, Wolfgang, 37n24, 50n62, 66n30, 93n32, 131
Schriver, Donald, 211n55, 226n21
Schroeder, David, 91n21, 92n26, 100n54, 101n58, 102nn60–61, 104n65, 122n37, 136n69, 162n35
Schürer, Emil, 42n31, n34, 42n34, 43nn37–38, n40, 45n44, 89n13, 203n31, 204n31

Scott, Bernard, 31n7, 39, 50n61, 93n29, 94n34, 98n48, 112n2, 182n3, 183, 189n29, 193n40, 193, 197n7, 198n8, 199n14, 204n39, 205n41, 207, 211n54, 222n8, 225n15, 229n31, n33, 234n42
Sellew, Philip, 94n33, 183n7, 207n47
Sellin, Gerhard, 29n2
Shaffer, Thomas L., 191
Shattuck, Michelle, 36n20
Shestowsky, Donna, 209, 210, 292n17, 298
Shigehiro, O., 163n37
Siebald, Manfried, 181n1
Singer, Peter, 122, 159
Singer, Tania, 271n31
Snodgrass, Klyne, 25n17, 26, 29n1, 31n9, 32n12, 33n15, 36n22, 50n62, 56n4, 57n8, 65nn26–27, 90n20, 93n30, 96n37, 97n43, 112n2, 114n7, 126n48, 182n4, 183n6, 185n22, 188nn27–28, 190n32, 195n2, 200n15, 202n23, 207n47, 225n16
Snyder, Susanna, 279n47
Soerens, Matthew, 22n9
Soloveichik, Meir Y., 60n14, 143n3
St. Jerome, 82
St. Paul, 71, 75, 146, 271, 272, 275
Stassen, Glen H., 92n28, 123n38, 126n48
Staub, Ervin, 91n22, 100n54, 107, 111
Steger, Michael F., 163n37
Stern, M., 43n39, 89n13, n15, 93n31
Strack, H. L., 64n23, 77n47
Strang, Heather, 6n8, 87n12, 295n22

Tacitus, 90n18
Theresa, Mother, 122
Thorburn, Malcolm, 301n32, 302n33, 310, 311n64
Tissot, Y., 182n4
Tolbert, Mary Anne, 185n20, 185n22
Tucker, Jeffrey, 33n15
Tunc, André, 155n18

Turner, Kathryn, 219n5
Turner, Nigel A., 212n59

Umbreit, M., 5n5

Van Ness, D. W., 5n3, n5
Varah, Chad, 21n7
Vass, Beck, 22n11
Via, Daniel O., 183, 184n11, 196n5, 207n47, 225, 227n24
Volf, Miroslav, 18n2, 200n17, 208, 222, 242n61

Wailes, Stephen L., 25n17
Ward, Bruce, 255n8, 256n10, 264, 271
Weil, Simone, 298
Wellford, Charles, 235n46
Wells, Samuel, 106n69, 125n44
Wilkinson, John, 82n1
Williams, Carol J., 152n9
Wilson, Stephen G., 29n2, 30n6, 33n16, 47, 48, 70n35, 77n49

Wink, Walter, 30, 30n6, 46n49, 99n51, 100n55, 116n16, 129n56, 132n64
Witherington, Ben, III, 31n7, 57n8
Wittig, Susan, 183n8
Woodward, Kathleen, 256n9, 257n11, 274, 275n38
Woozley, A. D., 157n23, 158n26, 162n34, 167
Wright, N. T., 23n14, 24, 31n9, 46n47, 77n49, 92n27

Young, Brad, 185n21, n23, 190n32, 197n7, 199n12, 201n20, 212n56, 238n55

Zehr, Howard, 5n5, 6n6, 87, 213, 229, 230, 317n89
Zimbardo, Philip, 85n9, 103n62, 136, 210n52, 236n47

Subject Index

Abraham, 55n1, 58n12, 121n34
actions, 38, 74–75, 95, 122–23, 127, 131–32, 161, 210–11, 220–21; *see also* behavior
    benevolent, 72–73, 76, 161, 262n22
    charitable, 20, 21, 134, 141
actors, 23–24, 52, 97n44, 104, 189, 192–93, 218, 236, 256, 277
    in parables, *see* characters
agape, 72; *see also* love
agencies, 6, 282; *see also* institutions
agency, personal, 164, 168, 221, 243, 276, 277
agents, 126, 129, 132, 164, 209, 267, 276, 315
    legal, 166, 168, 219, 282, 288, 296
    moral, 144, 160, 166, 218, 221, 263
aid, 21–22, 90, 91n23, 97, 104, 122, 152n9, 155; *see also* assistance, care, rescue, Samaritan laws
    in parable, 39, 50–51, 103, 126, 128
alien, 26, 77, 115
allegory, 25–26
altruism, 35n19, 97n44, 136, 160n31, 161–65
    and empathy, 265
    legal requirement, 159
    research on, 21, 94, 101, 105, 109–11, 271n31
ambiguities, ambiguity, 2, 18, 40, 48, 102, 279, 287
    in parables, 83, 183, 184n12, 206, 241
    in situations, 99–101, 136

America, Unites States of, 16–17, 191, 290, 305n46
analysis, prophetic, 17–21
Anglo-American law, legal system, 151–52, 153n12, 155, 157, 165
Anna (Tobit), 225
Antiochus IV, 117
antisocial behaviors, *see* behavior, antisocial
arena, 2, 21, 269, 282, 291, 293
assault, 175n56, 288
    of bandits, 36, 37, 86
assistance, 35, 50–51, 90, 156n21, 161, 165, 170, 273, 313; *see also* aid
Assyrians, 115
atonement, 58n12, 187–88, 191, 206, 211, 213–14
audience, Jesus' 22, 24, 40, 51–52, 82, 112, 126n50, 186, 188; *see also* hearers
Augustine [St], 25
Austin, Ashley, 284, 300
Australia, 156, 168, 279
autonomy, 20, 87, 149, 166–67, 171, 173–74, 256
    moral, 221, 224, 264, 266

Babylon, 114, 115, 182
bandits, banditry, robbers, 24–25, 36–37, 40, 82–84, 125, 133, 135
    violence of, 34, 36, 82–85; *see also* assault
banquet, 237–38, 240, 243
behavior and shame, 230, 231

Subject Index

behavior, behaviors, 61, 104, 105, 111, 136–37, 146–47, 195, 251, 262
   and context, 209–10, 293n17, 294, 298
   and law, 149, 175n57
   and motivations, 163, 221
   antisocial, 103, 103, 136, 231, 236
   brothers', 185n23, 187, 196, 221, 235
   criminal, 83, 162
   prosocial, 101, 102, 137
   repentant, 205, 208, 211
benefactor, 126, 197, 198, 203
beneficence, 166–68 *passim*, 171; *see also* Samaritan laws
benevolence, 72–73, 148, 159, 168, 255, 265n25
   divine, 121; *see also* God, favor of, love of, mercy of
   in legal processes, 262n22
blame, 107, 208–9, 211, 216, 229, 259, 292, 295, 299
   blamelessness, 261, 315
   blameworthiness, 151, 196, 262
bonds, relational, 122, 162, 174–75, 185, 208
brothers, 178–79, 182n3, 184–87, 192–96 *passim*, 201, 205, 212, 215, 234–42, 244–45
Bystander Effect, 101–6
bystanders, 152–53, 157–58, 167, 169

California, 152, 305
Canon, 59, 66n30, 71
care, 52, 104, 111, 140, 163–64, 256–57, 268, 273, 289
   duty of, 38, 54, 147–48, 268
   in law, 40, 152–53, 156n21
   ethics of, 24, 40, 302
   lack of, 202
   restorative, 40, 127–28, 165, 174
   Samaritan's, 125–28
Cash, Dave, 175n56
causation, 35n19, 168, 210, 299
celebration, 220, 227, 232, 239–44

change, social, 17, 18, 134, 135, 138, 209
chapter summaries, 54, 79–81, 106–10, 137–39, 173–76, 214–16, 242–45, 281–82, 319–22
character, 136–37, 147, 184, 262n22
   and law, 141, 146–47, 308
   moral, 20, 137–38, 146–47, 184, 209, 228
   of God, 51, 80, 121, 188, 233
   of love, 74, 80
   of parables, 250
   of Samaritan, 119, 121
characters, 27, 251
   Samaritan parable, 23–24, 27, 36–39, 57n8, 92, 106, 112, 130, 253
   Prodigal parable, 181–85, 192, 221, 224, 230, 235–36, 249
charity, 18, 50, 190, 206, 210, 273; *see also* actions, charitable; love
Christ, 3–4, 15, 18, 25, 37, 75–76, 147, 272–73, 321
Christchurch, 284
Christology, 25–27, 37n24, 187, 188n27
church, 7, 26, 30, 88, 273–74
   early, 25n17, 51n63
Church Fathers, 25
circumstances, 19, 52, 72, 96, 97, 132, 149–50, 161, 172–76
   situational, social, 92, 136, 155, 209–10, 263–64; *see also* factors
   victim's, 123–24, 128, 134, 137
citizen, citizenship, 77, 153, 162, 166–72 *passim*, 203–4, 233, 266, 269–79 *passim*
civilization, 147, 257, 272
civil law system, 154, 158n24
Claudius, Emperor, 117
cleanliness, 91, 96, 100; *see also* holiness; purity; requirements, ritual
clothes, clothing, 83–84, 85, 121, 123, 228

Subject Index

coercion, 166, 167, 171, 220–21, 314, 320
commandments,
    greatest, 32n12, 68–76 *passim*
    love, 26, 31–33, 64–67
common law, 147, 151–53, 156, 158n24, 172,
communities, community, 19, 20, 51, 76, 88, 132–33, 112–13, 236, 318–19
    covenant, faith, 3, 76, 80–81, 88, 109, 134
    moral, 250n1, 255,
    in parable, 196, 201–2, 205, 212–19 *passim*, 232–38 *passim*
    political, 147, 265–66, 271
    resistance to restoration, 234–36
    respectful, 305, 306, 310
    sense of, 260
compassion, 133–34, 222–24
    and action, 122–23
    and mercy, 262
    and personality, 136
    capacity for, 53
    cognitive structure, 258–62
    divine, 27n21, 121, 233, 321
    in Luke, 27
    New Testament terms, 253
    Samaritan's, 52, 73, 95
    want of, 108–9
compassionate conservatism, *see* conservatism
compassionate institutions, *see* institutions
Comte, Auguste, 162
concern, 19, 38–40, 96, 123, 190, 251, 253–54, 268–69, 283
    altruistic, charitable, 20, 163–64
    empathetic, 109, 111, 122
    lawyer's, legal, 45, 56–57, 108, 133, 140, 144, 297
    moral, 253–54, 274, 283
    personal, 102, 160–61, 260–61
    professional, 43, 95
confession, 208–13 *passim*, 216, 226–27, 229, 233, 243, 244
consequences, unintended, 126–27
conservatism, 109, 256n9, 274–75, 306, 313
considerations, 35n19, 255–56, 277
Constantine, emperor, 274
contrition, 207–8; *see also* repentance
Coponius, 117
corpse, 94–96, 98–101, 105–6, 151
correction of life, 206, 211–13
Corrections System, 239, 298
cost, expense, *see also* money
    financial, 94, 127, 221, 245
    non-material, 100, 105, 108–9, 244, 254
    of compassion, 264, 276, 280
    of Samaritan laws, 157, 163–64, 166, 170, 172
covenant, 28, 50, 58n12, 74, 76–77, 321
    community, 80–81, 130
    faithfulness, 34, 45, 130
criminal justice, 6, 23, 35–36, 53, 133, 191–93, 297–98, 302
    domain, sphere, 218, 235, 258, 313, 314
    ethics of, 193–94
    policies, 4, 297
    system, 209, 230, 233, 249, 251, 267, 269, 282
    theory, practice, 3, 50, 231, 256, 301, 311
criticism, of parables, 30–31, 32n12
culture, 32, 102, 150, 187, 257, 264, 273, 292
Cumanus, 117
Cutheans, 115
"cutting off," 202n23

death penalty, 64n25, 117n22, 192, 196
Decalogue, 59, 65–66, 200
deliberation, compassionate, 296

dignity, 40, 85, 91, 169–70, 197, 238, 257, 263, 273, 287
  restoration of, 76, 125, 128, 229, 230–31
disciples, discipleship, 28, 48, 56n3, 58n12, 72, 117–18,
disconnection, emotional, 86, 88, 311
disempowerment, *see* powerlessness; victim
disgust, 101n56
disposition, 185, 187, 209, 277, 293, 314
  rights of, 198, 199
disrespect, 196, 197–205
distance, moral, 159–61, 268, 288; *see also* partiality
distress, 40, 50, 101, 111, 163, 253–54, 262, 275, 300; *see also* Good Samaritan laws
distrust, 116, 203, 239
Donaghue v Stevenson, 147
dramatis personae, *see* actors
dualisms, 53–54
duty, 24, 38–40, 78, 91–92, 94, 97–99, 128
  failure of, 46, 47, 49
  legal, 143, 148, 151–53, 156n21, 157–61, 163, 168–71
  of care, *see* care, duty of

economics, 83, 143, 162, 256, 264, 275; *see also* circumstances; policies; resources
education, 165, 170, 173, 269, 270–72, 281, 297–98
efficacy, personal, 136
Eleazer, Eliezer, 43, 56, 116, 182n39
emergency rescue, *see* aid
emotions, 72–74, 120, 131, 223, 255–59, 261, 266, 269, 275–77; *see also* passions
  in law, 283–84, 286–88, 291–93, 296–98, 306–7
  negative, 34, 267

empathy, 136, 164, 222–24, 253, 269–72, 287–96 *passim*, 299–300; *see also* compassion
empowerment, 35, 128, 251, 313; *see also* power
enemies, enemy, 34, 52, 134, 135, 138, 148; *see also* neighbor love
  Jewish attitude to, 50–51, 77n 47, 90n18
  love of, 35n19, 49, 50–51, 72, 80, 313
  of God, 50, 97n44
engagement, 111, 120–23, 129, 136, 278, 287, 293, 301
environment, 128, 134, 136, 209–10, 277, 279
eschatology, 33–35, 48, 71, 251–52
Essenes, 60, 83
eternal life, 39, 44, 48, 55–58 *passim*, 64, 76–77, 80, 129, 131
ethics, 33–34, 64, 66n30, 106, 139, 140, 250, 270, 302; *see also* morality
  legal, professional, 35, 50, 108, 287
  medical, 21, 147, 277
Europe, European, 5, 98, 105, 154, 155n18, 158, 181, 186, 273
European Convention on Human Rights (ECHR), 169
European Court of Human Rights, 170
expectancy, 221–22
extensivity, personal, 35 n19, 136, 251, 281
extravagance, 34, 188, 205; *see also* money

factors, situational, 101–4, 109, 136, 164, 220–21, 259, 293n17, 295–96, 298
faith, 77, 85, 88, 258, 281, 306, 312; *see also* communities, faith
  -healing, 105
  loss of, 305

family, duty to, 94, 100, 202, 237, 245
family dysfunction, 185n21, n23, 188
father, 183–85, 208n50, 210–11, 225, 237–40, 242
  compassion of, 222–23
  disrespect shown to, 198–203, 220
  love of, 188–89, 220–21, 239–41
  restorative action by, 222–26 passim, 228–32
favor, divine, 206, 213n62
feast, 231–32
fiction, literary, 303
forces, situational, 53, 92, 106, 136, 209–10, 262; see also factors
forgiveness, 213n62, 226–33, 239, 243–45, 284–85, 306–7, 309–12, 317, 322
freedom, 20, 80, 149, 166–69 passim, 262–64, 265n25, 275
  and love, 80, 215, 220–21
friendship, 52–53, 215

Genovese, Kitty, 101–2, 153
Gentiles, 30, 77, 85n10, 91n24, 97, 114, 202–5 passim
Gandhi, Mohandas, 313
gift, gifting, 97–98, 200–201, 230
Glasgow City Council, 153, 169
Glassie, Nia, 154
God, 51, 74–75, 88, 123, 188–89, 210, 251
  character of, 51, 121, 188
  compassion of, 27, 121, 233, 260, 321
  enemies of, 50, 51, 97n44
  favor, goodness, grace of, 121, 188–89, 206, 213n16, 245, 252
  image of, 121, 186, 188 n29, 281
  justice of, 57, 233, 250
  love for, 26, 33n16, 64–76, 80, 119, 123–24, 128–29
  love of, 26, 33n16, 69, 80, 190, 233, 257, 272
  mercy of, 130, 190
  reign, sovereignty of, see kingdom of God
  will of, 33n16, 48, 59, 143, 149
Golden Rule, 38, 64, 68n32
Good Samaritanism, see Samaritanism
grace, 7, 26, 80, 191, 206n44, 211, 275, 322
  of Christ, 25, 26, 147
  of father, 184, 213–14, 245
  of God, 188n27, 189, 233, 252, 275
  of victims, 211, 216

haggadah, 66n30
halaka, halakic, 44, 45, 61, 96n39, 98, 143
harm, 149, 153, 155, 156n21, 162, 165–66, 168, 171, 174, 231
healing, 86, 128, 134, 208–9, 228, 231, 305–6, 309
hearers, Jesus' 30, 32, 35–39 passim, 83, 112–16 passim, 188, 196–201 passim; see also audience
heart, 73n43, 120–24; see also emotions; heart, soul, mind
heart, soul, mind, 64, 73–76, 119, 128
heaven, 58n12, 189, 191, 192, 195, 207, 210, 214
Hellenism, Hellenistic, 43, 63n20, 113, 114, 195, 196n4
Hemmings, Austin, 22
Herod the Great, 83
Holiness Code (Lev 19), 64, 89
holiness, 63n20, 89; see also cleanliness; purity
honor, 56n3, 57n9, 77n49, 85, 112, 119, 197–99, 200n16, 213–16 passim
  father's, 217, 243–44
  professional, 100, 128, 173
  reintegrative, 228–33
hope, 86, 221–22, 265n25, 288–89, 309, 317
Huckleberry Finn, 304
human rights, see rights, human

humiliation, 85, 128, 213, 227, 230–31, 316
humility, 58, 124, 224–26, 263, 315
hurry, cultural valuing of, 103–4, 106

identification, 50, 71, 97, 253, 254, 283, 288, 294
identity, 87, 122, 129, 137, 186, 222, 224, 235–36, 272, 294
  covenantal, religious, 24, 85, 104–5, 132
  human, 164, 174, 215, 263
  and repentance, 191, 215–16, 241, 244

image of God, 37, 121, 188 n29, 189, 281
imagination, 182, 191, 266n25, 270–71, 280, 284, 297
imprisonment, 126, 156; see also prisoners; prison
impurity, pollution, etc, 91, 94–98, 100, 105, 116, 120, 130, 151, 205
inheritance, 57, 196–200, 201–2, 215, 222, 238, 245
injury, disrespect, 197–205 passim
Injury Prevention . . . Act, 152n9
injustice, 17-18, 34, 146, 193, 234, 241, 260, 278, 289, 296, 313
inn, 118, 124–25, 127, 128, 134
innkeeper, 36n22, 118, 119, 126–27, 134
institutions, 175n56, 269, 275–78, 282, 284, 302, 306–7, 318, 320
integrity, 198, 226–28, 236, 265–66
intensity, emotional, 73–74, 187, 191, 262, 292
interpretation of parables, 25–26

Jericho, 39, 40, 82, 89, 118
Jericho road, 16, 18, 20, 21, 52, 89, 103, 133–35
Jesus, 22–28, 43, 50–51
  attitude to law, 33n16, 43, 47–49, 61–64
  legal reasoning of, 142–47
  source of parables, 29–30, 78–79
  teaching on love, 64–68, 71–76
  teaching on neighbor, 76–79, 321
  as victim, 37
Jews and Samaritans, 112–18, 138
Johannine love command, 27
John (Baptiser), 57
Josephus, 63n20
Judaism, 59, 60, 68n32, 97n44, 109, 113, 120n32, 143, 196
  law summarized in, 32n12, 63n20
judge, merciful, 219–33
judges, 287, 289–90, 293–94, 297–300; see also compassion, judicial
judgment, 109, 128–33, 151, 158, 167, 211, 265n25, 286, 288–90, 296–98
  cognitive, 259–61, 270
  divine, 51, 114n10
  moral, 151, 162, 202, 255
judgmentalism, 234–36
jurisprudence, 71, 100, 134, 142, 148, 150, 191
jurors, 209, 283, 287, 290, 292, 294, 296, 299–300, 315
justification, 89, 157, 201, 305, 311, 312
justice, 16–17, 124, 241, 218–19, 242, 252, 289–90, 310–12
  and compassion, 276–80, 312–19
  and law, 145–47
  and love, 164, 221, 278, 313–14, 316
  and violence, 134–35
  biblical, 138–39, 146n5; see also Torah
  criminal, 3–7, 50, 53, 133, 191–93, 230–31, 233, 235, 251, 256
  eschatological aspect, 251–52
  institutional, 297–99
  of God, 57, 138, 188, 190, 193–94, 217, 233, 250
  relational, 242, 310–12

justice (*continued*)
  restorative, 3–7, 35–53 *passim*, 40, 87, 191–94, 208, 216, 231, 241, 252, 301–19
  retributive, 243, 244, 278
  ritual, *see* cleanliness
  theory, 17, 35, 41, 141, 213, 216

King, Martin L, 15–20 *passim*, 131, 134n66, 139, 176, 313
kingdom of God, 24, 31, 33–34, 48, 55, 67, 189, 251;

label, labeling, 53, 113, 137–38, 235–36
language, legal, 289–91
law, 26, 35, 40–49 *passim*, 62–76, 124, 130–33, 145–47, 290; *see also* justice; Samaritan laws; Torah
  and love, 4, 49, 71–76, 128–29, 145
  and morality, 21, 147–51
  and religion, 143–45, 147–51
  Anglo-American, 151–56 *passim*, 165
  biblical, Jewish, 46–47, 57n9, 70–76, 92, 97–98, 116, 142–47 *see also* Torah
  criminal, 162; *see also* criminal justice
  divine and human, 24, 78, 123, 141–42
  duty to aid in, 155n21
  interpretation of, 49, 289–90
  penal, 157, 165–72 *passim*, 283n1
  relativizing of, 71–76
  torts, *see* tort law
  Western, 74, 139, 141, 146–48, 150, 160, 173
law and the prophets, 59, 68,
laws, symbolic, 172, 174–75
Laws, Michael, 154n15, 285, 301
lawyer, 41–47, 55–57, 128–32, 137–38, 140, 144–45, 148, 158
legal profession, 41–43, 47, 140, 142, 158, 287, 296; *see also* judges

legal reasoning, 99–101, 255, 284, 286
  Jesus' 41, 47, 142–47, 151
legislation, 59, 99, 139, 144, 149, 152n9, 155, 158; *see also* Samaritan laws
Levite, 46, 89n13, 96; *see also* priest and Levite
liability in rescue, 152–53, 155, 156n21
liberalism, political, 19–20, 78, 149, 165–73, 218, 255–56
liberty, 149, 156, 165–67, 170–71, 220–21, 275; *see also* freedom
life, 59–62, 211–13, 241, 245, 271n32, 277–80
  political, public, 17, 229, 250, 255, 265n25, 269–70, 276
limits, of compassion, 291–95
literature, 135, 181, 191, 198, 270, 272–73, 281, 308; *see also* narrative; parables
  ancient & classical, 182n3, 202n24, 203, 274
  Jewish, rabbinic, 55n1, 58n12, 63, 65, 66, 112n3, 117, 120n32, 190n33, 202n24
  pastoral, Christian, 51n63, 65n28, 66, 202n24
love, 18, 32n2, 35n19, 46, 52, 80n51, 125, 127–33, 160n31, 258, 272
  and justice, 164, 276, 277–78, 313–14, 316
  and punishment, 297
  commands, 31–33, 64–70, 71–76, 144–46
  for God, 71–76, 129
  God's, 187–90, 233, 257, 273, 321
  Jesus, example of, 26, 76
  of enemies, 50–51, 313
  of friends, 51
  of neighbor, *see* neighbor
  restorative, 139, 219
Lucifer Effect, 136
Luke, themes, 86, 184n20, 189–91, 223n10, 232–33

malfeasance, 105
Mandela [N], 305n46
medical aid, 105, 152n9, 155n19, 170
medical ethics, *see* ethics, medical
medicine, 123, 277
mercy, 108–9, 120n32, 123–24,
　　128–33, 141, 262; *see also* compassion; environment
　　and justice, 217–19, 249
　　of God, 27n21, 58n12, 130, 189–91
　　restorative, 46–47, 132, 138, 145
might/strength, *see* heart, soul, mind
Middle East, Eastern, 51, 109, 124,
　　188n29, 198, 201n20, 203, 225,
　　237n54, 238n55
mind, 60, 73n43, 77, 148, 160, 197,
　　235, 288, 298; *see also* heart,
　　soul, mind
Mishnah, 42, 58, 60, 61, 98, 115n11,
　　117n2
Mitchell v Glasgow CC, 153n13,
　　169n50
money, 23, 49, 274; *see also* cost
　　Prodigal's, 195, 203, 212, 216, 227,
　　238, 245n63
　　Samaritan's, 118, 126
morality, 72, 104n66, 108, 139, 147–
　　49, 161–63, 166, 167, 250n1,
　　273; *see also* ethics
Mount Gerazim, 114, 117
mutuality, 215, 221, 279n46, 306, 310,
　　312, 315

Nain, widow of, 121
narrative, 19–20, 23, 33, 36, 59,
　　182–89 *passim*, 245, 272–75,
　　303–4
　　personal, 280–81, 290, 291, 293,
　　300,
neighbor, 21, 38, 45, 50, 117–19, 138,
　　147–48
　　aid to, 90, 92, 97–98
　　love of, 32n12, 34, 39, 46, 64–79
　　passim, 127–31, 135, 144–45,
　　265

neighborliness, 24
New Zealand, 4, 22, 27, 152n9, 154,
　　155n19, 175n56, 205, 233,
　　276n39, 284, 307n52
Nietzsche, F, 255, 258, 264
nomikos, *see* lawyer
nomos, 44, 49n59, 59; *see also* Torah
nonfeasance, 152–53
nonviolence, 306, 320
norms, 63n20, 85, 96, 104–5, 116, 123,
　　145, 193, 198, 276

objections to Samaritanism, 157–73
obligation, 71–76, 78, 97–98, 139,
　　on offenders, 205–14
offenders, 4, 53, 136, 191, 205–14,
　　230–31, 294–95, 300–303,
　　306–8; *see also* victims
offender, serial, 192, 229–30, 234,
　　307–9
　　restoration of, 205–7, 216–17,
　　227–31 *passim*, 244–45, 249,
　　310; *see also* repentance
oil, 23, 40, 118, 123–24

Palestine, Palestinian, 51, 61–63 *passim*, 125, 188, 196, 219, 250
parables, 24–28, 183, 187–92
　　ancillary aims, 2
　　and modern justice, 192–94,
　　249–52
　　as legal reasoning, 47
　　authenticity of, 29–31, 184n20
　　cultural legacy of, 21–23
　　eschatological function, 33–34
　　Jesus' use of, 250
　　legal perspective, 40–49
　　Lost Coin, 224
　　Lost Sheep, 224
　　of restoring justice, 35–53 *passim*,
　　192–94
　　realism & unrealism, 34–35, 183,
　　251, 320–21
parents, 105, 132, 160, 164, 196, 200,
　　214, 268

Subject Index

partiality, problem of, 161, 268-69, 281, 299n91–92
passion, passions, 26, 37n23, 74, 75, 121, 218; *see also* God, love of; love;
    of legal system, 259, 265n25, 286–88
paterfamilias, 200, 219
Pelagianism, 58, 63, 77n49
penal system, *see* prison
performance, 31, 44, 63, 92, 108, 277, 309
    moral, 24, 227, 242, 255
perpetrators, *see* offenders
personality, personal character, 73n43, 74, 75, 80, 92, 111, 128, 133–37
    group-oriented, 186
    of father, 221
    of sons (parable), 187, 234
    Samaritan's, 120
    traits, 92, 104, 121, 136–37, 209, 234, 262n22
perversity problem, 271n32
Pharisees, 42, 57, 60, 77, 96, 144, 184, 191, 234n42
Philo, 63n20
philosophy, 21, 35, 147, 162, 181, 263, 265
philanthropy, 21, 24, 63n20, 97, 147, 276
pigs, 204–5
pity, 223, 253, 261, 263, 293
Plato, 271n32
police, 46n48, 133, 158, 209
policies, policy, 17, 144, 150, 250, 275, 279–80, 297
    political, social, 19, 14–50 *passim*, 171, 173, 176, 250
    public, 19, 23, 53, 141–51 *passim*, 218
possessions, 120, 123, 195, 199, 200, 202, 215, 245, 263
post-Enlightenment, 19, 20n3, 149, 263

power, 124, 136, 162, 168, 191, 218, 221, 229, 262, 264, 271
    eschatological, 35, 251–52
    of compassion, 254, 276, 279
    of law, 147, 161, 167, 175n57, 219, 297
    of love, 139
    of stories, 19, 26, 119, 192n39, 245
    restorative, symbolic, 175n57, 213, 229, 231, 239
powerlessness, 37, 84, 87; *see also* victims
practice, practices, 21, 57, 72, 85, 104, 130, 151, 271
    ethical, moral, 18, 137, 187, 271
    in Judaism, 59–61, 63, 114, 130, 197, 201, 204
    institutional, 277–80
    legal, 35–53 *passim*, 139, 157, 172–76 *passim*, 243, 250, 256
    in court, 293, 295–96
    theory & practice, 18, 151, 209, 258, 286
    of Jesus, 57, 96, 190
    rabbinic lawyer's, 45, 77, 129, 145
    restorative, 6, 35, 132, 191, 218, 301, 303, 310, 315
    Samaritan, 113–15, 118–19
prayer, 64n23, 85, 88, 93, 98, 114n10
priest and Levite, 52, 89–90, 93–94, 100, 128, 145, 173–74
    Bystander Effect, 105–6
    professional neglect, 89–99 *passim*, 106
    professional obligation, 95–99
    self-justification, 138
priests, 42–43, 45–46; *see also* Levite; priest and Levite
prison, 84, 128, 136, 175n56, 284, 285
prisoners, 39, 233, 273, 274
prodigal son
    acknowledgement of sin, 209–10
    modern views of conduct, 195–96
    offending of, 200, 205
professionals, legal, 287

projection, imaginative, 291–92, 296
prophet, prophets, 44, 59, 108, 130; see also King, Martin L; law and the prophets
property, 73n43, 91n24, 97n42, 123, 152, 193, 196–202 passim, 221, 235, 307n52; see also possessions
proportionality, 292–93, 302
prosocial behavior, see behavior, prosocial
prostitutes, 193, 195, 196n4, 201, 235, 239
psychologists, psychology, 21, 94, 107, 122, 136, 186–87, 268
　social, 85, 101–2, 147, 162, 209, 277, 291, 295–98 passim; see also altruism
punishment, 85, 91, 158, 191, 214, 230–31, 233, 243, 262, 297–98, 317–19
purity, 95, 96–97, 113, 115–16, 119, 123, 132, 146, 210
　concerns, 52, 57, 62,78, 89

Qumran, 77n47, 96n39

rabbi, rabbinic, 32, 59–60, 62–64, 73n43, 95n36, 114–17, 205–6; see also Eliezer, Rabbi
　legal discourse, 40–44 passim, 66n30, 77n47, 96n39, 98, 143–44
　tradition, 98n44, 112, 143–44, 182n3, 190n33, 197
rape, 88, 280, 292
rationalists, economic, 264–65
realism, unrealism, see parables, realism & unrealism
reason, 256, 258–59, 263, 265n25, 276, 282, 286
reasoning, legal, see legal reasoning
reconciliation, 185n23, 186–87, 213–14, 216, 219–21, 224, 232, 311–12; see also humility

redaction, redactional, 29, 30nn3, 6, 32n12, 49, 79, 184n20, 190n32
refugees, 279–80
reign of God, 34, 188, 194; see also kingdom of God
relationship, 105, 139, 210–11, 214–16, 242, 269, 272, 277, 279n46
　and law, 146–49 passim, 153, 174, 290
　father and sons, 196, 199, 207–8, 222–23, 226–28, 232, 237–38,
　interpersonal, 46, 52, 78, 87, 146, 185–87, 251
　just, right, repaired, 305, 310–12, 322
　special, 160
religion and law, 147–49
repentance, 190, 205–14, 230, 233, 241–44; see also contrition
requirements, ritual, 33n16, 62, 78, 96, 100, 106, 151
rescue, 103, 105, 107–8, 120–21, 167–69 see also care; aid
　duty to, 92, 97, 101, 122, 151–61, 163, 170–71, 173–76 passim; see also Samaritan laws
resources, economic, 16, 201, 202
respect, 89, 124, 131, 159, 215, 220–21, 231, 257, 263, 302–11 passim
　for deceased, 99
　for law, 71, 172, 175n57
　of father for sons, 224, 243
　negative, 46, 148
responsibility, 105, 119, 133, 136, 165, 213, 216, 265
　breach of, 153, 154, 158
　diffusion of, 102
　individual, 102–3, 100, 108, 127, 132–37, 187, 196, 221
　legal, 43n37, 89, 97, 130, 168, 175, 289, 292, 302
　moral, 27, 38, 161, 208–11, 268, 270
　religious, 46, 65, 147

responsibility (*continued*)
   social, 21, 39, 66, 144, 160, 170, 172, 299, 320
restitution, 155n19, 161, 164–65, 206, 211–13, 294
restoration, 216, 227–28, 234–42, 244–45, 249 see also offenders; victims
restorative justice, 4–7, 35–53, 87, 241, 245, 252, 301–19
   and coercion, 314–17, 320
   and confession, 208
   critique of, 303–19
   goal of, 302
   restitution, 211–13
   spiritual ideals, 306–7
   theory, 4, 191–94, 208, 212–13, 216, 231, 310–11
retribution, 203n26, 218–19, 267, 285, 294, 318
retributivism, 310
revenge, vengeance, 75, 117, 223, 267, 293, 313, 318
right relation, 309–12, 314; see also relationship
righteous, the, 92, 244, 245
righteousness, righteous, 34, 139, 194, 217, 219, 245; see also justice; self-righteousness
   legal, legalistic, 58, 129, 241, 244
rights, 38n26, 76, 78, 167, 196, 215, 227, 236, 278
   civil, 15, 21, 139
   human, 5, 17, 20, 22, 169–70, 276
   legal, 129, 170,
   of estate disposition, 198–99
ring, 228–29
risk, in Samaritan laws, 157–58, 171–72, 175
ritual, 24, 26, 33n16, 46n47, 78; see also purity
robbers, see bandits
robe, 228
Rousseau, 255

rule of law, 147, 172, 175n57, 219, 284, 286–87, 297

Sabbath, 61, 74, 114n10, 144–45
Sadducees, 42, 60, 115n11
salvation, 25, 48, 57, 63, 77, 115, 132, 188, 275
Samaritanism, 21, 113, 139, 159
Samaritan laws, 35, 151–73
   objections to, 157–73
   value of, 172–73
Samaritans, 21n7, 22–23, 39, 51, 57, 77, 98, 112–19, 138
sandals, 39, 229, 243
scholars, scholarship, 2, 25, 32n12, 63n22, 113, 162, 188n29, 192n39, 197, 212, 256–58
   gospel, 26n20, 29–30, 39, 47–48, 61, 65–66, 70, 95–96, 182–84, 190–92, 204n35
   Jewish, Torah, 42, 60n14, 89, 142, 197
   legal, 10, 108, 142, 152–53, 191, 252, 286, 302–3
Scripture, 41n30, 55n1, 57–60, 90, 92
   rabbinic exposition of, 63, 72, 89, 97, 99, 121n34, 190, 206
security, 7, 87, 105, 133, 236, 286
self-awareness, 226, 296
self-interest, 144, 162–64, 279, 309
self-realization, 265–66
self-righteousness, 63, 71, 236–39, 261
self-sacrifice, 22, 28, 52, 146, 160n31, 163
sentence, sentencing, 4, 284–86, 290, 293, 295, 297
servants, 124, 187, 207, 212, 214, 223, 227–29, 235n44, 238, 240
setting, literary, 30
shame, shaming, 10, 85, 205, 229–32, 233, 243, 264, 316
Shechem, 114, 117
Shema, 63, 64n23, 69, 73n43, 98

sin, 24, 58n12, 146, 164, 190–91, 195, 206, 210–12, 271n32; *see also* confession
sinner, sinners, 26, 45, 91–92, 121, 188, 190–92, 206n45, 207, 215, 239, 241
situations, situational factors, *see* factors; forces
social analysis, 17–21
social policy, *see* public policy
societies, society, 16–17, 53, 83, 97n44, 135, 162, 209, 233, 236, 264, 269–76 *passim*, 294
    Jewish, Middle Eastern, 43, 89, 93–94, 124n43, 186, 199–201, 243
    Western, secular, 19, 20–23, 23, 147–48, 165, 172–73, 186n25, 229, 249–50, 255–56, 274
sonship, restoration of, 228–31
soul, *see* heart, soul, mind
St Michael's, Kelburn, 27–28; *see also* the cover
St Paul, 71, 75, 84, 146, 271, 272, 275
Stanford Prison Experiment, 136
state, duties of the, 170–71
status, 38, 78, 89n13, 118–19, 148, 197, 212, 263
    covenantal, 76, 77n49,
    filial, 228, 240
    identity, and ethnicity, 52, 85 +n10, 91, 113, 120
    neighbor, 130, 138
    social, 47, 76, 83, 120, 280
stories, story, 19–20, 34–40 *passim*, 108, 135, 182–87, 250–51, 270, 272, 274 *see also* narrative
victims,' 280, 295, 314
strangers, 53, 84, 102, 148, 160,
    help to, 122, 141, 159, 161, 167,
    laws regarding, 153, 174
    love to, 35n19, 148,
    kindness of, 164, 278
strength, *see* heart, soul, mind
Strohmeyer, Jeremy, 175n56

suffering, 230, 252, 253–54, 259–65, 268–80 *passim*, 287–95 *passim*, 299–300, 315–16
sympathy, 83, 253, 262, 286, 290–92
systems, systemic issues, 94, 133–37, 203n31, 276–77

Talmud, 60, 143
teacher, 32, 42–43, 45, 56, 60, 89–90, 165, 195n3; *see also* rabbi; priest and Levite
temple, Jerusalem, 42n36, 43, 46, 89–90, 92–93, 95, 100–108 *passim*, 115–17 *passim*
    worship, 123–24
test, 45, 56, 67, 96, 128, 148n7
themes, of parables, 24, 55, 86, 186
theology of parable, 187–89; *see also* Father; God
theory, 166–72 *passim*
    ethical, 161, 258, 268, 270–71
    justice, 191, 213, 216, 231, 250, 301– 303, 310
    legal, 21, 41, 47, 258, 286; *see also* jurisprudence
    political, 145, 276, 278
    and practice, 35, 49, 191, 209, 258, 286, 310
therapies, therapeutic, 4, 134, 210, 227n25, 290, 306
Tobias (Tobit), 225
Torah, 26, 31–33, 43–46, 58–62, 139, 143–44, 150; *see also* Jesus, legal reasoning; law; love, commands
    chief demands, 62–76
    neglect of, 94–99
    Samaritan observance, 113, 115–16, 123
tort law, 35, 38n26, 147, 152, 156, 158
tradition, traditions, 18n2, 30–32, 142–43, 73, 150, 166n43, 255–56, 302n33
    biblical, 130, 146, 150, 187–90, 197, 210, 215, 311

372 Subject Index

tradition, traditions (*continued*)
   Christian, 20, 27n21, 65, 72, 142, 273
   dominical, 29, 32
   Gospel, 25, 26, 31, 32n12, 41, 43, 71, 143, 188
   hermeneutic, 59–63; *see also* allegory
   Jewish, halakic, 51n63, 58n12, 60, 61, 72, 121, 190
   Markan, 32n12, 42, 49, 69, 78, 79
   Matthean, 32n12, 42, 49. 69
   philosophical, 20n3, 131n58, 165–71 *passim*, 257
   rabbinic, 97n44, 121, 143, 190n33, 197
   Synoptic, 32, 63–71 *passim*; 73n42; 78–79
   textual, 44, 61, 73n43, 143, 204n35
   Western, 19, 21, 166, 186, 257
transformation, 6, 9, 18, 52, 71, 73n44, 134–36, 206, 319n91
   human, 149, 194
   inner, moral, 138, 147, 206, 228, 241, 306
trauma, traumatology, 8, 37, 86, 87,
truth, 6, 19, 124, 147, 219, 249, 258, 303, 315
   legal, Torah, 71, 282, 287, 304
   moral, spiritual, 20, 126, 150, 162, 174, 298
Tutu [D], 305n46

Unforgiving Servant, 274
United Kingdom (UK), 170
United States, USA, US, *see* America
utilitarianism, 155n17, 166n43, 310

values, 6–7, 19–20, 91n22, 104–5, 167, 229, 250, 257, 320
   and law, 46, 63, 128, 142, 150–51, 162, 172, 296
   compassionate, 275, 279,
Vermont, 156

victimization, 36–40, 126, 227, 239, 259, 267, 307n52, 313
victim, victims, 4, 18, 38–40, 53, 86–88, 280, 284–85, 292–95, 298; *see also* violence
   and offenders, 231, 251, 288, 300–18 *passim*
   changed circumstances, 124, 133–37
   disempowerment, 37, 84, 87
   embittered, 239–42
   father as, 192
   impact statements, 293–95
   point of view of, 36–38
   restoration of, 86, 128, 133, 139, 174, 210–11
   retribution against, 298, 319
Victim Support, 307n52
violation, 84, 96, 158, 167–69, 175 238
violence, 34, 83–86, 134–35, 294, 314, 320
   collective, 38, 52, 116–17, 261
   domestic, 292, 310–12
   sexual, 175n56, 288
vision, 3, 19, 24, 257–58, 265–66, 278, 311
   restorative justice, 303, 307, 315, 320
vulnerability, 37, 86, 88, 159, 176, 260, 276, 298, 298–301 *passim*, 315

war, 15–17, 22, 39, 105, 135, 256, 273
welfare [individual], 38n26, 73, 108, 111, 123, 136, 140, 164, 170, 215
   community, public, 202, 254–56, 274
   state, system, 203n31, 279, 282
wine, 40, 114n7, 118, 123–24
Woods, Emma and Nayan, 284–85, 300–301
Woolworth, FW, v Wilson, 287n8
worldview, 60, 134, 250, 266
worship, 73n43, 89, 90, 94n35, 112n3, 114, 115, 123–24, 189